Events Time-Line

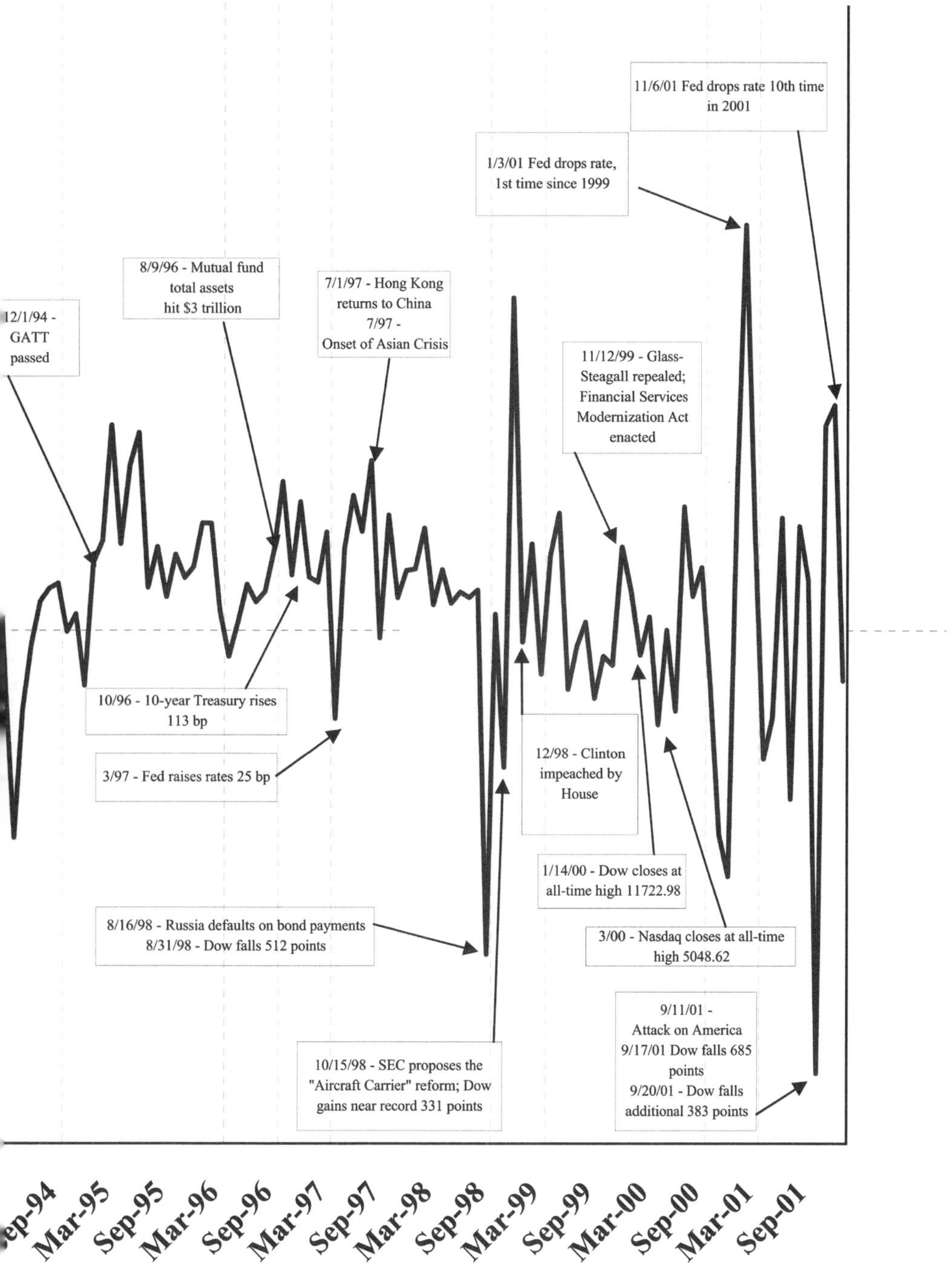

11/6/01 Fed drops rate 10th time in 2001
1/3/01 Fed drops rate, 1st time since 1999
8/9/96 - Mutual fund total assets hit $3 trillion
7/1/97 - Hong Kong returns to China 7/97 - Onset of Asian Crisis
12/1/94 - GATT passed
11/12/99 - Glass-Steagall repealed; Financial Services Modernization Act enacted
10/96 - 10-year Treasury rises 113 bp
3/97 - Fed raises rates 25 bp
12/98 - Clinton impeached by House
1/14/00 - Dow closes at all-time high 11722.98
8/16/98 - Russia defaults on bond payments 8/31/98 - Dow falls 512 points
3/00 - Nasdaq closes at all-time high 5048.62
9/11/01 - Attack on America 9/17/01 Dow falls 685 points 9/20/01 - Dow falls additional 383 points
10/15/98 - SEC proposes the "Aircraft Carrier" reform; Dow gains near record 331 points
ep-94
Mar-95
Sep-95
Mar-96
Sep-96
Mar-97
Sep-97
Mar-98
Sep-98
Mar-99
Sep-99
Mar-00
Sep-00
Mar-01
Sep-01

BEYOND

JUNK BONDS

HG
4523
.Y34
2003
LFJ3

BEYOND

JUNK BONDS

Expanding High Yield Markets

Glenn Yago
Susanne Trimbath

R96

OXFORD
UNIVERSITY PRESS

2003

OXFORD
UNIVERSITY PRESS

Oxford New York
Auckland Bangkok Buenos Aires Cape Town Chennai
Dar es Salaam Delhi Hong Kong Istanbul Karachi Kolkata
Kuala Lumpur Madrid Melbourne Mexico City Mumbai Nairobi
São Paulo Shanghai Taipei Tokyo Toronto

Published by Oxford University Press, Inc.
198 Madison Avenue, New York, New York 10016

www.oup.com

Library of Congress Cataloging-in-Publication Data
Yago, Glenn
Beyond junk bonds : expanding high yield markets /
Glenn Yago, Susanne Trimbath.
p. cm.
Includes bibliographical references and index.
ISBN 0-19-514923-8
1. Capital market. 2. Finance. 3. Securities. 4. Economic development. I. Trimbath, Susanne. II. Title.
HG4523 .Y34 2003
332.63'234—dc21 2002154174

9 8 7 6 5 4 3 2 1

Printed in the United States of America
on acid-free paper

Preface

When *Junk Bonds: How High Yield Securities Restructured Corporate America* was published by Oxford University Press in 1991, the high yield market had entered a period of great uncertainty. The stock market had crashed; Congress took away the tax deduction for interest paid on high yield bonds; savings and loan associations, as well as most insurance companies and pension plans, were prohibited from investing in high yield bonds; Drexel Burnham Lambert went out of business; and securities regulators, tax authorities, courts, and even economists were debating whether "junk bonds" were debt or equity. Following all of this negative news, the global economy was entering what would turn out to be one of the longest, most robust expansions in memory. More than ten years later, as *Beyond Junk Bonds* goes to press, another period of possibly even greater uncertainty lies ahead of us; uncertainty compounded and added to by the terrorist attacks of September 11, 2001, and the specter of a global recession that was already under way but that could only be exacerbated by the economic impact of the attacks and subsequent military actions. By June 2002, market uncertainty was indicated by a record negative return spread for high yield bonds over 10-year Treasuries that reached 1000 basis points and since narrowed to 800 basis points by November 2002. Furthermore, the level of defaulted debt bolted to $64 billion at year end 2001. By mid-2002, the defaulted debt in the speculative grade bond market already stood at $45.6 billion, not including the WorldCom default in July 2002 of $31.0 billion. Nevertheless, signs of resiliency in the high yield market, as we detail later in this volume, are beginning to appear as distressed turnarounds, restructurings, and refinancings are underway.

This book is the story of what happened in between. It is a success story, by and large—the story of the success of the market for high yield securities and the companies, industries, and even sovereign nations that used the expanded access to capital provided by the high yield market to grow and prosper. It is the story of how high yield securities moved beyond being called "junk." This book is, in fact, more than just a "story." A story could be told largely in chronological order. A topic as broad as "high yield markets" defies attempts at blow-by-blow coverage. Indeed, there are multiple time lines at work.

We take an in-depth look at some critical events. Many of those events relate to capital market regulations. Some events are more closely tied to the market players on the buy side (mutual funds, brokers, institutional investors, etc.). Companies and nations (the sell side) will always require some source of financing. The supply side of the capital markets will probably always be there. The question, however, is whether those in need of capital can be satisfied by private (bank) or public (market) sources.

The first part of this book finishes the work started in *Junk Bonds* and introduces the high yield market of the 1990s. The Tax Reform Act of 1989 was just one of a string of regulations that had the effect of restricting both the buy side and the sell side of the market for high yield securities (see chapters 2 and 3). Regulatory limitations resulted in a mismatch between jobs and capital. In other words, the companies that were creating jobs were unable to get the financing they needed because job creation came with a level of risk that regulators deemed unsuitable for the financial institutions that were holding an increasing share of U.S. financial assets. We demonstrate the impact of those regulations in chapters 3 and 4 with an empirical examination of the timing of the market disruptions. The technical details of the rigorous methodology applied to the data in order to identify the temporal distortion are in appendix B. In the text, however, we include enough details to convince even the most cynical reader that the market distortions at the end of the 1980s were not "naturally occurring." The high yield market did not fall; it was pushed into a price decline from which it swiftly recovered, but not without considerable disruption to companies and investors along the way.

Despite the government's best efforts to thwart it, the high yield market did recover. After the 1989–1990 disruption, money flowed back into mutual funds, capital markets recovered, and innovative firms were once more able to receive the financing they needed to grow. Not only did the market recover, but it began to expand and grow in new directions, as is detailed in chapters 5 and 6. In chapter 7 we go into some detail about the innovations in the structure of securities that originated and expanded in the high yield market, some of which were adapted to investment grade issuers as well. (A more complete list of security types is in appendix C.)

An important debate started with the 1989 Tax Reform Act that continues today: Are high yield bonds debt or equity? The answer holds importance for legal, regulatory, and accounting purposes that reach beyond tax implications. It will also impact high yield debt's place in the nearly fifty years of debate on the importance of corporate capital structure. In chapter 8 we offer a view of the important role of high yield debt in capital structure. We follow up with an analysis of the implications of the Miller-Modigliani capital structure proposition for the development of the high yield market in the same chapter. A wide variety of research reports came out of those turbulent years at the end of the 1980s. Bibliographies, sorted by topic, are available, with the more technical and empirical papers summarized in tabular form, in appendix D.

The 1990s were filled with relatively good news for high yield markets both in the United States and overseas. High yield bonds were vilified in the 1980s on two counts. The first was that they were used by empire-building managers with self-aggrandizement in mind and by takeover artists with bust-ups in mind. Actual evidence in chapter 9, contrary to the sound bite version of the 1980s, shows that corporate efficiency was enhanced through the market for corporate control. There is also additional evidence here that regulatory interference in the capital markets had a deleterious effect on the ability of the market for corporate control to discipline poorly performing firms. The second sound bite used against high yield financing is that the firms which issued the debt became mired in interest payments that weighed them down so badly they could barely survive. We present a substantial amount of evidence to the contrary. We show how firms were, and are, able to use high yield debt to rebuild broken balance sheets in ways that preserve assets, revenue streams, and, perhaps most important, American jobs. Also in chapter 9 we present evidence on five well-known companies that were high yield issuers in the 1980s. These companies, plus the industry discussed in chapter 10, were some of the most important contributors to the ten-year economic expansion that is the reason the U.S. economy still sustains its economic resilience and fortitude. Chapter 11 outlines new directions for financial innovations in the high yield market and beyond.

NOTE ON DATA

The print and electronic publication of news, information, and data on the high yield market expanded enormously in the 1990s. In 1989, beyond the credit rating agencies, only two or three investment firms regularly published market analyses that focused on high yield securities. By 2000, not only had the number of firms publishing reports expanded, but each of these firms was producing specialty magazines for market segments such as the telecommunications, retail, and food industries, plus Europe, Canada, Asia, and Latin America.

For all the expanded coverage of the market, there remain major differences in the measurement of the high yield market. In mid-1999 we surveyed the research departments of four investment firms. The results were dismaying: the U.S. market was somewhere between \$315 billion and \$649 billion—a discrepancy of \$334 billion! Oddly, the higher valuations on the U.S. high yield market were qualified as excluding certain segments (split-rated securities and / or convertible securities), while the lowest figure was given without qualification. The discrepancies were even greater in the European high yield market, which was only becoming organized when the survey was taken: between \$17 billion and \$43 billion. The survey respondents could offer no explanation for the differences. We go into more detail on this topic in chapter 2.

The choice of metrics for discussing the high yield market can be problematic. Published reports will alternatively refer to the volume, growth, value, or return when reporting on the health of the high yield market. A serious problem exists even with what should be simple measures of volume and value—not all published measures of size are the same. The "size of the market" can alternatively mean "all outstanding" or "outstanding less defaults," and it may or may not include sovereign bonds or fallen angels. Measuring defaulted securities may be the most difficult issue of all, since bondholders may be able to make some recoveries even after the rating agencies have listed the issue in technical default. One source may include municipal and sovereign bonds in the total value of defaulted issues, but another may not.

Throughout this book the reader will find a wealth of data in the form of charts, tables, and graphs. We generally limited our sources to two primary providers of information in each category. For firm-level data (including aggregated firm data) we relied on Compustat Industrial/Research files and Securities Data Corporation Platinum Service; for credit ratings and default rates (including the value of rated and defaulted debt) we used Standard and Poor's and Moody's; and for market summaries and mutual fund data we generally relied on the publications and indices of Merrill Lynch and Shearson Lehman. This is not to imply that these sources are better than any others. The intention is only to minimize the potential for discrepancies.

In our view, the most important event of the 1990s for the development of the high yield market was the implementation of the Fixed Income Pricing System (FIPS) by the National Association of Securities Dealers (NASD).[1] Most important, the reporting and dissemination of information reduce opacity, which will promote even more robust markets. In 1994 high price, low price, and volume aggregates for a selection of actively traded high yield bonds were disseminated as a result of FIPS. Broad acceptance and utilization of trade data have the potential to reduce, and possibly eliminate, high yield data problems in the future. The high yield market has always been research intensive and event driven. We hope this volume makes a contribution to understanding the central importance of high yield financial innovations within and beyond the junk bond market to building a more prosperous future.

1. Chapter 8 contains a complete discussion of the development and importance of FIPS and its successor system, TRACE (Trade Reporting and Compliance Engine).

Acknowledgments

This book was a collaborative effort and reflects our joint authorship as equal contributors. Kay Ma was our data manager for this project. She also helped keep us abreast of current market conditions, especially with news of the European high yield market. In addition to gathering data and preparing graphic material, Kay organized the efforts of the several research assistants and research analysts who worked on the project. We gratefully acknowledge the assistance of Cindy Lee, Don McCarthy, Juan Montoya, and Ed Phumiwasana in gathering data and preparing the many charts and tables included in this volume. Don also prepared background material on collateralized debt obligations for use in chapter 7. Cherie Boyer was very helpful in manuscript preparation.

Robert Pace was instrumental in the early stages of planning the book and identifying relevant data sets. Ori Kanot prepared the material for the case studies in chapter 10, including developing the layout for tables used to track original issue high yield securities.

We also acknowledge the cooperation and assistance of Barbara Bassano at NASD; Richard Morrissey at Credit Curve; and Lorraine Spurge and Wendy Shafer at MetWest Financial. Paul Donnelly at Oxford University Press also assisted us. Thank you for your faith and patience during the process.

We are personally indebted to the many people in our lives who are supportive of our efforts and who encourage us on a daily basis. These include our colleagues James Barth, Betsy Zeidman, Glenn Whitman, Roman and Halina Frydman, and Don Siegel. We've benefited greatly from discussions and work with other financial researchers and practitioners, including Ed Altman, Chris Andersen, Elliot Arsarnow, Ted Barnhill, Robert Bartley, Joe Bencivenga, Bob Beyer, Joe Cole, Sam DeRosa-Farag, Dan Fischel, Marty Fridson, Stuart Gilson, David Goldman, Nigel Holloway, Michael Jensen, Mitch Julis, Jim Laurie, Les Levi, Walter McGuire, Jim Moglia, Lisa Montessi, Art Penn, Larry Post, Randolph C. Read, Frank Reilly, Anthony Ressler, and Ken Taratus. The manuscript benefited from comments by Tim Opler, Ann Rutledge, and an anonymous reviewer. Richard Sandor and Michael Walsh's work and collaboration on environmental finance found its way into chapter 12.

The late Nobel laureate and intellectual giant of financial economics, Merton Miller, was a source of considerable inspiration during his visits to the Milken Institute. We miss him. Most of the business history perspective reflected in this book emerges from the prolific and perceptive writings of Robert Sobel. Our last collaboration with him was in organizing the conference "Democratizing Capital," cosponsored by the Roosevelt and Reagan presidential libraries in 1998; he passed away not long thereafter. His fascination with the high yield market and his encyclopedic grasp of historical parallels are impossible to replace. Another great loss during work on this book was the untimely death of *Forbes Global* editor Laurence Minard. He encouraged the publication of our work on financial innovations at home and abroad. The loss of numerous financial innovators working at the World Trade Center on September 11 was a blow to the human and knowledge capital that has supported the expansion of high yield markets and financial innovation. Their memories are our blessings.

We have had the considerable good fortune to be associated with the Milken Institute, and thereby have enjoyed the professional colleagueship of its chairman, Michael Milken. We want to express our gratitude to him for his encouragement of our work to further understanding of and research on capital structure, and financial innovation and its relationship to economic growth. We should emphasize, though, that the opinions and analysis in this book are our own. We absolve him and the Milken Institute from any errors of fact or interpretation in this book. Mike remains the pioneer of modern financial innovation, and has the arrows in his back to prove it. With good humor, enormous patience, and his legendary genius, he has provided continuous intellectual challenge to our work at the Milken Institute, and we are most grateful for his inspiration. Our friends and family deserve our thanks. Susanne especially thanks Rachel, Sue and Barry, and L. and R. Glenn expresses his thanks for inspiration, support, and encouragement to L. J., Sylvia, Noah, Gideon, and Dena Yago. While many individuals helped us prepare the statistical and factual material that appear in this book, any mistakes are ours alone.

Contents

BEYOND

JUNK BONDS

1

Where Do We Go From Here?

The high yield market has always been an event driven market. If we reconstruct and decode the high yield market of the 1990s, it will give us important insights into emerging market patterns today. As 2002 draws to a close, financial markets in general, and high yield markets in particular, are faced with greater uncertainty than at perhaps any other time in history. Bond markets around the world, already jittery from a deceleration in worldwide economic activity, are struggling to find direction in the aftermath of the September 11, 2001 terrorist attacks. Any attempt to compare the impact of these attacks against previous events in history will be flawed because the combination has never been seen before: an act of war committed in the continental United States during a recession. The December 1941 Japanese attack on Pearl Harbor (Hawaii was then a U.S. territory rather than a state) occurred in the middle of an eighty-month expansion in the U.S. business cycle. Iraq's August 1990 invasion of Kuwait, which resulted in the involvement of the United States in a military action, occurred at the end of a ninety-two-month expansion. This time U.S. military involvement comes at a different time. The certainty of a global economic slowdown became obvious well before the terrorist attacks, with the bottoming out of the market for technology securities, the sector that was seen as driving the previous expansion. The U.S. annual average productivity growth between 1996 and 2000 was 2.5 percent. The rate was substantially greater than the average 1.4 percent annual productivity growth seen from 1973 to 1995. The "New Economy" technology sector was largely responsible for the unprecedented growth in productivity seen in the years leading up to 2001.

The multitude of influences occurring from September 11 through the time of this writing (August 2002) have generated a complex matrix of potential reactions in the bond market. A federal budget on the brink of being "balanced," a two-year reduction in marketable public debt, and an economic downturn were followed in rapid succession by the devastation of the travel/tourism and insurance industries; a "shooting war" of unknown duration and involvement; loose monetary policy with a federal funds rate below the rate of inflation, fiscal stimulus spending, industry bailouts, federal disaster relief spending, the elimination of the "long bond" (thirty-year Treasuries) and the re-creation of the "war bond"; low consumer confidence; labor productivity that continues to rise, albeit at a reduced rate; the ongoing and recurring "high alerts" for additional terrorist attacks; and the potential for disruptions in overseas supply and distribution chains. All of these have combined to create such uncertainty that no matter how cheap money becomes, it continues to sit on the sidelines assessing the options, reviewing the risks, fearful that the rewards won't materialize.

In table 1-1 we attempt to sort out the effects of individual events and circumstances on the market for high yield securities. Unfortunately, little if any of the federal stimulus and relief monies have yet been distributed, making it difficult, if not impossible, to judge the magnitude of those positive effects. Nor have any of the potential threats after September 11 and the distribution of anthrax in the Postal Service materialized, again making it impossible to judge the magnitude of those negative effects. The final element of uncertainty is specific to the high yield market: the April 2001 court decision that high yield debt is not equity for legal purposes and the November 2001 Financial Accounting Standards Board (FASB) review of the distinction between debt and equity for accounting purposes.

What we do know is that U.S. corporate bond issuance through August 2001 had already surpassed the full-year record set in 1998, largely spurred on by falling interest rates. By September, however, global bond issuance slowed, becoming truly anemic after September 11. The high yield market was particularly hard hit, with spreads widening by 170 basis points in the first two weeks after the attacks. This increase comes on the heels of the roller-coaster ride in yield spreads that went from 417 basis points in June 2000 to 955 in November. The late 2000 rise in yield spreads was likely a reaction to the inverted yield curve that was increasingly evident.[1] A subsequent yield spread decline in early 2001 followed the initial rate cuts made by the Federal Reserve.

By September 25, 2001, Standard and Poor's RatingsDirect Commentary was tallying the damage done to the credit markets:

- Nine U.S. airlines were downgraded or had their ratings put on CreditWatch with negative implications.
- The Port Authority of New York and New Jersey was placed on CreditWatch with negative implications.
- Every North American airport and airport-related special facility was put on CreditWatch with negative implications. (European airport ratings remained unchanged.)
- Thirteen commercial aerospace companies—airplane manufacturers; engine producers; suppliers of aircraft systems, components, and materials; and vendors providing aviation support—were put on CreditWatch with negative implications.
- Twenty-one North American lodging companies were put on CreditWatch with negative implications. (One European company had its outlook revised from positive to stable.)

1. An inverted yield curve is generally considered to be a predecessor of recession.

Table 1-1. Ups and Downs in the High Yield Market

Event	Positive effect	Negative effect
Economic downturn	Improved quality from "fallen angels"	Increased defaults
Fiscal stimulus and disaster relief spending, "war bonds"	Support businesses in affected regions, support affected industries	Inflationary pressure on prices and return on investment, steepening yield curves from government bond issuance
Low consumer confidence	None	Reduced consumer spending puts pressure on corporate revenues in cyclical sector
Balanced federal budget, reduction in marketable public debt	Funds available for corporate market	Elimination of budget surplus would erase positive effects
Elimination of the "long bond"	Unknown	Unknown
Equity market decline	Refinancing debt with equity more attractive	Reduces supply of equity financing
Loose monetary policy, reduced interest rates	Lower prices for new issues; higher yields for older issues	Inflationary pressure could help noncyclical sectors
Rising labor productivity	Facilitates restructuring and cost-cutting	Potential upgrades could reduce supply
Industry bailouts	Avoids defaults in airlines, travel, insurance, etc.	Potentially supports otherwise inefficient firms in affected industries
"Shooting war"	Revenue in defense, technology, transportation	Increase uncertainty for investors
Business disruptions from additional attacks	None	Increased defaults, loss of capital assets, higher risk premiums
Debt-equity distinction	Current rulings argue for interest deduction	Final rulings could go either way

- The ratings of five gaming companies were placed on CreditWatch with negative implications, and one outlook was revised to negative from stable.
- The ratings outlooks on two cruise lines were revised to negative, and the rating on another was lowered with the outlook still negative.
- Eastman Kodak Co. (whose business is closely related to vacations) had its commercial paper placed on CreditWatch with negative implications.
- More than a third of rated retail companies had already either been placed on CreditWatch with negative implications or bore a negative outlook (only supermarkets and drugstores, key noncyclical retailers, were unaffected).
- Walt Disney Co., the owner of those great vacation destinations, was placed on CreditWatch.
- Nineteen insurance companies were put on CreditWatch with negative implications, and another three were downgraded.

Standard and Poor's named more than fifty "fallen angels" in 2001, affecting over $100 billion of debt worldwide.[2] Since 1987 no more than forty fallen angels had been named in any year, affecting less than $40 billion in debt. The largest angels to fall in 2002 were AT&T Canada, Inc. ($3.3 billion), Goodyear Tire & Rubber Company ($3.0 billion), Nortel Networks, Ltd. ($3.3 billion), and Sierra Pacific Resources ($3.6 billion). Between October 2001 and April 2002, twenty-three new names were added to the worldwide list of "potential fallen angels," those BBB– rated issuers with uncertain futures. None were upgraded.

Although 2000 may have been comparable to 1991 in terms of ratings changes and market activity, including the tightening of credit and the prelude to a recession, no one can say if 2002 will turn out to be like 1992 because of the uncertainty induced by the unprecedented events of September 2001. Not all of the news is bad news as we enter the second year of the new millennium. There is at least anecdotal evidence of large cash positions sitting on the sidelines globally. Therefore, this recovery could be very significant. Once there is a consensus on the turnaround from the 2001 recession, the upside potential of the global economy will be very strong, indeed.

The following chapters review the market, regulatory, macroeconomic, and political uncertainty that have characterized the high yield market since 1990. In revealing the patterns and the market's reaction to them, we provide the landmarks for navigating the expanding high yield markets.

2. A fallen angel is an issuer whose credit rating falls to BB+ and below from BBB– and above.

2

Junk Bonds Then And Now

Since the late 1970s, the high yield securities market has represented the most creative, expansive, and sometimes controversial laboratory of financial innovation in the history of the United States. In the early 1990s we learned that rumors of the high yield securities market's demise, like Mark Twain's death, were "an exaggeration."[1] Twain is also thought to have said that history doesn't repeat itself, but it does rhyme. In retrospect, we find that much of the financial technology which fueled the high yield market was subsequently transferred into private equity and securitization, where it fueled waves of market, technological, and economic innovation. It infused the capital structure of corporations in the initial public offering (IPO) and secondary equity markets. There is rarely a term sheet to be found in the venture capital market or all of private equity investing[2] that does not contain features of subordinated debt, payment-in-kind provisions, or other financial innovations incubated in the high yield market of the 1970s and 1980s. The explosive growth of the markets for collateralized debt obligations and other derivative instruments began in the high yield market as well. The centrality of merging corporate strategy with the management and design of appropriate capital structures to execute growth strategies proved out the central hypothesis of high yield financial innovation—it was possible to manage the spectrum of instruments in corporate finance to empower owners, managers, and employees in financing their futures.

In short, capital structure mattered as a firm and its investors sought to realize high yielding business strategies. No longer could one assume only the term and rate structure of debt independent of equity. All features of corporate debt contracts became inextricably linked to the broader picture of corporate capital structure and its purpose and objective in business strategies—pursuing new product and process technologies, new markets at home and abroad, and business combinations with (sometimes elusive) synergies in the mergers and acquisitions market.

1. The rumors about the death of high yield were obvious in such headlines as *The New York Times*, May 13, 1990: "Market Sees That Junk Bonds Are, Well, Junk" and *The Wall Street Journal*, October 19, 1989: "U.S. Economy: House Built on Junk-Bond Sand." Mark Twain's note of June 1, 1897, to the London correspondent of *The New York Journal* was "The report of my death was an exaggeration."

2. "Private equity investing" became the politically correct way to refer to leveraged buyout funds, which have merged with venture capital as an asset class.

In this context, we've learned a great deal since the early 1990s not only about the development and application of financial technologies, but also about how they can be effectively regulated—or not. We've also learned how regulations can distort markets and generate the opposite of their intended effects. Financial markets represent a learning system for practitioners and policy makers alike. In refining our understanding of what works and what doesn't, the prospects for financing the future increase. There are also lessons to be learned from what is now established as a critical part of our capital market system—the securitized business loan market. At the beginning of the 1990s, an array of regulatory chokeholds on capital formation arose. The reversal and restructuring of regulation in the ensuing years enabled the next wave of capital formation among high yield firms and the new markets and technologies.

A BRIEF HISTORY OF THE HIGH YIELD SECURITIES MARKET

The advent of the modern-day high yield market derives from the financial conditions of the United States in the early 1970s. The disappointing performance in the early and mid-1970s of traditional investments in long-term, fixed-rate mortgages and government and corporate bonds, as well as common stocks, resulted in the search for new investment opportunities. (Much of this discussion derives from Yago 1991a.)

In fact, it was the credit crunch of 1974 that truly caused a revolution in the capital marketplace. By then, political and economic developments at home and abroad had brought an abrupt end to the pattern of postwar prosperity that most Americans had taken for granted. An array of factors converged to grind productivity to historically low levels. The ineluctable rise and concentration of the largest corporations began to pause and later to decline. The national government's "guns and butter" policy, defined during the Johnson administration and continued under Nixon, sought to finance both a major war in Southeast Asia and an aggressive expansion of social services at home. These events, along with the lifting of wage and price controls, produced a level of inflation previously unseen in the American experience (figure 2-1).

Consumer price increases were exacerbated by the 1973 oil shock. It was in this context of turmoil that monetary officials tried to brake the acceleration in consumer prices. Three decades of interest rate stability came to an abrupt end—short-term borrowing costs doubled in less than two years. Declining economic activity sent equity prices into a two-year slide that reduced the market value of U.S. firms by more than 40 percent. Banks, concerned about their own capital inadequacy caused by the effects of declining asset values in both real estate and the stock market, curtailed lending to all but the largest and highest-rated companies (Milken 1999a). As yields in the open market rose above interest rate ceilings on bank deposits, deposited funds flowed out of the banking system. Deteriorating bank capital positions and declining asset values further constrained lend-

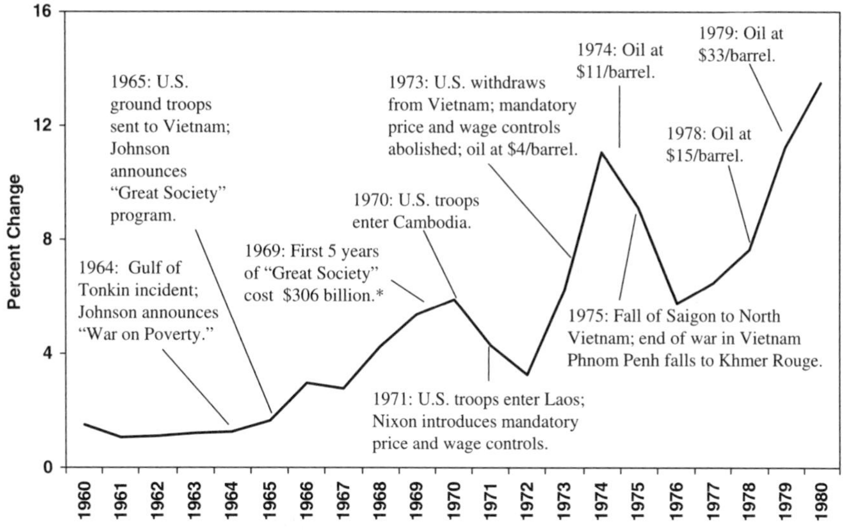

Figure 2-1. Guns and Butter: Inflation—U.S. Consumer Price Index Change, 1960–1980. In 2002 dollars. Sources: International Financial Statistics (IFS); Congressional Research Service; Milken Institute.

ing. In 1974, commercial bank loans shrank by $16 billion, or 20 percent, the largest single-year decline in twenty-five years. As the credit crunch spread, job losses increased, security prices of sound companies declined, and defaults increased in both real estate and retailing.

Under the circumstances, financial institutions canceled lines of credit and called in loans to existing customers, further exacerbating the drop in valuations of American businesses. Indeed, for most companies, money was unavailable at any price. Businesses were forced to reduce their levels of operation and cancel expansion plans, resulting in the largest reduction in private sector employment in the postwar period (Yago 1993).

By the end of the 1970s, patterns of corporate concentration, conglomerate diversification strategies, and global competition had led the U.S. economy into long-term economic stagnation. Stagflation and the misery index (unemployment plus inflation rates) characterized the economy of that decade.

Paradoxically, the companies with the highest returns on capital, the fastest rates of growth in both market share and employment, and the greatest contributions to technological and new product innovation had the least access to capital. Simply put, successful, growing, and profitable companies were denied the money they needed to operate and build. Troubled companies under new management were frozen out from raising capital to redeploy assets toward higher productivity operations. Investors were blocked from financing growth firms or firms seeking to restructure and redeploy assets. Circumstances also served to block investors from exiting from firms that pursued lower growth paths or negative net present value strategies.

The economic and financial disruptions of 1974 changed the way companies were financed and the way Americans were to look at their investments in future years. History and biography intersected in the person and career of Michael R. Milken. His prodigious body of work exemplified the nascent high yield market and set a standard for financial innovation in pioneering, renewing, and modernizing traditional industries.[3] Providing capital to businesses was one of the crucial challenges of the late 1970s and early 1980s. Asset managers and investment bankers were called upon to design transactions that could provide value in a time of volatile equity markets and interest rates. During this period, new industries needed money to grow. Older ones, such as automobiles, farm equipment, mining, and steel, needed huge sums to rebuild and adjust in order to survive. New firms and technologies in information, communications, health care, entertainment, and energy sought expansion and acquisition capital. Through new and innovative high yield securities, or structured finance adapted from the high yield market, money managers provided long-term, fixed-rate funds for businesses while earning higher rates of return for their clients. Aligning the interests of investors with those of entrepreneurs through corporate capital structure created a virtuous circle of investment that propelled the economy forward. Advances in corporate finance enabled the design of capital structures that would minimize the costs of capital coupled to the execution of strategic growth plans in an array of industries (Yago 1993).

Over the last quarter of the twentieth century, the revolution in corporate finance unfolded. Innovations in financial markets and institutions were designed to offer companies—large and small, new and established—access to capital that was previously available only to a select group of businesses. Increasingly, research and analysis of firms and industries suggested that the investment risks usually associated with new and renewing firms were less than what had been believed. By designing securities that would provide higher returns, their capital structure could compensate for any additional risk to investors while increasing the entrepreneur's chance for success. (See table 2-1 for a complete list of bond rating scales and definitions used to determine high yield.) Previously excluded firms, industries, and entrepreneurs were brought into the economic mainstream.

The high yield marketplace incubated some of today's most powerful and innovative corporations. Names like MCI, McCaw Cellular, Time-Warner, TCI Telecommunications, Mattel, Cablevision, News Corp., Barnes and Noble, and hundreds of others began within the high yield market and later graduated into the investment grade market. In many cases, their strategies and technologies infused larger corporate giants and taught them how to navigate through changing times.

3. For more on Milken's work, see his informative website, www.mikemilken.com. See particularly Walter and Milken 1973.

Table 2-1. Bond Rating Scales and Definitions

Moody	S & P	Fitch	DCR	Definition
Investment Grade—High Creditworthiness				
Aaa	AAA	AAA	AAA	Prime, maximum safety
Aa1	AA+	AA+	AA+	High grade, high quality
Aa2	AA	AA	AA	
Aa3	AA–	AA–	AA–	
A1	A+	A+	A+	Upper medium grade
A2	A	A	A	
A3	A–	A–	A–	
Baa1	BBB+	BBB+	BBB+	Lower medium grade
Baa2	BBB	BBB	BBB	
Baa3	BBB–	BBB–	BBB–	
High Yield Bonds Below Investment Grade—Low Creditworthiness				
Ba1	BB+	BB+	BB+	Noninvestment grade
Ba2	BB	BB	BB	Low grade, speculative
Ba3	BB–	BB–	BB–	
B1	B+	B+	B+	Highly speculative
B2	B	B	B	
B3	B–	B–	B–	
Predominantly Speculative—Substantial Risk or in Default				
Caa1	CCC+	CCC	CCC	Substantial risk
Caa2	CCC	—	—	In poor standing
Caa3	CCC–	—	—	
Ca	—	—	—	Extremely speculative
C	—	—	—	May be in default
—	—	DDD	—	Default
—	—	DD	DD	
—	D	D	—	
—	—	—	DP	

Split ratings describe securities rated differently by the two agencies: Split-investment-grade securities were rated investment-grade by one agency (BBB or higher) and below-investment-grade (BB and below) by the other. Split BB securities were rated BB by one agency and B or below by the other. Split B securities were rated B by one agency and Below-B by the other.

Moody—Moody's Investor Service; S&P—Standard & Poor's Corporation; Fitch—Fitch Ratings; DCR—Duff & Phelps Credit Rating Co.

There are, of course, some difficulties in measuring the size of the high yield market. Table 2-2 shows high yield new issuance statistics from different sources. They include figures from Securities Data Corporation (SDC), Credit Suisse First Boston (CSFB), Merrill Lynch (ML), Donaldson, Lufkin & Jenrette (DLJ), and Bear Stearns (BS). There are significant differences between data reported by the various companies. For example, SDC data include all markets, while ML and CSFB exclude private issues. (See table 2-3 for a complete description of each source.) The differences do not appear to follow any pattern or to have any consistent explanation. For example, in 1988 and 1996, DLJ reports more issues but less principal amount than ML. In 1991 and 1993, DLJ reports more of both, but in most other years reports less of both. Regardless of these differences, however, there is no denying the fabulous growth of the market for high yield securities in the last years of the twentieth century.

THE ETYMOLOGY OF "JUNK"

While the concept of high yield bonds has been around since bonds were first issued, the phrase "junk bond" is more recent. If you check ten reference guides for the definition of "junk bond," you will find ten very different answers (see appendix A). The earliest the phrase "junk bond" is used in print is a 1974 article in *Forbes* (see box 2-1). The article introduces the phrase in an effort to describe "a new angle in the bond market." The same companies that are listed as "junk bond" issuers in the 1974 article are described in *Forbes* in 1973 as "junk stocks." Articles printed between 1973 and 1974 about the debt of those companies and about the bond market in general do not use the term "junk bond." In the early 1970s, bond portfolio management was in its very beginning stages, hence the initial application of the word "junk" to stocks prior to its usage for bonds. The *Reader's Guide to Periodical Literature* first lists "Junk bonds" as a category in the March 1980–February 1981 volume, although it lists only "See Bonds" under the heading. "Junk Bonds" becomes its own category with the listing of full references in the March 1984–February 1985 volume. The 1974 *Forbes* article is listed in the *Reader's Guide* under "Bonds—Yields." (The only reference to "junk" in the 1974 *Reader's Guide* is "Junk cars, See automobile—wrecking.")

Among stock market professionals, the term "junk" became shorthand for describing those companies with highly recognizable names and highly rated securities that lost their good credit ratings. Those companies were also referred to as fallen angels, without quotation marks. *Forbes* ran a regular feature beginning in the 1950s that listed these companies as loaded laggards, though the reference was to equity and not debt securities. In this sense, "junk" is defined as something of poor quality or something of little value.

"Junk" was also shorthand for stocks that were simply out of favor. We find references to "the stock market junkman" who can have "happy scavenging" poring through the list of "junk-market specials." In Janu-

Table 2-2. High Yield New Issuance, 1977–2001

	SDC		ML		CSFB		DLJ		BS*	Average	Average
	Issues	Amount	Issues	Amount	Issues	Amount	Issues	Amount	Amount	Issues	Amount
1977	61	1,040	61	1,040	25	950				49	1,010
1978	81	1,553	82	1,579	50	1,450				71	1,527
1979	52	1,376	56	1,400	40	1,240				49	1,339
1980	44	1,426	45	1,429	40	1,360				43	1,407
1981	33	1,471	34	1,536	32	1,536				50	2,152
1982	50	2,669	52	2,692	42	2,562	49	2,400	4,414	58	3,300
1983	95	7,765	95	7,765	88	7,656	44	5,600	11,094	92	8,223
1984	131	15,239	131	15,239	132	14,652	111	12,700	15,670	141	15,308
1985	169	15,293	175	15,685	177	14,514	151	13,600	17,951	194	16,786
1986	218	31,866	226	33,262	223	34,119	221	30,500	40,165	269	38,087
1987	186	30,351	190	30,522	176	28,512	182	28,000	35,102	248	35,580
1988	154	30,520	160	31,095	157	27,632	162	26,600	30,012	264	37,221
1989	124	27,633	130	28,753	116	24,940	129	24,800	27,929	207	33,018
1990	11	1,589	10	1,397	6	684	11	1,600	2,717	54	3,685
1991	52	10,309	48	9,967	43	10,062	59	11,900	13,390	71	11,775
1992	262	42,066	274	43,566	236	39,648	267	40,600	42,761	271	42,200
1993	462	77,918	436	72,261	429	75,504	450	74,400	61,117	455	72,632
1994	314	48,397	272	42,333	255	43,095	246	39,200	37,400	290	42,626
1995	256	46,801	246	44,381	237	43,845	229	41,800	42,020	255	44,150
1996	486	85,852	359	65,912	410	79,130	379	65,800	66,213	424	73,042
1997	782	145,647	679	118,707	724	138,284	721	128,000	107,000	741	127,977
1998	891	171,309	720	140,889	—	—	—	—	—	839	156,960
1999	561	122,152	417	99,677	—	—	—	—	—	513	114,095
2000	318	59,320	181	50,215	—	—	—	—	—	263	55,224
2001	625	105,134	309	83,495	—	—	—	—	—	471	94,465

*Bear Stearns reports only amount issued.
"Issues" refers to number of issues during the year; "Amount" refers to the principal amount issued (in million U.S.$).
DLJ and BS may include some private market issues.
Sources: Securities Data Corporation (SDC); Merrill Lynch (ML); Credit Suisse First Boston (CSFB); Donaldson, Lufkin & Jenrette (DLJ); Bear Stearns (BS).

Table 2-3. High Yield Market Definitions

	Definition of High Yield Market
Securities Data Corporation (SDC)	High yield data can include straight (nonconvertible) debt. Public and private placements and Rule 144A may be flagged as "high yield." SDC defines an issue as high yield if the issue is rated BB+ and below by S&P or Ba1 and below by Moody's.
Merrill Lynch (ML)	High yield data include nonconvertible, corporate debt rated below investment grade by Moody's or Standard & Poor's. Excludes mortgage- and asset-backed issues, as well as non-144A private placements. Senior debt includes senior secured and senior unsecured issues. Subordinated debt includes senior subordinated, subordinated, and junior subordinated issues.
Credit Suisse First Boston (CSFB)	High yield data include public issues registered in the U.S. or issued under Rule 144A rated below investment grade by Moody's or Standard & Poor's.
Donaldson, Lufkin & Jenrette (DLJ)	High yield data include public issues registered in the U.S. or issued under Rule 144A rated below investment grade by Moody's or Standard & Poor's. Issues are straight corporate debt, including cash-pay, zero-coupon, stepped-rate, and pay-in-kind (PIK) bonds. Floating-rate and convertible bonds and preferred stock are not included.
Bear Stearns (BS)	High yield data include public offerings in registration, visible private deals (not including shelf registrations), as well as split-rated, nondollar, and emerging market corporate debt.

Note: CSFB bought DLJ in 2000. Their high yield indexes merged as of May 31, 2001.
Source: Milken Institute

ary 1973, *Forbes* interviewed two moneymen: John Neff from Wellington Management (a fund manager) and Robert Wade from Burnham & Co. The last six months of 1972 saw market advances coming almost entirely from growth stocks. When asked for his picks, Neff bucked the trend and insisted that he would "buy stocks that nobody wants and wait until other people do want them." Wade, on the other hand, believed that the win-

BOX 2-1 FIRST ARTICLE ON "JUNK" BONDS, *FORBES*, APRIL 1, 1974, p. 26

The Big Money in "Junk" Bonds

A new angle in the bond market where returns of 12% to 14% are not unusual—and the chance for capital gains is good.

As INTEREST RATES have inched downward, a small corner of the bond market—known among traders as the "junk index"—has been getting a heavy play from individual investors.

Since late January, for example, one of the two most actively traded straight interest bonds has been a "junk" bond, Recrion's 10's of 1984 (the other, no junker, was AT&T's 8¾s of 2000). The unrated Recrion issue is an obligation of the old scandal-scarred Parvin/Dorhmann Corp. Nevertheless it has run from 68 on Jan. 23 when it was first listed, to over 80 recently.

What makes an issue a junk bond? While there is no precise definition, they typically come out of mergers or exchange offers. Some traders extend this definition to include the bonds of highly leveraged companies whose issues are of questionable quality. Junk bonds are usually not sold through an underwriter, although a dealer-manager is often involved.

The issuing of straight interest junk bonds is typically a means of massaging the balance sheet. An exchange for common, for instance, leverages up a company and can produce instant earnings increases. This is because the after-tax interest cost is invariably less than the earnings attributed to the acquired common stock. Ten percent may sound like a high coupon rate, but it is low compared with the earnings involved if, say, the common acquired in a swap was selling at only five times earnings. The company must earn 40% pretax to cover stock with a P/E of 5. But it can save three-fourths of that cost if it can exchange that stock dollar for dollar for a 10% bond.

These so-called junk bonds can also be used to reduce potential dilution hanging over a stock. This is done by swapping a higher coupon straight bond for a lower coupon convertible bond or preferred.

Typically, junk bonds carry high coupons and are sold at deep discounts when they are first listed—the Recrion 10's had a current yield of 13.9% and a yield to maturity in excess of 15% when they were first traded.

Why the high yields? Junk bonds are not widely distributed and are more often than not unrated. Thus few institutions—the big factors in the bond market—will touch them. This means the bonds must carry enough of a premium to entice holders of the securities for which they are being offered to make the swap in the first place. In addition, the yield must also be high enough to make the bonds attractive in the secondary market.

Yields are highest when the bonds are first issued and generally decline as they are absorbed by the market. Thus the more seasoned junk bonds move less dramatically with changes in market conditions. But there are now new

(*continued*)

Box 2-1 continued

Bond	Coupon & Maturity		Price on 12/31/73	Recent Price 3/15/74	Current Yield	Standard & Poor's Rating
American Medicorp	$9^{1}/_{2}$s	'98	$71^{1}/_{4}$	79	12.0%	—
City Investing	$8^{1}/_{8}$s	'91	80	$83^{7}/_{8}$	9.7	B
Continental Investment	9s	'85	80	78	11.5	—
Crane	7s	'94	$74^{1}/_{2}$	$77^{3}/_{8}$	9.0	B
Fuqua	$9^{1}/_{2}$s	'98	$89^{1}/_{4}$	92	10.3	B
Great Western United	6s	'87	$58^{1}/_{4}$	62	9.7	—
Gulf & Western (A)	7s	'03	65	68	10.3	—
Jones & Laughlin	6¾s	'94	$72^{1}/_{4}$	70	9.6	BB
LTV	5s	'88	$45^{1}/_{8}$	49	10.2	CCC
LTV Aerospace	$6^{3}/_{4}$s	'88	$58^{1}/_{2}$	$66^{3}/_{8}$	10.2	BB
LTV Wilson	$6^{1}/_{2}$s	'88	$59^{1}/_{2}$	65	10.0	BB
Lykes/Youngstown (new)	$7^{1}/_{2}$s	'94	62	66	11.4	B
McCrory	$7^{3}/_{4}$s	'95	$61^{1}/_{8}$	$64^{1}/_{2}$	12.0	—
McCrory	$7^{5}/_{8}$s	'97	$60^{3}/_{4}$	$66^{1}/_{4}$	11.5	B
Rapid-American	$7^{1}/_{2}$s	'85	$69^{7}/_{8}$	$72^{1}/_{2}$	10.3	CCC
Rapid-American	6s	'88	$52^{1}/_{2}$	$57^{1}/_{4}$	10.5	CCC
Recrion*	10s	'84	68*	79	12.7	—
Reliance Group	$9^{7}/_{8}$s	'98	$74^{3}/_{4}$	$83^{1}/_{2}$	11.8	—
United Brands	$9^{1}/_{8}$s	'98	$83^{1}/_{2}$	$88^{1}/_{2}$	10.3	B
Warner Communications	$7^{5}/_{8}$s	'94	68	72	10.6	B
Western Union	$10^{3}/_{4}$s	'97	$85^{1}/_{2}$	$92^{1}/_{2}$	11.6	B
Whittaker	10s	'88	70	$80^{1}/_{8}$	12.5	B

*First traded Jan. 23, 1974

junk bonds coming out every few weeks—APL, M-G-M, Reliance Group and Gulf & Western all have new issues in the pipeline. Lately the prices of the newer junk bonds moved up smartly (*see table*) as interest rates tailed off. Who's buying junk bonds? Individuals; mostly businessmen. "These have proved to be generally excellent buys," says one trader. "Big money is being made in junk bonds." "If you're a businessman and you want to play the bond market," says another, "this is one way you can do it—especially if you're willing to take the leverage."

Yes, the leverage. There are no set margin requirements on fixed-interest bonds and many brokers will allow good customers to carry them on margins of 25% or even less. If a junk bond yields 14% and is bought on 25% margin, the buyer can get an effective yield of well over 20% on his cash investment (assuming he is paying 11% interest on his margin debt). And that is not taking into account the tax consequences; the appreciation, if any, can be a capital gain.

But what about the risks? "This is definitely not a game," *Forbes* heard repeatedly, "for widows and orphans." The leverage, of course, operates well

(*continued*)

Box 2-1 continued

both ways; if interest rates start going the other way, there will be a drop in junk bond prices, and with it will come margin calls. The result will be lots of sellers but no buyers—everybody will be in the same boat.

That's the market risk. Then there is the risk associated with investing in a given company. The investor has to decide if the extra risk is reasonable. How? By doing his homework on the company and the industry.

"Remember," explains a bond trader, "historically you are better off diversifying in low-grade bonds than in high-grade ones in terms of effective yield and risk. And, besides," he adds quickly, "if you can buy a bond that has, say, three times coverage and the company doesn't look like it's going belly up and it's yielding 14% for you, how bad are you going to go?"

Assuming, of course, that the nation isn't in for a major recession or a brutal credit crunch.

[Reprinted with permission.]

ning investment strategy for 1973 would be buying the same growth stocks that were favored by the market during the previous year, "and so does [*sic*] the majority of professional money managers." In the case of Neff's comments, "junk" would be defined as waste or discarded articles that may be used again in some form, much as one would refer to "junk art." Oddly enough, the director of research at Burnham did not favor "junk" stocks in 1973, although Michael Milken would be joining Drexel Firestone & Co. that same year. The two firms merged in 1974 to become Drexel Burnham & Co., a name that will forever be linked to the definition of "junk bonds."

CRITICAL EVENTS IN THE HIGH YIELD MARKET

Corporate, political, and economic events all converge in the high yield market to shape expectations about returns, performance, and prospects for firms navigating their way through the business strategies and objectives of rapidly changing factor, product, and consumer markets, using technologies that change just as rapidly. A time line of events that have affected this market is shown on the inside front cover of this book. The period 1989–1990 was often characterized at the time as the beginning of the end of the high yield market. In retrospect, it is clear that it was only the end of the beginning. The year 1989 was one of those critical years that occasionally appear (like 1968, 1945, and 1929) in which historical convergence creates the foundation for long waves of economic growth and change. The high yield market financed and catalyzed many of the cascading changes that defined the opening of this new century—new technology markets in communications and entertainment, new markets in transition economies, the management of international financial crises in Latin America and Asia, the opening of markets in the Far East, and so on.

Obviously, the history of the high yield market is marked by controversy. Some of the controversy, especially that surrounding Michael Milken and Drexel Burnham Lambert, worked its way into the very definition of the financial instruments (see appendix A). That critical year, 1989, began with speculation about what Rudolph Giuliani had in store for Milken. The incredible ninety-eight-count federal indictment against Milken on charges of racketeering and securities fraud in April provoked a collective gasp among Wall Streeters (*Time*, April 10, 1989, p. 42). As financial institutions were forced to sell their holdings of high yield securities, the ramifications of government interference in the market were just coming into view.

In his 1990 Nobel Laureate Address, Merton Miller vigorously defended the high yield market on theoretical and empirical grounds. "New markets and new developments," he said, "are always unsettling." Despite a spike in defaults that year, capital markets, as information systems with self-correcting feedbacks, have built-in controls against systemwide overleveraging. During 1989, the share of new high yield bonds rated B– or lower fell to 28 percent after averaging 62 percent for the two prior years. Additionally, high yield issuances in leveraged buyouts fell from 41 percent in 1988 to 25 percent in 1989.[4] Miller warned against any attempt to override the self-correcting mechanisms of the market:

> Recent efforts by regulators to override these built-in market mechanisms by destroying the high yield market and imposing additional direct controls over leveraged lending by banks will have all the unintended consequences normally associated with such regulatory interventions. They will lower efficiency and raise the cost of capital to this important business sector. (Merton Miller, Nobel Laureate Address, *Investors' Daily*, December 12, 1990, p. 30)

CAPITAL ACCESS AND HIGH YIELD FINANCIAL INNOVATIONS

The low and stable inflation, interest rates, and exchange rates of the 1950s and 1960s gave way to higher levels of financial market volatility in subsequent decades. Disruptive economic conditions in the 1970s created the response of the high yield market. With the credit crunch of 1974, growth companies sought new ways to increase their financial flexibility and the management of their capital structure. Chronic uncertainty accompanying increased market volatility plagued investors. Holding "riskfree" U.S. Treasuries during the late 1970s and early 1980s meant that investors could lose as much as 50 percent of their principal after inflation (figure 2-2).

4. This is significant since more than 65 percent of defaults in the spike year, 1990, derived from 1987 and 1988 issues when some incidents of overleveraging in the buyout market were evidenced. See Paulus and Waite 1990.

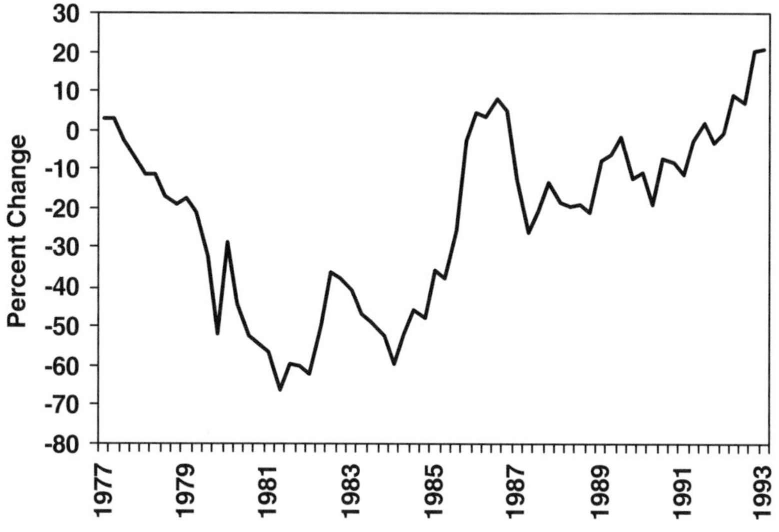

Figure 2-2. Quarterly Change in Market Value of U.S. Treasury Bonds, 1977–1993. Sources: Federal Reserve; Milken Institute.

Companies seeking long-term financing increasingly found investors willing to purchase diverse securities, including innovative issues of commercial paper, long-term debt, convertible debt, preferred stock, common equity, and derivative products related to these underlying assets. The convergence of corporate and investor demand was the impetus for the high yield market's evolution.

The noninvestment grade market gave small and medium-sized companies access to long-term capital previously available to only 800 (and thus less than 5 percent) of the 22,000 U.S. companies with sales in excess of $35 million. Efficient access to funds, coupled with a secondary market for restructuring balance sheets, provided flexibility in financial management, allowing companies to pursue changing corporate strategies. Firms were empowered to expand into new products, processes, services, and markets that unleashed an enormous potential for growth.

Prior to the development of the high yield securities market, growth companies with little or no credit history depended almost entirely on restrictive, short-term bank financing or relatively high-cost equity offerings to fund growth. After the 1981–1982 recession, over one-third of all public high yield new issues were from companies in dynamic, high-growth industries such as pharmaceuticals, computing equipment and semiconductors, cellular phone networks, long-distance telephone communications, cable television, and health services. During the 1980s, moreover, intensive users of noninvestment grade capital in such high-growth industries were found to exhibit one-third greater growth in productivity, 50 percent faster sales growth, and about three times faster growth in capital spending than U.S. industries generally.[5]

Another target of high yield securities innovation was the market for corporate control. Large blocks of capital were mobilized to gain control of undervalued corporate assets in relatively mature, slow-growing industries. Roughly 32 percent, or $579.7 billion, of total public high yield issuance was used to finance corporate control transactions (in primarily low growth industries) during the 1980s active period (figure 2-3). The academic research is quite clear about the impressive gains in corporate stock prices, operating cash flow, worker productivity, and cost efficiency that resulted from the restructurings of the 1980s. (See, e.g., Trimbath 2002, chap. 3, for a complete review of ex post changes at the firm level.) The heavily restructured manufacturing sector grew at 3.6 percent annually and regained the share of GDP it had during the 1960s at the height of U.S. manufacturing dominance.

A breakdown of the use of proceeds of high yield issuance shows different patterns in different periods. The use of high yield debt declined with the advent of federal government regulations relating to high yield funding for merger and acquisition activity. Although leveraged buyouts (LBOs) and refinancing of acquisition debt accounted for a large portion of the 1980s market, these two groups comprised only 10 percent of the proceeds of high yield securities issued from 1990 to 1999 (figure 2-4).

The late 1990s and 2000 once again saw bond issuance mainly for acquisition financing and capital expenditures, with these two categories

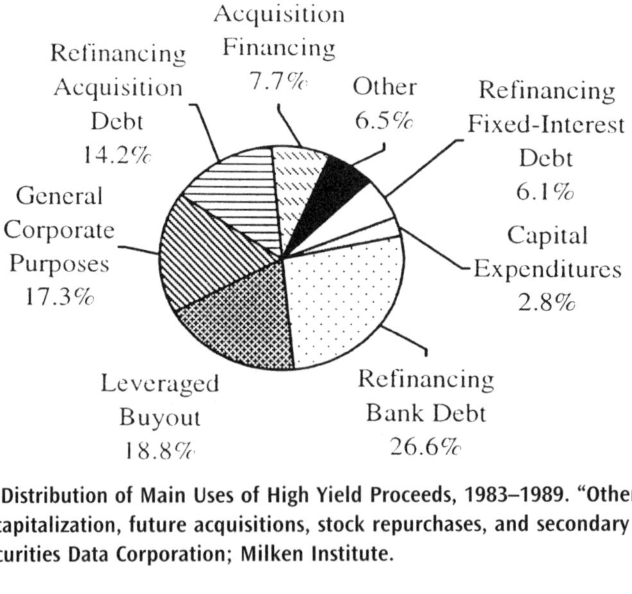

Figure 2-3. Distribution of Main Uses of High Yield Proceeds, 1983–1989. "Other" includes recapitalization, future acquisitions, stock repurchases, and secondary offerings. Sources: Securities Data Corporation; Milken Institute.

5. Generally, noninvestment grade companies accounted for virtually all of the 19 million net new private sector jobs created during the 1980s, while the largest, most creditworthy firms were responsible for 3.5 million net jobs lost over the same period.

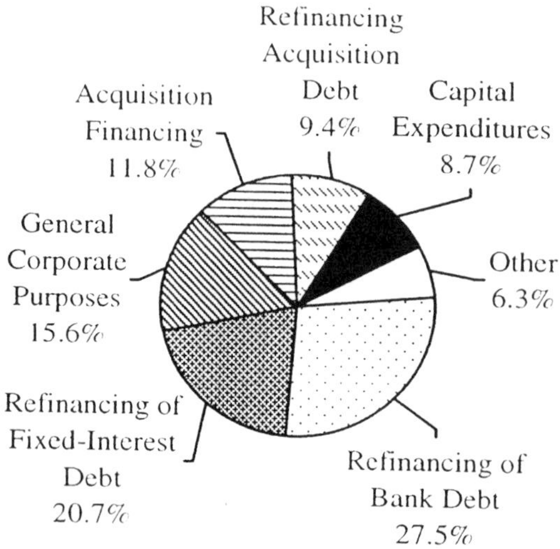

Figure 2-4. Distribution of Main Uses of High Yield Proceeds, 1990–1999. "Other" includes recapitalization, leveraged buyouts, future acquisitions, stock repurchases, and secondary offerings. Sources: Securities Data Corporation; Milken Institute.

growing to account for 50 percent of total issuance by 2000 (table 2-4). Another trend of note is the growth in issuance used for refinancing fixed-interest debt in the early 1990s, and its subsequent decline in the latter part of the decade. From its peak of 48 percent in 1991, the share of high yield proceeds used for refinancing fixed-rate debt fell to a low of 6 percent in 2000. Finally, refinancing bank debt has remained consistently important. Refinancing bank-related debt accounts for the single largest portion in the period 1981–1999 with 27 percent of total issuance.

Economic and flexible sources of capital are drivers of firm and industry growth. In addition to the newer industries mentioned above, older industries also benefited from innovative financing and the promotion of efficiency-enhancing restructuring and rebuilding activity. Innovations in capital structure and security designs have created an impressive array of financial instruments—ranging from commodity- and currency-indexed bonds to bond-warrant units, liquid-yield option notes, zero-coupon bonds, and payment-in-kind securities. (We discuss some specific innovations in chapter 7.) These enable companies to cope with volatility in commodity prices, exchange rates, interest rates, and equity prices. These innovations also allow investors to reduce their uncertainty about corporate exposures to financial risks. And, finally, they enable companies to raise capital on more favorable terms.

In short, the 1980s witnessed a resurgence in U.S. competitiveness linked to market-driven financial innovations. By the 1990s, continued volatility in domestic and international financial and product markets elaborated advances in financial technology and made them even more valuable to all firms. As we shall observe in chapter 7, the resurgence and expansion of the

Table 2-4. Breakdown of Use of Proceeds, 1983–2000 (Percent of Principal Amount)

	General Corporate Purposes	Capital Expenditure	Refinancing	Recap.	Stock Repurchase	Secondary Offering	Acqui. Financing	LBO	Future Acqui.
1983	25.0	15.9	55.7	0.0	1.9	0.0	1.1	0.0	0.0
1984	22.9	3.5	53.7	0.0	2.3	0.0	2.8	12.6	2.2
1985	34.9	0.0	43.7	0.0	1.3	1.3	5.9	3.9	9.1
1986	14.5	0.0	44.3	1.7	0.5	0.3	12.3	25.1	1.5
1987	7.5	0.0	45.4	8.8	1.7	0.0	7.2	27.6	1.8
1988	5.9	0.0	49.5	2.3	0.0	0.9	10.9	29.6	1.0
1989	10.5	0.0	36.4	5.6	0.0	1.1	13.7	32.7	0.0
1990	1.8	7.2	91.1	0.0	0.0	0.0	0.0	0.0	0.0
1991	24.9	0.2	71.8	0.0	0.0	0.0	0.0	3.1	0.0
1992	18.4	0.0	68.3	6.1	1.0	0.7	3.0	0.3	2.2
1993	15.1	1.4	70.1	1.3	0.8	0.4	5.9	0.4	0.3
1994	26.5	4.1	48.2	1.7	0.2	0.9	14.7	0.0	0.0
1995	14.8	7.9	53.7	0.0	0.0	0.0	16.5	0.0	2.8
1996	18.9	11.5	41.8	0.9	1.0	0.0	19.5	1.1	1.6
1997	20.5	15.0	40.1	2.2	0.3	0.0	17.1	0.9	0.4
1998	8.6	20.0	45.0	2.4	0.1	0.0	18.8	4.8	0.3
1999	6.4	20.0	46.4	0.3	0.4	0.0	22.1	3.7	0.7
2000	7.6	22.6	34.3	1.8	0.0	0.0	26.5	6.5	0.7

Sources: Securities Data Corporation; Merrill Lynch.

high yield market in the 1990s led to further changes in the use of funds in high yield financing and the structuring of transactions for firms in that market. We will spend time in chapter 8 understanding why and how practitioners in corporate finance came to understand that capital structure really mattered in the first place. The emergence of both the practical and the theoretical implications of the linkages between financial innovation and growth are important elements in the explanation of how economic values can be maximized through the application of financial technology.

JUNK BONDS NOW

Unlike the high default environment that began the 1990s, the historically large number of troubled credits and defaults in today's high yield market are advantaged by a historically low interest rate environment. While clearly in a funk of decline, new high yield issuance has not come to the abrupt shutdown that it did in the early nineties. Though the absolute size of defaults and distressed credits are at all time highs, they comprise a relatively smaller portion of the total market than they did in the early 1990s. Distressed credits (the proportion of bonds trading at spreads 1,000 basis points or greater than government bonds) comprised more than 60 percent of the high yield market in the early nineties, versus 30.6 percent today (figure 2-5). Until recently, there was a long term trend since 1990 of declining high yield secondary market distress. By contrast, the newer European high yield bond

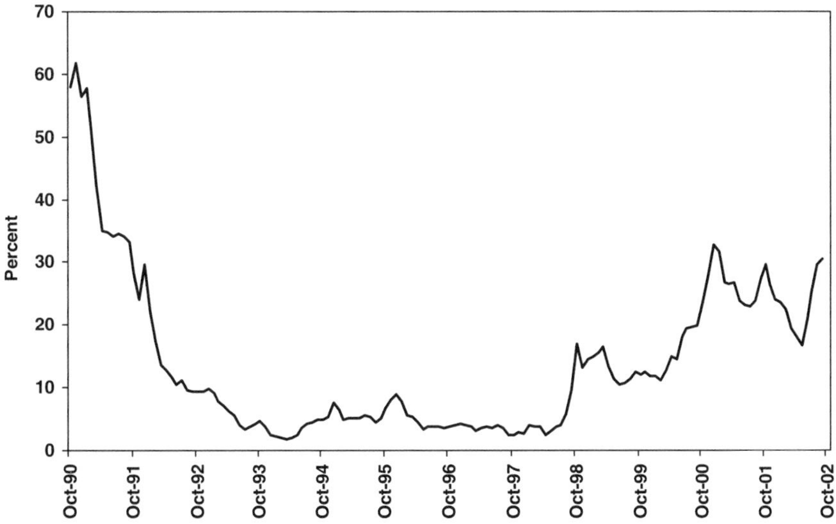

Figure 2-5. Distress Ratio, October 1990-September 2002. The distress ratio is the percentage of issues in the Merrill Lynch High Yield Master Index outyielding Treasuries by 1,000 basis points or more. Source: Martin S. Fridson, Chief High Yield Strategist, Merrill Lynch.

distress ratio stands at 46.8 percent, suggesting much less segmentation, maturity, and diversity (not to mention experience and regulations that inhibit restructuring) than the U.S. high yield market.

Another significant change is the recently increased prominence of fallen angels in the high yield market. The crisis in the high yield market is now more broadly characteristic of the problems of U.S. corporations. The total fallen angel inflow into the high yield market is highly significant and equal to half of the new issue volume during the same period in 2002, a new phenomenon since the advent of the new issue high yield market in the 1970s. The composition today is highly concentrated in the telecommunications area. The market value of the WorldCom, Qwest, and Global Crossing defaults alone instantly made telecommunications the largest industry sector in the high yield market. Telecommunications issuers constitute a massive 61 percent of defaults and have heavily influenced default rates. Removing telecommunications from default rate calculations lowers the issuer-weighted default rate to 8 percent. Once again, the high yield market has become a place where companies come to restructure, rehabilitate, and reinvent themselves in another business cycle.

The high yield market has always been an event driven market. The uncertainty of current economic conditions echoes the circumstances that preceded its previous recoveries. Broader problems in corporate management are reflected in the significant number of fallen angels into the high yield market. Clearly, the high concentration of securities issued under Rule 144A (144A issues) and telecommunications issuers at the market's issuing peak

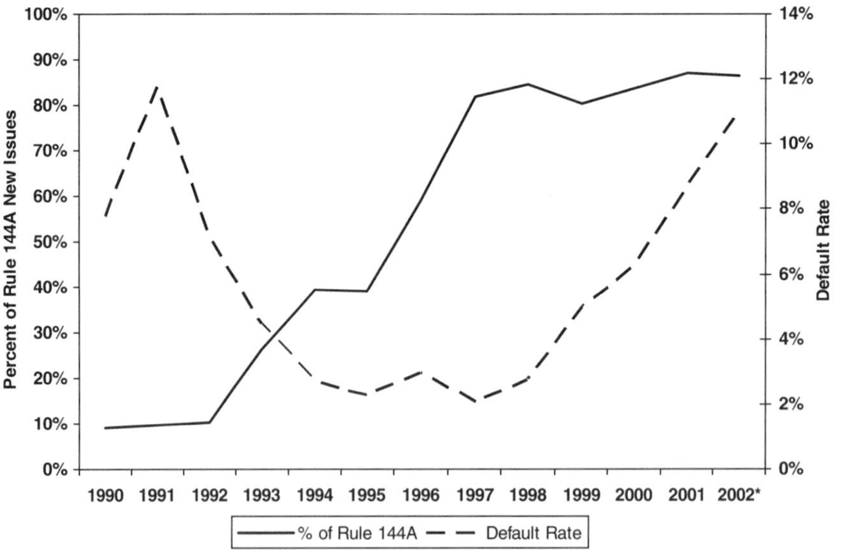

Figure 2-6. Percent of Rule 144A New Issues and High Yield Default Rate. *YTD 7/31/2002. Source: Securities Data Corporation, Moody's Investors Service.

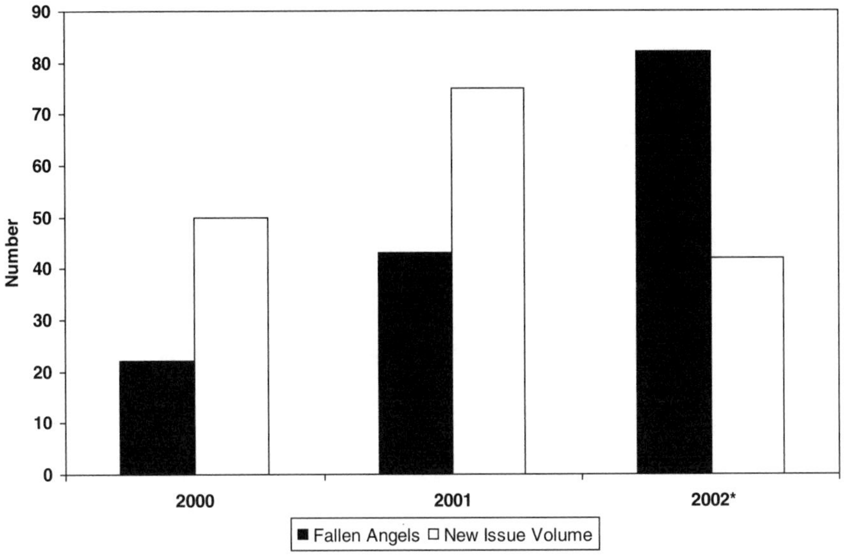

Figure 2-7. High Yield New Supply, 2000–2002. *YTD 8/30/2002 (data not annualized). Sources: Bear Stearns High Yield Index (BSIX); MW Post Advisory Group, LLC.

in 1998 increases the negative event risk of further downgrades and defaults. The peak of high yield issuance in the market was in 1998 with 891 issues at $171 billion volume of offering. At that time, 144A issues comprised 85 percent of the total number of issuances. Both the size and industrial concentration of those issuances (in telecommunications) suggests the subsequent basis of defaults (figure 2-6). However, the counter opportunity of positive events resulting from equity offerings associated with restructurings, mergers and acquisitions, and calls and tender offers are the mirror image of this market process that should lead to recovery in the high yield market.

The market of high yield credits is quite sensitive to negative events in both the general economy, geopolitical situation, and specific industry or company conditions. By the summer of 2002, numerous setbacks rocked the high yield market. Stock prices crumbled back to near September 11, 2001 lows. The fallout from the telecom industry, including several high-profile investment and high yield companies, chilled the market. Bank line maturities, renegotiations, and commercial paper setbacks put a temporary squeeze on corporate credits. Given major corporate defaults and accounting scandals, major credit rating agencies started to overhaul their reporting resulting in an all-time high downgrade ratio and the record number of fallen angels. The unusually high number of over 80 fallen angels in 2002 rose to more than $130 billion. Since the recent spate of corporate bond downgrades began in 1998, more than $223 billion of corporate bond issues have fallen from the investment grade categories into the high yield bond market overwhelming the number of new issues for the first time in over a decade.

3

Regulatory Choke Holds on Economic Growth

> The prices of the material factors of production, wage rates and interest rates on the one hand and the anticipated future prices of the consumers' goods on the other hand are the items that enter into the planning businessman's calculations. The result of these calculations shows the businessman whether or not a definite project will pay. If the market data underlying his calculations are falsified by the interference of the government, the result must be misleading.
>
> Ludwig von Mises, memorandum dated April 24, 1946

A fundamental mismatch exists between the sources of job creation and the sources of capital formation. U.S. financial history can be read as a long attempt to resolve that mismatch—from the early days of the Republic through the expansion of credit, land, and home ownership in the late nineteenth and early twentieth centuries until the revolution in corporate finance and capital markets that fueled the expansive U.S. economic growth beginning in the early 1980s. Financial technologies and market-based public policy innovations focused on resolving one problem: how to carve channels of capital from investors to the entrepreneurs who are the most important source of job, income, and wealth creation. The resolution of this mismatch underlies America's greatest economic policy challenge—to achieve the growth that will lower economic inequality to keep prosperity alive.

Flow of funds data reflect the relative contraction of financial institutional sources of capital and the expansion of capital market sources. The central point shown in figure 3-1 is that depository institutions' share of financial assets has been shrinking dramatically while that of nondepository institutions has grown to replace them. The explosive growth of the securities market (figure 3-2), the growth of the high yield securitized business loan market (figure 3-3), and the overall expansion of market capitalization (figure 3-4) illustrate the growth and maximization of value in the economy.

An earlier version of this material appeared as a Milken Institute policy brief under the title "The Jobs/Capital Mismatch: Financial Regulatory Chokeholds on Economic Growth" (1999).

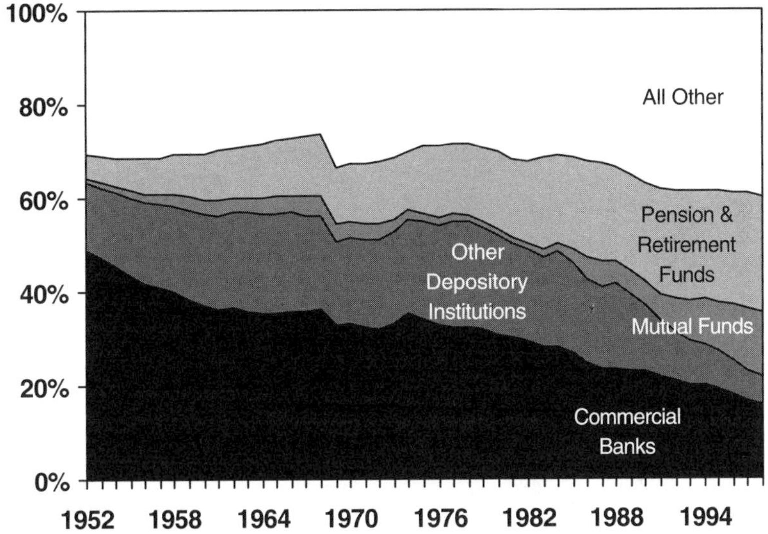

Figure 3-1. Percentage Distribution of Total Financial Assets Held by U.S. Financial Service Firms, 1952–1998. Source: Federal Reserve Statistical Releases, Flow of Funds.

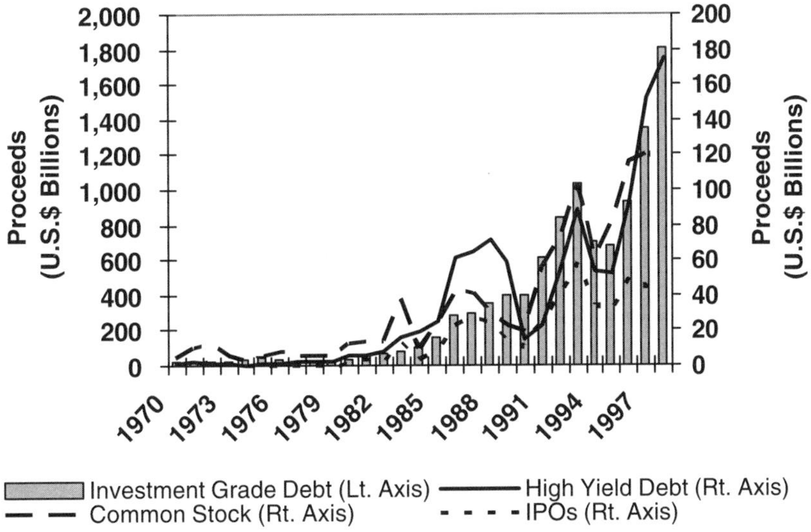

Figure 3-2. Securities Market, 1970–1998. Sources: Milken Institute; Securities Data Corporation.

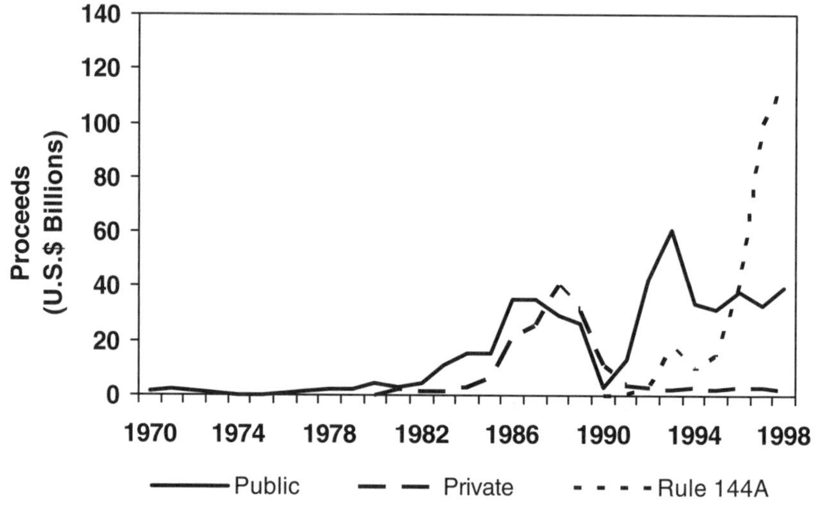

Figure 3-3. Securitized Business Loan Market, 1970–1998. Sources: Milken Institute; Securities Data Corporation.

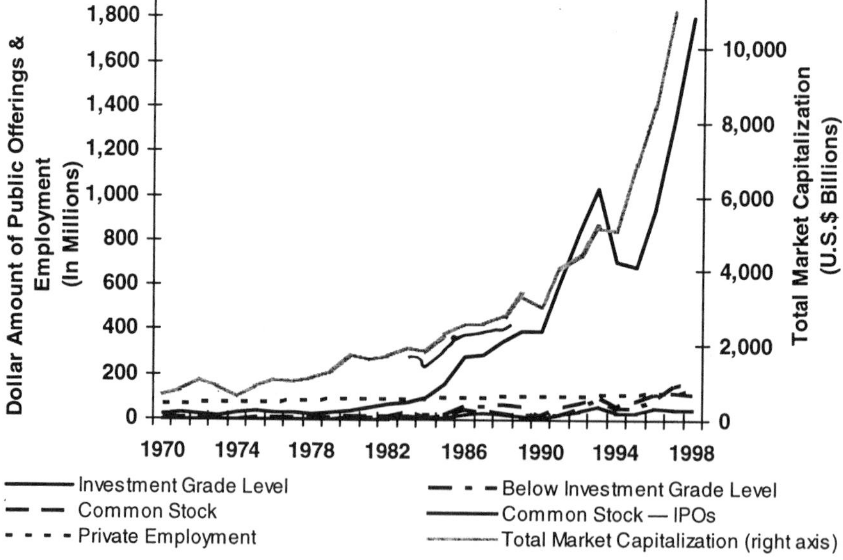

Figure 3-4. America's Working Capital: Public Offerings, 1970–1998. Sources: Milken Institute; Securities Data Corporation; Center for Research in Stock Prices (CRSP); Bureau of Labor Statistics.

These are all positive indications of the vibrancy of innovation and the spark points for economic and employment growth that can emerge when finance is linked to growth strategies by firms. For example, from 1990 to 1997, the growth in all forms of public offerings, besides high yield and investment grade convertible debt, rose over 90 percent. A picture of the linkage between the active management of capital structure and a strategy of growth emerges from these descriptive demonstrations of capital market experimentation and learning.

The sources of growth in employment, output, and profits are at the lower end of the size range of firms in the economy, where most innovation takes place. A wealth of entrepreneurial research continues to verify that fundamental pattern—growth emerges from a relatively small set of firms. The continued evolution of firms from that volatile segment fuels the pattern of business learning that supports aggregate economic growth (Birch, Haggerty and Parsons 1993). The complexity of this dynamic process generates a self-organizing pattern of increasing returns for the economy as a whole. (See Arthur 1990, 1994, 1995; Romer 1986, 1996a, 1996b.)

MEASURING BUSINESS FINANCE: THE PERSISTENCE OF SIZE ADVANTAGE

The structural shift from financial institutions to capital markets as the mechanism through which businesses finance their growth is striking and has fueled the process of increasing returns. However, as that change in the channels through which capital flows has taken effect, small businesses have participated less. In very general terms, the allocation of capital resources for growth financing suggests that while many financial technologies have developed to support emergent businesses, they have not always served firms equitably on the basis of size. This has been an ongoing problem in U.S. financial history that has been resolved in critical transaction points by financial innovation (Tufano 1989).

Although small businesses in the United States represent over 40 percent of total assets, debt, and net worth, the small business share of measurable business financing is less than 10 percent (table 3-1). Small businesses continue to rely mostly upon their own internal resources. Despite tremendous advances in the growth of the venture capital (see Lerner 1999; Lerner and Gompers 1998, 1999), mezzanine debt and corporate bond markets, and asset-backed securitization, the vast majority of small businesses do not have access to the valuations and financing technologies available to larger companies. The generalization of financial innovation toward a broader section of the business market remains unfinished work. We are still in the early stages of an era of entrepreneurial growth dependent upon the transfer of capital market financial technology to growth sectors in order to keep economic growth alive.

Here is the problem, then, as these data indicate: the increasing concentration of capital funds has moved toward nondepository institutions, particularly mutual funds, which have become the major repositories of

Table 3-1. Measurable Financing of Business

Small Firms	$ billions	Large Firms	$ billions
Commercial Paper	0	Commercial Paper	163
Commercial Mortgages	66	Commercial Mortgages	224
Commercial and Industrial Loans	98	Commercial and Industrial Loans	418
Trade Debt	233	Trade Debt	638
Finance Companies	91	Finance Companies	272
Initial Public Offering	10	Initial Public Offering	117
Venture Capital Pool	34	Venture Capital Pool	0
Bond Market	0	Bond Market	1326
Stock Market	0	Stock Market	5828
Bank Loans	98	Bank Loans	418
Total	630	Total	9404

Note: A "small firm" is a business with fewer than 500 employees.
Sources: Milken Institute; Small Business Administration; Federal Reserve, Flow of Funds.

capital. However, the remediation of those funds from savers to investors into the economy toward firms that offer the potential for returns and growth in employment and investment remains largely absent. The critical need of smaller firms for start-up, later stage, and operating capital remains. Trade debt and commercial mortgages remain the largest sources of finance. Small business is disproportionately dependent upon banks in comparison to larger firms: two-thirds of small firms that borrow get their funds from commercial banks.

However, since commercial banks participate in a declining share of the financial services market (going from a 51 percent share in 1950 to a 23 percent share in 1997), small businesses have been affected to a greater extent because they have fewer nonbank options than larger companies even as capital markets have become more user friendly. Despite the tremendous wave of financial innovation in the 1980s, we have only begun the era in which financial innovation can further advance economic growth and the democratization of capital.

THE ECONOMY IN THE EARLY 1990s: PRECIPITOUS RECESSION

In 1991, Robert Hall, the newly elected president of the American Economic Association and one of the nation's leading macroeconomists, framed his inaugural address about the inadequacies of existing macroeconomic theory in explaining the recession that opened the decade (Hall 1993). In the policy arena, a remarkable bipartisan consensus emerged about the existence of inadequate growth accompanied by growing inequality. While the explanations and solutions vary considerably, we now appear to share acknowledgment of this dual reality. Though many factors hampering growth may be structural in nature and require long periods of resolution—education, training, family and community structure—institutional factors surrounding the regulatory environment that create a choke hold on growth are mutable immediately. There are four sources of this regulatory choke hold that created a growth capital crunch in the early 1990s and that continue to hamper more equitable and faster economic growth—the overregulation of banking, insurance, thrifts, and mergers.

REGULATORY CHOKE HOLD I: BANKING REGULATIONS

As noted above, smaller growth-oriented businesses remain disproportionately dependent upon banks as their source of capital. These largely undercapitalized firms were particularly hard hit by regulatory measures taken during the late 1980s that now appear to have precipitated the recession. David Mullins, then vice chairman of the Federal Reserve, acknowledged this fact in 1993:

> Indeed, there is every reason to think that recent regulations and statutes may have changed the nature of supervision and regulation. The process has become progressively more standardized and mechanical, more dependent on documentation, analytical formulas, and rigid rules as opposed to examiner judgment. This may have disproportionately affected small business lending, which often takes the form of character and cash-flow loans, requiring judgment, and where the bank's return comes through knowledge and a working relationship with the borrower. These loans may be heterogeneous in nature, and they may be less amenable to the increasingly standardized nature of supervision and regulation. (*Federal Reserve Bulletin*, May 1993)

Increasingly, the empirical research record supports earlier arguments that the banking sector played a precipitating role in the 1990 recession and that certain sectors were unable to participate in the recovery. In 1989, only bank lending slowed down, while other credit forms continued to grow. Later, growth of all forms of credit slowed. Large banks accounted for up to 50 percent of the lending slowdown and initiated the 1990 recession (Lown, Peristiani, and Robinson 2001). Overall, economic activity in small businesses shrank relative to that of larger businesses in the opening years of the decade, especially relative to the long swing of economic recovery since the 1981–1982 recession.

Economic activity grew more slowly (as measured by employment, payrolls, and firm formation) among smaller businesses. The relatively slower growth of firms at the lower end of the size distribution coincided not only with the national recession but also with the bank capital crunch. Smaller, growth-oriented businesses were particularly susceptible to these shocks. The increased capital pressure that banks felt in the late 1980s led them to change their portfolios, just as they had done during earlier credit crunches in 1974 and 1932 (Bernanke 1983). Banks reduced loan holdings by about eight times the amount their capital declined or was reduced by regulatory redefinition of risk-leveraged ratios. Since small business borrowers have fewer substitute lenders available to them than larger businesses, the reduction in loans produced a larger negative change in economic activity. Small firms have lower debt: equity ratios than larger firms, so that loans to smaller businesses have a larger multiplier effect on total financial resources available to the firm. Hence, the contraction of credit induced by the crunch magnified recessionary effects that echoed throughout the macroeconomy (Hancock and Wilcox 1993; Yago 1993).

There were both federal and state regulations of banking throughout this period that resulted in the temporary shutdown of a long period of economic growth. From 1989 to February 1993, commercial and industrial lending fell by 8 percent or $50 billion—the reverberation of that impact was considerable. Bank regulators in 1989 issued guidelines to implement the risk-weighted capital measurements system proposed in 1988 by the Basel Committee on Banking Regulations and Supervisory Practices. Under those risk-based capital standards, banks must adhere to two risk-based capital ratio requirements: Tier 1 capital must be composed of at least 8 percent risk-weighted assets, and total capital must be composed of at least 8 percent risk-weighted assets. Therefore, the 0 percent risk bucket is composed only of government securities. This enabled, or forced, banks to shift lending from the private sector as an asset class to the U.S. Treasury and other government securities in order to preserve their capital base without reducing deposits. By contrast, the 100 percent risk bucket had an asset: capital ratio of 12.5:1. All private sector asset-based commercial and private loans are in this category, backed by equity and producing income.

This technical recitation of the regulatory factors that produced additional capital pressures upon banks requires some comment. Despite what we can observe to be the enormous economic policy consequences of these measures, they were implemented without statutory review by Congress or the administration. The Basel Accords were an enactment of central bank authority alone, without any democratic mechanism of policy review. Figure 3-5 demonstrates the induced capital pressure impact of Basel risk-based capital standards upon business lending. The gap reflected in this figure shows the difference between the expected level of loan activity, resulting from changes in business cycle demand for loans, and the actual level, resulting from the regulatory changes. In short, structural changes in the policy rules connecting bank balance sheet information and examination ratings resulted in lending restrictions after 1989 that were independent of measures of aggregate economic activity, real estate prices, and yield spreads (Bizer 1993; Hall 1993). Controlling for changes in economic conditions, actual loans declined precipitously from their expected levels.[1]

1. See Lown, Morgan, and Rohatgi 2000: "it appears that risk-based capital requirements combined with stricter bank examination standards contributed to a credit crunch and adversely affected the monetary aggregates" (p. 68).

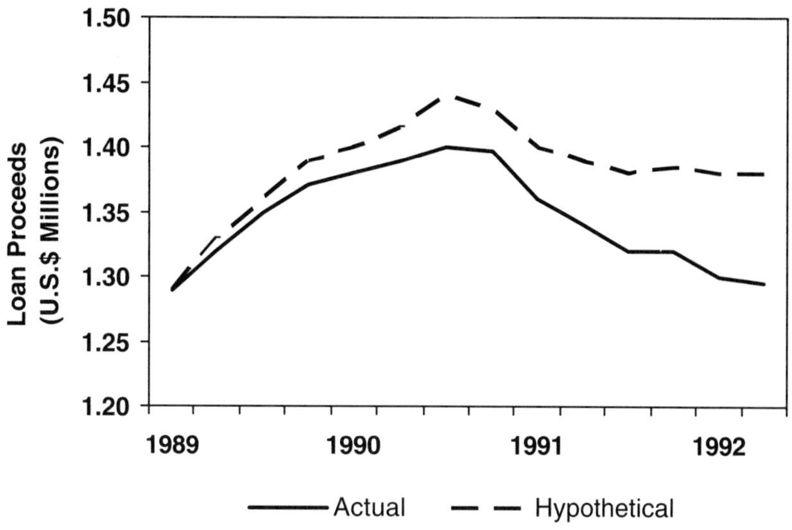

Figure 3-5. Hypothetical Impact of the Change in Capital Standards, 1989–1992. Sources: Milken Institute; Securities and Exchange Commission.

State-level banking regulation further amplified the constricting effects of financial regulations on economic growth activity. Empirical studies across states indicated that statewide branching, interstate banking, bank holding company presence, absence of usury limits on corporate borrowing, and a regulatory environment that reduces bank operating costs improved the performance of a state's economy as measured by population/employment ratios (Krol and Svorny 1993). Hence, state-level banking overregulation could further amplify the negative effects of contracted lending demonstrated above.

Nowhere was this more obvious than in the commercial and industrial lending of commercial banks. As figure 3-6 indicates, the long-term secular trend of commercial and industrial loans as a percentage of overall bank portfolios declined throughout the 1990s. Despite a recovery in the overall number and value of loans, the aggregate move away from business lending as a category of banking activity requires further concern and scrutiny, especially since it remains the greatest single source of capital for growth firms.

Aside from commercial and industrial loans, acquisition-related debt available from commercial banks was at one time a significant source of senior debt for ownership change, specifically in divestitures of business units from large to smaller firms, business sales by retiring owners, and leveraged employee and management buyouts (Yago 1990). In the late 1980s a series of restrictive rules for banks was issued by the U.S. Treasury limiting highly leveraged transaction (HLT) loans. Such loans had become increasingly common as firms changed ownership and sought to actively

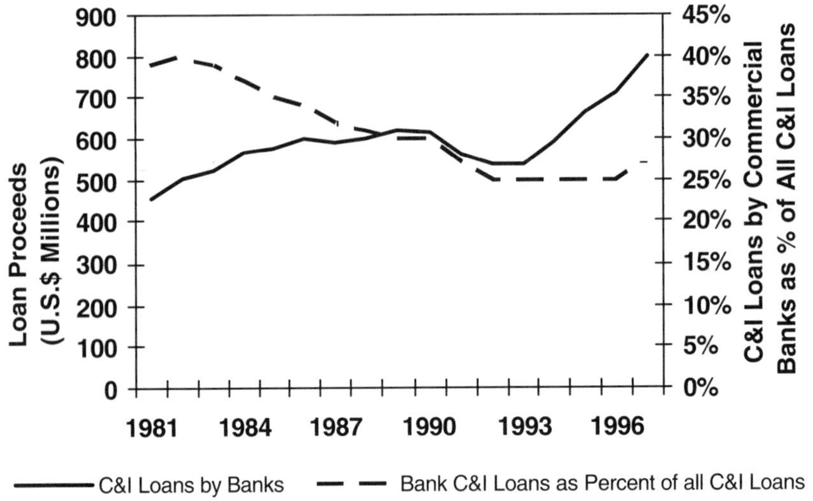

Figure 3-6. Commercial and Industrial (C&I) Loans Made by Commercial Banks, 1981–1996. Sources: Milken Institute; Federal Deposit Insurance Corporation (FDIC).

manage their capital structures. The impact of the regulations was to reduce that flexibility to manage capital structures in order to accomplish new objectives. Though they were later rescinded, the chilling effect of these regulations continued to restrict acquisition-related bank financing, as seen in figure 3-7. The impact of the regulations was to shut down this source of business finance.

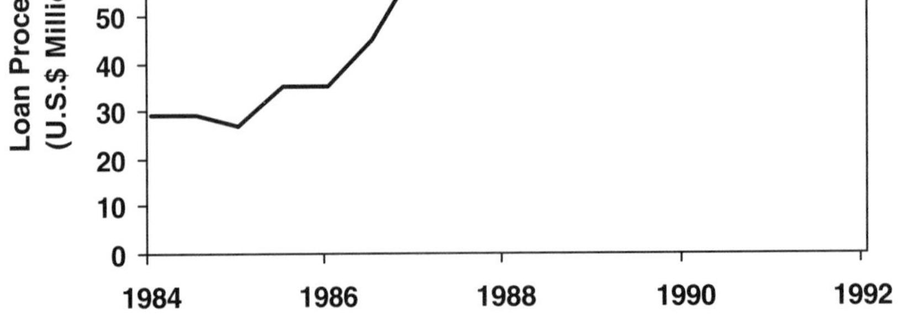

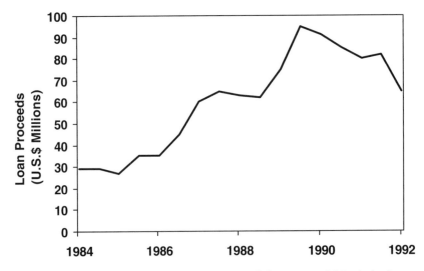

Figure 3-7. Highly Leveraged Transaction Loan Proceeds by Commercial Banks in the United States, March 1984–March 1992. Sources: Milken Institute; FDIC.

It is important to note that the high yield market, as a source of public subordinated debt, enhanced senior lending from banks. The simultaneous constriction of bank lending and regulatory freeze of the high yield market directly precipitated recessionary pressures on the economy as a whole.

REGULATORY CHOKE HOLD II: INSURANCE REGULATIONS

Insurance companies have long been important sources of institutional investment. As regulatory pressures increased on other financial institutions and institutional investors, insurance regulators became swept up in the wave of activity that stigmatized asset categories and the businesses that depended upon them.

Under the threat of federal preemptive legislation in the late 1980s, state insurance commissioners jumped on the regulatory bandwagon, first in New York and Delaware and later throughout the country. The National Association of Insurance Commissioners (NAIC) introduced finer distinctions in the credit ratings of corporate bonds. Under the old rating system, many securities (especially public bonds) with credit quality equivalent to BB or B agency ratings received an investment grade rating from NAIC. In the initial year of reclassification, insurers reported that below-investment grade bonds rose from 15 percent of total bond holdings in 1989 to 21 percent in 1990. By the following year, the level of reported holdings of non-investment grade bonds jumped more than 40 percent.

Insurance companies report the ratios of their book capital to levels of capital that are adjusted for risk. As an insurer's ratio falls below 1, successively stronger regulatory actions are triggered. Below-investment grade securities carry risk weights much higher than those on investment grade bonds and even commercial mortgages. As a result, major insurance companies' participation in that market during this critical opening period of the 1990s was virtually eliminated (see figure 3-8). Similarly, the private placement market dried up during this period. As figure 3-9 indicates, the private placement market never recovered the position it enjoyed as a source of investment capital a decade earlier.

In short, these changes in risk-based capital standards associated with the changes in classifications made it too expensive for insurance companies to invest in growth businesses. As insurance ratios fell and strong regulatory action was triggered, the chilling effect upon growth investment became apparent. Insurance portfolio compositions changed radically as a flight to perceived safety ensued. Securitized business loans, which historically had proved substantially less risky than commercial mortgages, were put at a great disadvantage within those portfolios.

REGULATORY CHOKE HOLD III: THRIFT REGULATIONS

The period 1989–1991 saw a dramatic change in the economic relationships that drove the high yield market. The structural economic relations that

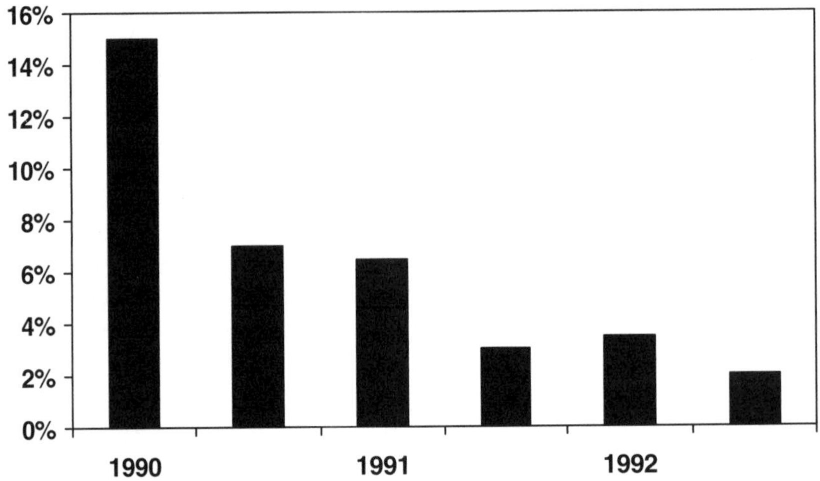

Figure 3-8. New Commitments to Purchase High Yield Private Placements as a Percentage of Total New Commitments by Major Life Insurance Companies, 1990–1992. Note: Each bar represents a six-month period. Sources: Milken Institute; American Council of Life Insurance.

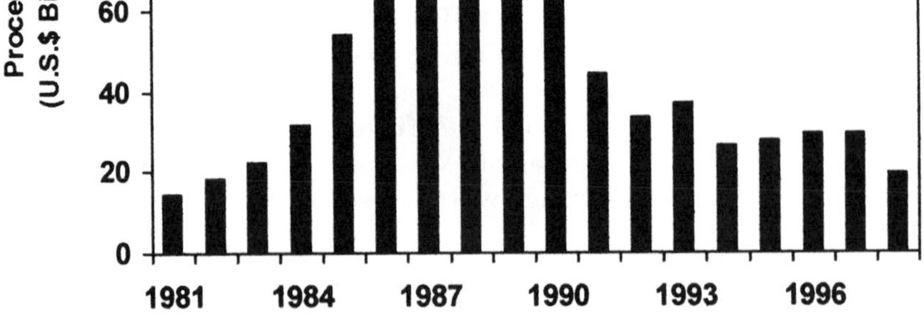

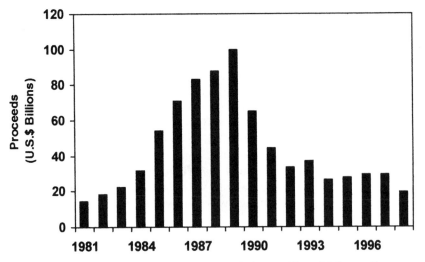

Figure 3-9. Gross Issuance of Private Placement Debt by Non-Financial Corporations, 1981–1998. Sources: Milken Institute; Securities Data Corporation.

drove the market through the 1980s included the relationships between cyclical factors, credit quality, defaults, and competitive market yields. These relationships were severely disrupted, and the high yield market entered a period of unpredictability that corresponded to increases in government regulatory intervention, climaxing with the introduction of Financial Institutions Reform Recovery and Enforcement Act (FIRREA). (See Barth, Trimbath, and Yago (2003) for a fuller discussion.)

In the next chapter we present the results of an econometric test of a model that, prior to late 1989, was robustly capable of explaining high yield market behavior. We present proof that the market entered a period of instability precipitated by the timing of thrift regulatory events. These regulatory restrictions on thrift investment reduced the market's ability to self-correct in response to changes in economic conditions. The result was a politically induced temporary collapse in the public high yield market (figure 3-10). The impact of the regulatory destabilization was dramatic. In 1990, the average high yield bond traded at 66 percent of its face value. In 1989–1990, the Merrill Lynch High Yield Index registered its only negative return of the decade (–4.36 percent).

The combination of notable defaults in the summer of 1989 combined with these regulatory events to create a "bank run." Investors made large net withdrawals from high yield mutual funds (figure 3-11). Thrift legislation induced a massive sell-off by the fourth quarter of 1989, creating further surpluses in supply. A temporary shutdown of the new issue market ensued (figure 3-12).

During the 1980s, the high yield market had combined the flexibility of the private debt market with liquidity and capital structural advantages

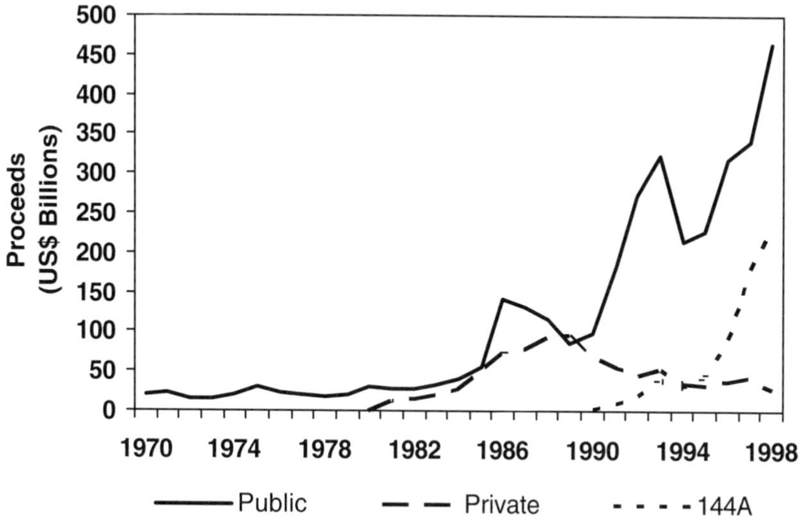

Figure 3-10. Issuance of High Yield Bonds by Non-Financial Corporations, 1970–1998. Sources: Milken Institute; Securities Data Corporation.

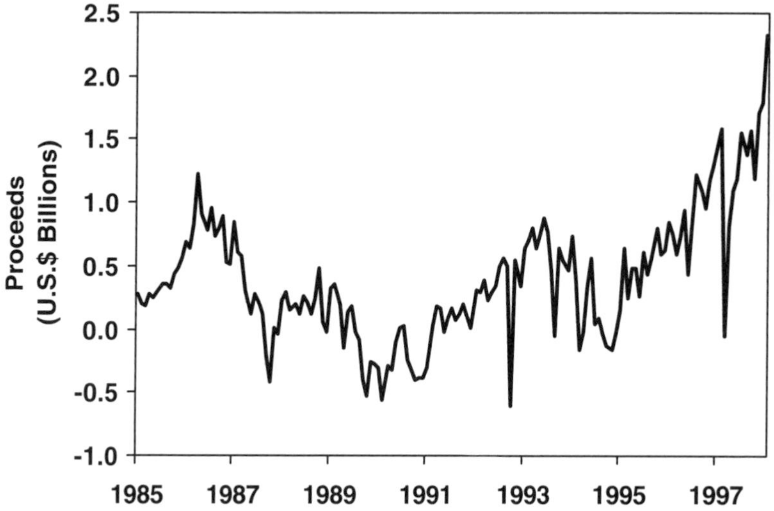

Figure 3-11. Net Capital Flows into High Yield Bond Mutual Funds, 1985–1997. Sources: Milken Institute; Investment Company Institute.

of the public debt market. As Barclay and Smith (1996, p. 24) correctly note, the first recessionary test of the high yield market was during 1981–1982, not 1989–1990.

In the early 1980s, Milken and others used the 3(a)9 exchange offering (debt-equity swap) as an alternative to Chapter 11 bankruptcy filings. Interest payments could be reduced (e.g., through zero coupon, PIKs, or equity swaps),

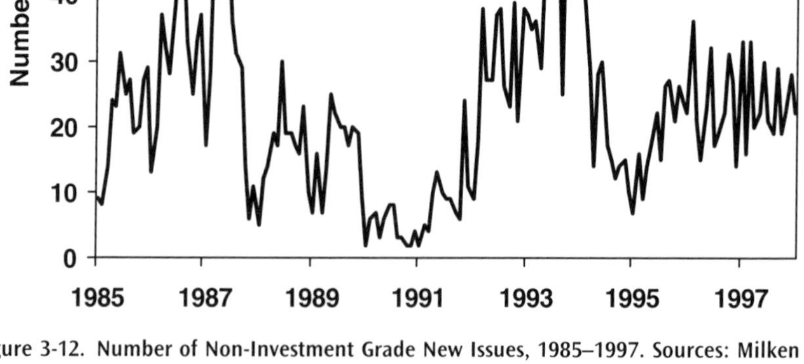

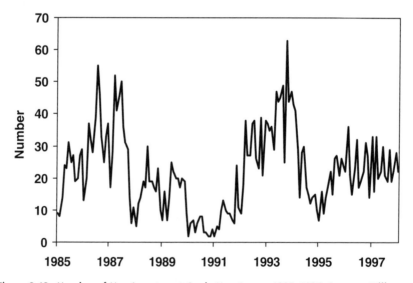

Figure 3-12. Number of Non-Investment Grade New Issues, 1985–1997. Sources: Milken Institute; Securities Data Corporation.

maturities stretched, and other capital structure adjustments made to remove financial distress and enable economic recovery (see chapters 4 and 5). Disruptions induced by regulatory and prosecutory actions in 1989–1990 eliminated market liquidity and flexibility for workouts and refinancings.

REGULATORY CHOKE HOLD IV: MERGER REGULATIONS

Considerable economic evidence demonstrates that expansion and change in ownership of firms are highly associated with growth in productivity, employment, market share, and value maximization. (See Trimbath (2002, chap. 3) for a summary of the literature on postmerger performance.) Explosive growth throughout the 1980s was associated with the expansion of ownership through entrepreneurial revival, expanded employee and management ownership, and buyouts by active investors. Several factors converged to accelerate the patterns of ownership change and the related improvements in firm performance: succession planning by retiring owners who started their businesses after World War II, the linkages between active investors and owner-managers that were forged to create value through the buyout movement, and legislative and tax measures that furthered employee and management buyouts.

The variety of performance measures associated with ownership change and its linkage to aggregate growth are now better understood. (See Yago, Lichtenberg, and Siegel 1989; Bhagat, Shleifer, and Vishny 1990; Kaplan 1991; Easterwood and Seth 1993; and Trimbath, Frydman, and Frydman 2001.) In manufacturing plants that were either divested or restructured through buyouts, productivity growth was about 14 percent higher than that of other plants in the same industries (Lichtenberg 1992). In plants with significant management participation, productivity growth was 20 percent higher. Research and development expenditures were also higher than in comparable industry facilities.

Firms experiencing ownership changes have higher employment and wage levels, as well as greater productivity increases, than firms that do not change hands (Brown and Medoff 1988). Layoffs have turned out to be higher when entrenched managers defeat a takeover bid than when takeovers are successful (Yago 1991a). In a sample of 286 plant closings, only 48 (17 percent) were made by takeover targets before, after, or during the bid—and only twenty-two of these forty-eight were targets of hostile bids (Blackwell, Marr, and Spivey 1990). Labor productivity is positively affected by large firm mergers, without reducing employment (Trimbath 2002). In short, job losses do not appear to be attributable to ownership change, and they are amplified by the absence of change.

This general trend does not, however, obviate the fact that there were (and are) poorly structured transactions that resulted in job losses. For example, defensive LBOs and corporate acquisitions in which entrenched managers took on more debt to defend against takeovers produced less than stellar results. Within the high yield market, two-thirds of the "distressed credits" in the 1980s were issued in the last few years of the decade when deal-hungry merger and acquisition departments overpriced issues in poorly structured, fee-driven transactions (Fridson 1991c). During that time, entrepreneurial buyouts that added strategic economic value were superseded in the LBO market by defensive, financially driven buyouts. On an aggregate basis, job losses most often occurred at the middle management level. Administrative staffs were often cut as overhead was reduced, while production plant workers were largely unaffected (Lichtenberg and Siegel 1987; Lichtenberg 1992).

Concerning other types of salutary impacts of ownership change, the empirical record is also quite informative. The net impact of buyouts on the U.S. Treasury has been positive when one includes the increased tax payments of the new debt holders and those shareholders who sold their stock in the targeted companies. The combined firms' future higher income from productivity increases also has contributed to the tax base (Jensen, Kaplan, and Stiglin 1989).

Postacquisition corporate performance suggests that returns to acquirers in unrelated conglomerate acquisitions were lower than returns in related acquisitions (Healy, Palepu, and Ruback 1992). The improvement in returns was not the result of simple price changes but represented real economic gains. Cash flows of merged or acquired companies increased after the mergers, but sales margins did not (Karpoff and Malatesta 1989). Asset productivity, and not monopoly pricing, improved cash flows, further suggesting that consumers were not hurt by mergers and acquisitions.

Restrictive regulations on ownership change that emerged during the late 1980s contributed dramatically to the shutdown of growth in the early 1990s. Anti-takeover legislation in thirty-eight states passed in a matter of months. (This legislation is discussed in more detail in chapter 9.) The wave of restrictions on highly leveraged transaction eliminated an important source of ownership change financing. Changes in the tax treatment of employee stock ownership plan debt and acquisition-related financing inhibited the pattern of ownership change and reduced the flexibility of capital structure management necessary to accomplish it.

As most research in corporate finance in the 1990s amply demonstrated, ownership change can promote market discipline and the incentives requisite for maximizing positive net present value investments that spur growth. What the regulatory restrictions on ownership change did was to eliminate or at least distort market discipline. This resulted in high costs to the economy through excess diversification, rent-seeking behavior by managers, and other value-destroying behavior. Growth in jobs, income, and wealth creation suffered. The result was a decline in liquidity, monitoring, and competition. Capital allocation inefficiencies resulted, and prosperity faded (Rajan and Zingales 1995, 1998). Measurably, Morck, Acs, and Yeung (1997) found that anti-takeover laws resulted in excess diversification that reduced capital value by an estimated $481 billion. (See also Morck, Shleifer, and Vishny 1990.)

REINVENTING FINANCIAL INSTITUTIONS AND RESTRUCTURING REGULATION

As has frequently been observed, commercial financial institutions are still the primary providers of capital to small businesses. This dependence persists despite the structural shift of financial assets to nonbank institutions and capital markets. Pension funds, mutual funds, and other nondepository financial services firms have become the leading repositories of capital, yet the ability to recycle that massive shift in the flow of funds into small business and growth firm investment capital remains an unmet challenge. Meanwhile, the asset portfolio problems that besieged many banks and thrifts in the early 1990s resulted in onerous demands by regulators upon banks that have limited their capacity to fulfill their historic role as the major small business finance source.

Several public and business policy initiatives suggest the direction of future efforts to recapitalize the small business finance market. To address the problem of equity capital, the federal government, through the Small Business Administration (SBA), set up venture capital intermediaries to attract funds (e.g., general and specialized small business investment companies). These entities are licensed to make both equity and long-term debt investments. Other specialized efforts in the venture capital market have linked to these efforts or expanded them through the varieties of structured transactions they have developed (Bygrave and Timmons 1991).

Similarly, pension fund managers have discovered excellent yields in the category of "alternative investments" that could include elements of securitized small business finance. While only 4 percent to 6 percent of pension fund portfolios are invested in alternative vehicles, they have experienced some of the highest yields. Financial advisers have suggested that many private pension funds could double their current portfolio positions in currently illiquid investments and maintain those yields. Mutual funds also continue the search for higher yielding investments. In short, all elements of the nonbank channels of capital suggest an important source for future small entrepreneurial business investment.

This requires, however, a substantial rethinking of the role of financial institutions. In the past, commercial financial institutions acknowledged their obligation to lend to small businesses and accepted regulations limiting their ability to behave as active investors in exchange for limited competition, cross-subsidization, and a regulatory and accounting regime that allowed them to operate in an innately cyclical business on a highly leveraged basis. Specifically, banks face a structural discontinuity in their ability to serve this function as a source of small business finance because these conditions have changed. Losses as a percent of bank income have skyrocketed in recent years, reflecting the widely observed fact that the process of small business lending has put banks into the position of taking equity risks without receiving equity rewards. (See Young 1993; Iannoconi 1993; Phillips 1995.)

In short, new types of institutions could emerge either within the Bank Holding Company Act or future enabling legislation that would allow financial institutions to become more directly involved in venture / buyout association forms of equity investing with related performance-based compensation and an investment partnership culture. These entities could interact well in alliance with traditional banks, insurance companies, and other financial institutions in structuring debt components of firm finance as well as diversifying risk. Similarly, diversifications of risk would enable these nonbank institutions to serve as reinsurance companies for small business finance (Chew 1998; Jensen 1991).

FINANCIAL TECHNOLOGY TRANSFER FOR SMALL BUSINESSES

Building upon the structural changes in the relationship between financial institutions, small businesses, and capital markets, a major effort is necessary to create the policy infrastructure for developing and expanding secondary markets for debt and equity investments. At the present time, there exists no ready avenue for liquidity for investments in small businesses by banks, investment companies, and the like (Phillips 1995). The development of a secondary market for small firm equity and debt would inject liquidity into the system and attract more funds for small business growth (Chen 1993).

This is a crucial area of policy development to fund small business in the twenty-first century. It could be accomplished without government guarantees by utilizing the existing financial technologies that have developed in the high yield market, mortgage-backed securities market, and IPO market in recent years. In the case of small business loans, intermediaries could gather and pool loans into portfolios constructed to diversify the risks inherent in those assets, industries, and firms (e.g., owner succession, repayment character, cash flow deficiency, etc.). Asset pooling could be on the basis of industry, asset maturity periods, firm size, and owner characteristics, thereby reducing the risk perception in the capital markets allocated to any individual asset.[2]

Utilizing recently developed risk management techniques, risk variables could be identified and insured against through the derivatives markets. Lenders could securitize small business assets and use them as collateral for bond issuance. Collateralized loan obligations would be a useful tool. Similar activities could be taken in the equity markets or by creating hybrid securities for small businesses. What would be required in the small business equity market is, again, standard and acceptable methods and vehicles for valuing and pricing equity assets. Proxy variables for dividends (e.g., net profit less a reinvestment reserve, divided by the number of shares outstanding) for small and new firms could allow for pricing nominated as earnings multiples.

2. Aside from the developments of securitization, the guaranteed portion of SBA loans, this logic of structured finance is also to be extended to the development of a secondary loan market for community and economic development lenders in California, South Carolina, and Minnesota.

In summary,

- Developing secondary markets would add liquidity to small business equity and investors would greatly increase the flow of investment funds to institutions that originate those assets.
- Investment originators could create derivatives to contain the risk or speculate in those markets.
- Investment originators could issue bonds or certificates using small business loans as securities; REIT-like structures also could be used.

CONCLUSION

Policies should create conditions to enable market solutions to the substantial capital access barriers facing entrepreneurial growth businesses. These policies should specifically remove regulatory barriers to allowing banks to establish nonbank investment functions for subordinated debt and equity financing. They should also remove regulatory barriers on pension funds and insurance companies that discriminate against investing in companies on the basis of size. Investment professionals should be encouraged to develop initiatives to encourage capital market innovations that will serve smaller firms. Finally, steps must be taken to eliminate tax barriers (e.g., capital gains tax, estate tax) and lower transaction costs for ownership change in order to encourage employee, minority, and management equity involvement, and mergers and acquisitions among small businesses.

In the next chapter, we extend the discussion started here about the regulatory distortion of the high yield market.

4

The End of the Beginning

> A broad political persecution was ultimately aimed at the linchpins of the debt market—Drexel Burnham in particular—in which virtually every arm of the Federal Securities laws was used as a lever to constrain entrepreneurial financing. By 1990, . . . the financial market that spawned the booming entrepreneurial market of the 1980s lay in shambles.
>
> John Pound (1992a)

During 1989 and 1990, the high yield market experienced an unprecedented, precipitous, and largely unanticipated decline. While a considerable amount of research has been done about market breaks in the equity markets (Mitchell and Netter 1989; Bennett and Kelleher 1988; Securities and Exchange Commission 1988), in this study we seek to identify the relative role of fundamental economic, institutional, regulatory, and structural factors that precipitated sharp, temporary declines in the high yield bond market. While several events and economic conditions are candidates for the cause of the devaluation of high yield security prices during this period, we provide evidence which suggests that specific regulatory events exacerbated the temporary contraction of liquidity and trading in the market, resulting in the price collapse.

Sharp price drops resulted in major declines in high yield indices. These indices, which included deferred interest and payment-in-kind as well as conventional cash-coupon bonds, declined to result in a –4.36 percent total return, the only negative return for the market over an entire decade (Fridson 1991a). A confluence of technical factors affected the market to produce chaotic selling pressure during 1990. These factors included the following:

- Forced selling by insurance companies and thrift holders due to regulatory requirements
- Associated sell pressure from other institutional investors (e.g., pension funds)
- Unusually high mutual fund redemptions
- The bankruptcy filing of Drexel Burnham Lambert, thought to be the primary high yield market maker
- A reduction in liquidity due to tightened credit.

These technical factors, coupled with the economic conditions of an oncoming recession and the political factors of the Gulf War, magnified market factors that exacerbated credit quality deterioration and increased defaults (First Boston 1991).[1] Though the high yield market's decline was substantial relative to its "normal" performance, real estate and mortgage markets fell roughly four times as much—36.6 percent and 41.6 percent, respectively, during late 1989–1990 (DeAngelo, DeAngelo, and Gilson 1993). Despite the more substantial drop in these asset categories and the greater proportional price collapse in the equity markets during the 1987 crash, the high yield market appears to have been targeted by the press for adverse publicity, and subsequently for heightened regulatory attention in the national and state legislatures (Jensen 1991).

Specifically, newspapers and magazines repeated the story that non-investment grade debt was bad for America. For example, *Financial World* in 1988 called U.S. companies like National Gypsum, whose credit rating recovered in less than five years, the "walking wounded" (*Financial World*, April 19, 1988, p. 24). In fact, out of millions of businesses in the United States only about 800 are "investment grade." Most of us work for non-investment grade companies. Another myth is that the 1980s was a time of greed. In this case, it was the Canadian business magazine *Maclean's* that called 1989 "a vintage year for greed and stupidity" (December 25, 1989, p. 46). In fact, charitable contributions, adjusted for inflation, doubled during the 1980s, even as changes in the tax laws made those contributions less advantageous to the givers.

By early 1991, as we shall see, the high yield bond market rallied, and continued to improve substantially with average market returns that outstripped all other asset categories in 1991 and 1992. But in 1990, the average high yield bond was trading at 66 percent of face value. These considerable discounts combined with the factors mentioned above to produce the lowest new issuance level of the decade for the high yield market. Ironically, the 1987 and 1988 quality deterioration that resulted from market conditions was over by 1989. Adverse supply factors and a paucity of new demand created a liquidity crisis in the market and sharp price drops.

STRUCTURAL AND CYCLICAL FACTORS AFFECTING THE HIGH YIELD MARKET

The development of a liquid market for original issue subinvestment grade bonds represented an important institutional and structural shift in the flow of capital from intermediated bank borrowing, strapped by restrictive covenants and regulations, toward publicly traded business loans (Taggart 1990; Benveniste, Singh, and Wilhelm 1993). In this chapter we briefly describe the methodology we have used to examine whether several catastrophic events occurring near the end of the 1980s caused structural

1. See Yago 1993 for further analysis and detail on the array of financial regulations introduced during 1989. Also see Meakin 1990.

changes in the market for high yield securities.[2] Critical changes in supply, demand, and returns all reflect both cyclical and structural factors influencing the high yield market. We begin with a descriptive analysis of monthly data on the supply of high yield issues, indices of rates of return, and capital flow in high yield bond mutual funds. The data on monthly returns derived from the Merrill Lynch High Yield Index (inside front cover) show that the steepest declines occurred during the last quarter of 1987, the second and third quarters of 1989, the third quarter of 1990, and the spring of 1991. The time line of important events includes the passage of the thrift bailout bill, which affected this market.

Data on the number of new issues are shown in figure 4-1. The high yield market experienced a precipitous decline in new issues during the fall of 1989 and did not recover until the spring of 1991. Net capital flows in high yield bond funds are presented in figure 4-2. It is interesting to observe that substantial withdrawals of funds occurred *before* the steep reductions in either returns or the supply of new high yield issues. Figure 4-3 indicates that negative media sentiment concerning the high yield market appears to have had a deleterious influence on net flows into high yield mutual funds independent of changes in returns during the first three quarters of 1989.[3] There was overwhelming negative sentiment from 1987 through the beginning of 1990. However, to sort out the factors that influence changes in the high yield market more precisely, we need to further specify the economic factors that influence changes in supply and returns.

EXPLAINING VOLUME AND RETURNS IN THE HIGH YIELD MARKET

Evidence from the high yield and other securities markets leads us to hypothesize that the rate of return or month-to-month change in the rate of return on high yield issues is a function of the default rate on these bonds, the high yield spread over Treasury securities, credit availability, fluctuations in stock market indices, and general economic performance (Yago 1991b; Altman 1991; Blume, Keim, and Patel 1991).

We conjecture that an increase in the default rate on high yield debt will reduce the attractiveness of these securities to potential investors. On the other hand, higher spreads should increase the relative attractiveness of, and thus the demand for, high yield debt. This occurs because higher spreads imply an increase in the relative rate of return. We also postulate that the demand for high yield securities is lower during periods when credit conditions are relatively tight. An increase in stock prices is expected to stimulate increases in prices of high yield issues because the market value of firms with outstanding debt will be higher and be-

2. All technical material relating to the econometric analysis in this chapter can be found in appendix B. For ease of presentation, we primarily discuss only the results in this chapter.

3. The sentiment index uses 1,486 news stories about high yield bonds and codes them as positive or negative, weighing them based on different newspapers, magazines, and journals. See Salomon Brothers, *The High Yield Market Survey*, February 4, 1994, 16 for a complete description.

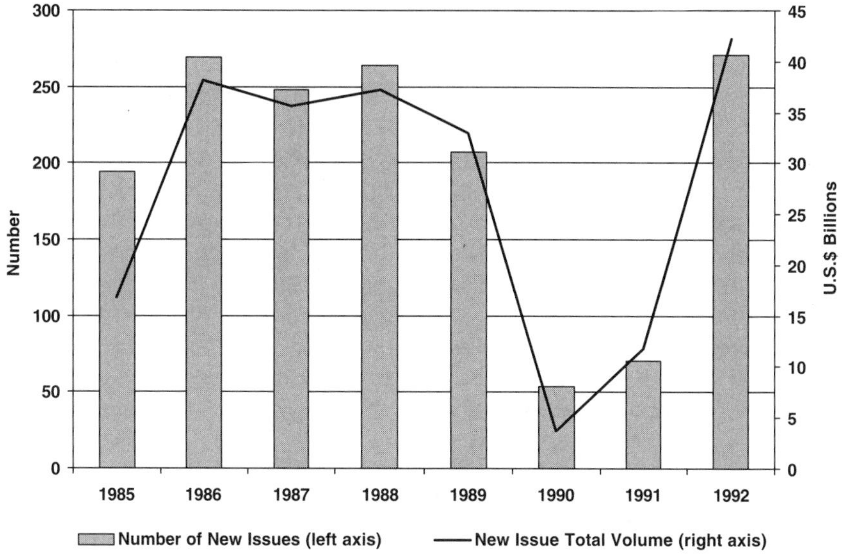

Figure 4-1. High Yield New Issuance, 1985–1992. Source: Securities Data Corporation.

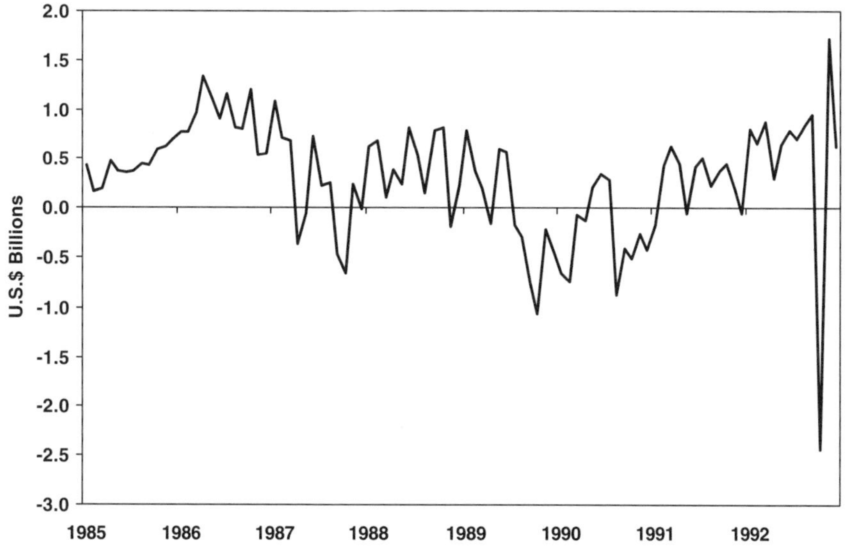

Figure 4-2. Net Capital Flows into High Yield Bond Funds, 1985–1992. Source: Investment Company Institute.

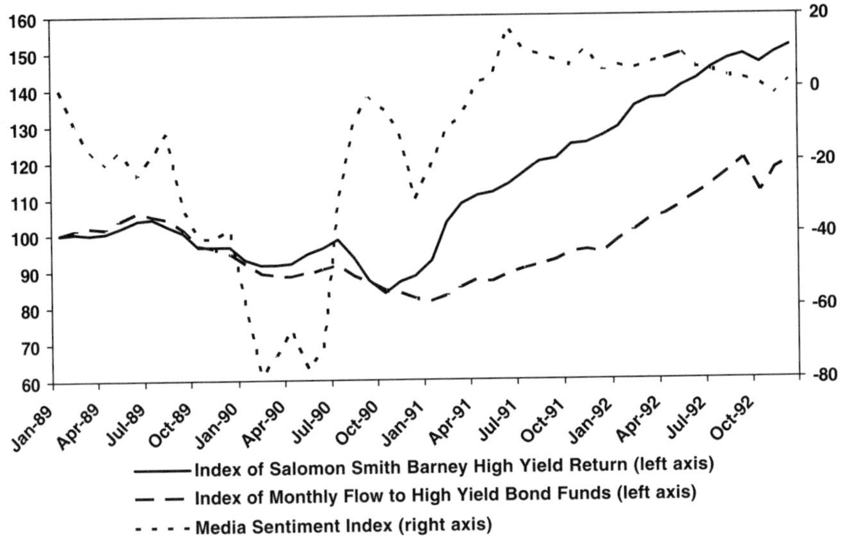

Figure 4-3. Media Sentiment and Net Capital Flows into High Yield Mutual Funds, January 1989–October 1992. Sources: Salomon Smith Barney; Milken Institute.

cause investors will have greater perceived or actual wealth. Both of these factors should increase the demand for high yield debt. A recession or a downturn in the economy is alleged to reduce the supply of and demand for these securities because during these periods, potential investors and firms offering this debt may be greatly concerned about the probability of repayment.

We also can analyze the determinants of the number of high yield issues and capital flows in funds that are devoted to these securities. Our hypothesis is that the higher returns should induce additional investment in high yield securities. An expansion in leveraged buyout (LBO) activity is assumed to increase the number and value of high yield issues, since in part these securities have been used to finance corporate control changes.

The interested reader will find the details of our data descriptions, descriptive statistics, a matrix of correlation coefficients, regression models, and the regression results in appendix B. The evidence shows that the most powerful determinant of returns in this setting is the average value of the spread.[4] Spreads are widely used by investors for selecting among alternative asset classes. However, issues of credit analysis, liquidity, and performance of nonfixed-income securities and markets should be considered in further modeling the market. Our finding is not inconsistent with studies of different time periods that did not include the high yield market through 1990 and 1991 (Fridson and Cherry 1991b).

4. In this case we used the spread or difference between the yields on high yield bonds and Treasury bonds.

EVIDENCE OF DISTORTIONS

An analysis of the structural stability of the regression equations provides evidence of regulatory destabilization, that is, evidence that the regulations at the time had a destabilizing effect on the market for high yield securities. The usual practice in assessing whether regression coefficients change across time is to use prior information concerning the true point of structural change in the nature of the relationship. The researcher identifies an event or set of events that is hypothesized to cause a structural change, estimates separate regressions, and examines whether the results are significantly different before and after the event. This is the so-called Chow test (1960).

We prefer a test developed by Brown, Durbin, and Evans (1975) that does *not* require prior information concerning the true point of structural change. An attractive property of the Brown-Durbin-Evans test is that it allows the data to identify when the true point(s) of structural change occurred, thereby eliminating the potential for the researcher to bias the results by selecting the event. This test has been employed on time series data to analyze the demand for money (Heller and Khan 1979) and to examine whether the returns to research and development investment vary by firm size (Link 1981a, 1981b; Lichtenberg and Siegel 1991).

We calculated the Brown-Durbin-Evans test and include the empirical results in appendix B. On the following pages we present graphs of the test statistics for the level and month-to-month change in returns and the number of high yield issues. Each chart includes two horizontal lines representing the 95 percent and 99 percent "confidence regions." Where the difference between the actual and expected value of the test statistic passes into this "confidence region," we find support for our hypothesis that structural changes occur at that point, within the respective levels of confidence.[5]

INTERPRETING THE RESULTS

The results presented in figures 4-4 to 4-6 reveal that structural stability was not part of the landscape. Let us consider and interpret these important empirical findings in light of the political and economic history of the period. In all three cases (for returns, issues, and mutual fund capital flows in the high yield market), the test statistic "breaks" the confidence bound toward the end of 1989 or at the beginning of 1990, only to return in 1991. In other words, the functional economic relationships between cyclical factors, credit quality / defaults, competitive market yields, and so forth that drove the high yield market during the 1980s changed measurably. Functional relationships appear to be restored by late 1991 as the market recovered from regulatory destabilization and responded to more economic

5. Again, the interested reader will find a more technical explanation of this test and the results in appendix B.

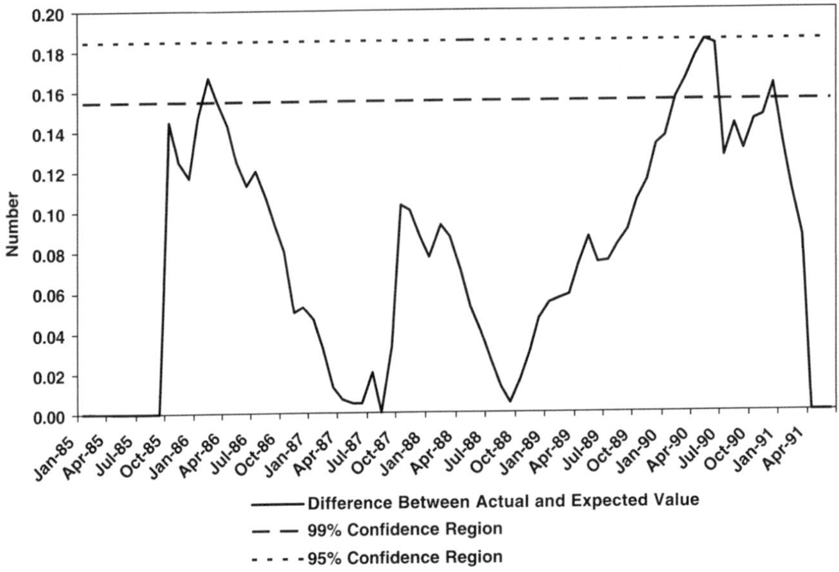

Figure 4-4. Dependent Variable: Merrill Lynch High Yield Index Level, January 1985–June 1991. Sources: Merrill Lynch; Bloomberg.

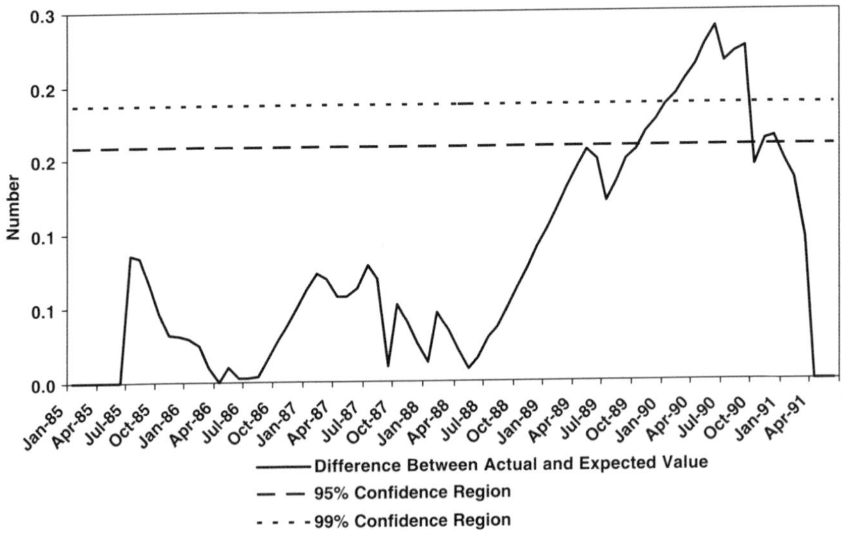

Figure 4-5. Dependent Variable: Month-to-Month Change in Merrill Lynch High Yield Index, January 1985–June 1991. Sources: Merrill Lynch; Milken Institute.

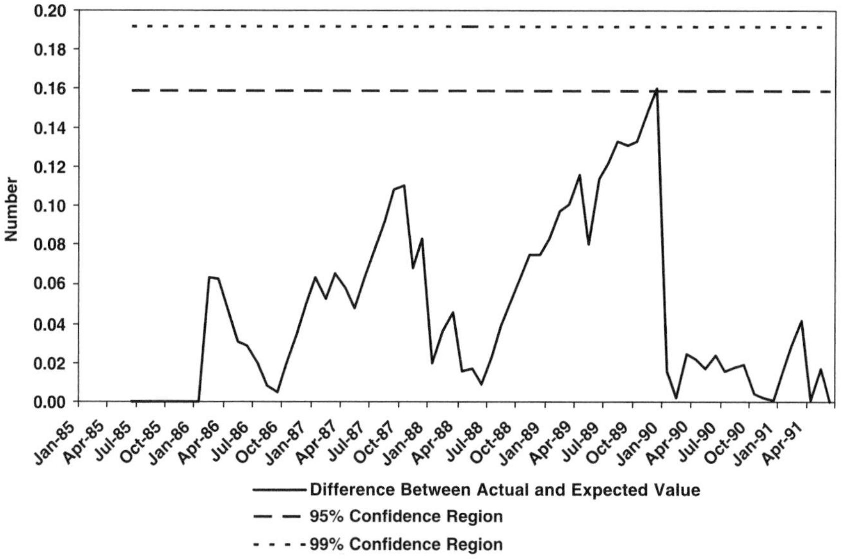

Figure 4-6. Dependent Variable: Number of High Yield New Issues, January 1985–June 1991. Sources: Securities Data Corporation; Milken Institute.

fundamentals in the marketplace. This leaves unanswered important questions about the further specification of models of the high yield market and whether or not permanent malformations of the market resulted, in terms of its capacity to affect sectoral and aggregate economic growth. Nevertheless, the enhanced selectivity of the market even after its recovery suggests that there may be further evidence to be explored that growth sectors of small and medium-sized businesses which were the backbone of the high yield market during its ascendance remain underserved.

The period in which the market broke from econometric models of its performance was also a period of dramatic increases of government regulatory intervention in the high yield market. As a result of changes in the rules of the game through selective enforcement and prosecution, new regulations, and increasingly punitive actions, significant events occurred that unhinged the market from economic dynamics and the capacity of the market to self-regulate in response to changes in default rates, credit quality, and relative yield spreads. These events, in turn, generated a politically induced temporary price collapse in the high yield market.

The events that led to this regulatory reaction began earlier. The Business Roundtable, which at the time was headed by General Motors chairman Roger Smith, was particularly active in those efforts. The Roundtable's "tender offer reform" committee began active lobbying against the high yield market. By the autumn of 1985, senior SEC officials were invited to visit Representative John Dingell of Michigan and his staff. Dingell, who headed the committee with oversight responsibilities for government operations, was concerned about the lack of government success in uncovering irregularities associated with takeovers and its failure to stop raiding activity. And the congressman, whose wife worked in public relations for General Motors in Washington, identified strongly with the agenda set forth by the Business Roundtable in stopping "the raid on Corporate America." According to at least one former SEC official who attended the meetings, Dingell and his staff made it very clear that certain individuals—an investment banker, a risk arbitrageur, and a corporate raider—were to be investigated and indicted.

By May 1986, the insider trading scandals erupted, and in October, Ivan Boesky was indicted. Boesky's subsequent bargaining with the U.S. attorney led to press stories regularly linking Michael Milken, Drexel, and Carl Icahn, based on leaks and innuendo. Former SEC chairman John R. Shad, who later was head of Drexel when it went into bankruptcy, had made a courtesy call in 1985 on his old friend, Drexel's vice chairman and CEO, Frederick Joseph, and assured him that Drexel was not being singled out. Though Drexel was to be confronted with numerous charges of SEC violations in 1987, Shad promised Joseph that he would be in good company, since other Wall Street houses would have similar problems. Yet, no other investment firms were ever charged. (For more on this point, see Yago 1991b.)

The array of factors cumulating to create this regulatory effect climaxed with the introduction of the Financial Institutions Reform, Recovery, and Enforcement Act (FIRREA) in the fall of 1989.[6] The market had previously absorbed and adjusted to discounts resulting from the "bad cohort" credit quality deterioration that peaked in 1988, the politically induced negative media sentiment about the "junk" market, and even the investigation and indictment of some market participants. Nevertheless, there resulted an array of regulatory events that were either announced or enacted in 1989 that appear to have badly damaged the high yield market independent of economic factors generally found to affect changes in securities demand and returns in this and other markets. Moreover, the political pressures on the high yield market now appear to have been part of an overall trend toward the constriction of capital credit flows to U.S. businesses associated with general declines in commercial and industrial business lending.

In retrospect, the high yield market appears to have been targeted for special regulatory action that resulted in restrictions of the flow of capital to firms and the suppression of both supply and demand as a result of legislated and regulatory sell-offs by insurance companies, thrifts, and other financial institutions subject to government regulation. The high yield market—issuers, mutual funds, investors, and intermediaries—appears to have been caught up in a financial regulatory wave that had independent depressing effects on other areas of investment that produced an overall

6. The act is commonly referred to by its initials, FIRREA, pronounced "firey-ah."

capital crunch in the economy. Evidence of such a contraction in investment capital flows to the private market that places the events affecting the high yield market in a broader context is accumulating. Examples include the following:

- Bernanke and Lown (1991) found that capital ratios help explain aggregate regional differences in bank lending; risk-based capital ratio changes introduced in 1989 logically would be expected to depress bank lending as well.
- Peek and Rosengren (1993) found that in New England banks, restrictive capital regulations had a significant negative impact on bank size and loans.
- Bizer (1993) reveals structural changes in the policy rules connecting bank balance sheet information and examination ratings that resulted in post-1989 lending restrictions independent of measures of aggregate economic activity, real estate prices, and yield spreads.
- Zycher (1993) demonstrates that leverage ratio regulations had a disproportionate impact on smaller manufacturing firms.
- Lown, Morgan, and Rohatgi (2000) present evidence that new capital rules and other regulations led banks to decrease their lending to businesses and consumers, generating a credit crunch and recession.

Changes in examination practices, the proliferation of restrictive lending regulations (e.g., limits on highly leveraged transactions), and changes in risk-adjusted capital ratios compelled banks to downgrade existing assets, accept credit risks more cautiously, and reduce lending. With intermediated bank lending constricted and the disintermediated public corporate debt market shut down for new entrants and restricted for refinancing, there seems to be considerable evidence emerging in this analysis and others to support the argument that contractions in aggregate economic activity beginning in 1989–1990 were politically induced by an excessive and selectively applied wave of financial regulation. This suggests that growth objectives of economic and regulatory policy would be well served by an honest assessment of the cumulative and independent effects of regulations in altering the structural economic dynamics of emerging and complex market systems based on financial innovations that contribute to capital access and lower capital costs for the vast majority of U.S. businesses.

The regulatory manipulation that culminated in 1989–1990 created a dark spot in the financial landscape not only because of the turmoil it generated but also because the resulting distortion cast a shadow deep enough to leave lasting doubts about what really lay beneath. The analysis presented here is supported by more than anecdotal evidence of disruptive regulatory manipulation at corresponding times.[7] Despite these regulatory

7. Empirical analysis that does not acknowledge this structural break can do so only by assuming it away.

restrictions, many high yield companies recovered in the subsequent years, as we show below.

CAUSES AND CONSEQUENCES OF FINANCIAL DISTRESS

After ten years of continuous economic expansion in the United States, several industries were in poor health as 2001 drew to a close. Steel, travel, theater, and health care were among the hardest hit. A significant number of firms experienced chronic problems; for others the distress was sudden and acute. Although business failures are normal, even sometimes desirable, events in a capitalist economy, too many can signal vulnerability or a pocket of distress. On the one hand, if the economy is becoming overheated, distressed events can play a positive role in keeping a lid on pressures that could lead to longer-term problems. Alternatively, a rise in corporate bond default rates can signal deterioration in overall credit quality.[8] Furthermore, losses to investors could dampen overall growth statistics and portend other problems.

In recent years, a number of companies and countries have experienced difficulty in growth and operations due to balance sheet problems. Though many of them were successful in raising financing in the past, capital markets have been closed to them recently and their debt has sold at significant discounts. Recent examples include Xerox (downgraded from Baa2 to Ba1 on December 1, 2000), Edison International (downgraded from A3 to Baa3 on January 5, 2001), Southern California Edison (downgraded from A2 to Baa3 on January 5, 2001), and Argentina (downgraded from B3 to Caa1 on July 13, 2001). As the economic outlook becomes more uncertain, and the volatility of equity and debt values increases, refinancing and investing become more art than science.

Fixing the balance sheet will remain the corporate challenge for the immediate future: $147 billion in U.S. speculative grade bonds and loans will mature between 2001 and 2003. Banks are shutting down access to capital for speculative grade companies because of modifications to capital requirements. The capital market is drying up for high yield bonds as well as new equity offerings. In the midst of these conditions, Chapter 11 filings by corporations increased by 11 percent in 1999 and an additional 6 percent in 2000.

INDUSTRY IMPACT

Some industries are more sensitive to economic conditions than others. Figure 4-7 shows the changing impact by displaying the sectors of the twenty largest U.S. bankruptcies from 1995 to 2001. Consumer cyclical firms were hard hit in 1997; large technology firms suffered more in 2001.

8. For a thorough discussion of the factors believed to impact default rates in the high yield bond market, see Altman, Hukkawala, and Kishore 2000.

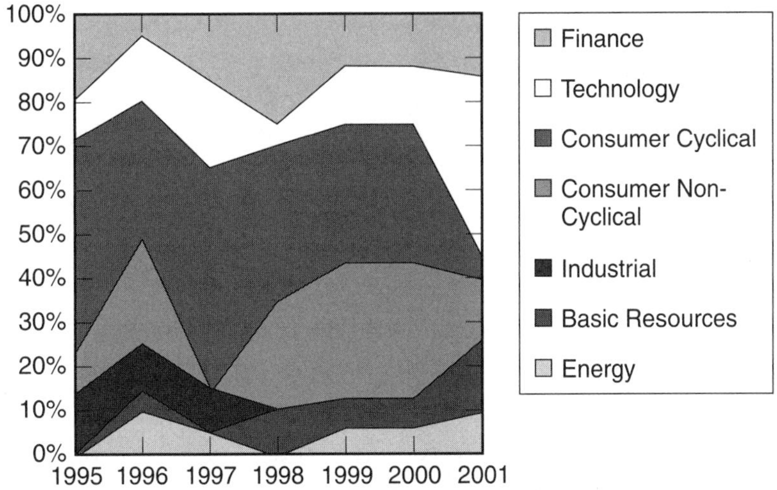

Figure 4-7. Sector Share of Twenty Largest Public U.S. Bankruptcies, 1995–2001. Sources: BankruptcyData.com; Trimbath 2000; Milken Institute.

In 1999, in addition to the general manufacturing and miscellaneous industries (each with fourteen defaulting issuers), such sectors as energy (twelve), retailing (twelve), communications (ten), health care (eight), leisure/entertainment (eight), and transportation (eight—mainly shipping) led the way. The energy sector's doldrums were mainly early in the year, while retailing and textiles continued to be a chronic problem. Industries such as communications and health care were new leaders in defaults, reflecting the frenetic new issuance in the former and the excess capacity and governmental regulatory fee-related factors in the latter. Hence, despite an ebullient economy, driven by technology and productivity growth, a number of sectors have been ailing, and some will continue to do so. Others, like energy and shipping, appear to have experienced the peak of defaults. Retail, insurance, supermarkets, drugstores, and textiles/furniture had the highest default rates in the 1991–1998 period. Steel, health care, theater chains, and retailers were vulnerable in 2000. Retailers recovered somewhat in 2001, and steel, health care and theaters were joined by travel in 2002.

With about $700 billion of debt, the perils facing the telecom industry could threaten the health of our economy. Major corporate defaults in this sector include Worldcom, Global Crossing Iridium, Globalstar, ICG Communications, Northpoint, and GST Telecommunications. The telecom industry is an interesting and challenging study. Telecoms were funded by high yield, but that source of financing is unavailable now. Current analysis is focused on defining what the real assets are and who will be the most likely buyers for those assets when liquidity returns.

RESTRUCTURING FOR RECOVERY

One of the unique features of U.S. capital markets is the availability of reorganization under Chapter 11, which allows companies to continue to operate while they recapitalize. In 1991, Knowledge Exchange (Santa Monica, California) published a list of the largest U.S. firms in the high yield market, which they called the "High Yield 500." Twenty-four of those firms were reorganizing under Chapter 11 that year. These were not necessarily the new, young firms often associated with the new-issue high yield market. Yet they were also large employers.

Of the twenty-four members of the High Yield 500 who were in Chapter 11 bankruptcy in 1991, twenty continued operations: three completely recovered and went on to investment grade ratings, nine were merged into other firms, and eight continue to operate. Reorganizing just these twenty companies had the potential to conserve more than 369,000 jobs.[9] Their stories are briefly summarized below.

Fully Recovered

Federated Department Stores (FD). First goes below investment grade in April 1988. Long-term rating recovers in November 1998.

Interco (FBN), name changed to Furniture Brands International on March 1, 1996. Falls below investment grade in December 1988. Moves back to investment grade in April 2000.

Southland Corp. (SE), name changed to 7-Eleven on April 29, 1999. In September 1992 short-term issuer credit rating is moved to A1+, highest rating. In April 2000, S&P Long Term Issuer Credit rating moves to investment grade (BBB) for the first time since November 1987.

Merged Assets

Allied Stores Corp. Falls below investment grade in February 1987. Merged into Federated Department Stores in February 1992.

American Healthcare Management. Merged with OrNda HealthCorp in 1994.

Carter Hawley Hale Stores. Emerged from Chapter 11 in October 1992. Changed name to Broadway Stores in June 1994. Merged with Federated Department Stores in October 1995.

Circle K Corp. (CRK). Merged with Tosco Corporation in June 1996.

Doskocil Companies. Emerged from bankruptcy and changed name to Foodbrands America in April 1995. Merged with IBP in 1997.

Forum Group. Merged with Marriott International in 1996.

National Gypsum Co. Emerged from bankruptcy in 1993. Merged with N G Acquisition (Delcor) in September 1995.

Public Service Company of New Hampshire. Became the first investor-owned utility to declare bankruptcy since the Great Depression. Restruc-

9. The four liquidated companies are Best Products, First Capital Holdings, Lionel Corp., and Pan American World Airways, representing 64,411 jobs.

tured under the Federal Energy Regulatory Commission in January 1989. Merged into Northeast Utilities (CT) in June 1992.

Revco D S. Emerged from bankruptcy in June 1992. Merged into CVS Corp. in May 1997.

Continuing Struggles

Ames Department Stores (AMESQ). Entered bankruptcy in 1990 and emerged in 1992. In March 2001, Moody's downgraded its long-term issuer rating to Caa3, below investment grade. Reentered Chapter 11 in August 2001. In April 2002, they are nearing completion of an agreement of reorganization.

Continental Airlines Holdings (CAL). Entered bankruptcy 1990, emerged 1993. Name changed in April 1993 to Continental Airlines. Remains below investment grade. Condition worsened by the impact of the events of September 11, 2001, on the travel industry in general and on airlines in particular.

LTV Corp. (LTVCG). Emerged from bankruptcy in 1993. Reentered Chapter 11 in 2000 with $6. billion in assets.[10] In April 2002, International Steel Group, a company controlled by distressed asset investor Wilbur Ross, completed the acquisition of LTV's steel assets, and plans to restart its plants as soon as possible.

Lomas Financial Corp. (SIEN). Name changed to Siena Holdings. Reentered Chapter 11 in 1995 with $310.78 million in assets and emerged effective March 1997. Creditors' trust scheduled to terminate June 2002.

United Merchants & Manufacturers (UMMF). Reentered Chapter 11 in February 1996 with $58.43 million in assets. Removed from NYSE in March 1996. Filed Form 15 (termination of SEC share registration) in June 1997. Delisted from Nasdaq's OTC bulletin board in March 2000.

WTD Industries (TRES). Filed bankruptcy in January 1991, emerged November 1992, completed reorganization in the fall of 1998, was renamed TreeSource Industries. Back in Chapter 11 in October 1999 with $54.99 million in assets. Bondholders took control of all assets in prepackaged deal; emerged from bankruptcy January 2002. Filed Form 15 (termination of SEC share registration) in February 2002 (delisted).

Salant Corp. (SLNT). Reentered Chapter 11 in 1998 with $233.4 million in assets. Emerged from bankruptcy May 1999 (case closed November 2001).

JPS Textile Group (JPST). Name changed in June 1999 to JPS Industries. Filed prepackaged Chapter 11 plan of reorganization in August 1997, which was confirmed in September 1997.

CHALLENGES AND OPPORTUNITIES IN 2001 AND BEYOND

A new record was set in 2001 with a total of 1,437,354 bankruptcy filings, a 14 percent increase over 2000. Chapter 7 liquidations continued as the

10. Twenty-five U.S. steelmakers have entered bankruptcy since 1998.

most prevalent filing, followed by wage earner reorganizations under Chapter 13, then business reorganizations under Chapter 11, with farmer reorganizations under Chapter 12 pulling up the rear.

Chapter 11 filings by public giants like K-Mart and Enron brought bankruptcy to the forefront of national attention in the early 2000s. It's not just technology companies that are suffering, though they are still filing for bankruptcy in record numbers. With the recession under way—and officially acknowledged—we see the impact on other industries as well. Retail and travel are helping to fuel the rise in Chapter 11 filings nationally.

The increasingly fragmented ownership of bank loans and bonds is creating new challenges and opportunities for trading and investing in discounted debt instruments. Moody's predicted a healthy increase in defaults for 2001. Equity valuations, though still high, are volatile and lower than 2001. Interest rates are still relatively low, but uncertain even after six consecutive reductions in the Fed Funds rate during the same number of months. The naysayers are predicting a sustained economic downturn, and analysts are finding all the statistics they need to prove it. The National Bureau of Economic Research (NBER), which usually waits months if not years before "declaring" a recession, bent to popular pressure in October 2001. It dates the official peak of the last expansion (and the beginning of a recession) at March 2001.

Investors need to distinguish between businesses that are suffering financial distress induced by poor management and those that are suffering from a lack of access to capital (Andrade and Kaplan 1998). Regardless of the cause, restructuring means firms can survive financial distress and prosper. Thus, supporting the high yield securities that enable firms to restructure will continue to be a successful strategy.

5

Participants in the Recovery

We have discussed the factors that triggered the temporary price collapse of the high yield market. We now turn to the question of when and how first movers returned to the market and renewed it with activity that far surpassed issuance and performance over previous decades. The high yield market was in disarray in 1990 as Drexel Burnham Lambert, then a primary, but by no means dominant, underwriter and market maker filed for bankruptcy and several types of financial institutions were forced to liquidate their holdings. A healthy future for the market seemed unlikely to many. New high yield bond issuance all but disappeared in 1990, and there was considerable concern about the very survival of the market as 1991 commenced. With additional pressure exerted by liquidity concerns, spreads over U.S. Treasuries reached a historic high of ten percentage points (see figure 5-1). Most analysts expected high default rates on outstanding issues as sources of capital for refinancing maturing debt all but disappeared. They were not disappointed. The one-year default rate on speculative grade bonds began a rapid ascent to previously unseen heights. The higher default rates were reflected in rates of return. High yield investors lost 4.4 percent in 1990—the first negative annual return in a decade.

What happened in 1991, however, was a complete reversal. Although default rates peaked in July 1991 at 13 percent (figure 5-2), they fell just as quickly, so that a more "normal" default rate of less than 6 percent was achieved before the end of 1992. There was also a sharp decline in the interest rate spread at original issue, and the market for new issues rebounded, with thirty-three companies raising almost $10 billion in forty issues. The new issue market's recovery was derived mainly from $6 billion of issuance used to repay leveraged buyout (LBO) debt. Although this was a year of revival, the 1991 proportion of total new issue straight corporate debt comprised by high yield bonds was still fairly low at about 6 percent, considerably below the record years of 1987 and 1988, when high yield accounted for 25 percent of total corporate bond issuance.

Recovering from its near collapse at the end of the 1980s, the high yield market enjoyed a period of remarkable and virtually uninterrupted growth in the 1990s. Almost every year saw record-breaking new issuance levels. Issuers from seventy-two countries on six continents floated high yield debt in the United States. The contrast between the 1980s and the 1990s is evi-

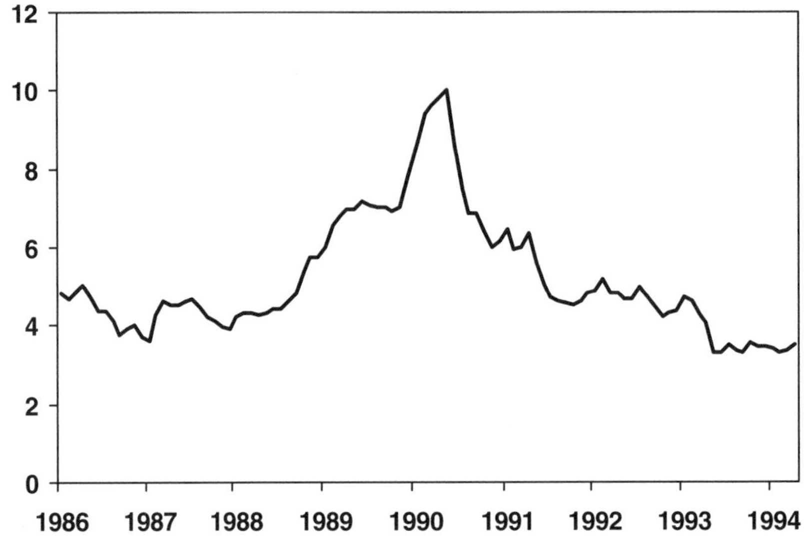

Figure 5-1. High Yield Spread over Treasuries, 1986–1994. Sources: Federal Reserve; Merrill Lynch.

denced in the annual increases in the value of new issues for high yield securities in the U.S. market (see figure 5-3 and figure 5-4). The value of new issues increased by about $3.75 billion each year from 1979 through 1989. In contrast, the growth of issuance during the recovery years of the 1990s was more than double that at $8.68 billion per year.

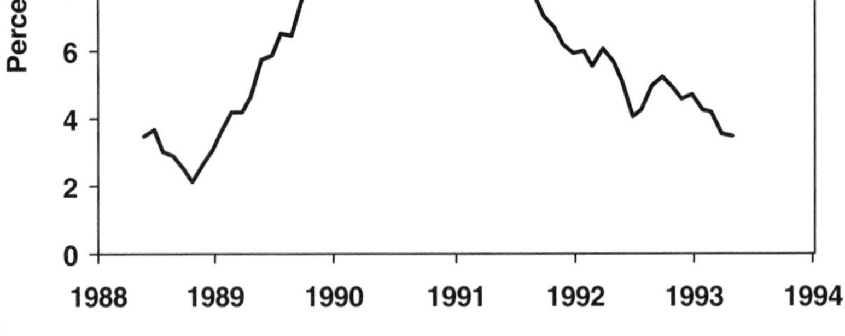

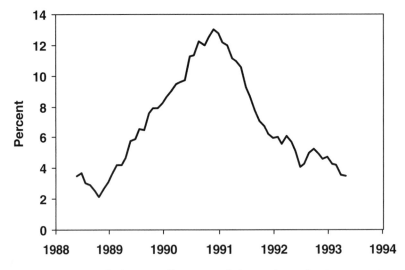

Figure 5-2. One Year Default Rates: All U.S. Speculative-Grade Bonds, 1988–1994. Source: Moody's Investors Service.

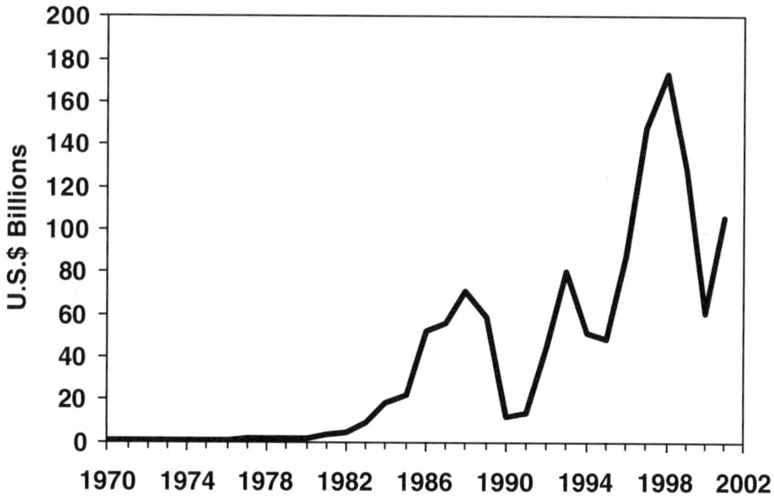

Figure 5-3. Historical Perspective on U.S. High Yield Market: Value of New Issues, 1970–2002. Source: Securities Data Corporation.

The issuers in this decade of growth came from a number of industry groups. The initial 1991–1993 participants in the recovery of the high yield market, including media and telecom firms, continued to contribute greatly to the growth, accounting for 37 percent of new offerings, and were joined by entities from such diverse industries as consumer products, energy, and financial services. Firms in the technology and energy sectors dramatically

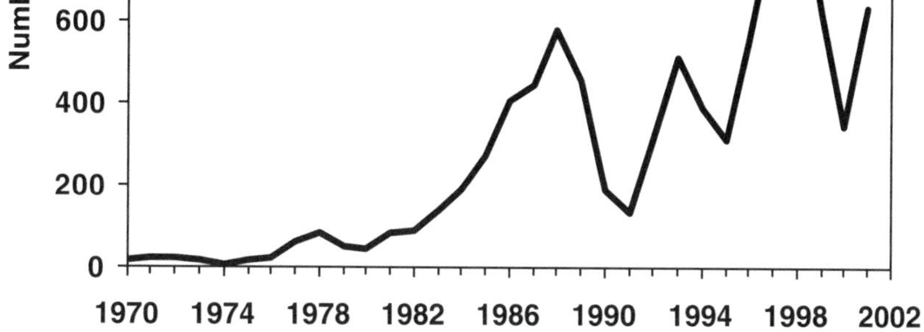

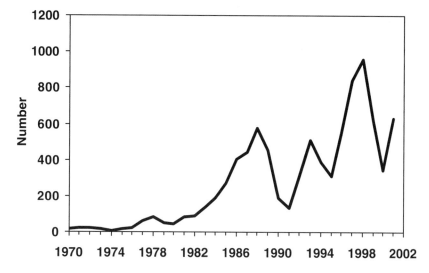

Figure 5-4. Historical Perspective on U.S. High Yield Market: Number of New Issues, 1970–2002. Source: Securities Data Corporation.

increased participation in 1994–1998 as the economic expansion was taking hold.

During the recovery years, the high yield market underwent dramatic, measurable changes. The quality of issues available increased significantly even though the yield spread of high yield bonds over Treasury bonds was still as high as ever. In 1988, roughly 60 percent of the high yield bond market was rated B or below by Standard & Poor's. By 1994, only about 20 percent of the market was rated B or below. In 1993, 19 percent was the average return to mutual funds investing in the high yield bond market, the only market where investors could earn a double-digit return that year from interest income alone.

The transition from near collapse to a healthy and respected market that continues to provide excellent earnings opportunities for investors and access to capital for otherwise excluded borrowers is a story that requires two viewpoints to tell. On the one hand, volumes periodically dried up, leaving investors scrambling for liquidity. On the other hand, the cause of those illiquid spells was often the transition from a market of corporations that were troubled, even bankrupt, to one characterized by healthy and streamlined issuers.

The initial period of the transition of the high yield market began in October 1990 and ran through January 1994, during which time the market posted positive monthly returns virtually without exception (see figure 5-5). As we will discuss later, the setback of 1994 typified the "good news/bad news" duality of the market. After 1994, the resurgence continued unabated to the end of the decade, as high yield financing virtually left behind its "junk" moniker.

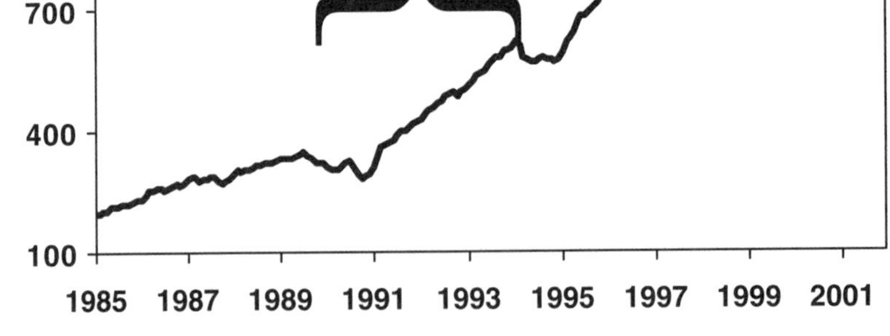

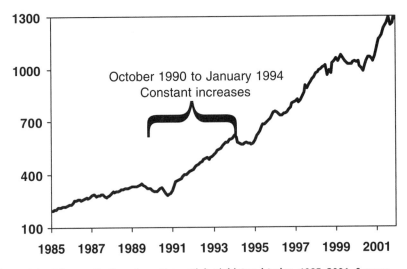

Figure 5-5. Salomon Brothers Long-Term High Yield Bond Index, 1985–2001. Source: Bloomberg.

A number of factors allowed this resurgence:

- Increased quality of issuers as the economy recovered
- Upgraded firm credit ratings
- Eased monetary policy that reduced interest rates from 6.75 percent in 1991 to 3.0 percent in 1992
- Equity markets opened to high yield issuers
- Business cycle advances that increased demand for investment products
- Defaults and distressed credits cleared as restructuring continued and workouts of poorly structured transactions were carried out
- Increased interest in overseas issuers.

THE U.S. MARKET: QUALITY JUMP-STARTS THE RECOVERY

By the end of 1991, the high yield market in the United States had not only survived the financial dark ages of the late 1980s but had grown to over $200 billion, a figure that would more than double over the next seven years to $580 billion by the end of 1998 (figure 5-6). New issues totaled $10.5 billion for the first four months of 1992, and the second quarter broke the record for a single quarter's new issuance at $12.5 billion, as the market's rebound took hold. Total market size, however, remained constant in 1992 despite new issuance volume as firms redeemed or recapitalized substantial amounts of debt. The exciting growth of the market was displayed in new records for annual new issue volume in 1993 and again in 1997.

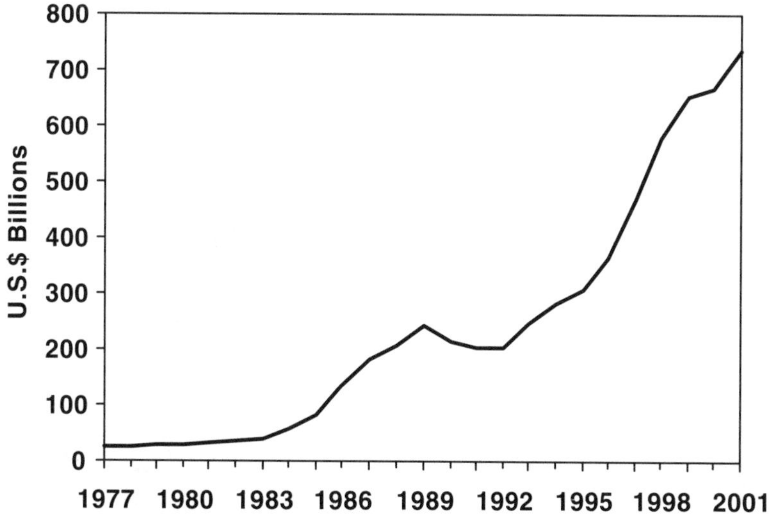

Figure 5-6. U.S. High Yield Amount Outstanding, 1977–2001. Sources: Credit Suisse First Boston; The Bond Market Association; Venture Economics; Portfolio Management Data (PMD).

The quality of issues in the high yield market dramatically improved. For example, Duff & Phelps/MCM upgraded twenty-three companies in January 1992 and downgraded just six. Over that year, rating upgrades outpaced downgrades by nearly four to one, continuing a trend of improving quality that had started the previous year. The increase in quality meant a decrease in new supply for investors as competition to buy new high yield issues put downward pressure on original issue interest rates and on the availability of high yield for investors. Figure 5-7 illustrates these and other issues that show the impact of macroeconomic conditions on the high yield market. This figure shows why, by 1992, medium- and higher-quality issuers were able to improve their finances through reduced interest costs—at times significantly. These issuers were also aided by the rising equity market and by crossover buyers. Because they could issue equity more cheaply than debt at the time, many companies tapped the equity market and reduced their debt, creating the conditions required for upgrades. In addition, crossover buyers—traditionally investment grade purchasers—switched to better quality noninvestment grade companies, in search of yield and return. (In fact, some crossover buyers may have continued purchasing the debt of companies whose ratings temporarily fell below investment grade.) These buyers would accept lower yields than traditional high yield buyers usually would, putting further downward pressure on the issuing interest rates of high yield companies. This new opportunity to issue debt at lower than usual costs encouraged refinancing, which added to the new issue volume while allowing the size of the total market to remain constant.

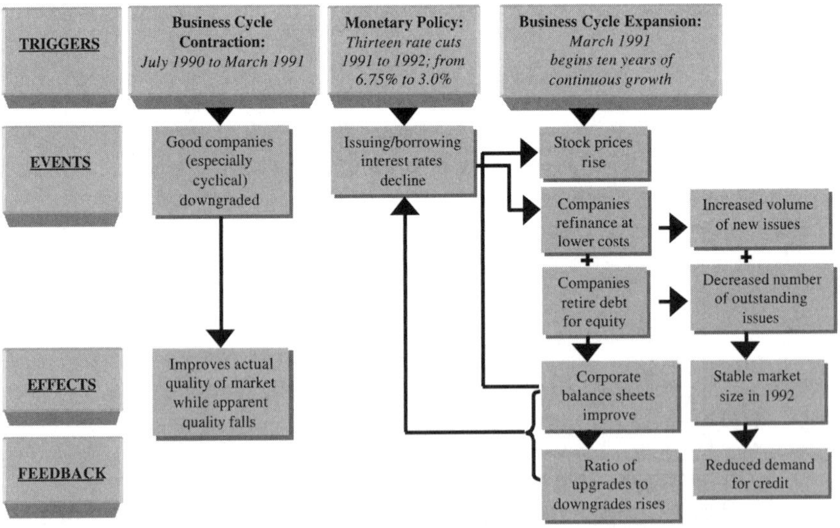

Figure 5-7. The U.S. Economy in Transition: Macroeconomic Effects on the Size and Quality of the High Yield Market. Source: Milken Institute.

The high yield bond market was healthier in 1992 than at any time in almost three years. In the third quarter of 1992 the default rate on high yield debt dropped to 0.2 percent, far below the 4.2 percent seen in January 1991. The first nine months of 1992 saw a refinancing boom set off by lower interest rates that retired 11 percent of the high yield market. By the end of the year, many of the better companies had already refinanced most of their higher-cost debt. As interest rates on new issues trended toward 13 percent later in the year, refinancing activity slowed dramatically. In fact, more than $2 billion in prospective high yield bond deals were pulled off the shelf before ever reaching the market in the third quarter of 1992, adding to the equilibrating effects of refinancing versus retiring existing debt that left the market size flat.

The new issue market became increasingly weighted toward bonds that financed acquisitions and capital expenditures. Although riskier than refinancings, the new high yield issues still presented good investment opportunities. With the tax law changes of 1989 (Trimbath 2002), acquisition financing shifted from debt to syndicated bank loans; by 1993 the predominant use of high yield proceeds was refinancing, with 62.3 percent of the proceeds used in refinancing either bank debt (31.5 percent) or fixed interest debt (30.8 percent).

In another form of refinancing debt with equity, several firms that were acquired through highly leveraged transactions in the 1980s were reissued to the public during this period. These transactions contributed to the general improvement in corporate balance sheets that raised the overall quality of issues in the high yield market. With few attractive new acquisitions available, leveraged buyout players put their cash to work deleveraging. These financiers viewed capital in terms of supply and demand: with equity plentiful but credit scarce, it was the moment to substitute equity for debt to make the deals less highly leveraged, as Milken had publicly called for before being sidelined by legal issues (Milken 1992). By putting fresh equity into distressed situations, the dealers could negotiate with lenders and get them to accept lower interest rates, postpone maturities, or scale back their principal. Some buyout firms used their equity to re-leverage their companies at more favorable terms. For example, in May 1992 New York's Kelso & Co., the firm that pioneered the use of employee stock ownership plans to help finance buyouts, put $14 million in additional equity into the recapitalization of Mosler, a manufacturer of security systems it had bought in 1986. In the process, Kelso got bankers to put back in $80 million of scarce senior debt, debt that Mosler had already paid off. According to IDD Information Services, the volume of reissued targets reached nearly $1 billion in 1992. Notables selling equity to retire debt around this time included KKR/Safeway ($112.5 million, April 1990), First Chicago et al./Air & Water Technologies Corp. ($68 million, August 1989) and First Boston et al./First Brands Corp. ($95 million, December 1989).

All these events helped the quality of new issue corporate debt to remain the lead story in the 1990s. While securities in the lower end of the quality scale, rated B or lower, comprised nearly 80 percent of new issues in the high yield market in 1989, the average from 1992 through 1998 was only about 60 percent (see figure 5-8). The share of the high yield market composed of BB-rated debt (the higher end of the quality scale) peaked in 1991 at nearly 60 percent of rated issues. Though this was extraordinary, the percentage of total new issuance rated BB did not fall below 30 percent for the next decade—a level two-thirds higher than 1989's record low of 19 percent.

Despite this improvement in quality, 1994 brought little good news for the market. High yield new issues returned to favoring the lower rating grades that year: bonds rated B or lower accounted for 75 percent of new issue ratings in the first half of 1994, compared with 48 percent for the first six months of 1993. That was still short of the annual average of 84 percent for the 1987–1989 period, but not enough to maintain the positive gains in the indices. (See discussion below on high yield mutual funds.) Overall, downgrades in the first two quarters of 1994 fell 13 percent year-on-year, to 39 percent (figure 5-9). Upgrades, which had soared past downgrades in the same period of 1993, fell 20 percent, to 43 percent, although they still outnumbered downgrades. However, these events were not to be the portent of an ongoing decline in the quality of new high yield issues or the overall quality of the market. By the end of 1994, the market settled into a comfortable 60/40 split around the B rating and stay there for the foreseeable future.

In the first half of 1994, twenty-three Moody's downgrades affecting $10.1 billion of debt were attributable to special events such as mergers,

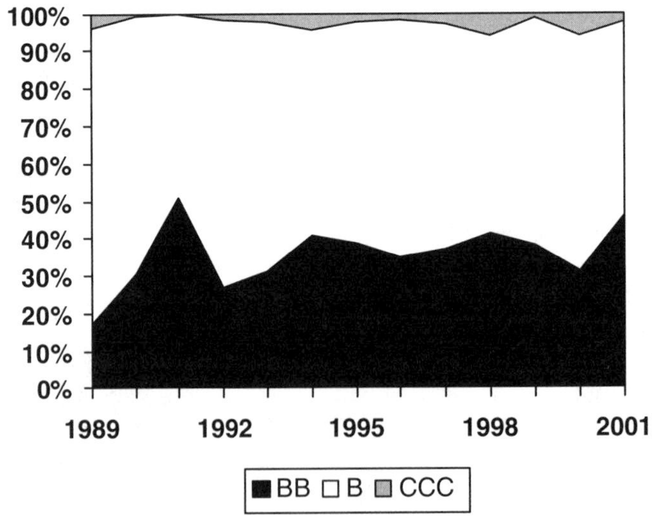

Figure 5-8. New Issues by Credit Rating, 1989–2001. Note: Based on Standard and Poor's ratings. BB includes BB+ and BB–; similarly for B and CCC. Source: Credit Suisse First Boston.

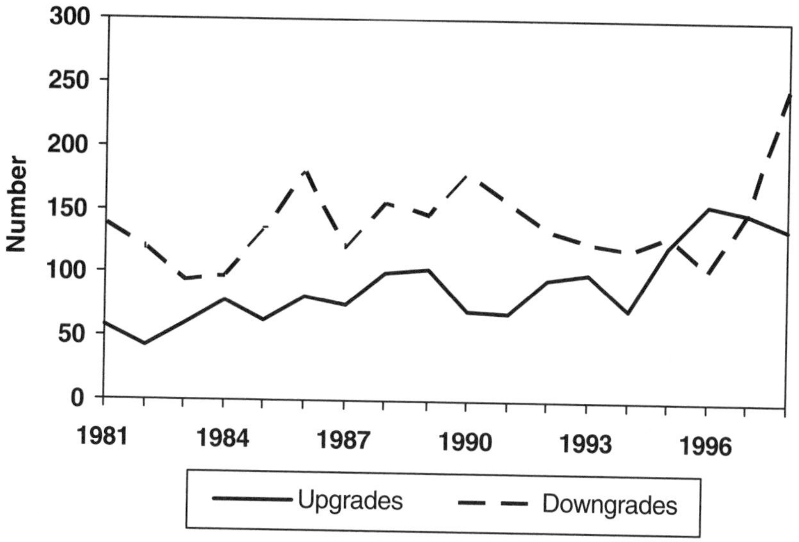

Figure 5-9. Number of Downgrades and Upgrades, 1981–1996. Source: Standard and Poor's.

equity buybacks and other recapitalizations, or litigation. (See chapter 4 for a discussion of the impact of litigation on downgrades and turnarounds.) This compares with nine such downgrades in the first half of 1993 (and twenty-nine for all of 1993), twenty-eight for 1992, and only nineteen in recession year 1991. The largest downgrades of debt in 1994 were triggered by two mergers: Viacom/Paramount ($960 million tumbled below investment grade) and James River/Jamont Holdings (ratings lowered on $2 billion of bonds to below investment grade). Both buyers went on to fully recover their investment grade status (see boxes 5-1 and 5-2).

U.S. ECONOMIC INDUSTRIES AND SECTORS

The proportion of the high yield market occupied by any one industry will vary across time as market forces and macroeconomic conditions evolve. It is the nature of this segment of the market for corporate finance that the issuing firms will generally fall into one of two categories. Lower credit ratings at original issue are usually assigned to borrowers who are either unproven or distressed. Once these borrowers enter the market, they may remain active issuers by refinancing their original issues either to service their debt prior to improving their finances sufficiently to raise their credit rating or to take advantage of declining interest rates.

In late 1990, the U.S. economy was entering a period of economic correction after several years of expansion. The National Bureau of Economic Research identified July 1990 through March 1991 as a period of economic contraction. Economic conditions during the subsequent expansion brought

BOX 5-1. DOWNGRADED BUT NOT OUT I: VIACOM RECOVERS

Viacom Incorporated

In July 1994 Viacom purchased Paramount Communications, one of the world's largest and oldest producers of motion pictures and television shows. The deal, which cost approximately $8 billion, elevated Viacom to the fifth-largest media company in the world. It also lowered Viacom's debt rating to "junk" status. The acquisition of Paramount vastly expanded Viacom's presence in the entertainment business, giving it a motion picture library that included classics such as *The Ten Commandments* and *The Godfather*. Moreover, Viacom gained ownership of Simon & Shuster, one of the world's largest book publishers.

Later that same year, Viacom expanded into a new segment of the entertainment industry by acquiring Blockbuster, the owner, operator, and franchiser of thousands of video and music stores. The Blockbuster group of subsidiaries was one of Viacom's fastest growing enterprises; by 1997, Blockbuster boasted 60 million cardholders worldwide and over 6,000 music and video stores.

Viacom's acquisition of Paramount and Blockbuster gave the company thriving new enterprises but left the company with significant debt. To both relieve that debt and focus the company's energies, Viacom divested itself of several non-core businesses. In 1995 the company sold the operations of Madison Square Garden for $1.07 billion. In 1996, the company spun off its cable systems. Although this represented a break with Viacom's origins as a cable provider, the deal relieved the company of $1.7 billion in debt. The following year, Viacom left radio broadcasting by selling its ten radio stations. This approximately $1.1 billion deal reduced Viacom's debt even further.

Although Viacom was no longer a cable service provider, and had expanded into the motion picture and video rental market, its cable networks remained a significant portion of its business. MTV Networks, which included MTV, Nickelodeon, and VH1, accounted for almost $625 million in operating profits in 1997, approximately 32 percent of Viacom's estimated earnings for the year.

The following year, on October 13, 1998, Viacom's long-term debt rating moved into investment grade territory. On March 26, 2001, Merrill Lynch Capital Markets issued a long-term buy recommendation for Viacom with a twelve-month price objective of $100 from the then current price of $43 (Gale Group 2001).

Moody's Rating Actions

6 APR 1995 Moody's upgrades Viacom's long-term debt ratings to Ba2 (senior unsecured) and B1 (subordinated).

3 AUG 1995 Moody's assigns Ba2 ratings to bank credit facilities of Viacom and Viacom International.

(continued)

22 JAN 1996 Moody's confirms ratings of Viacom and Viacom International (senoir at Ba2) following announcement by Viacom of senior management changes.

1 JUL 1997 Moody's confirms ratings of Viacom and Viacom International (senoir at Ba2) following announcement by company of worsened expectations for Blockbuster unit.

23 SEP 1997 Moody's confirms ratings of Viacom and Viacom International (senior at Ba2) following announcement by company of sale of interest in USA Networks.

13 OCT 1998 Moody's upgrades long-term debt ratings of Viacom, senior unsecured to Baa3, short-term to Prime-3.

24 MAY 2000 Moody's upgrades viacom's and the former CBS Corporation's senior unsecured debt ratings to Baa1 from Baa3.

16 NOV 2000 Moody's upgrades viacom's ratings to A3 from Baa1 (senior unsecured).

out inflationary pressures that, by increasing product prices, increased the revenue stream for firms in the cyclical industries. As we shall see, the changing economic conditions affected some industries differently than others. (See the flow chart in figure 5–7.)

The consumer products, energy, technology, and financial services sectors were disproportionately active in the high yield market in the 1990s compared to their overall representation in the U.S. economy (table 5-1). During the early part of the recovery, it was the noncyclical and financial services sectors that were relatively more active in the high yield new issues market. The participation of firms in the energy, technology, and cyclical consumer products sectors gained momentum after the initial recovery, moving the market forward.

The increased participation of firms from the cyclical sector in the later period reflects of the dynamics of inflation in the 1990s. Although average inflation was relatively low during the entire 1991–1998 period, the average in 1994–1998 was substantially higher (2.6 percent, compared to only 1.8 percent) than in 1991–1993 (based on the GNP implicit price deflator). An average of forty-five cyclical firms participated in the high yield new issues market in the earlier years of lower inflation, compared to an average of sixty-eight firms in the period of relatively higher inflation. In a period of rising prices, these firms were experiencing increasing revenue streams, allowing them to support the debt-servicing payments on new issues of high yield securities during a period when the business cycle was on an upswing. By comparison, participation by firms in the consumer noncyclical sector remained fairly constant across the two periods (adjusted for the difference in the number of years in each period, about fifty firms per year).

BOX 5-2. DOWNGRADED BUT NOT OUT II: FORT JAMES CORP. RECOVERS

James River Corporation of Virginia

In 1994, following three years of losses, most analysts were recommending that investors sell their James River stock. The purchase of European paper towel and tissue manufacturer Jamont N.V. resulted in the downgrade of its debt to below investment grade. Just a year later, however, James River defied expectations and returned to profitability. The improvement reflected increased efficiencies and an upturn in demand for the firm's products. The 1995 recovery was led by a 60 percent increase in sales in the firm's U.S. consumer paper business, which accounted for about 45 percent of the company's revenue. In an irony not lost on bond investors, Jamont N.V. reported a tenfold increase in profit for the period. Earnings from communications paper jumped to almost $200 million, after a $35 million loss in 1994, mostly because of stronger demand for office products. James River merged with Fort Howard in 1997 to become Fort James. The chairmen of the two companies estimated that the merger would result in about $150 million in savings in 1998, resulting from economies of scale and efficiencies created by the combined operations. Fort James's credit rating was raised to investment grade in 1998 (Gale Group 2001).

Moody's Rating Actions

20 MAY 1997 Moody's confirms debt ratings of James River, senior unsecured at Baa3; upgrades Fort Howard, senior unsecured to Baa3.

29 JUL 1997 Moody's assigns Baa3 to guaranteed revolving credit facility of Fort James Corporation.

19 SEP 1997 Moody's assigns Baa3 to senior unsecured notes of Fort James Corporation.

18 JUN 1998 Moody's raises debt ratings of Fort James Corporation: senior unsecured to Baa2; short-term rating to Prime-2.

26 APR 1999 Moody's confirms Fort James's ratings at Baa2.

2 AUG 1999 Moody's confirms ratings of Fort James Corporation; senior unsecured at Baa2. Changes outlook to positive.

Table 5-2 shows where the greater number of firms in each sector participated. Note that of the technology and energy firms issuing high yield, substantially more of them issued after 1993, when the U.S. economy was well into expansion. Technology was being applied in virtually every sector, as would be seen in the unprecedented growth of productivity that followed. Figures 5-10A and 5-10B demonstrate a similar surge in the technology sector's participation by showing that the proportion of all firms issuing high yield that were in the technology sector rose from 10 percent in the early part of the recovery to 18 percent during the ensuing expansion.

Table 5-1. Sectoral Distribution of Firms in High Yield Market versus Fortune 500

Sector	1991–1993 High Yield	1993 Fortune 500	1994–1998 High Yield	1998 Fortune 500
Basic Resources	9.4%	16.2%	6.5%	16.9%
Consumer Cyclical	17.9%	22.6%	16.1%	22.7%
Consumer Noncyclical	19.7%	16.8%	12.5%	15.8%
Energy	5.7%	5.0%	7.4%	5.1%
Industrial	15.8%	16.2%	14.3%	16.5%
Technology	9.6%	12.3%	17.2%	12.1%
Financial Services	13.7%	6.9%	18.2%	7.0%
Other	8.2%	4.0%	8.0%	4.0%

Source: Trimbath 2000.

U.S. COMPANIES

Of the most active companies in the 1991–1993 initial period of the recovery, all stayed in the high yield original issuance market for the later years of the recovery, though mostly at a reduced rate of issuance (table 5-3). Only News America, United Airlines, Time Warner, Delta Air Lines and Owens-Illinois made the top twenty in both periods. Four of those five are in cyclical industries.

HIGH YIELD BOND FUNDS DURING THE TRANSITION YEARS

Mutual funds have always been important to the high yield market's buy side. Mutual funds owned at least 30 percent of all high yield bonds during the early 1990s. Battered by a wave of defaults and bad publicity, a majority of high yield bonds lost more than 40 percent of their value between 1988 and the end of 1990. As a group, high yield funds compiled a deplorable

Table 5-2. Number of Firms Participating, 1991–1998

Industry	1991–1998	1991–1993	1994–1998
Financial Services	485	104	381
Consumer Cyclical	474	136	338
Technology	433	73	360
Industrial	420	120	300
Consumer Noncyclical	411	149	262
Other or Unclassified	229	62	167
Basic Resources	207	71	136
Energy	198	43	155

Source: Trimbath 2000.

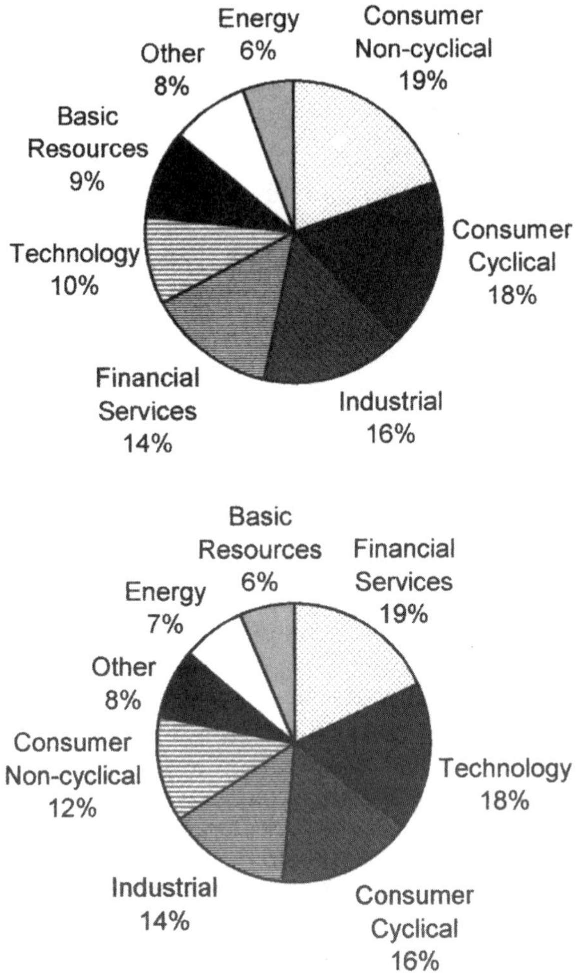

Figure 5-10 Top. Distribution of High Yield New Issues, 1991–1993. Bottom. Distribution of High Yield New Issues, 1994–1998. Sources: Securities Data Corporation; Milken Institute.

–12.3 percent return over those years. No other class of funds had given so poor a performance, yet a nucleus of investors kept faith in the market and their money in high yield funds. Indeed, redemptions accounted for $8.6 billion of the $15.7 billion drop in total high yield fund assets that occurred following June 1989, when assets in the funds peaked at $35.2 billion (figure 5-11). The decline was short-lived: by 1992 high yield bond funds had enjoyed a sixteen-month spree of improving returns, and net flows to high yield mutual funds had again become positive (figure 5-12). The annual performance of these two measures is summarized in Table 5-4.

Table 5-3. Active U.S. Companies

Number of Issues	Company Name	Sector
During the Recovery Years 1991–1993		
11	News America Holdings	Cyclical consumer products
9	Kroger	Noncyclical consumer products
8	United Airlines (UAL Corp.)	Cyclical consumer products
8	Time Warner	Cyclical consumer products
8	Tele-Communications	Cyclical consumer products
7	Stone Container Corp.	Industrial
7	Safeway	Noncyclical consumer products
7	Delta Air Lines	Cyclical consumer products
7	Continental Cablevision	Cyclical consumer products
6	Owens-Illinois	Basic resources
6	Chrysler Financial Corp.	Financial
5	Georgia-Pacific Corp.	Basic resources
5	Comcast Corp.	Cyclical consumer products
	19 companies tied at 4 each	
Active During Expansion Years 1994–1998		
17	CMS Energy Corp.	Energy
15	United Airlines (UAL Corp.)	Cyclical consumer products
14	Time Warner	Cyclical consumer products
13	Great Southern Bancorp	Financial
13	News America Holdings	Cyclical consumer products
10	AMERCO	Financial
9	Cablevision Systems Corp.	Cyclical consumer products
9	Delta Air Lines	Cyclical consumer products
9	Niagara Mohawk Power Corp.	Energy
8	Black & Decker Corp.	Basic resources
8	Cleveland Elec. Illuminating	Energy
8	Intermedia Communications	Cyclical consumer products
8	Nextel Communications	Technology
7	Adelphia Communications Corp.	Technology
7	CalEnergy Co.	Energy
7	Commercial Mortg. Acceptance Corp.	Financial
7	Owens-Illinois	Basic resources
7	Tenet Healthcare Corp.	Noncyclical consumer products

Sources: Securities Data Corporation; Milken Institute.

1991

At least twenty high yield funds brought in new managers to revive their fortunes in 1991. Some of the larger funds to do so included the $105 million Alliance bond fund high yield portfolio, the $299 million American Capital High Yield Investments fund, the $593 million Dean Witter high yield securities fund and the $556 million First Investors high yield fund.

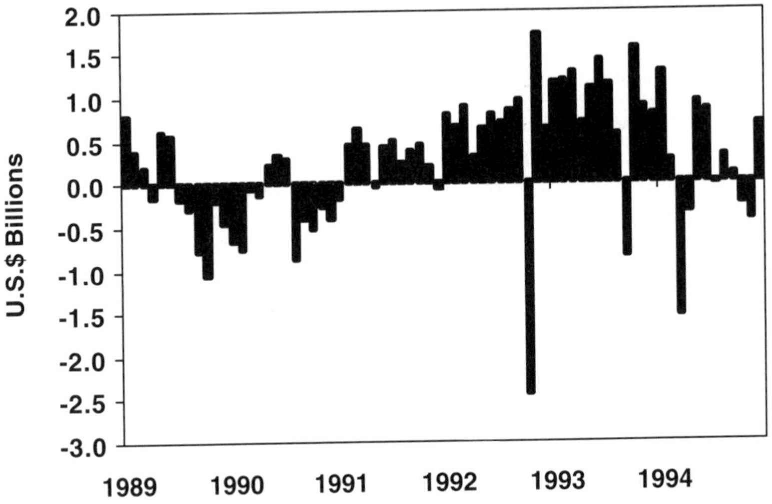

Figure 5-11. Monthly High Yield Mutual Fund Net Flows, January 1989–December 1994. Source: Investment Company Institute.

Many experts expected defaults to skyrocket, drawing many middle-tier bonds into the lowest tier. Meanwhile, they anticipated that the ongoing flight of thrifts and insurance companies from the high yield market would tend to depress prices of upper-tier high yield bonds for months to come. But some fund managers picked the right upper-tier issues, bought them cheap, and scored a rich payback when the companies redeemed the bonds.

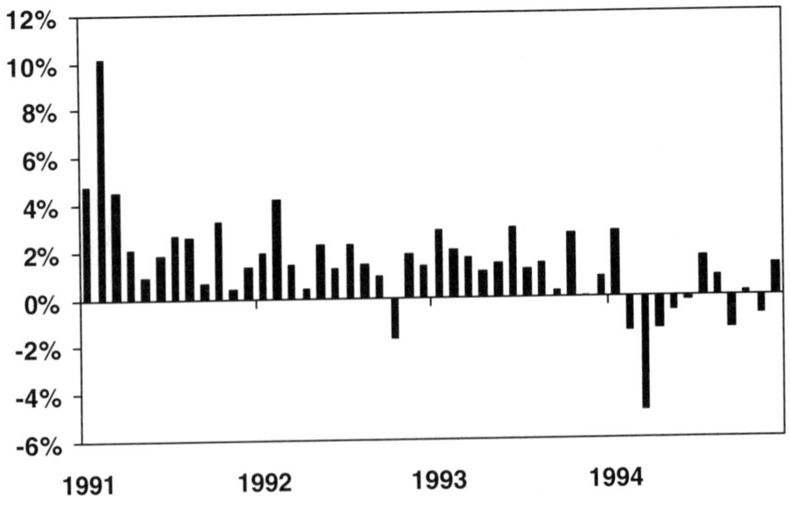

Figure 5-12. Monthly Returns for Salomon High Yield Indices, 1991–1994. Source: Bloomberg.

Table 5-4. Index Performance and Fund Flows, 1991–2000

Year	Annual Change in Index	High Yield Funds (total flows)
1991	36.50%	3.39
1992	16.90%	5.79
1993	16.54%	10.94
1994	–6.40%	1.75
1995	26.44%	11.06
1996	6.93%	15.48
1997	17.05%	21.97
1998	6.91%	19.89
1999	–1.22%	4.25
2000	3.50%	

By March 2001, the index had already gained 9.3 percent over December 2000.
Source: Bloomberg. Total flows are from *Merrill Lynch Extra Credit*, January / February 2000, p. 57.

In 1991, investment recommendations shifted to convertible bond funds that invested in fixed-income securities that could be exchanged for a specified number of shares of the issuer's common stock. As a result, they combined some of the growth potential of stocks with some of the safety of bonds. When the market went sour in 1990, convertible funds actually lost more than the average equity portfolio (7.6 percent versus 6.3 percent). The reason was that about two-thirds of convertible issuers were small companies, which stock investors dumped hard in 1990. In 1991, though, small stocks were hot—and so were convertible funds. As of early May 1991, these funds were up 15.4 percent for the year. Convertibles offered a way to profit from the small-stock advance while collecting generous yields (an average of 5.8 percent that year) and shouldering only about half the risk of small stocks.

1992

A major reversal in the market came in October 1992 when, after a buying spree that had been going on for nearly two years, investors redeemed more than $1.9 billion in high yield bond fund shares. It was a virtual stampede. Much of October 1992's outflow was triggered by market-timing investment advisers, who had bought large blocks of high yield bond fund shares during the rally. By October the average high yield fund's rise of 16 percent looked so good that these hot-money managers decided to lock in their returns. Vanguard's high yield bond portfolio lost $531 million in net redemptions—more than a quarter of net assets; T. Rowe Price's high yield fund had $239 million in net redemptions; Financial Bond Shares, $95 million in net redemptions. The stampede had a beneficial side effect, however: it made high yield bonds a little cheaper for buyers. The average yield climbed to 4.3 percentage points over ten-year Treasury bonds at the end of October 1992, up forty-one basis points from the gap at the end of August. At the same time, Treasury yields were moving up during this presidential election year as the market began discounting Clinton's victory.

1993

For smart investors, however, the sell-off of October 1992 represented an opportunity. The economy rebounded in 1993, and the lowest-grade securities of cyclical firms performed best. High yield bonds were a good place to be for return-hungry investors. The year 1993 was to be the last of three consecutive great years for high yield investors. Returns were bolstered by three factors: the recovery from the ultralow prices following the 1990 market collapse; the emergence of many issuers from bankruptcy; and the dramatic declines in long-term interest rates. By year-end 1993, there were eighty-one funds with a total of $46.8 billion of assets, compared with sixty-six holding just $17.3 billion at year-end 1990. And they performed spectacularly. For example, high yield bond funds in existence from 1991 through 1993 earned an average of 24.2 percent a year: 37.3 percent in 1991, 17.5 percent in 1992, and 18.9 percent in 1993. Obviously, those returns far exceeded the bonds' interest rates. Funds pulled in much of those outsize returns by buying bonds that were selling well below face value and then just riding them up.

1994

A slow, steady hissing sound could be heard as the air went out of high yield bond funds' returns in 1994 as the ready supply of reasonably decent discounted bonds was running out. Many issuers had recovered their financial health or emerged from bankruptcy, and that trend, combined with the decline of overall interest rates, dried up the pool of solid discounted high yield securities available for investment. Between 1990 and 1994, some of the largest high yield issuers emerged from bankruptcy, recovered their credit ratings, or had their debt paid off in a merger. Of the 1991 "High Yield 500," the firms moving beyond the high yield designation included the following:[1]

- Southland Corporation (SE), whose short-term issuer credit rating moved to A1+, the highest rating, in September 1992
- Allied Stores, which first fell below investment grade in February 1987 and merged into Federated Department Stores in February 1992
- American Healthcare Management, which merged with OrNda HealthCorp in 1994
- Carter Hawley Hale Stores, which emerged from Chapter 11 reorganization in October 1992

1. Other High Yield 500 firms emerged from bankruptcy during the period, but did not achieve investment grade issuer ratings before the end of 1994. A review of the fate of many of the High Yield 500 firms is available in chapter 4.

- National Gypsum Company, which emerged from bankruptcy in 1993
- Public Service Company of New Hampshire, which became a private subsidiary of Northeast Utilities (CT) on June 5, 1992
- Revco D S, which first fell below investment grade in November 1986, emerged from bankruptcy June 1, 1992.

Long-term interest rates (ten-year Treasury bonds) declined from 9.11 percent at the end of 1988 (prior to the market disturbance caused by the collapse of the high yield market) to 5.8 percent at the end of 1993. The resulting fall in the available yields on other fixed-income investments drove up prices in the higher yielding below-investment grade debt market.

THE NON-U.S. ISSUES: EMERGING AND CONVERGING

Before 1991 a total of just seventeen issues raising $1.9 billion were recorded outside the United States. In only seven years, from 1992 through 1998, the value of high-yield bonds issued worldwide was 72 percent of the total dollar amount issued for the more than twenty years since 1970. After the market's bottoming out in 1990, 1992 was a year of new records in both volume and value. There was some backsliding in 1994–1995, but even then the volume remained not far from 1986's peak. The annual increase in non-U.S. new issues in the high yield market averaged about $6.17 billion from 1992 through 1998 (figure 5-13). Privatization of state-owned industries, infrastructure development, and capital investment drove worldwide demand for long-term capital. International issuers became increasingly familiar with the benefits and depth of the U.S. bond markets (table 5-5).

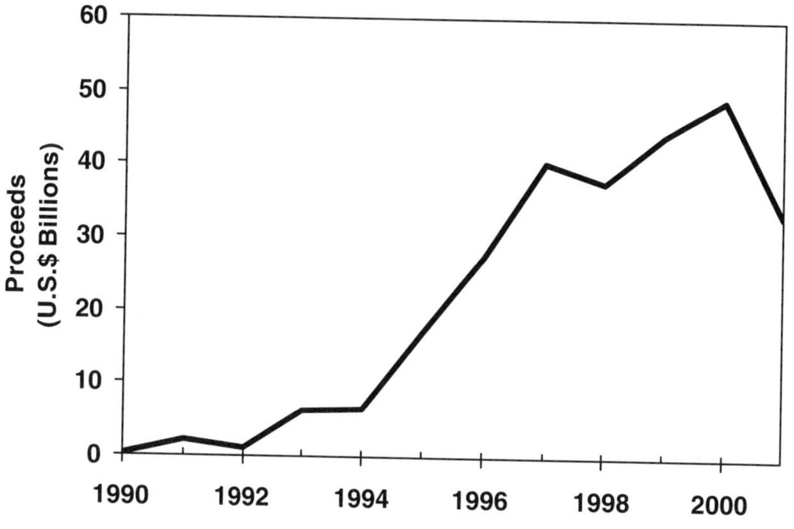

Figure 5-13. Historical Perspective on Non-U.S. High Yield Issuance Market, 1990–2001. Source: Securities Data Corporation.

Table 5-5. Number of Foreign Corporations Issuing High Yield Debt in the United States, 1991–1998

	Corporate Issuers	
Nation	1991–1993	1994–1998
Canada	25	93
Mexico	5	49
Argentina	2	43
United Kingdom	0	41
Brazil	0	29
Netherlands	0	19
India	0	16
Philippines	0	14
Bermuda	3	11
Australia	0	8

Sources: Securities Data Corporation; Milken Institute.

In the early 1980s, Michael Milken was one of the first to urge securitizing Latin American debt. His exhortation was followed in the 1990s by a greater participation in the high yield market by Latin American firms. The number of Yankee bonds (dollar-denominated securities sold in America by foreign issuers) launched by companies rated below investment grade began to grow in 1992, when Donaldson Lufkin Jenrette estimated there was $450 million worth of such issues. In 1993 there was $2.7 billion worth—about 5 percent of all new high yield issuance. The foreign-currency debt issued by all Latin American firms (64 percent of it by private-sector firms) hit a record $25 billion in 1993: Mexico accounted for 36 percent of it, and Argentina and Brazil for 25 percent each (table 5-6).

In January 1994, Yacimientos Petrolíferos Fiscales (YPF), an Argentine oil company, launched a $350 million, ten-year Yankee bond. It was at least three

Table 5-6. Active Nations During the Recovery Years, 1994–1998

No.	Sovereignties
18	Argentina
7	Mexico
7	Turkey
6	Republic of Venezuela
5	Republica do Brasil (Brazil)
5	Russian Federation (Russia)

Sources: Securities Data Corporation; Milken Institute.

times oversubscribed, with only about one-third of the buyers thought to be traditional investors in high yield bonds. The YPF issue was priced to yield 8.03 percent, or 232 basis points, over ten-year U.S. Treasury bonds. That is almost exactly where the global bond issued by Argentina itself was trading. Two other issues that attracted attention in early 1994 were those of Bariven, the financial subsidiary of the Venezuelan oil company, which traded at a spread of 370 basis points, and Copeni, a Brazilian petrochemical company owned by Petrobras which was priced at 495 basis points over Treasuries. Brazilian corporate bonds yielded more than Mexico's at the time simply because Brazil's sovereign credit rating was lower. (See box 5-3.)

BOX 5-3. THE MYTH OF THE SOVEREIGN CEILING

A strange feature of the high yield market for emerging market issuers in the early 1990s was that the rating agencies did not (ordinarily) grade even the healthiest company higher than its country of origin. The rating agencies at that time took a more conservative approach to rating sovereign issues than American corporate ones. The limit set by the credit rating of government issues was commonly referred to as the "sovereign ceiling." Because of this, buyers of emerging market issues were sometimes able to buy up investment grade assets with speculative grade yields.

That changed significantly at the end of the decade. In 1997, Standard and Poor's rated fourteen Argentine firms higher than the Argentine government, in essence piercing the "sovereign ceiling." Moody's reacted negatively and suggested the move was irresponsible. In response to Moody's criticism, Standard and Poor's noted that "despite its frequent use in the market, the term 'sovereign ceiling' is a misnomer and the image it conveys is a misleading one. Standard & Poor's assesses the impact of sovereign risk on the creditworthiness of each issuer and how it may affect the ability of that issuer to fulfill its obligations according to the terms of a particular debt instrument" ("Understanding Sovereign Risk," *CreditWeek*, January 1, 1997).

In 1999, a partially guaranteed issue of the Electricity Generating Authority of Thailand received credit ratings from both Standard and Poor's and Moody's that were above the sovereign ceiling: A3 and A– as compared with Ba1 and BBB ratings for the sovereign debt of the kingdom of Thailand. The sovereign ceiling issue came to a full head in 2001 when both Moody's and Standard and Poor's issued several press releases in June and July clarifying their position on rating certain issues above the sovereign.

On June 7, 2001, Moody's Investors Service issued a press release announcing that it was placing the long-term foreign currency bonds and notes of thirty-eight issuers in thirteen countries on review for upgrade: "The reviews are the result of a change in the rating agency's long-standing approach to

(*continued*)

Box 5-3 continued

rating the foreign currency bonds of debt issuers that will now permit ratings of bonds and notes of some issuers to exceed their country ceilings."

For a thorough and informative discussion of ratings methodology and cases where corporate foreign currency debt ratings exceed the sovereign foreign currency debt rating, see "Sovereign Risk and Ratings Above the Sovereign," *Credit Week*, August 1, 2001.

Table 5-7 lists the non-U.S. companies that issued bonds in the high yield market at a rate that would put them on a par with the most active U.S. issuers shown in table 5–3. These issuers would be instrumental in the development of their domestic high yield markets. Roger Communication issued the first high yield bond in the Canadian market in February 1996. A high yield market in Europe grew from less than $1 billion in 1990 to more than $20 billion in 2000. We review the development of markets outside the United States in chapter 6. For now, we turn our attention to an empirical analysis of the impact of high yield on the market for corporate control.

CONCLUSION

Several important conclusions can be drawn from analyzing the participants in the high yield market recovery of the early 1990s. Though sidelined by political controversies in the high yield market, Milken had warned as early as 1986 about the need to deleverage balance sheets and build liquidity, which is precisely what the new cohorts of high yield issuers did in the early 1990s. He had admonished leveraged buyout companies and investment bankers that attempted to simply "xerox" capital structures which had been appropriate for another period. Those which failed to deleverage were found in the default category of the markets (Milken 1992). By the beginning of the 1990s, equity values exceeded debt by up to $1 tril-

Table 5-7. Active Non-U.S. Companies, 1991–1998

1991–1993	1994–1998	Company Name	Sector	Country
4	5	Rogers Communications	Technology	Canada
—	8	Philippine Long Distance Tel.	Technology	Philippines
3	13	PEMEX	Energy	Mexico
—	5	Banco Nacional de Comercio Ext.	Finance	Mexico
—	5	Banco Safra SA	Finance	Brazil
1	5	Cia Cementos Mexicana (Cemex)	Industrial	Mexico
5	0	Gulf Canada Resources Ltd.	Energy	Canada

Sources: Securities Data Corporation; Milken Institute.

lion, up from $160 billion a decade previously. Reduced interest costs also improved the outlook for new high yield issuers. Capital structure could be managed and improved as market conditions advanced in favor of new issues. Despite exogenous events such as the regulatory disruptions of FIRREA and the Gulf War, the new issue market returned, based on linking the needs of investors and entrepreneurs in a renewed high yield market. New industries and new countries entered the high yield market as it recovered, extending the theory and practice of capital access.

6

New High Yield Markets

> That financial markets contribute to economic growth is a proposition almost too obvious for serious discussion.
>
> Merton Miller (1998)

The use of high yield securities for corporate financing was greatly expanded during the 1990s by issuers from Latin America, Asia, and Europe. The rise of Latin American issuers in the Yankee Bond segment of the high yield market was spurred on by the privatization of telephone monopolies beginning in late 1989. But European firms in particular, in addition to issuing bonds in the U.S. market, were increasingly able to issue bonds on local markets. As new high yield markets developed, fundamental distinctions in the lender / borrower relationship became apparent. Asian borrowers relied primarily on "relationship borrowing," which did not require the public disclosure of information. Creditor rights issues came into play in Europe, where the legal role of bond creditors under insolvency was not as clearly defined as it is under U.S. bankruptcy laws. Both bond covenants and creditor rights in bankruptcy would come to play important roles in the development of high yield markets outside the United States.

We briefly mentioned some of the developing high yield markets in our discussion of the participants in the recovery (chapter 5). Before we focus on the development of non-U.S. markets for high yield bonds, it is useful to review the countries from which national and corporate borrowers were driven to the U.S. markets for capital. These would also be the countries most likely to develop high yield markets of their own.

YANKEE BOND UPDATE

The foreign corporate and government issuers that avail themselves of the deep, liquid capital market in the United States represent the full spectrum of size, location, and creditworthiness. They range from defaulted Argentina in the south to burgeoning Canadian technology firms in the north; from Australia and New Zealand in the far Pacific to British telecommunications and media firms just across the Atlantic from New York. Foreign corporations often issued larger securities in the United States than domestic issuers. By 1997, when European issuers combined with other foreigners to account for nearly 20 percent of the U.S. high yield market, the average security issued by a foreign corporation was $234 million, compared to an average issue for a U.S. borrower of only $167 million—about 70 percent as large.

Argentina and Brazil combined to account for nearly 90 percent of all high yield bonds issued in the United States by South American corporations in the 1990s. Argentina accounted for eighteen sovereign bonds and forty-three corporate bonds issued in the U.S. high yield market during the recovery years of 1994–1998. In its third year of recession by 2001, the Argentine financial system experienced asset quality and external funding problems, and the expectations of a near-term recovery faded. External funding sources had been closed to Argentine issuers, and the steep fall in domestic deposits caused a harsh credit crunch, resulting in asset quality deterioration.[1] The stressful environment surrounding the 2001 downgrade of Argentina to "SD" (selective default) by Standard and Poor's, following the announcement of a debt restructuring, was the result of a prolonged deterioration of the country's financial condition. Banks in Argentina, however, remained at the CCC+ level, indicating that they retained a reasonable chance of continuing normal operations after a default on the Argentine sovereign debt, particularly after the announcement of a debt restructuring unaccompanied by a debt moratorium. The terms of Argentina's exchange offer of November 6, 2001, extended the maturity of each affected obligation by three years and reduced the coupon on the affected bonds to 7 percent or less.

The surge in activity by Canadian issuers in the U.S. market is generally attributed to the "crowding-out" effect. The Canadian government had been running fiscal deficits for more than twenty years. (Canada ran a deficit consistently from 1975 to 1997.) Domestic demand was insufficient to support a Canadian high yield market. Canadian corporate issuers in the U.S. high yield market accounted for the largest number of issues in the 1990s, with 118 in just five years. The issuers were spread out over a range of industries: technology, media, hotels, airlines, and energy. Rogers Communications, a technology firm, was one of the most active Canadian firms in the U.S. high yield market, financing over $4 billion during the 1990s, enabling it to fund a major expansion program that would not have been possible otherwise.

Prior to 1990, there was little corporate bond issuance in Australia. Between 1990 and 2001, the share of corporates in the total bond market in Australia made an amazing increase from 16 percent to 47 percent, well above the global average (tables 6-1 and 6-2). While a reduction in total government debt contributed to this increase in share, there was a substantial increase in the total value of corporate bonds issued in Australia as well. Australian corporations accounted for nearly 3 percent of all high yield bonds issued in the United States between 1993 and 1997.

1. Argentine issuance of corporate and sovereign high yield bonds in the United States fell from thirty-one issues with a combined principal of $8.3 billion in 1997 to zero in 1998.

Table 6-1. Australian Corporate Bond Market, 1990–2001

Year	A$	% Total	% Change
1990	16.0	16.1	—
1991	23.0	21.2	43.8
1992	45.4	25.5	97.4
1993	42.4	20.6	–6.6
1994	40.0	17.9	–5.7
1995	40.2	16.9	0.5
1996	50.6	19.8	25.9
1997	70.1	26.0	38.5
1998	76.9	28.6	9.7
1999	108.3	35.8	40.8
2000	144.7	44.2	33.6
2001	168.5	47.2	16.4

Source: "Size & Structure of the World Bond Market: 2002," *Merrill Lynch Fixed Income Strategy*, April 2002.

The Yankee Bond issuers from the United Kingdom turned out to be from the same sectors that would take the lead in the rapidly approaching European corporate high yield market: telecommunications and media. The first high yield bond in Britain was issued in 1995. Two notably successful British deals launched that year were TeleWest, a cable company, and Independent Newspapers, a publisher.

THE EUROPEAN HIGH YIELD (EHY) MARKET DEVELOPS

By 1997, investors in Europe had begun to show an interest in bonds with lower than investment grade ratings (figure 6-1). Their interest was stimulated by three factors: reduced government bond yields, the looming elimination of arbitrage opportunities through the European Monetary Union, and a lower cost of credit risk worldwide. Although the development of the market there disappointed some watchers, by 2001 even some U.S. firms, like Levi Strauss, were issuing high yield bonds in the European market.

In the late 1990s, most developed countries had reduced government bond yields significantly through a commitment to controlling inflation and budget deficits.[2] In the United States ten-year government bonds yielded around 6.4 percent; in Japan, around 2.2 percent; and in continental Europe, between 5.5 percent and 6.5 percent. Hungry for better rates of re-

2. The Stability and Growth Pact, adopted at Amsterdam in 1997, formally capped deficits in the European Union at 3 percent of country GDP.

Table 6-2. Composition of Domestic Bond Markets

	Corporate	Government
U.S.	30.3%	50.3%
Euroland	41.6%	48.4%
Japan	16.1%	74.2%
U.K.	5.1%	36.1%
Canada	21.6%	69.2%
Switzerland	31.4%	19.0%
Denmark	69.6%	26.9%
Australia	47.2%	31.3%
Sweden	47.2%	46.8%
Norway	46.5%	43.0%
New Zealand	0.0%	64.5%
Average	32.4%	46.3%

Source: "Size & Structure of the World Bond Market: 2002," *Merrill Lynch Fixed Income Strategy*, April 2002.

turn, investors turned to the high yield market. In 1997, $108,850 million and 573 tranches sold in the EHY market. At the same time, investors saw the coming end of interest and exchange rate arbitrage opportunities with the implementation of the European Monetary Union in 1999.[3] Finally, the cost of increased credit risk had fallen so that the yield spread on emerging market bonds dropped by half (400 basis points) in the twenty months from January 1996 to August 1997.

In 1999, the size of the bond market in the United States was 1.52 times GDP and only 0.99 in Europe, where banks continued to dominate the financial landscape at 1.82 times GDP (table 6-3). The total fixed income under management in Europe was about $4 trillion in January 1999. Less than 0.82 percent of all assets under management in Europe were high yield securities. Possibly because of the size of the market, or due to the level of sophistication of EHY investors, the European market experienced much shorter cycles initially. In the United States the high yield market ran on a three-to-five-year cycle. But when the European market was disrupted in the summer of 1998, the market went through a complete cycle in six months.

The launch of the euro set the dial to warp speed. Corporate mergers and acquisitions in Europe surged. In the first half of 1999, Europe's debt market grew 18 percent. A new bond market based on the Euro sprang up in a matter of months. The increased merger and acquisition activity promoted by the reduction of cross-border differences in Euroland is considered by most

3. The euro became legal currency in January 1999, although coins and bills were not available until January 2001. By 2002, the Euro was accepted as legal tender in twelve of the fifteen European countries.

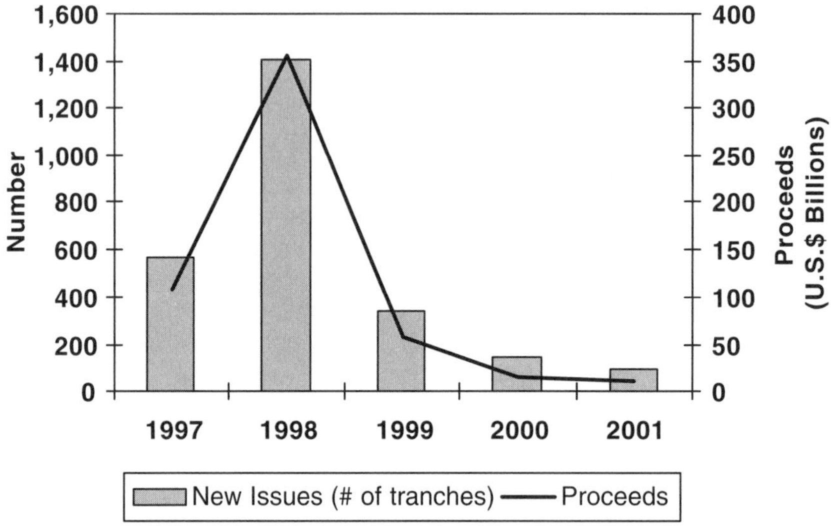

Figure 6-1. The European High Yield Market, 1997–2001. Sources: Securities Data Corporation; Milken Institute.

Table 6-3. European Financial Systems

	Bank Assets / GDP	Bonds / GDP	Equity / GDP
Austria	193%	78%	16%
Belgium	242%	123%	79%
Denmark	na	158%	67%
Finland	86%	40%	245%
France	166%	57%	112%
Germany	207%	114%	68%
Greece	117%	65%	99%
Ireland	357%	28%	87%
Italy	114%	111%	72%
Luxembourg	2957%	na	183%
Netherlands	238%	88%	175%
Portugal	210%	45%	58%
Spain	153%	54%	91%
Sweden	122%	68%	144%
U.K.	283%	75%	182%
U.S.	56%	156%	153%

Sources: *International Financial Statistics;* Merrill Lynch, *Emerging Stock Market Factbook;* World Bank; Milken Institute.

to be a contributing factor to the development of the EHY market. Nottingham University's Centre for Management Buyout Research in the United Kingdom reported an increase in corporate control transactions in the late 1990s financed by bonds. In 1997, there were 660 management buyout and buy-in deals in the United Kingdom worth £10.4 billion, an increase by value of one-third over a year earlier. In addition to being a less expensive form of capital than equity or bank loans, high yield bonds also allowed companies to increase leverage up to 70–80 percent of total funding, compared with 50–60 percent using traditional senior/mezzanine structures. The progress of the European Union indicated a continuing phase of corporate control activity. Europe was at the stage the United States had reached in the mid-to-late-1980s, when the high yield market first took hold. Most industry analysts believe that Europe has at least three to five years of restructuring ahead of it in every sector.

The abolition of the advance corporation tax (ACT) and the removal of the ACT tax credit refund on dividends paid in the United Kingdom also encouraged stock repurchases and the increased use of leverage.[4] With the ACT distortion removed, interest payments were made before taxes, encouraging the use of debt financing. Another factor driving demand in Great Britain was the tax advantages linked with savings schemes such as PEPs (personal equity plans) and their successor ISAs (individual savings accounts), which favored investments in bonds.[5]

Interest in high yield bonds in the European Union was initially strongest in the United Kingdom, Germany, Italy, and Spain. France and the Netherlands began to enter the market from the buy side in mid-1999. The immediate problem for European investors is to develop the internal expertise of credit appraisal that is so essential for managing high yield investments. This role would be fulfilled by the expansion of dedicated high yield bond funds.

The expansion of the EHY market paused in 1998 in the immediate aftermath of the Russian crisis. But market watchers were optimistic again during the recovery in April 1999, predicting five-year growth to £250 billion or more as a result of the wave of capital market reforms and corporate restructuring unleashed by the introduction of the euro. By March 2001, the EHY market was coming close to self-sufficiency, only to be stillborn at the beginning of the most recent recession as returns on both euro- and sterling-denominated high yield debt suffered (figures 6-2 and 6-3). Most of the issuers in the EHY market had been telecom and media (mostly cable) companies (70 percent of issues in 1999). Telecom was particularly hard

4. Corporate leverage ratios rose to 60 percent, levels more common in the United States and continental Europe.

5. PEPs and ISAs are personal retirement plans, similar to IRAs in the United States. Continental Europe remains wedded to the traditional combination of social security funded out of general government revenues and private pensions funded out of corporate earnings. Hong Kong has required its citizens to save in individual, privately managed retirement accounts since 2000. Provident funds—compulsory defined contribution individual accounts that are managed by the government—are common in Asia. Chile switched from a pay-as-you-go public pension system to a defined-contribution privatized system in 1981.

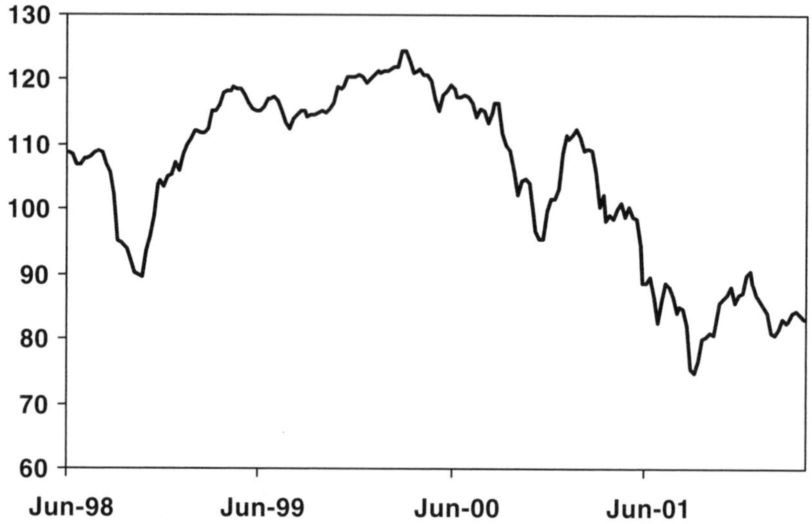

Figure 6-2. The European High Yield Market: Total Rate of Return Index (Euro-Denominated Debt), June 1998–May 2002. Sources: Merrill Lynch; Milken Institute.

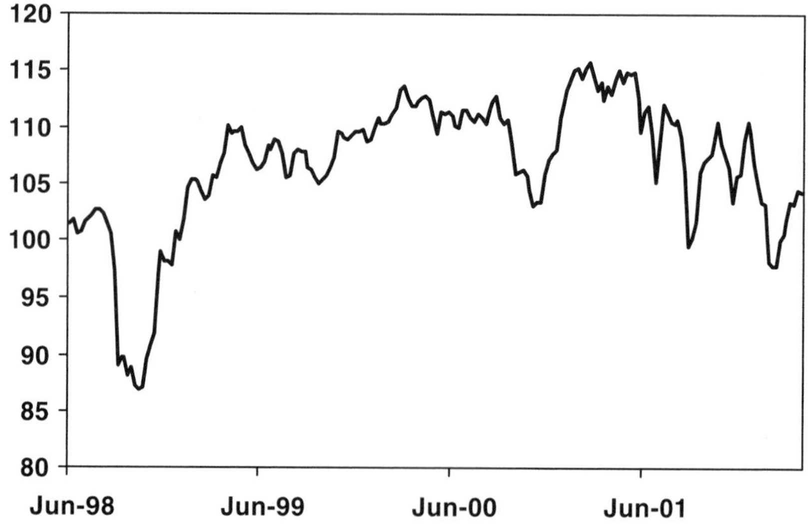

Figure 6-3. The European High Yield Market: Total Rate of Return Index (Sterling-Denominated Debt), June 1998–May 2002. Sources: Merrill Lynch; Milken Institute.

hit by the recession. Media companies would be among the hardest hit in the aftermath of the terrorist attacks of September 11 in the same year.

By late 2001 (even before September 11), the EHY market appeared to have broken into a number of pieces that were becoming increasingly isolated. The most active piece was the market around fallen angels such as Marconi and Xerox's Euro credits. European investors found the upside potential enticing. In contrast, the EHY market for telecom and cable debt was shrinking rapidly, with few corporates seeing any active trading. The active sell-side activity in those issues in prior years left little demand unfilled. The market set new record lows in July 2001, but even those records would be short lived. U.S. issuers with large European operations (like Tokheim, a maker of petroleum pumps) were able to raise capital in the EHY market.

The buy side comprised mostly retail investors looking for income and institutions looking for new yield opportunities. But U.S. investors were an important buy-side ingredient in the successful development of the EHY market. U.S. investors accounted for a "large dollar tranche and a smaller euro segment" critical on offerings above €350 (Euro) million. The large U.S. interest was, in fact, the primary reason for issuing U.S. dollar tranches in the EHY market. This is also why most EHY bonds were registered with the U.S. Securities and Exchange Commission (SEC). Meeting SEC requirements in order to place a full bond issue could eventually become a deterrent to the growth of the market, however, as European countries bulk at quarterly (versus semi-annual) financial reports, U.S. auditing standards and reporting in English. By late 1999, fortunately, small single tranche issues of €150 million to €250 million could be comfortably sold in Europe with just a tiny share going to U.S. investors who did not need to play a critical role in completing the deal. ("Growing Fast—and Growing Up as Well," *Financial Times*, October 29, 1999, Leveraged Finance Supplement.)

Prior to the Russian crisis, U.S. mutual funds proprietary books and hedge funds formed the bulk of the European investor base. A year later, U.S. mutual funds still dominated with a 60 percent share, but insurance companies and European banks and money managers had become more prominent. By 2001, pension funds, European mutual funds, and retail investors rounded out the composition of the EHY market buy side.

The composition of the buy side would prove to have an important influence on market volatility, producing telling results in the differing attitudes on both sides of the Atlantic. A 1999 EHY market issue by Weight Watchers offers a keen example of the differing reactions of U.S. and European high yield investors. The euro-denominated portion of the deal rose to a price of 102 percent of face value in the first week of trading, while the dollar-denominated portion fell to 99 percent of its launch price in spite of the fact that they were offered at the same yield.

EHY Bond Funds

The summer 1998 liquidity crisis from Russia's debt default and the near-collapse of the hedge fund Long Term Capital Management prompted many Wall Street firms to cut their debt exposure—creating illiquid trading in many bonds. As a result, institutional investors were unable to sell bonds when they needed to. In the year after the trough of the near collapse of the EHY market (October 1998), one fund (M&G) saw its value swell from £30 million to £426 million. At least ten high yield funds were opened in Europe between June and October 1999, with an estimated $200 million flowing in each month during the period. The EHY funds outperformed their U.S. counterparts during 1999, when the U.S. market was beset by liquidity concerns. From January to September 1999, EHY funds returned 6.1 percent, compared to 0.56 percent for U.S. funds. At the same time, EHY had lower default rates than the United States. The EHY funds were generally split across several asset classes, though some specialized in high yield only. Except for the U.K., most European countries had larger shares of fixed income in mutual funds than in the United States (17.5 percent in 1999). In Spain, for example, 57 percent of mutual funds were fixed income or mixed.

Several of the factors described so far led market analysts to make comparisons between the EHY market of 2000 and the U.S. market of 1980. The United States had about 200 issues then, compared to little more than 100 in Europe. The top two sectors accounted for around 60 percent in each of the compared markets, and there was strong concentration on the buy side in both cases. The United States underwent tax reforms in 1986 and again 1989 that played key roles in the development (and demise) of the high yield market; the removal of the ACT tax credit in the U.K. was expected to stimulate the market. There are a few other statistical and circumstantial similarities. However, there was one important difference: bondholder rights in bankruptcy.

Absence of Harmonized Insolvency Regime

The clarity of bankruptcy rules in the United States underpins capital markets in general, bond markets specifically, and the high yield market in particular. The secured debt of borrowers subject to the U.S. Bankruptcy Code generally can receive ratings one to three notches above the corporation's rating (S&P). Without clear foreknowledge of the associated risks in a security, market participants cannot accurately price their investments for borrowers. The EHY market, in contrast, comprises competing bankruptcy jurisdictions, regarded by many as an impediment to development.

The question of structural and contractual subordination is emerging as a key issue in EHY market development. This is a complex legal issue that centers on the position of debt issues within the capital structure of issuers. In the United States bank debt and bonds are issued by the same entity within a corporate family. In the United Kingdom, as an example of the EHY market, high yield bonds are often issued at the ultimate holding company level without benefit of security; bank debt is raised at a subsidiary level, benefiting from upstream guarantees provided through the Companies Act. Under this structure, the bond investors cannot clearly identify the subordination in order to assess the overall asset base of the issuer in regard to the level of risk they are assuming.

Furthermore, there is no room at the European bankruptcy table for unsecured creditors (i.e., bondholders). Under British bankruptcy law, the bank lenders appoint a receiver who takes charge of all the assets of the corporation—from holding company to subsidiary. The bondholders rank below the issuer for claims on the assets of the firm. This is, of course, the worst case scenario, where the bonds were issued at the ultimate holding company level. The British bankruptcy procedures are generally creditor friendly, however, which should encourage a resolution to this issue that will be beneficial to the development of the high yield market there. The French bankruptcy code, on the other hand, is much less friendly to bondholders.

The French insolvency process makes it difficult for creditors to access the economic value of secured property in a reasonable time frame. If a company does not liquidate after declaring insolvency, an observation period of up to twenty months can ensue during which no debt can be paid, *irrespective of the contractual agreement for that debt.* (See Standard and Poor, *Global High Yield Bond & Bank Loan Ratings*, Summer 1999, for a fuller description of these complex issues.) This complete disregard for bond covenants will hinder the development of the high yield market in France.

So far, the EHY market has not experienced a significant default event. Most observers believe that Europe will not run with the big high yield dogs until it is tested in that fashion. In 2001, all EHY defaults were initially assigned speculative grade ratings—no investment grade issue defaulted, a pattern that emerged in Standard and Poor's annual survey of European ratings performance three years in a row. However, European default rates are moving closer to the global average, and the overall penetration of bond ratings in Europe has continued to increase—as more issues and issuers are rated, the numbers of events should even out. Still, BBB-rated bonds account for 34 percent of the U.S. bond market, but less than 30 percent in the U.K. While 20 percent of all European rated bonds outstanding are in the "speculative grade" category, 33 percent of new issuer ratings in 2001 were speculative grade, indicating a rising trend.

Transnational Bankruptcies

Perhaps no one event more clearly exemplifies the combined impact of the strong U.S. presence in the EHY market and the lack of clear bondholder rights in insolvency than the bankruptcy of NTL. On April 16, 2002, the British cable group NTL said it had reached agreement in principle with an unofficial committee of its public bondholders on a comprehensive recapitalization. The recapitalization would result in the conversion of approximately $10.6 billion of debt into equity. To implement the proposals, NTL filed a prenegotiated recapitalization plan in a Chapter 11 case under U.S. law. Under the proposals, the members of the unofficial committee, which held over 50 percent of the face value of NTL's public bonds, committed to providing up to $500 million of new financing to the company's operations. The U.S. bondholders were largely cable companies and their representatives. Because the proceedings took place in U.S. bankruptcy courts, the bondholders were given a role in the negotiations. The existing equity holders received only the option to obtain warrants with the right to buy more equity. In the end, the U.S. cable company bondholders got control of the British cable operator without firing a shot.

CANADA'S MARKET DEVELOPS

About half of all Canadian corporate bonds were historically issued in the United States (Hartzheim 2000) (table 6-4). Canadian firms had been issuing high yield bonds since 1980—just not in Canada.[6] In other words, the supply side of the high yield corporate bond market in Canada had been robust for more than one decade. Therefore, the story of the birth of a market for high yield securities in Canada must include an assessment of changes in the demand side of the equation. The demand-side factors include a reduction in inflation, lower interest rates as government deficits turned to surpluses, and the attenuation of barriers restricting the purchase of below-investment grade bonds by institutional investors.

Inflation in Canada reached levels in excess of 12 percent in 1980 before retreating to 4 percent in 1984 and remaining under 6 percent through the end of the decade. To combat the return of inflation, the Bank of Canada announced in January 1988 that the control of inflation would be a primary objective of monetary policy. As credit was tightened, the bank rate reached 13.04 percent in 1990. This increase in short-term rates inverted the yield curve, and a severe recession followed. Canadian monetary policy was effective, however, with inflation remaining under 2 percent after 1992.

Meanwhile, the supply of net new Canadian government bonds peaked at C$56.4 billion in 1993 and then began a steady decline to C$9.7 billion in 1998 as deficits were reduced and / or eliminated at every level of government. The declining supply of government bonds put increasing pressure on investors to substitute corporate bonds in their portfolios, fueling the demand side for corporate bonds in general and high yield bonds in particular.

Institutional factors play a large role as impediments to the development of a vibrant public market for high yield debt in Canada. Insurance companies and pension funds are restricted from holding non-investment grade bonds.[7] The banks are strong and can provide competitively priced loans to firms. The fact that such a high percentage of bonds for Canadian firms were issued in the United States eliminated the potential for fallen angels (former investment grade bonds) in the Canadian bond

6. In a move that may have encouraged the earlier development of a domestic high yield market in Canada, Drexel Burnham Lambert received Canadian Department of Finance approval in May 1988 to establish a securities subsidiary in Toronto, an action it had pursued since 1986. See "Drexel Burnham's Canada Unit," *Wall Street Journal* April 29, 1988, p. 3(W). Also see "Junk Bond Initiator Drexel Ready to Open Canadian Office," *Financial Post*, May 12, 1988, p. 29, cited in Hartzheim 2000.

7. Since 1986, some firms were able to sell lower rated debt in the Canadian private market, which is fairly vibrant. Institutional investors would sometimes purchase lower grade debt in the private market, where they could better influence the terms of the deal.

Table 6-4. Foreign Issuers in the U.S. High Yield Market, 1971–2001

Year	Issued in the U.S.	By All Foreigners	By Canadians
1971	101	1	0
1972	71	0	0
1973	27	0	0
1974	11	1	0
1975	28	1	0
1976	57	1	0
1977	96	1	0
1978	117	0	0
1979	108	0	0
1980	161	5	2
1981	170	1	0
1982	182	0	0
1983	296	4	3
1984	261	2	2
1985	414	1	1
1986	671	6	0
1987	622	10	2
1988	667	15	4
1989	555	13	3
1990	261	20	7
1991	220	6	3
1992	437	18	9
1993	689	49	19
1994	479	97	14
1995	385	60	32
1996	729	150	26
1997	1067	257	35
1998	955	151	27
1999	603	117	13
2000	347	95	6
2001	636	99	16

Source: Security Data Corporation.

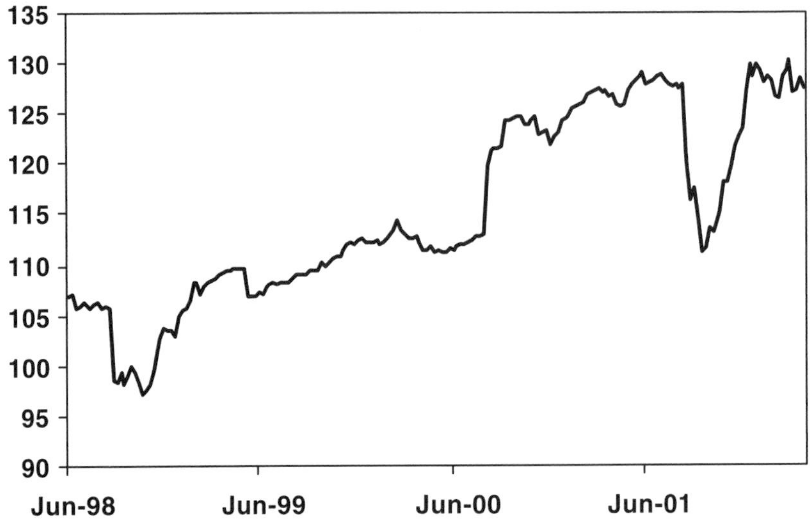

Figure 6-4. The Canadian High Yield Market: Total Rate of Return Index, June 1998–May 2002. Sources: Merrill Lynch; Milken Institute.

market that could have stimulated the development of a secondary market. Finally, Hartzheim (2000) provides some evidence that the growth in mutual funds assisted in the development of the public high yield market in Canada. As investors sought better rates of return, they shifted deposits from banks into mutual funds, similar to the experience in the United States.

Rogers Communications, mentioned earlier, issued the watershed high yield bond in Canada in February 1996, its tenth issue in five years. In 1996, three firms sold a total of C$308 million in non-investment grade bonds in the public market in Canada, representing 3.7 percent of total corporate bonds placed in Canada. In 1997, the volume rose to C$2.1 billion and represented 15.5 percent of the market. The Canadian high yield market leveled off at only C$788 in 1998, the year of the Russian debt crisis, and then expanded again as almost half that much (C$344 million) was issued in just the first two months of 1999. Similar to the experience in Europe, issuance was concentrated in a few sectors. Communications and media accounted for 62 percent of all high yield corporate bonds placed in the public market between 1996 and 1998.

By 2002, the share of all bonds raised by Canadian firms in Canada was 35 percent (C$7.5 billion) through April, substantially below the historical rate of 50 percent. Unfortunately, none of the C$3.3 billion raised from the "speculative-grade category" was issued in the domestic market ("Canadian Corporate Bond Issuance: Northern Light Flickers," *Standard and Poor's Global Fixed Income Research*, May 1, 2002). Most of it was raised in the U.S. market. U.S. firms are also getting a growing slice of the underwriting business in

Canada because issuers there prefer access to the more liquid American markets. The most active in Canada are Merrill Lynch Canada, Salomon Smith Barney Canada, Morgan Stanley Canada, J.P. Morgan Canada, CSFB Canada, and Goldman Sachs Canada. Most of them are also underwriting high yield bonds. The weak demand from Canadian investors continues to drive companies to hire New York firms to get their debt into the hands of U.S. investors. One industry observer was quoted in *Canadian Business* as saying, "There aren't many deals the Canadians don't have the clout to underwrite, but that's not the point. It's having access to other capital markets, whether it's Tokyo or London, or placing high yield debt to somebody in Kuwait. That's what you need, but the Canadians aren't there [in the overseas markets] in size" (*Canadian Business* 74, no. 13 [July 9, 2001]: 151). Despite the lack of volume, however, the total rate of return in the Canadian high yield market has done quite well, especially compared to that in Europe (figure 6-4).

ASIA ATTEMPTS TO BREAK THROUGH

Most of the issues mentioned so far as detrimental to the development of deep, liquid markets for high yield securities also apply throughout Asia and South America. Bankruptcy proceedings in Asia can take as much as seven years to provide compensation to creditors. The status of creditor rights in South America and Asia is mixed, as seen in table 6-5. High levels of government borrowing, and the resulting crowding-out effect, absorb a disproportionate amount of available capital. As table 6-4 showed, a substantial number of high yield bonds issued in the United States are placed by foreign corporations. The dominance of banks in providing capital, the lack of the analytical sophistication necessary to evaluate credit investments, and ease of access to foreign markets through domestic offices of U.S. global financial services firms all have the impact of holding back high yield market development. In Asia, however, two additional issues arise that are specific to the region: interlocking bank-corporate relationships and cultural taboos against bankruptcy.

In Japan they are called *keiretsu*. In Korea they are *chabol*. For simplicity, we'll call them "the interlocks." In any country where banks dominate as a source of capital, public capital markets are less likely to develop unless there is some competitive advantage in either price or service. Under the interlocks, the role of banks is much stronger. In addition to dominating as a source of capital, the banks in an interlock have equity interests in the companies they finance and the companies they finance have an equity interest in the banks and in each other. These relationships eliminate the need for the public release of financial information from corporations. The members of the interlock can keep the information "private," at least within the interlock. In fact, the members probably have access to more information about the companies they invest in than the investors in public markets anywhere in the world. The companies in an interlock usually have other business relationships (e.g., supplier-buyer, vendor-customer, etc.).

Table 6-5. Creditor Rights in Asia and Latin America

Asia	
Hong Kong	4
Indonesia	4
Malaysia	4
Singapore	4
South Korea	3
Thailand	3
Japan	2
Taiwan	2
South America	
Ecuador	4
Chile	2
Brazil	1
Argentina	1

Note: Higher scores are better, with 4 being the best.
Sources: La Porta et al. 1998; Inter-American Development Bank; Milken Institute.

The idea of maintaining private information in the interlocks is related to the taboo against bankruptcy because it incorporates the extreme importance of reputation in many Asian cultures. By not making information public, the corporate mangers can avoid the embarrassment of revealing poor results. Far more than simply appearing to have managed the firm inefficiently, poor results are more of a personal reflection than one would find in most Western cultures. Bankruptcy is not an option in a culture where failure is unacceptable.[8]

These roadblocks do not have to be fatal factors in the development of high yield bond markets in Asia. As investors come to accept a broader range of security types, instruments can be structured in ways that balance the perceived risk/reward ratio. It is possible for structured finance to compete effectively with bank loans for providing corporate capital. The U.S. bankruptcy code evolved from a system that at one point in time refused to allow any form of debt forgiveness. Whether or not cultural norms evolve and adjust, systems can be structured that are focused more toward aligning incentives under which entrepreneurs are given the opportunity to fail, in return for the opportunity to succeed.

8. For example, Japanese retail giant Sogo Group's vice president committed suicide in April 2000 after the company revealed losses of more than $1 billion for 1999.

7

Extended Markets and Innovative Extensions

> Clearly, the traditional bond investment is evolving into new forms as investors try to improve their relative performance. The menu is larger than it has ever been, and there is something for everyone willing to break the old habit of buying fixed-rate, investment grade securities of companies whose best years often are behind them.
>
> Drexel Burnham Lambert,
> *The Case for High Yield Bonds* (1984)

Financial innovation is the engine driving the financial system toward improved performance in the real economy—targeting the improvement of product and process technologies and their application for the improved efficiency and productivity of both labor and capital. The conventional view of financial instruments is based upon the categorical distinction between debt and equity. However, financial innovations have evolved less as distinct categories than as a range of financial technologies involving characteristics of both. In the high yield market, innovative debt securities emerged that added value by reallocating risks among investors, increasing liquidity, reducing agency and transaction costs, reducing tax exposure, and escaping regulatory choke holds.

Financial innovation had many precedents in earlier centuries. In each historical period, the structuring of finance enabled efficient allocation and subsequent diversification of risk among a wider group of investors. In fact, the proliferation of financial technologies derived from earlier periods of economic development and trade that also required new instruments for entrepreneurs and investors. In understanding the historical roots of financial innovation, we can come to grasp how new geographic, product, technology, and process markets came to be included in the high yield asset class and create even newer structured finance products in other asset classes. The lessons of the high yield market went beyond its borders.

The Dojima rice market in Osaka was a forward market in the seventeenth century and a fully developed futures market by the eighteenth century. Options and contracts resembling futures were commonplace in Amsterdam in the seventeenth century. Organized futures exchanges rose in London and Frankfurt shortly after the American Civil War. The Chicago Board of Trade was founded in 1848, and the New York Cotton Exchange in 1872 (Merton 1992b). In the corporate securities market generally, and in the bond market specifically, a great deal of innovation was associated with the transition from transportation bonds to industrial bonds in the nineteenth and early twentieth centuries. These innovations were applied during the advent of the new issue high yield bond market. In fact, financial innovation often demonstrated and enabled a "first mover advantage" among early adapters, who were able to finance corporate strategies and capture market share based upon resources mobilized through these innovations (Tufano 1992; Mason et al. 1995). The comparative advantage afforded by adoption of financial innovation to forge resources to execute corporate strategies enables companies to prevail in rapidly changing competitive environments.

Richard Sandor has identified a seven-stage process for market development generally:

- A structural economic change that creates a demand for new services
- The creation of uniform standards for a commodity or security
- The development of legal instruments that provide evidence of ownership
- The development of informal spot markets (for immediate delivery) and forward markets (nonstandardized agreements for future delivery) in commodities and securities where "receipts" of ownership are trades
- The emergence of securities and commodities exchanges
- The creation of organized futures markets (standardized contracts for future delivery on organized exchanges) and options markets (rights but not guarantees for future delivery) in commodities and securities
- The proliferation of over-the-counter markets (Richard L. Sandor, "Getting Started with Pilot: The Rationale for a Limited-Scale Voluntary International Greenhouse Gas Emissions Trading Program," White House Conference on Climate Change, October 6, 1997).

The pace of revolutionary change in the international financial system since the 1970s is, however, unprecedented. Continuous global trading from Tokyo to Frankfurt to London and New York, the expansion of the corporate bond market to include noninvestment grade credits, structured finance and securitization, financial futures, swaps, asset-backed securities of every kind from mortgages to recreational vehicles and credit cards, LBOs (Leveraged Buy-Outs), MBOs (Management Buy-Outs), ESOPs (Employee Stock Ownership Plans), CBOs (Collateralized Bond Obligations), CLOs (Collateralized Loan Obligations)—all abound in a financial world that would have been inconceivable in the 1950s.

The shrinkage of the world economy after 1929 and the prolonged depression undermined innovation in financial instruments and markets

(Miller 1986, 1992). The rise of the regulatory role of government also suppressed financial innovation, except in the government-sponsored sector, where special housing-related instruments flourished (through Fannie Mae and Freddie Mac issuance), and in the U.S. Treasury market, where new instruments became the leading short-term liquid asset for banks and corporate treasurers. During the 1950s and 1960s, when inflation was low, interest rates were stable, and the United States faced little international competition, financial planning was not a primary concern for corporate managers. Financial innovation was largely ignored because financing, for many companies, involved little more than balancing the corporate checkbook. The rise of the high yield market in the 1970s gave birth to an explosion of financial innovation that seems striking only in contrast to the dearth of major innovations that preceded it during the long period of economic stagnation that began in the 1930s.

Market-induced, as opposed to government-sponsored, financial innovation emerged in earnest only in the 1970s. Financial innovation was brought on by the persistent inflation and rising interest rates that caused people to withdraw their funds from banks. As funds flowed to capital markets through mutual funds, and directly to bond and equity markets, an array of instruments relevant to future financing emerged.

During the recession and credit crunch of 1974, many companies (especially small and medium-sized enterprises and emerging firms) learned that capital access was no longer guaranteed on the basis of profits or success. With dramatic changes in the world economy, companies required innovative securities to provide them with the financial freedom necessary to survive and grow. They required securities that would enhance their flexibility in managing the capital structure of their firms in changing times and securities that would finance their objectives for accomplishing corporate growth strategies.

THE CORPORATE FINANCE REVOLUTION

Interest rate volatility and the frequency of tax and regulatory changes were key factors in producing a fertile period of financial innovation. The deregulation of the financial services industry in the 1980s and the increased competitiveness globally within the financial services industry also converged to generate product differentiation in the financial markets. For investors, these new financial instruments were needed to generate higher (after-tax) returns at a given level of risk, enhance liquidity through a secondary market, and provide better returns. For entrepreneurs and established corporations, the objective of financial innovation was simply to lower the cost of capital.

On the other hand, investors demanded flexibility in the daily management of their portfolios. Matching the needs of corporate managers with investment managers through the capital markets created value through financial innovation. In the early days of the new issue high yield market,

Michael Milken was often fond of saying that the best investor is a good social scientist—the importance of finance in society lies in its ability to unlock potential in people. In an increasingly information-based economy, value results from people addressing and solving the needs and problems of society. Consequently, both investment managers and corporate managers became astute observers of the changing needs and tastes revealed in social, economic, and political trends.

From these social and economic changes, market requirements for financial innovation emerged and market growth for these securities occurred. The primary function of a financial system is the allocation and deployment of economic resources across time and space in uncertain environments. Capital markets enable the basic cash-flow cycle whereby household savings are channeled into capital investments by firms and then returned to households (via security repurchases, dividends, and interest payments) for consumption and further recycling into new savings (Merton 1990, and 1992a). From the investor's point of view, companies produce only one product—cash. Cash payments to investors become more complicated because they occur in the future (have time value) and are uncertain (have risk value) (Brealey and Myers 2000). Investors might prefer certain types of securities based upon their investment preferences associated with time and risk. A central goal of innovative financial management is to maximize the total value of securities sold for a given amount of cash returned, depending upon time and the performance of the company (its rate of return).

Debt and its derivative forms in various hybrid securities create tax advantages (through deductibility), but are accompanied by a greater risk of bankruptcy for the firm because of the requirement to continue to make fixed payments even when earnings are negative or low. Firms need to match the cash flows on assets to the cash flows on liabilities because their enterprise value is defined as the present value of the assets owned by the firm (Walter and Milken 1973). Firm values vary over time as a function of firm-specific factors such as project success and broader macroeconomic variables such as interest rates, inflation rates, and aggregate demand. The financing mix afforded a firm by innovations in managing its capital structure are critical.

FINANCIAL INNOVATION AND GROWTH

Until very recently, standard economic growth theories excluded any meaningful role for the financial sector and financial innovation in influencing long-term growth. Savings by households are "assumed" to be transformed into productive investment. Most research focusing upon the nexus between finance and growth has focused upon microeconomic models of how financial institutions alleviate borrowing constraints, such as monitoring managerial agents, mobilizing savings, and/or leading to specialization and efficiency. In fact, recent theoretical and empirical work elaborates upon how the financial systems and innovations within them create channels for growth in the economy as a whole. The production of financial innovations continuously improves the efficiency of the financial intermediation process that transforms savings into investment. Investments, in turn, enable research and development activities in the technological sector and applications to the economy as a whole. By financing the most promising productivity-enhancing activities and enabling the diversification of risks associated with innovative activities in the real economy, the probability of successful innovation and growth is enhanced (Chou and Chin 2001).

CATEGORIZING FINANCIAL INNOVATIONS

Corporate managers and investment managers have a wide range of tools available to them as they go about the business of capital markets. We've gathered a glossary with the definitions of the tools of the finance trade into appendix C. In this section we elaborate on some of the more recent, more innovative financial instruments that evolved with and from the high yield market. Some remain exotic instruments used only by the most expert specialists. Others have become common features of the financial landscape.

Bond-warrant units offer an example of a financial technology that proliferated. These securities were originally employed in the 1960s by corporations that exchanged them for the assets of companies they were seeking to acquire. For example, in 1968 Loews Theatres exchanged $400 million in fifteen-year, 6.875 percent bonds and 6.5 million of its warrants in the acquisition of Lorillard, one of the five major cigarette companies. In February 1969, General Host Corporation exchanged $160 million in fifteen-year 7 percent bonds and 6.6 million warrants in connection with its investment in Armour and Company. Almost $1.5 billion of this type of transaction was completed in the late 1960s and early 1970s for the purpose of acquisitions and investments in lieu of cash.

By the 1980s, these securities were being directly underwritten, and became a significant and independent source of new money for growing companies. In 1983, equity markets were continuing to recover from the recent recession, finally surpassing levels seen ten years earlier. While stock prices were rising, equity market values were still considerably below replacement costs. As a result, companies were reluctant to dilute the ownership of existing shareholders by issuing new common stock. At the same time, long-term interest rates, though declining, were still historically high and many companies resisted lengthy commitments at such high interest rate levels.

Enter financial innovation with instrumentation to resolve the problem. A bond-warrant unit is a hybrid security combining equity and debt components to provide both investors and corporations with an attractive alternative under those macroeconomic conditions. From the standpoint of the corporation, a bond-warrant unit made the dilution of ownership more attractive because it was exercisable above the current market price. These instruments substantially reduced borrowing costs in almost all cases to single-digit interest rates, and in many cases to below the prevailing U.S. government rates. Finally, these instruments allowed a company to extend maturities for repayment beyond what it could have had in a straight debt offering. At the onset of this innovation in 1983, almost $3 billion was raised by over thirty-five noninvestment grade companies through the issuance of bond-warrant units.

Other examples included MGM's sale of $400 million in 10 percent bond-warrant units to refinance the bank debt used in its acquisition of United Artists. Golden Nugget sold $250 million in bond-warrant units in order to gain the financial flexibility to expand operations. One of the largest of the offerings was undertaken by MCI, which issued $1 billion in ten-year bonds with a coupon of 9.5 percent, substantially below what U.S. Treasuries were yielding at the time. Up to that point, MCI's management had been faced with the constant, time-consuming task of negotiating for short-term capital to build its long-distance network. With the bond-warrant offering MCI obtained the financial freedom and capital structure flexibility to build a revolutionary fiber-optic telephone network long in advance of the profits the network subsequently achieved.

Zero-coupon, payment-in-kind (PIK), and split-coupon securities represent another financial tool often used by companies in new industries with unique needs. Firms like McCaw Cellular, Turner Broadcasting, and Viacom International were investing virtually all of their current cash flow to expand their cellular telephone networks, cable television programming, and cable television systems, respectively. (McCaw and Viacom are covered in detail as case studies in chapter 9.) These and other firms required financial tools that would help them obtain the money needed to build their companies before they had any positive cash flow on their financial statements. McCaw Cellular was able to issue $250 million in twenty-year discounted convertible debentures paying no cash interest for five years, thereby enabling the company to retain needed cash flow for expansion. Turner Broadcasting issued $440 million in zero-coupon notes that deferred interest payments until maturity. Viacom issued $370 million in PIK securities that enabled the company to have the option of paying interest in additional securities rather than cash.

Commodity-linked securities are another example of financial innovation. For example, in 1980 Sunshine Mining issued the first silver-backed, commodity-indexed bonds in 100 years. These unique securities were linked to the price of silver. The interest payment on the bond was about half of what Sunshine would have otherwise had to pay for a straight debt issue and about 3 percent below what U.S. Treasuries were paying at the time. By issuing securities that allowed investors to share in any increase in the price of silver, Sunshine was able to raise low-cost, long-term capital enabling it to survive. Sunshine undertook four such offerings, raising a total of $120 million. During periods when silver rose in commodity value, these securities traded as high as 45 percent above their original face value. An equivalent dollar investment in silver itself produced inferior returns compared with those obtained by owning the Sunshine securities.

In all of these cases, high yield debt innovations involved some form of *risk reallocation*—adding value by transferring risk away from issuers or investors to those institutions better able to bear them. For example, zero-coupon bonds enable interest to be effectively reinvested and compounded over the life of the debt issue at the yield to maturity at which the investor purchased the bond. For pension funds concerned about "reinvestment risk" when attempting to reinvest interest payments received on straight debt issues, this is a considerable advantage. Interest rate risks were also managed during periods of rising and volatile interest rates through adjustable rate notes and floating rate notes. By adjusting interest payments to correspond to changes in market rates, floating rates reduced the lender's principal risk by transferring interest rate risk to the borrower—this was particularly appropriate for credit card companies and banks.

Price and exchange rate risks were managed by commodity-linked bonds. As in the case of Sunshine, principal repayment and sometimes coupon payments were tied to prices of commodities like oil or, silver, or a specified commodity price index. Such bonds are structured to enable a commodity producer to hedge its exposure to a sharp decline in commodity prices and, hence, revenues. To the extent that interest or principal payments are associated with changes in a company's revenues, the structure of the security reduces the volatility of cash flow. These innovations increase the company's debt capacity by shifting debt service burden from times when it is least able to pay to times when it is most able to pay. Similar to shifting interest rate risk, dual currency bonds, indexed currency option notes, principal exchange rate-linked securities (PERLS) and reverse principal exchange rate linked securities (reverse PERLS) can be used to reallocate currency risk.

Other sources of value enabled through financial innovation include enhanced liquidity through structured financial products (which we discuss at the end of this chapter); reduced agency costs from protecting against inherent conflicts of interest between managers, stockholders, and bondholders (e.g., interest rate reset notes, credit sensitive notes, floating rate, rating sensitive notes, puttable bonds, and increasing rate notes); reduced transaction costs from reduced underwriting commissions (e.g., extendable notes, renewable notes, remarketed reset notes), and reduced taxes (e.g., zero-coupon bonds); and reduced regulatory choke holds (e.g., equity contract or commitment notes, variable coupon renewable notes, and commodity-linked bonds). Numerous preferred stock innovations, convertible debt innovations, and equity innovations have also permutated from the new ideas in securities structuring first advanced in the high yield market (Finnerty 1992; Ross 1989; Fabozzi 1989).

THE RISE OF THE PRIVATE PLACEMENT MARKET: RULE 144A

Adopted by the SEC in April 1990, Rule 144A permits private placements to be freely traded among "qualified institutional buyers" (QIBs).[1] It was designed with the intention of attracting foreign issuers dissuaded by the illiquidity premiums of the traditional private placement market and the registration requirements of the public market (Carey et al. 1993). As shown in figure 7-1, while foreign bond issuance in the United States grew rapidly in the 1990s, it is not obvious that this growth was in response to Rule 144A because growth of the foreign component was robust in the public market as well. Figure 7-2 shows the rapid growth of emerging market issuance in the market for high yield debt over the 1990s. Again, it would not appear that Rule 144A could be directly linked to that increased activity.

An unintended consequence of Rule 144A, however, was the issuance of securities by domestic, below investment grade firms that used it as a vehicle for quick issuances to raise funds as soon as securities were marketable. When the bonds were subsequently registered, investors benefited from liquidity on the public market. The most striking observation of research about the 144A market is the rapid growth of this domestic component of the market (Fenn 2000). Table 7-1 shows that the use of Rule 144A by below investment grade domestic issuers increased from 16 percent in 1993 to nearly 80 percent by 1997. The trend continues, and some analysts have suggested that ultimately all high yield debt will be issued through the Rule 144A market (*Investment Dealers' Digest*, 1997).

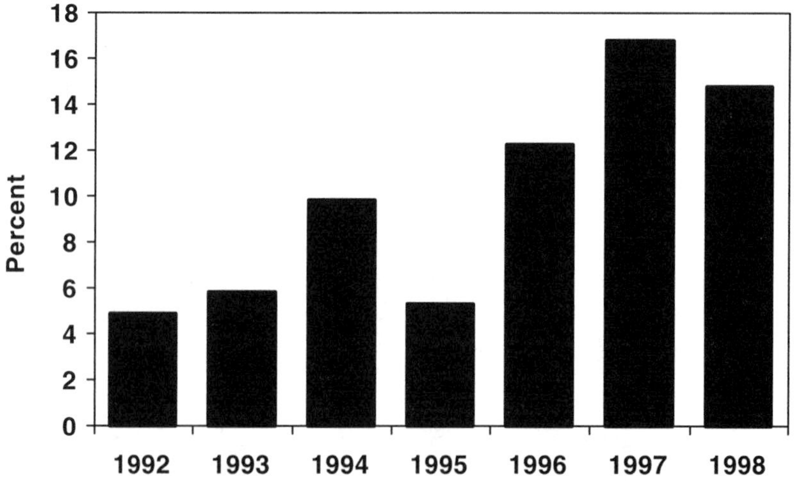

Figure 7-1. U.S. Foreign Issuance of High Yield Rule 144A Securities as a Percent of Total Issuance by U.S. Nonfinancial Firms, 1992–1998. Source: Securities Data Corporation.

1. The development of Rule 144A, and its importance for understanding the development of the high yield market, are discussed in detail in chapter 8.

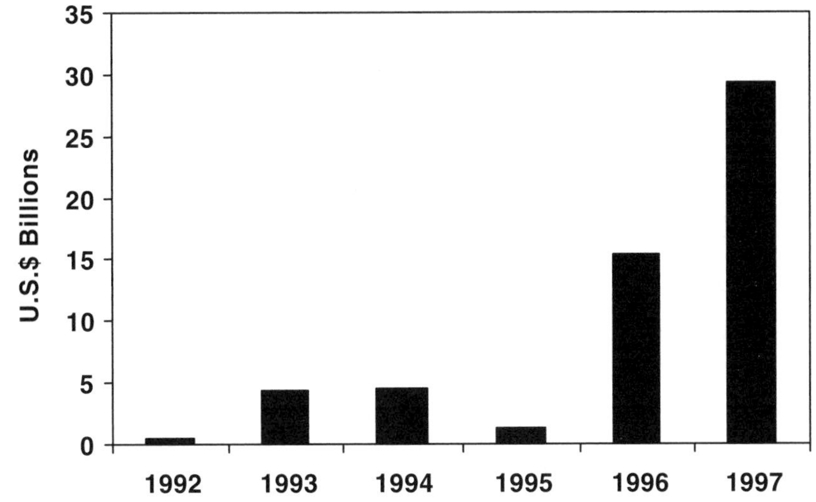

Figure 7-2. U.S. High Yield Emerging Market Corporate Bonds: Proceeds Raised, 1992–1997. Source: Securities Data Corporation.

Lower rated issuers relied most heavily on the Rule 144A market. As shown in table 7-2, the upper three rating classes—split investment grade, BB, and split BB—issuance under the Rule 144A accounted for less than 30 percent of the total, while for the lowest rated bonds, the share of Rule 144A issuance exceeded 60 percent. Two alternative hypotheses that might have motivated this pattern have been investigated. The first is that tight financial constraints for low rated firms necessitated speedy issuance. Al-

Table 7-1. Public and Rule 144A Below Investment Grade Securities Issuance by U.S. Nonfinancial Firms, 1990–1997

	Total Issuance ($mil)		Share of Issuance (%)	Average Issue Size ($mil)	
Year	Public	Rule 144A	Rule 144A	Public	Rule 144A
1990	3,104	0	0	141	—
1991	19,732	11	0	247	11
1992	40,559	490	1	166	163
1993	60,482	11,425	16	174	197
1994	31,746	3,500	10	182	109
1995	24,593	8,053	25	202	161
1996	34,943	28,824	45	190	188
1997	21,527	78,325	78	215	198
Total	236,686	130,628	43	187	195

Sources: Securities Data Corporation; Fenn 2000.

Table 7-2. Public and Rule 144A Below-Investment-Grade Securities Issuance of U.S. Nonfinancial Firms, by Rating Class

Rating Class	Public Securities ($mil)	Rule 144A Securities ($mil)	Total ($mil)	Rule 144A Share (%)
Split investment grade	41,489	15,890	57,749	28
BB	58,746	20,816	79,562	26
Split BB	30,016	10,904	40,920	27
B	106,954	120,807	227,760	53
Split B	8,048	12,721	20,760	61
Below-B	4,053	9,412	13,465	70
Total	249,306	190,550	440,216	43

Note: Rating class describes ratings assigned at time of issue by Moody's and S and P. BB, B, and Below-B rated securities were rated BB, B, and Below-B, respectively, by *both* rating agencies, or by one agency if only one agency rated the bond. Issurance from January 1990 through May 1998
Sources: Securities Data Corporation, Fenn 2000.

ternatively, these firms may have been less likely (as compared to their higher rated counterparts) to establish shelf registrations under which public bonds could be issued quickly.

To investigate these hypotheses, Yago and Ramesh (1999) looked at registration outcomes for all domestic, below investment grade Rule 144A securities in the eighteen-month period from January 1, 1996, to June 30, 1997. Bonds issued prior to this period were likely to have been retired at the time of the study, while bonds issued after this period would not yet have been registered. Of the 307 below investment grade securities in the study that were issued under Rule 144A, 305 remained on the Bloomberg system in mid-1998. As shown in figure 7-3, 97 percent of these were registered within three to seven months. This finding reinforces the hypothesis that issuers used the rule to facilitate speedy issuance rather than to avoid due diligence.

On the premise that lack of registration might imply less disclosure and provide less time for due diligence, investors might require premiums to compensate for perceived lower credit quality and higher risk. Empirical findings, however, suggest the contrary. Apart from the finding that most securities were subsequently registered, there is also no evidence of greater premiums on first time bond issues under Rule 144A after controlling for ratings and other issue characteristics. Vanishing yield premiums also imply that investors regard them as no less liquid than their public counterparts.

Requiring securities registration at the time of issuance in the high yield market would be costly to issuers and of little apparent value to investors. Company registration, on the other hand, allows the SEC to emphasize the quality of ongoing disclosure, providing valuable information to investors. Company registration was recommended in an SEC advisory report as an alternative to the current transaction and securities-based registration pro-

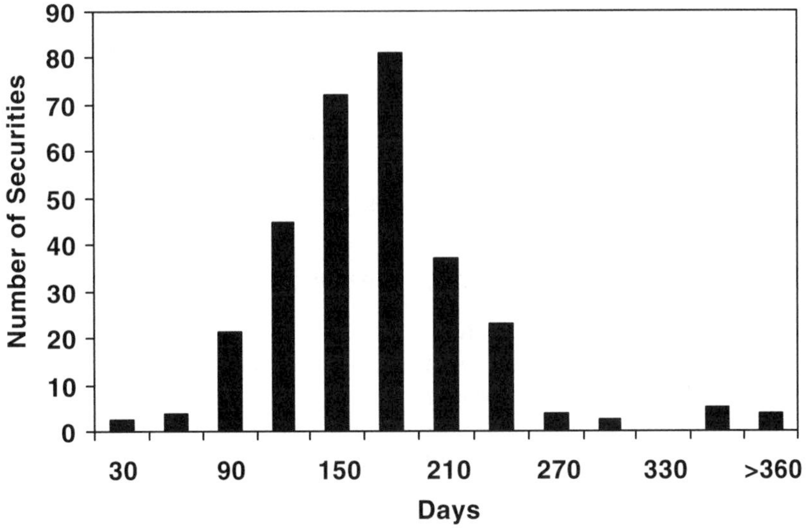

Figure 7-3. Distribution of Number of Days to Register Rule 144A Securities. Sources: Securities Data Corporation; Bloomberg.

cess (Securities and Exchange Commission 1996). According to this recommendation, public firms would be required to register as companies on a one-time basis. Subsequent securities issues would not have to be registered separately, thereby expediting issuance. An argument in favor of this recommendation is that it would retain the simplicity of the current issuance procedure because Rule 144A already permits companies to avoid transaction-based registration.

EFFICIENCY GAINS FROM RULE 144A

Rule 144A created huge gains in efficiency and cost effectiveness because issuers of corporate debt no longer had to make separate purchase agreements directly with institutional buyers, as they had done earlier to ensure private placement exemptions for their offerings. Nor were they required to grant buyers shelf registration rights for multiyear periods to cover resales. Rule 144A securities could be registered through an exchange offer or through ex post shelf registrations. The latter procedure is more difficult because it requires that the holders of securities at the time of registration be named in the prospectus.

This process of shelf registration has been described in some detail. According to this study, resale shelf registration was much more cumbersome for both the issuer and the buyer. For instance, insurance company buyers were subject to regulations that restricted their holdings of securities. If an insurance company wanted to maintain the bonds in its portfolio for an extended period, it would have to sell its holdings in keeping with shelf registration rules and then repurchase them "off the shelf" from another institution. This was an inefficient and costly process for the buyer, and the issuer was also required to maintain an effective shelf registration statement for a multiyear period, with its attendant costs and risks. This changed with Rule 144A, so that purchasers of privately placed bonds were able to obtain freely tradable securities without passing them through an intermediary. The issuer was able to discharge its obligations in a single registration.

IMPLICATIONS OF THE "AIRCRAFT CARRIER" PROPOSAL

In 1998 the Securities and Exchange Commission proposed to overhaul U.S. securities laws and reduce private placements by encouraging companies to issue stocks and bonds through public offerings. The proposal, so cumbersome it was dubbed the "aircraft carrier," would have shut off the private placement market that had flourished since the introduction of Rule 144A, raise transaction costs, and limit access to capital for firms issuing high yield securities. Although the "aircraft carrier" proposal was never adopted, portions of it continue to show up in subsequent SEC rulemaking.[2] Therefore, it is important to note the main arguments against making certain changes to disclosure rules.

The optimistic view of the proposal was that it would reduce the number of private placements by making public offerings faster and simpler for some companies.[3] This is because, under the proposal, the SEC would review only offerings by companies with a market capitalization of less than $250 million. An alternative view, however, is that overseas companies would be worst hit by the elimination of the two-step exchange offer (involving a private placement that is subsequently converted into a public offering of debt or equity). This would remove what used to be a training ground for foreign companies.[4] Moreover, smaller companies would still be scrutinized.

The smaller issuers that would be exempt from scrutiny would be those with a one-year reporting history, provided they agreed to limit their offerings to Rule 144A QIBs. The buyers, in turn, would have to buy restricted securities for their own investment purposes without possibility of resale.

2. In 2001, for instance: "(I)n the Securities Act Reform Release (aircraft carrier), we propose new rules, forms and amendments. . . . Some of these proposals are republished in this release for the convenience of readers, as follows: portions of proposed new Forms C and SB-3 and proposed new Rules 166, 167 and 425." Proposed Rule: Regulation of Takeovers and Security Holder Communications, Securities and Exchange Commission, 17 CFR Parts 200, 229, 230, 232, 239, and 240, (Release No. 33-7607; 34-40633; IC-23520; File no. S7-28-98), RIN 3235-AG84, Regulation of Takeovers and Security Holder Communications. Additionally, in 2002: "I should only point out, on these new proposed time periods on the 10-Qs and 10-Ks that basically the same proposal was made as part of the Aircraft Carrier proposal, about three years ago." John White, Esq., Cravath, Swaine & Moore, transcript of Roundtable Discussion on Financial Disclosure and Auditor Oversight, March 4, 2002. (The full text of this document is available at http://www.sec.gov/spotlight/roundtables/accountround030402.htm.)

3. The opinion was held by a partner, Frank Goldstein, with Brown & Wood LLP in Washington and quoted in the *Wall Street Journal* in an article by Judith Burns, "'Aircraft Carrier' Overhaul Aims to Curtail Surge of Private Placements" (January 5, 1999).

4. According to Sara Hanks, a partner at Rogers & Wells's Washington office; also quoted in the article by Judith Burns in the *Wall Street Journal* (January 5, 1999). (See note 3.)

If the offered securities did not "come to rest" in the hands of QIBs, eligibility for registration of the offering would be lost retroactively. This would be a devastating outcome that would render an offering illegal after the fact. To prevent such an outcome, issuers would find it necessary to adopt contractual measures to restrict the transfer of ownership and other precautionary measures. Rule 144A was originally designed to circumvent precisely these contractual complications that would have to be reinstated under the "aircraft carrier" proposal.

Moreover, the inability to subsequently register securities that a QIB acquired under Rule 144A would make these offerings less attractive for private issuers and QIBs. As a result, Rule 144A transactions would be available only to public companies. This is a significant restriction because many small companies and most high yield issuers that currently raise capital under Rule 144A are not "seasoned" by SEC standards.[5]

STRUCTURED FINANCE: COLLATERALIZED DEBT OBLIGATIONS

Collateralized debt obligations (CDOs) are relatively recent financial innovations that are created to take assets subject to credit risk and restructure them into new debt securities in order to achieve economies for the seller. A special purpose vehicle (SPV), referred to as the "issuer," buys the assets with the simultaneous issuance of new liabilities. The new liabilities are issued chiefly in the form of high-grade bonds, with subordinated or equity tranches containing most of the original assets' credit risk (see figure 7-4). SPVs are structured to be bankruptcy remote.

CDOs use a structure wherein the holders of the most senior debt have priority access to principal cash flows or redemption proceeds of the SPV assets until their claims are satisfied, and then the next most senior debt holders have access to ongoing cash flows or redemption proceeds, and so on. While this sequential waterfall structure is most common, other structures are possible. The second most common liability structure is prorata, meaning that investors in different tranches of debt are entitled to receive a share of principal cash flows proportional to the size of their tranche in relation to the total transaction.

To insure the health of senior noteholders' claims, some CDOs make use of sequential principal payments as described above. Another protective measure is overcollateralization with a trigger, to divert principal cash flows originally due to the subordinate tranches to the senior security noteholders when the portfolio fails certain performance tests; for example, when the market value of the CDO's assets falls below a certain percentage of value in excess of par, which guarantees a minimum level of overcollateralization in a CDO whose main source of protection comes from prices of the bonds in portfolio ("market value CDO"). When an overcollateralization trigger has been breached, the principal proceeds may not be reinvested in new collat-

5. To be seasoned means that the issuer is required (a) to have a one-year reporting history under the Exchange Act and (b) to have filed at least one annual report.

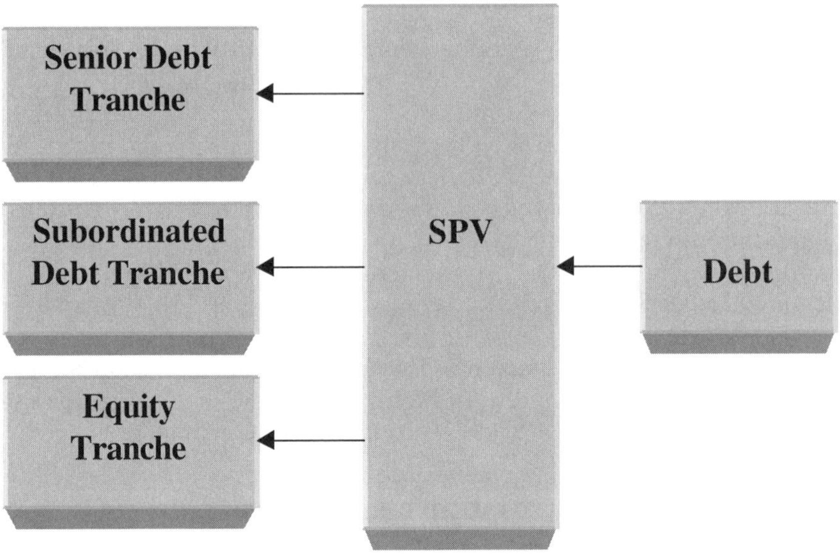

Figure 7-4. Generic Collateralized Debt Obligation. Source: Milken Institute.

eral but must be used to pay down the amounts of debt outstanding until the target level of cushion to the senior noteholders is restored.

In incomplete or imperfect markets or in the presence of capital requirements, CDO structured products add value by increasing the liquidity of (usually) high yield debt offerings, and reducing the amount of regulatory capital a bank is compelled to hold (Duffle and Gârleanu 2001). One important use of CDOs is to pool a group of smaller issues. Individual bond issues may be a too small in size to attract sufficient trading volume or may be otherwise illiquid. Securitization though the creation of a CDO commonly increases liquidity, and thus both reduces the liquidity risk of firms trading them and decreases bid-ask spreads on the securities.

Another use of CDOs involves the use of an SPV to shift part or all of a loan portfolio off a commercial bank's balance sheet into a collateralized loan obligation (CLO). Removing loans has the beneficial effect of allowing the bank to free up expensive regulatory capital that it would otherwise be compelled by regulation to hold. The value of CDOs is reflected in the rapid increase in their issuance in the 1990s (figure 7–5).

CDOs can be categorized as either balance sheet or arbitrage transactions. The first type is often driven by a bank's desire either to reduce its credit exposure to a specific borrower or group of borrowers or to free up regulatory capital, and the second by the desire of purchasers of the equity tranche to profit from conditions of "overselling" in the high yield bond market represented by yields that overstate the actual riskiness of the debt. Both types of CDO can be further divided into cash flow and market value obligations, with market value CDOs being based on debt that is marked-to-market. A further division can be made on the basis of whether the CDO involves the

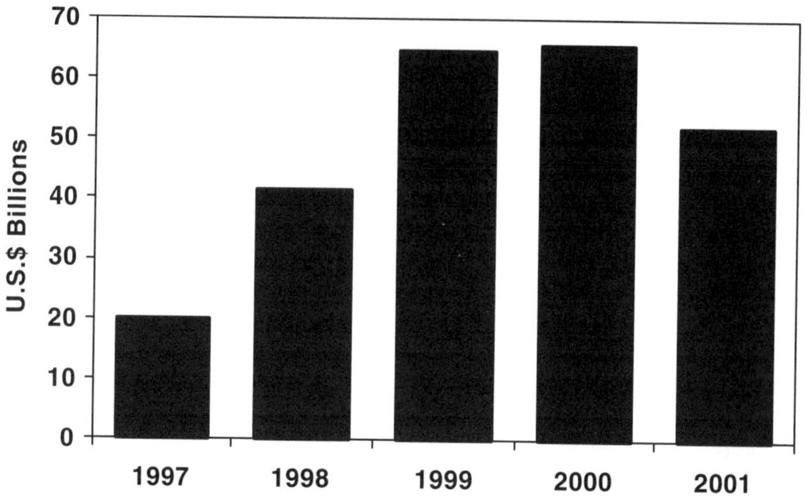

Figure 7-5. U.S. Collateralized Debt Obligation Issuance, 1997–2001. Sources: Thomson Financial; Securities Data Corporation.

actual transfer of debt or is a based on the use of credit derivatives such as default swaps. According to JPMorgan, balance sheet CDOs and arbitrage CDOs were used about equally between 1987 and 2000, while just 10 percent of the market is composed of market value CDOs. Nine percent of CDOs created between 1987 and 2000 are synthetic balance sheet obligations, and a further 4 percent are synthetic arbitrage CDOs (table 7–3).

CDOs can involve the purchase and repackaging of any type of fixed income security, but chiefly involves bank loans and high yield bonds. More recently, finance professionals have created CDOs based on emerging market sovereign bonds, on investment grade debt, and on securities issued as part of other CDOs. A more recent innovation is synthetic CDOs, which allow a commercial bank to divest its credit risk exposure on a bond or loan portfolio while retaining the debt on its balance sheet. Such CDOs involve a credit derivative contract between the holder of the debt and an SPV that then legally assumes the credit risk on the portfolio. A summary of the volume of CDOs issued based on various securities is presented in table 7–4.

Table 7-3. CDO Volume by Structure

Structure	Percent of Volume 1987–2000
Balance sheet, cash flow, cash	41
Balance sheet, cash flow, synthetic	9
Arbitrage, cash flow, cash	36
Arbitrage, market value, cash	10
Arbitrage, cash flow, synthetic	4

Source: JP Morgan Securities 2001.

Table 7-4. CDO Volume by Underlying Security Type

Security	Percent of Volume 1987–2000
Loans	63
Bonds	25
Asset backed / mortgage backed securities	9
Emerging market debt	3

Source: JP Morgan Securities 2001.

Table 7-5 suggests that loan-based CDO use is concentrated in balance sheet obligations. We discuss loan- and bond-backed securities in some detail below.

COLLATERALIZED LOAN OBLIGATIONS

Seventy percent of CLOs are balance sheet obligations that are typically initiated by commercial banks either seeking to shift part of their loan portfolio off their books or to remove the credit risk of their part of their loan portfolio while keeping the assets themselves.

The vehicle for shifting loan portfolios is a balance sheet CLO in which a bankruptcy-remote SPV is created to purchase the bank's loan portfolio and then split its cash flows into tranches of highly rated bonds and unrated equity. The structure for such a CLO resembles that of the generic CDO (figure 7-4). The debt in question is the loan portfolio (or part there-

Table 7-5. CDO Volume by Structure and Underlying Security

Structure/Security	Percent of Volume 1987–2000
Balance sheet (cash flow)	
Loans	45
Bonds	3
Asset / mortgage backed securities	2
Arbitrage (cash flow)	
Bonds	19
Loans	16
Emerging market debt	3
Asset / mortgage backed securities	2
Arbitrage (market value)	
Asset / mortgage backed securities	4
Loans	3
Bonds	3

Source: JP Morgan Securities 2001.

fore) of a commercial bank, and typically a trustee and a portfolio manager receive fees from the SPV to carry out oversight and management functions. The portfolio manager may also hedge the interest rate risk of the loan portfolio.

The vehicle for the transfer of the risk of a portfolio rather than the entire portfolio is a synthetic CLO, the structure of which is shown in figure 7-6. A synthetic CLO closely resembles a cash CLO with the simple difference that the transaction between the SPV and the commercial bank in a synthetic CLO is a credit derivative.

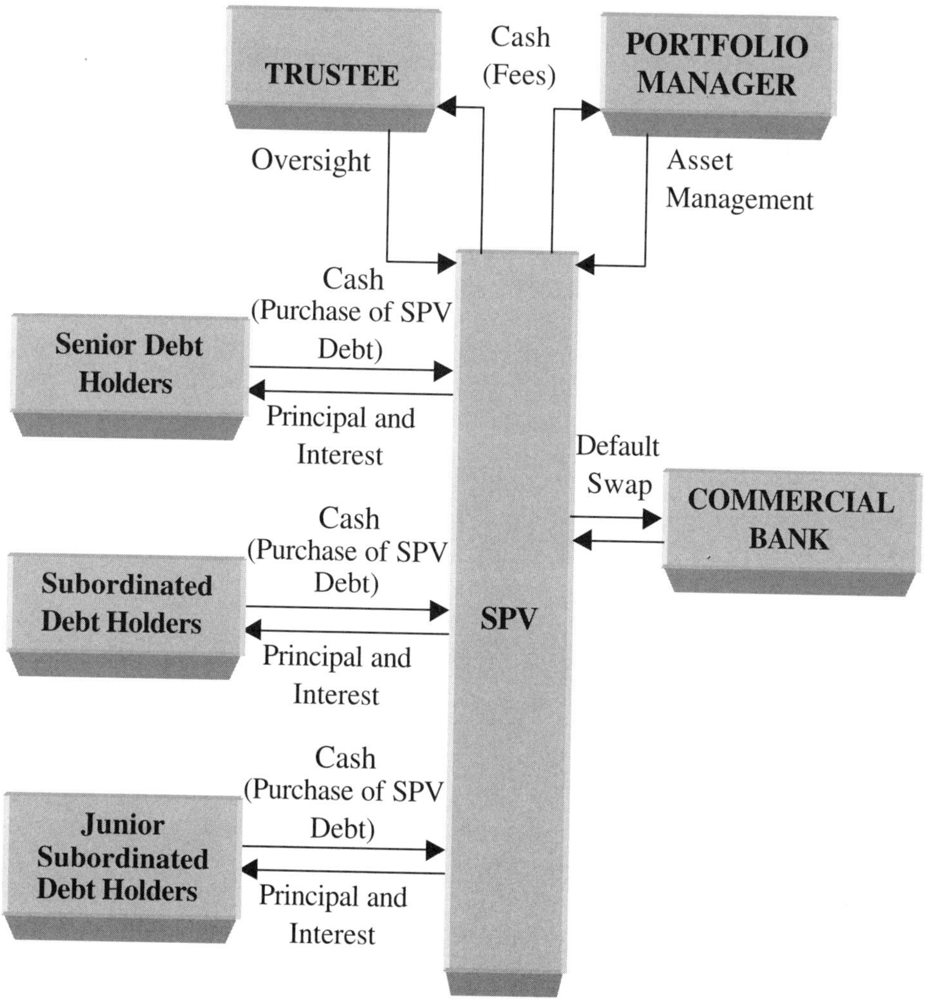

Figure 7-6. Synthetic Collateralized Loan Obligation Structure. Source: Milken Institute.

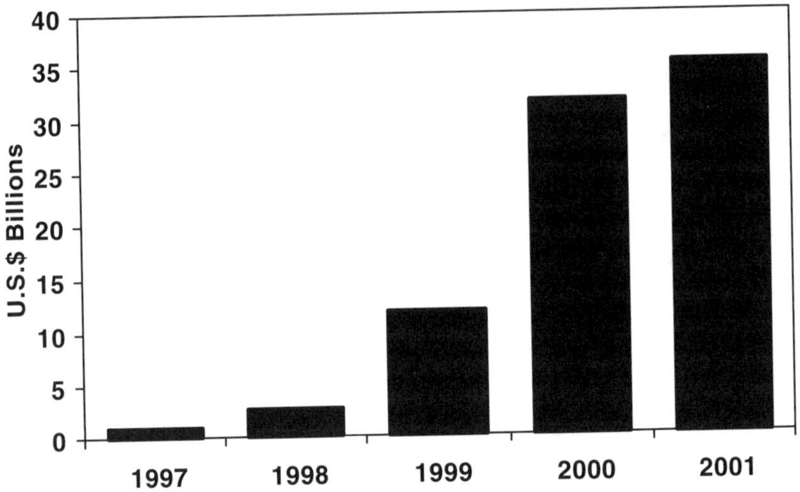

Figure 7-7. U.S. Collateralized Bond Obligation Issuance, 1997–2001. Source: Securities Data Corporation.

COLLATERALIZED BOND OBLIGATIONS

Collateralized bond obligations (CBOs) were introduced as a vehicle for the securitization of high yield corporate debt, although rapid growth in their use did not occur until the late 1990s (see figure 7-7). One attraction of securitizing high yield bonds was a liquidity effect. Illiquid high yield bonds could be bought up and bundled together; then their cash flows could be reissued by SPVs in a more liquid issue.

Unlike CLOs, which are primarily balance sheet transactions, more than 75 percent of CBOs are arbitrage vehicles. To a large extent, therefore, the CBO market is driven by high yield and (to a much lesser extent) emerging market spreads that junior unsecured debt investors in a CBO seek to capture. As the spread of high yield bonds over CBO cost of funds widens or narrows, the attractiveness of CBOs to investors waxes and wanes. The narrowing of high yield spreads in the mid-1990s decreased the attractiveness of high yield securtitizations and led to the structuring of CBOs based on emerging market debt that now accounts for over 7 percent of arbitrage CBOs. The subsequent growth in spreads through 2001 may achieve an increase in high yield asset securitization, but this may well be limited by the modest levels of new high yield bond issuance.

The basic structure of a CBO—common to both cash and market value obligations—is presented in figure 7-8. It is also possible, and can be useful—particularly for CBOs based on emerging market debt—to swap the bond portfolio from local currency into the currency in which the CBO is denominated to remove currency risk.

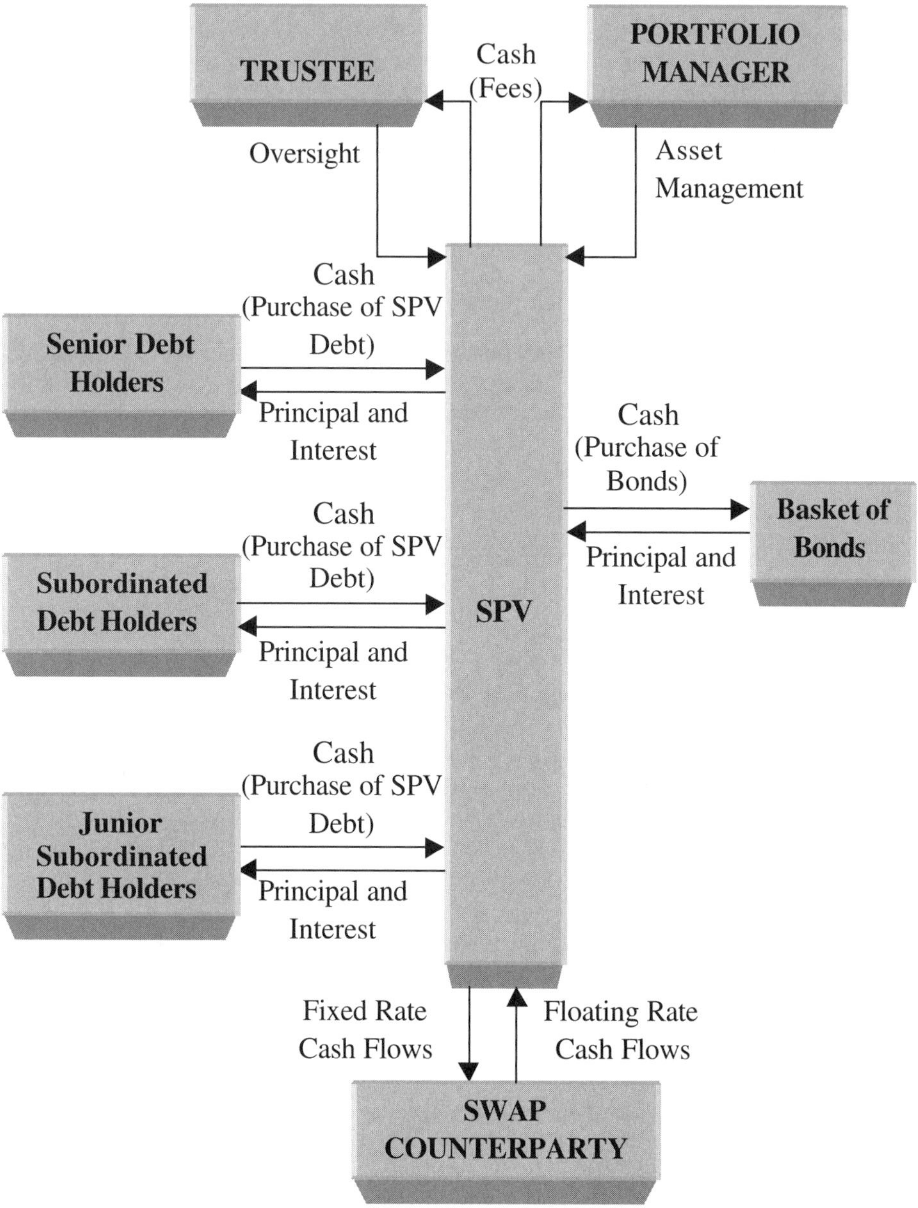

Figure 7-8. Collateralized Bond Obligation Structure. Source: Milken Institute.

8

Why Capital Structure Matters: The Corporate Finance Revolution

> Through new, high leverage, limited-liability securities, firms might enhance their own value (and the social welfare) by offering risk and return combinations that fully-liable investors could not hope to achieve on their own.
>
> Miller and McCormack (1989)

Although economists have been talking about the importance of capital structure since the 1950s, they have tended to make the same Chicago-style assumption: they assume we have capital. By the 1990s, discoveries in financial economics combined with practical innovations in the financial marketplace to clarify all that mattered in corporate capital structures. The sources and uses of capital became more than sections on the accounting statement. The difference in the cost of issuing debt or equity capital moved further and further apart as a result of legal, regulatory, accounting, and tax code changes. What matters in corporate finance also turned out to matter for the structure of financial systems. In this chapter we focus on the corporation's choice between debt and equity, and look at the blurring of differences in the definitions of debt and equity, which are the subject of current debate.

No longer could capital structure be taken for granted as some inherited attribute of a business's history or strategy. Any claim on either internal or external funding had to be justified and linked to plans to enhance the productivity of the firm and to the promise of maximizing shareholder value in that firm. In a related way, the attributes of a firm's capital structure came to be understood in relation to the macroeconomy. And no longer can firm finances be separated from productivity at the aggregate level of a firm's primary industry. Concurrently, no longer can the fate of aggregate demand and supply factors and macroeconomic growth be abstracted from how an entrepreneur can finance growth at the firm level. Capital structure came to be understood as a critical aspect of business management along with other core disciplines that could build the value of a firm (Walter and Milken 1973; Milken 2003). Term and rate are no longer the only negotiable aspect of a company's debt. Equity issuance is more than a discrete decision in financial management or a simple celebratory watershed in a business's history.

Microeconomic issues of how to finance the firm are integral to and reflective of changes in the macroeconomy. In short, the dichotomy between these subfields of economics has come to be understood as artificial and obsolete. Similar to the discovery in particle physics that the secrets of the universe are contained within a single atom and its substructures, economists began to appreciate the linkages between understanding an individual firm's capital structure and how that aggregates to an understanding of the dynamics of the economy as a whole, capital markets, and financial institutions. Simply put, economists made a quantum leap toward a full understanding of how firms' capital structures and the ability to finance them accelerate the economy as a whole (Gertler and Lown 2000).

Since the 1990s, these issues have been reflected in debates about the relative efficiency of different national financial systems—market based systems (with widely dispersed shareholders and a market for corporate control) and bank based systems (with large bank and intercorporate holdings). With the transition economies of Central and Eastern Europe and the former Soviet Union seeking appropriate financial models, this emerged as a central issue. With Japan's long-standing financial problems and Europe's persistently high level of unemployment, concerns about the links or divisions between financial markets and institutions as providers of capital are key to understanding how new waves of economic growth and capital formation can occur.

Market experience revealed, and academic research confirmed, the importance of capital structure after the wave of corporate restructuring that accompanied the fusion of capital and corporate strategies. Research in corporate finance showed that average stock price reactions to announcements of a variety of U.S. restructuring activities—takeovers, LBOs, spin-offs, and large stock buybacks—were consistently positive. Follow-up studies of restructured companies proved the market's positive expectations were accurate. Research on LBOs, large leveraged recapitalizations, large strategic mergers, and a number of studies on corporate spin-offs and divestitures all by and large vindicated the market's initial endorsement of restructuring as expressed in positive stock price reactions. Comparable shareholder gains and operating improvements were demonstrated for similar restructuring transactions in the United Kingdom.[1] Capital structure matters, it can be actively managed, and we can demonstrate and monitor its impacts upon both firms and the overall economy (Walter and Milken 1973). Capital structure became the fundamental issue in the nexus between corporate strategy and structure and the financial scaffolding upon which they rest.

To understand the importance of capital structure, we need to understand how the market was able to separate good risks from bad risks through liquidity and active trading. This effort required expertise on the part of market participants. It was necessary to monitor corporate performance closely so that if the firm faced financial difficulty, its capital struc-

1. See Kaplan (1989, 1997) and Andrade and Kaplan (1997) on the affect of LBOs on corporate governance and efficiency; Denis and Kruse (2000) on managerial discipline and restructuring; and Healy, Palepu, and Ruback (1992) on large strategic mergers and corporate performance. See also Wright, Wilson, and Robbie (1997, 1998) on management buyouts in the United Kingdom.

ture could be rebuilt and diversified efficiently across investors with the appropriate taste for risk and reward inherent to those situations.

A BRIEF HISTORY OF CAPITAL STRUCTURE THEORY AND RESEARCH

We can't discuss capital structure without reminding ourselves that Merton Miller and Franco Modigliani were the first to focus on the financial structure of firms in a way that created a linkage to the cost of capital and the ability of the firm to attract external funds. (See Miller and Modigliani 1958, 1961 and 1963.) The message of the Miller-Modigliani propositions (M-M) is that there is no "magic" in leverage or dividends. M-M showed that if we make some simplifying assumptions—if we ignore taxes and bankruptcy costs and assume that managers behave the same way if the firm is leveraged with 10 percent debt or 90 percent debt—then there is no good reason to expect changes in corporate leverage and dividend payout ratios to affect the value of the firm. The practical import of the M-M propositions is what they say about why financing decisions *might* matter. Given a level of total capital necessary to support a company's activities, how can capital be divided between debt and equity to maximize the firm's current value?

The M-M propositions say, in effect, that *if* corporate financing and dividend decisions are going to increase corporate values, they are likely to do so for the following reasons: (1) they reduce the taxes paid by the corporation or its investors; (2) they reduce the probability of costly bankruptcy (including the expected costs of underinvestment from overleveraging); (3) they send a positive signal to investors about management's view of the firm's prospects; or (4) they provide managers with stronger incentives to invest wisely and operate efficiently. Miller started the process of relaxing some of the assumptions underlying the M-M propositions by exploring issues like the tax benefits of debt and the signaling effect of dividends in later work. It is in this sense that the M-M framework laid the groundwork for the modern theory of corporate finance: directing scholars and practitioners where to look for the *real* effects of financial decisions.

The major shift in showing why capital structure and dividend policy mattered was instigated by the work of Michael Jensen and William Meckling (1976). They focused academics and practitioners alike on the potential loss in value caused by the separation of ownership from control in large public corporations. Conflicts of interest between management and shareholders could be controlled or made worse by corporate capital structure and dividend choices. A decade later, Jensen's research reflected a major insight into the patterns of corporate restructuring that were under way in America. In his seminal article, "Agency Costs of Free Cash Flow, Corporate Finance and Takeovers" (1986), Jensen was able to link ownership structure and the organizational dynamics within the firm to its capacity to maximize shareholder value. The argument, stated briefly, was that highly leveraged acquisitions, stock buybacks, and management buyouts of public companies were adding value by squeezing excess capital (i.e., "free cash flow") out of organizations with few profitable growth opportunities. The customary practice was for corporations to reinvest excess capital into their core businesses even while expected returns to capital at the margin were falling lower and lower. The alternative practice of diversifying into unrelated businesses had been a major driver of the industrial conglomeration movement that characterized the late 1960s and 1970s. The question was, and remains, how to finance the exit of both financial capital and human capital from unproductive overcapacity. How could financial strategies and structures enable capital to move out of declining industries and into more vital ones?

Perhaps the most direct statement of this perspective was Jensen's presidential address to the American Finance Association, "The Modern Industrial Revolution, Exit, and the Failure of Internal Control Systems" (Jensen 1993). The technological changes of the last twenty years created remarkable increases in productivity, but also enormous overcapacity and obsolescence in many sectors of the economy. Because of the increasing globalization of business and the resulting interdependence of national economies, squeezing out excess capital and capacity had become the most formidable problem facing all economies. The pace of technological change created enormous pressures on senior managers. They must continuously encourage innovation and constantly be prepared to move people and capital out of maturing operations and into more promising ones. As a result, capital efficiency became a prime function of management.

Though these problems first appeared in U.S. corporations during the restructuring movement of the 1980s, they were easily observable in overseas markets and corporations as well. Many of the problems of transition economies in the former Soviet bloc represent these challenges well. Because of capital market transformation and the flexibility of financial innovation, the transitions occurred in the United States—though not without major disruptions. Japan, in contrast, still struggles with the rigidity of the capital structure of its firms, its capital markets, and its financial institutions. By the late 1980s, Japanese firms were flush with cash from successes in their export wars. They were also paying only nominal dividends and were prohibited from making stock repurchases, two ways by which U.S. corporations could return value to shareholders. Consequently, Japanese firms were either overinvesting in their core businesses, in misguided attempts at maintaining market share, or they were diversifying through acquisitions into completely unrelated businesses, just as U.S. corporations had done two decades before. Often they would do both. Excess capital and the lack of appropriate capital structure management again created these problems.

As the early insights brought capital structure's centrality to corporate strategy into view, the research also reflected this increasing complexity. Most recently, a steady stream of research has come from Clifford Smith and his colleagues at the Simon School of Business Administration in Rochester, New York (Barclay, Marx, and Smith, forthcoming; Smith 2001; Barclay and Smith 1996, 1999). Capital structure is complex. The decades-old term and rate debates have given way to consideration of complex capital structures addressing issues of leverage, maturity, priority, callability, convertibility, and whether or not the debt is public or private. Smith's work has been most definitive in explaining how and why capital structure decisions affect corporate valuations. In terms of debt contracting costs, he found that companies with more growth options (high market to book ratios) have significantly lower leverage than companies with fewer growth options. Growth companies have shorter maturity debt than assets-in-place firms. Finally, growth firms have tended to concentrate their obligations among high priority classes. In terms of taxes, Smith found that firms facing high tax rates are more likely to issue debt. In terms of leverage, he found a negative relationship between past profitability and leverage, and a small relation between future earnings changes and leverage. In terms of maturity, he found that undervalued firms did not use less short-term debt, while in terms of priority, they used less senior debt.

As capital structure is managed, Smith's data on the costs of adjusting capital structure are also instructive. Basically, adjustment costs differ by the type of transaction. Costs of equity issues are higher than those of debt. Costs of share issues are higher than those of share repurchases. Adjustment costs exhibit fixed attributes in addition to being sensitive to the scale economies of the financial system. Equity offers are rare while bank loans are common. The optimal adjustment of the capital structure frequently involves overshooting the target cost of capital. This means that firm managers must focus upon determining the optimal capital structure for the economic balance sheet. Capital structure, therefore, is not fixed. It is a trajectory over the life of the firm. As the costs of deviating from the target exceed the cost of adjustment, managers must adjust their capital structure.

In all of these cases, information costs are critical to financing decisions. The role of financial institutions and capital markets is key to overcoming these problems. It is in this context that the rise of the high yield market can be best understood. The market for innovative high yield securities emerged at the nexus of changes in both information technology and financial technology. During the early 1970s, the market may have appeared to be inefficient precisely because of the high information costs in the sectors of distressed credits and growth firms in new markets that could not obtain bond ratings or have their financial information widely disseminated to investors.

The high yield market of the late 1970s and the 1980s can be best understood as a market whose main accomplishment was overcoming information costs by separating good risks from bad risks through liquidity and active trading, monitoring companies' performance closely, and then reorganizing them among investors if they encountered financial difficulty. Small and medium-sized companies with high information costs required accurate valuation of their equity and debt. Overcoming information asymmetries is a pricing and information problem. That was key to the rise of the high yield market and the proliferation of its financial innovations throughout all securities markets in subsequent years.

BOX 8-1. FIXED INCOME PRICING SYSTEM: FIPS

In October 1989, the Senate Committee on Banking, Housing, and Urban Affairs sent a letter to the chairman of the SEC expressing concern about, among other things, the lack of transparency in the high yield bond secondary market and suggesting the possibility of developing a quotation system for those securities. In his response, Chairman Breeden (1990) stated that the commission shared the Senate's interest in improving the availability of information concerning price and liquidity in the high yield bond market.

The value of bonds changing hands is substantial. In 1990, an estimated $15.7 billion in corporate debt changed hands every day. Of that, $7 billion to $10 billion was investment grade and $0.5 billion to $1.5 billion was high yield. Compare that to the daily average of $6.2 billion in equities traded on the NYSE in the same year. The NYSE accounted for only 0.5 percent to 1 percent of total corporate debt trading volume in 1990, largely because few debt issues were eligible for listing. The majority of corporate debt, and high yield in particular, was traded in the over the counter market. To put the bond market in perspective, consider that the average price of an equity share on the New York Stock Exchange at the time was about $37, while bonds traded with a minimum face amount of $1,000. The average trade of high yield bonds was valued at about $1 million to $3 million, whereas the average trade in investment grade bonds was a bit bigger, between $2 million and $5 million. Therefore, although the volume of trades (and hence the number of market participants) in the bond market was small, the total daily value of transactions could be quite significant.

If the information key to the development of deep, liquid bond markets was to become available, it would require far-ranging changes in the existing market infrastructure. During April 1990, as Rule 144A was passing final rulemaking, the SEC made initial contact with the National Association of Securities Dealers (NASD) to initiate the development of a facility to capture trade reports for secondary trading in high yield debt. One of the main obstacles to an investment in infrastructure to support this disclosure was the high market concentration. Too few users meant that the development costs of the system to individual users could be prohibitively high. In 1989, the seven largest underwriters accounted for almost 90 percent of the offerings in the high yield market. That left too few users at the time to support the cost of developing and implementing a system. By March 1991, however, the NASD had substantially completed development of its Fixed Income Prototype System (later renamed the Fixed Income Pricing System, FIPS), a rules-based regulatory reporting/ surveillance facility to capture trade reports for a small list of representative actively traded issues. FIPS would also provide limited dissemination of information in the form of high, low, and volume aggregates for those issues. The developers recognized that mandating increased transparency for the large segment of the market that is illiquid might further reduce dealer participation. Mandatory disclosure was therefore practicable only where a "critical

(*continued*)

Box 8-1 continued

mass" of market participants existed. It was decided that the efforts to increase transparency in the high yield market would focus, at least initially, on the forty to fifty most actively traded securities (SEC 1991).

Daily high and low prices of thirty-five actively traded high yield securities became public information in April 1994.* Yankee bonds, convertible bonds, medium-term notes, and Rule 144A private placement issues are excluded under FIPS rules. There were 3,000 issues in the FIPS database in June 2001. All NASD member firms transacting business in high yield debt securities must register as FIPS participants and report all trades in covered securities. Reporting is mandatory for the fifty most active issues (within five minutes of the trade). Trades in all other issues must be reported by end of day (and there is no quotation obligation with these issues). At the time of this writing, there is no long-term storage of historical hourly data available to the public, although NASD is aware of the importance of this data for research purpose.

FIPS is a screen-based system operated by The Nasdaq Stock Market, Inc., that enables Nasdaq to collect and disseminate hourly cumulative and end of day aggregate information on eligible high yield corporate bonds. Quotes are displayed by market makers in the FIPS fifty bonds.

A FIPS participant is any National Association of Securities Dealers (NASD) member that is registered as a FIPS dealer or broker. A FIPS dealer is a broker-dealer with end accounts. A FIPS broker is an interdealer broker. Participation in FIPS is mandatory for NASD members trading FIPS mandatory or nonmandatory bonds.

The obligation to report a transaction in FIPS bonds depends on the role of each party in the trade. In transactions between

- A FIPS dealer and a FIPS broker, only the broker reports the trade.
- Two FIPS dealers, only the sell side dealer reports the trade.
- A FIPS participant and nonparticipant, only the FIPS participant reports the trade.

The FIPS 50 list represents some of the most active and liquid issues currently trading, and as particular issues no longer represent their sector or industry, they are replaced with more representative issues. Nasdaq (and some market data vendors) disseminate quotations on an hourly basis during FIPS operating hours.

Each hour, Nasdaq and market data vendors disseminate summary transaction information that includes the high and low execution prices and volume for transactions reported in that hour and cumulatively in FIPS mandatory bonds, aggregated from individual transaction reports made by members. In addition, an end-of-day summary is disseminated with the day's overall high and low prices and cumulative volume. Transaction information in FIPS nonmandatory bonds is monitored by Nasdaq for surveillance purposes only and is not disseminated publicly.

*By April 10, 1995, thirty-nine bonds were subject to dissemination in the form of aggregates. The list was expanded to fifty issues at least by November 30, 1996, although the "official" date is uncertain. The list of mandatory bonds is reviewed and subject to change every three to four months. Revisions take into account those issues with the highest volume and trade count.

COST OF CAPITAL, LEVERAGE, AND LIQUIDITY

The corporate finance revolution catalyzed by the rise of the high yield securities market demonstrated that a company could reduce its cost of capital and raise its stock price by increasing the liquidity of its securities. Slicing and dicing the capital structure of the firm according to firm strategy and investors' differentiated interests created financial innovations and new securities that would increase a firm's investor base, create new trading venues for its securities, and, most important, increase the amount and quality of information to investors (Amihud and Mendelson 1988, 2000).

Solving the capital structure puzzle—how a firm divides its capital along the debt-to-equity continuum to support its business strategy and activities in a way that maximizes current firm value—became central to the nexus of financial and business strategy in setting the leverage ratio for a given firm. As Smith and his colleagues have shown, CFOs have come to understand both the costs associated with deviating from a target optimal capital structure and the costs of adjusting back toward that target as they weigh external financing decisions and the costs and scale of various financings. (See Barclay and Smith 1999; Smith and Watts 1992.)

The available evidence on the size and variation of capital costs indicates that information, transaction, and other costs all fall with transaction size. Small and medium-sized firms have traditionally been at a disadvantage in terms of external financing, and that issue has been only partially resolved by the advent of the new issue high yield securities market, the expansion of private equity, the complexity of capital structure in venture capital transactions, and the initial public offering market (which is highly cyclical). It has been well demonstrated that long-term public debt issues, particularly for below investment grade companies, are less costly than equity (Datta, Iskandar-Datta, and Patel 1999).

An optimal capital structure offers the highest net benefits for shareholders. Efficiency gains from restructuring in companies with abundant free cash flow have been demonstrated. Substituting debt for equity, especially in noninvestment grade firms, has been shown to add value by creating incentives to increase future cash flow and return excess capital to investors. The expected benefit of debt financing and its availability increase when corporate taxable earnings and free cash flow are large and predictable. Default and bankruptcy risk has proved greatest in the high yield market and elsewhere in the capital markets when this is not the case.[2]

THE HIGH YIELD MARKET AND THE REAL ECONOMY

The relationship between financial markets, complex capital structure, and economic growth has become increasingly apparent. The diversity of fi-

2. The theory and evidence on these points are available in Jensen (1986), Grossman and Hart (1982), and Stulz (1990). More recent evidence is available in Opler, Saron, and Titman (1997).

nancial instruments available, the increasing variegation of corporate capital structure, and the resulting diversification benefits of financial markets have converged. The broadest possible spectrum of financial markets helps a country avoid overreliance upon commercial banking or upon any one market for its growth and development needs. The United States as the late Merton Miller showed, has made itself less vulnerable than in the past to credit crunches, and has created a more efficient capital allocation process by substituting dispersed and decentralized financial markets for banking (Miller 1998; Stulz 1999).

Just as the high yield market began its remarkable recovery in 1991, popular and professional realization of the centrality of finance in providing the means and methods to empower the future became more accepted. Coincidentally, Nobel laureates in financial economics were first awarded that year. The relationship between finance and growth has been increasingly appreciated ever since. No longer is high yield finance, or finance in general, considered a technical backwater of economics and business; it is now central to the core competencies of building companies in a new economy and renewing older economies. Both neoclassical and Marxist economists considered finance to be something far away from the production factors that determined the shape and direction of economic growth. They viewed finance as something that goes on above the heads and behind the backs of most of the population. As business news became more widely available and stock prices were followed like baseball box scores, the appreciation of the relationship between corporate finance, financial institutions, and capital markets became more widespread. The impetus to make finance and financial markets more transparent, responsive, and accessible emerged, not simply as an issue of finance and economics but also as a major public policy concern.

Simply put, credit market frictions significantly amplify shocks to the economy. Cash flow, leverage, and other balance sheet factors have a major influence on investment spending (Fazzari, Hubbard, and Petersen 1988; Hubbard, Kashyap, and Whited 1995). Similarly, evidence has accumulated about the impact of investment spending on inventories and employment (Sharpe 1994; Carpenter, Fazzari, and Petersen 1994). There is a central role for credit market conditions in the propagation of investment. Credit problems of businesses resulting in forgone expansion plans or insolvencies, collapsing asset prices, runs on banks, bank failures, and rising debt burdens are not mere reflections of past problems: they depress economic activity directly. Whether we are trying to understand the Great Depression or, more recently, the causes and consequences of the Asian financial crisis, the mechanisms through which credit market crunches affect the overall economy are becoming increasingly appreciated.

Over the 1990s, the knowledge base about finance and its linkages to the real economy grew. Financial factors are now understood to amplify and propagate changes in the business cycle. Decisions about capital structure and corporate strategy coincide into what has come to be known as the "financial accelerator" of the economy as a whole (Gertler and Lown 2000). This notion is a major contribution to our understanding about the role of finance in the economy in general and the specific role of the high yield market in particular. Credit market crises increase the costs of credit and reduce the efficiency of matching lenders and borrowers. Both theoretically and empirically, recent work has demonstrated the existence of the financial accelerator whereby developments internal to credit markets propagate and amplify shocks to the general economy (Bernanke, Gertler, and Gilchrist 1996). Business cycle dynamics are greatly influenced by this financial accelerator.

The linkages between the means and methods of financing firms and the future of the economy as a whole have become increasingly clear. Frictions in financial markets can damp or fuel economic growth. Information costs, regulation, contract enforcement costs, and tax regime changes in financial markets drive a wedge between the cost of external funds and the opportunity cost of internal funds (referred to as the "premium on external funds").

If firms are to innovate and grow, they must escape the fate of self-financing and mobilize external funds. Capital access and its costs are driving factors for the economy. The premium paid for external funds affects the corporate borrowers' balance sheets inversely and amplifies borrower spending, in turn affecting the business cycle.

Economic growth occurs on the margins. It is on the edges of the economy, in firms large and small, that innovation occurs. New entrants into capital markets seeking external funding drive demand for new product, process, and technology markets, and subsequently for the derived demand in the economy as a whole. The increasing centrality of the high yield securities market, as a component of capital structure managed by new firms, industries, and countries entering the global capital markets, is suggested by recent empirical research.

High yield spreads appear to have significant explanatory and predictive power for the business cycle with a one-to-two-year lag, particularly high yield bond to AAA corporate bond yield spreads. Figure 8-1 shows the yield to maturity of the Merrill Lynch High Yield 175 index over the yield of the Lehman Brothers Government Bond Index.

Other leading indicators, such as commercial paper spread or the Federal Funds rate, have been found to be less satisfactory in empirical studies (Lown, Morgan, and Rohatgi 1999; Mishkin 1991; Gertler and Lown 2000). Figure 8-2 shows estimations of GDP gap based on high yield spreads as compared to commercial paper spreads.[3]

Firms in the high yield market are more credit constrained than their investment grade counterparts. Their lack of access to capital is more likely

3. GDP gap is the deviation of actual GDP growth from the long-term trend of GDP growth. The estimations are based on a simple bivariate ordinary least square regression equation of the form $Y=\alpha+\beta X+e$, where Y is GDP gap, X is either high yield spread or commercial paper spread, α and β are estimated coefficients, and e is a normal error term.

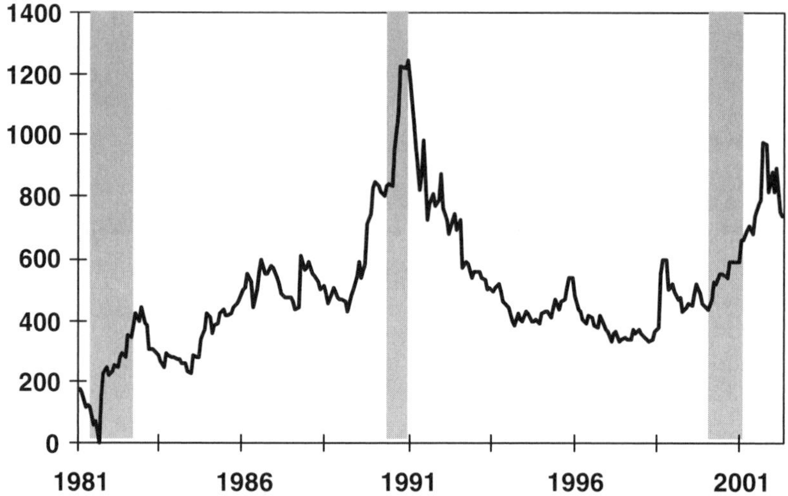

Figure 8-1. The High Yield Bond Spread and U.S. Recessions, 1981–2001. Spread measured as the difference between the yield to maturity of the Merrill Lynch High Yield 175 Index and the Lehman Brothers Government Bond Index. Shaded dates represent NBER defined contractions. Sources: Merrill Lynch; Lehman Brothers; NBER; Milken Institute.

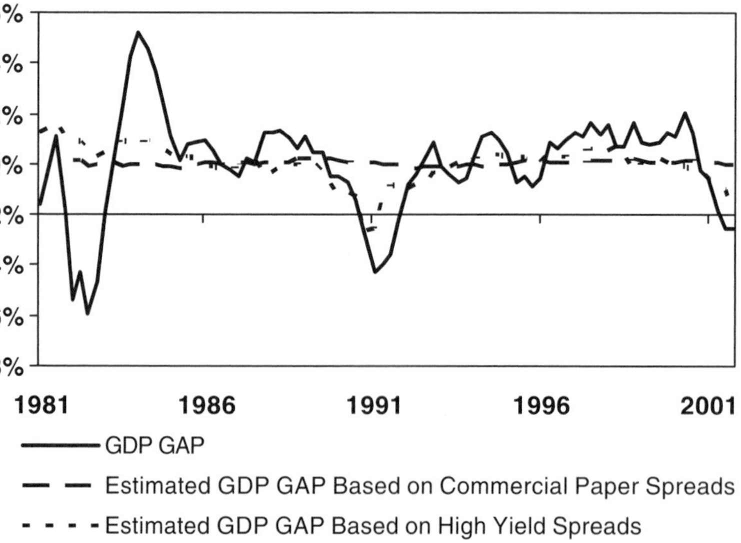

Figure 8-2. The High Yield Bond Spread as a Predictor of Economic Activity, 1981–2001. Source: Lown and Gertler 1991.

to reflect an impending recession. The high yield market, and more generally the market for high yield financial innovations, represents a kind of "canary in the coal mine" for the economy as a whole. The extent to which firms can depend upon the cost and access of external funds to finance growth determines the course of the economy as a whole. Thus, when the high yield market stops singing, it signals the coming credit crunch that has the potential to trigger a recession.

While the high yield market represents only a portion of those firms with imperfect access to credit markets, the spread on high yield debt—the premium that noninvestment grade firms must pay for capital—is closely correlated with the premium on external funds that smaller, bank-dependent firms face. Hence, it represents that additional cost of capital—which we explained earlier as the premium for external funds. The high yield spread improves the ability of economic models to explain variation in total output. In short, it is a measure of the financial accelerator in the economy as a whole. Sensitive to default risk, the high yield market detects a greater variety of factors influencing the macroeconomy. This is largely because the segmentation of the high yield market reflects, and is a refraction of, the complexity of the capital structure of firms in that market (Reilly and Wright 1992).

IMPLICATIONS OF RECENT DEVELOPMENTS

The high yield market has exhibited impressive growth since 1980, increasing in new issuance volume from under $1.5 billion in 1980 to over $105 billion in 2001. With the increase in volume has come an increase in the number of issues. In 1980, there were just forty-three new high yield issues. The growth of the high yield market is illustrated in figure 8-3, which shows the peak of the market in 1998 with 839 new issues and a volume of $157 billion.

The increase in the size of the high yield market has been largely due to the strong growth of the public and Rule 144A markets (figure 8-4, table 8-1). After the turmoil of the late 1980s, the private placement market was to a great extent replaced by the public market—which rapidly recovered from its early 1990s lows—and the market for Rule144A high yield debt. The mature high yield market can also be distinguished from the market of the early 1990s by the disappearance of payment-in-kind and deferred interest bonds and by the emergence of multicoupon bonds and floaters. This change in the structure of the market can be seen in figures 8-5 and 8-6. As the stock of payment-in-kind and deferred interest bonds has dwindled, there has been a trend against the issuance of subordinated debt. As issuers appear to increasingly favor senior debt, the importance of subordinated issues—which in 1992 accounted for more than a third of the market—has fallen. In 1998 and 1999, subordinated debt accounted for zero and 2 percent of the market, respectively (table 8-2). Although 2000 saw a recovery in subordinated debt, it now accounts for slightly less than half of its 1992 market share.

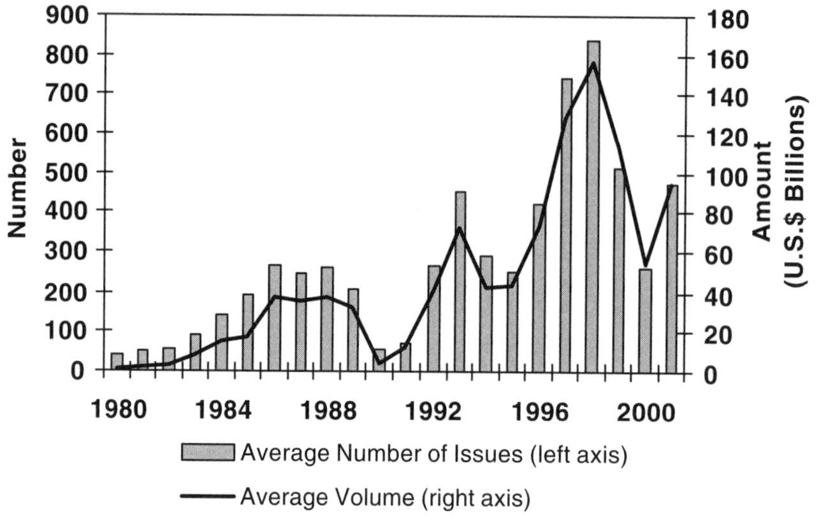

Figure 8-3. Number of High Yield Issues and High Yield Issuance Amount, 1980–2001. Sources: Merrill Lynch; Credit Suisse First Boston; Milken Institute.

The demand for high yield debt has exhibited increased variance and an increased volatility of flows of money into high yield bond funds, as seen in figure 8-7. Prior to 1992, the market exhibited little volatility, but the maturing of the market has changed this characteristic. The flow of funds into high yield debt is now marked by a high level of variance.

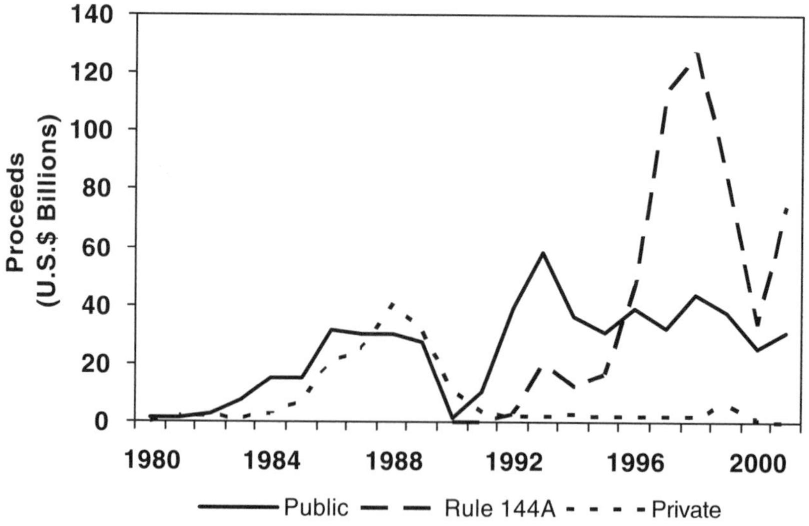

Figure 8-4. High Yield New Issuance by Market, 1980–2001. Sources: Securities Data Corporation; Milken Institute.

Table 8-1. High Yield New Issuance by Market, 1977–2001

	Public		Rule 144A		Private	
	% Issues	% Principal Amount	% Issues	% Principal Amount	% Issues	% Principal Amount
1977	100	0	0	100	0	0
1978	100	0	0	100	0	0
1979	100	0	0	100	0	0
1980	98	0	2	100	0	0
1981	39	0	61	43	0	57
1982	56	0	44	60	0	40
1983	68	0	32	86	0	14
1984	69	0	31	83	0	17
1985	62	0	38	69	0	31
1986	54	0	46	61	0	39
1987	42	0	58	54	0	46
1988	27	0	73	43	0	57
1989	27	0	73	47	0	53
1990	5	1	94	12	2	87
1991	35	4	61	74	3	24
1992	76	9	15	88	6	5
1993	67	24	9	73	25	2
1994	49	32	19	71	24	5
1995	51	32	17	63	33	4
1996	36	53	11	45	53	3
1997	17	76	7	22	77	2
1998	14	79	7	25	74	1
1999	18	74	8	29	66	5
2000	15	77	8	42	56	2
2001	13	86	1	29	70	0

Sources: Securities Data Corporation; Milken Institute.

The changing fortunes of the high yield market are reflected in the changing spread of high yield bonds over Treasuries (figure 8-1). The narrow spreads of the early and mid-1980s exploded into double digits in the later 1980s and the early 1990s as the bankruptcy of the main underwriter of, and market maker in, the bonds, Drexel Burnham Lambert, was compounded by the worsening fortunes of the U.S. economy.

Patterns of restrictive regulations inhibited change and growth in the economy through restrictions on changing capital ownership, commercial bank lending, savings and loan lending, insurance companies' lending, and

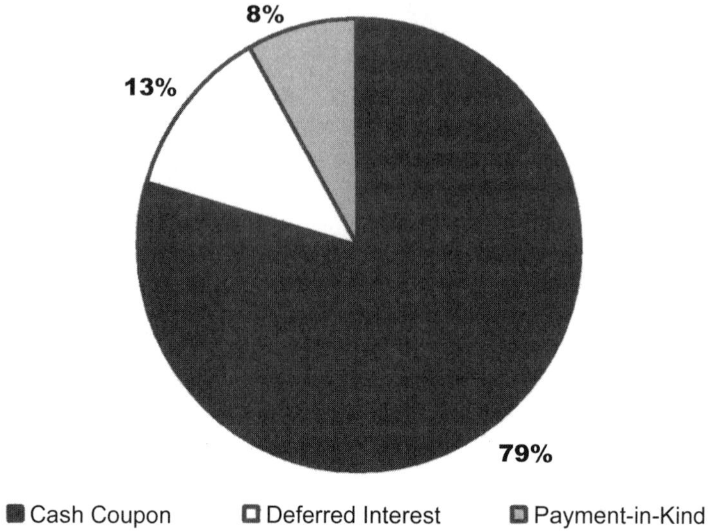

Figure 8-5. Distribution of High Yield Market by Coupon Type, 1990. Source: Merrill Lynch.

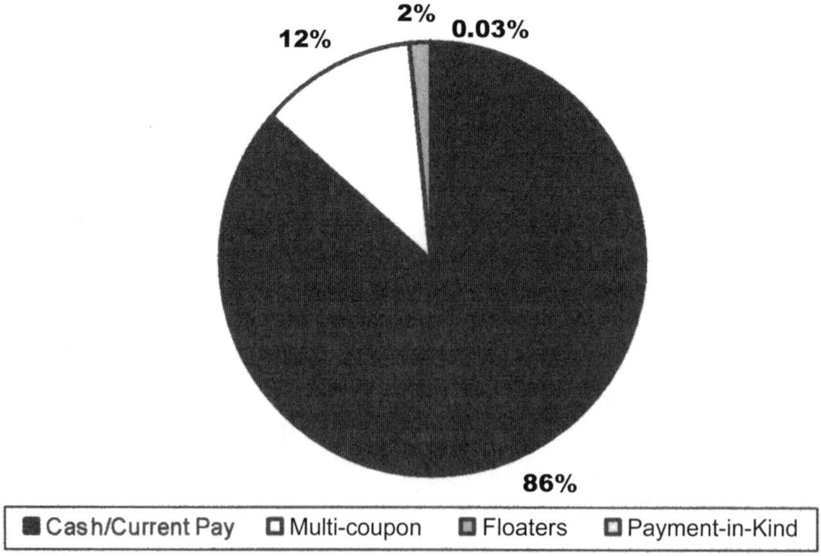

Figure 8-6. Distribution of High Yield Market by Coupon Type, 2000. Source: Merrill Lynch.

Table 8-2. Distribution of High Yield Bonds by Seniority, 1990–2000 (percent)

	Senior Secured	Senior Unsecured	Senior Subordinated	Subordinated	Discount and Zero Coupon
1990	10	27	33	21	9
1991	3	43	24	24	6
1992	22	12	25	34	7
1993	6	22	31	28	13
1994	23	35	23	14	5
1995	15	27	52	3	3
1996	16	17	37	17	13
1997	16	48	24	4	8
1998	18	61	18	0	3
1999	11	47	31	2	9
2000	8	29	37	16	10

Source: Altman, Resti, and Sironi 2001.

mutual fund investing, as well as through discouragement of investments by pension funds. Additionally, changes in tax codes and other regulations introduced rigidities both in corporate capital structure and in capital markets, further inhibiting the adaptive capacity of corporations both to finance expansion and to adjust to downturns (table 8-3). In all cases, sometimes disparate and at other times related policy initiatives converged to create barriers to new capital ownership and capital access. Policy-induced

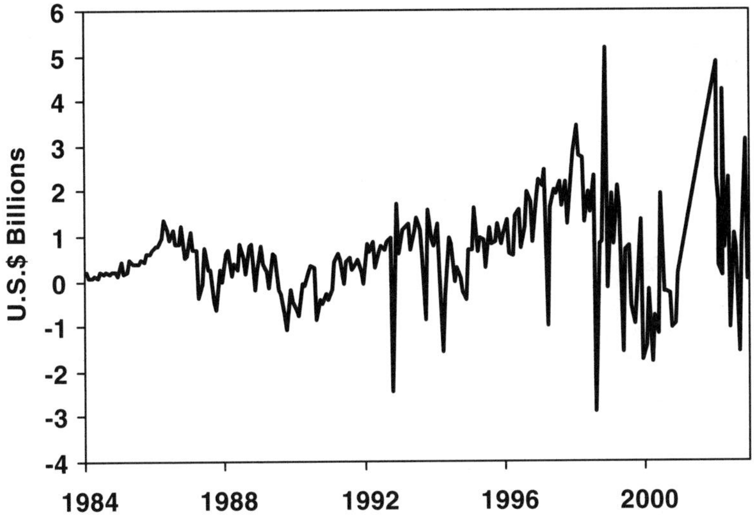

Figure 8-7. Net Capital Flows into High Yield Bond Funds, January 1984–March 2002. Sources: Merrill Lynch; Investment Company Institute; Milken Institute.

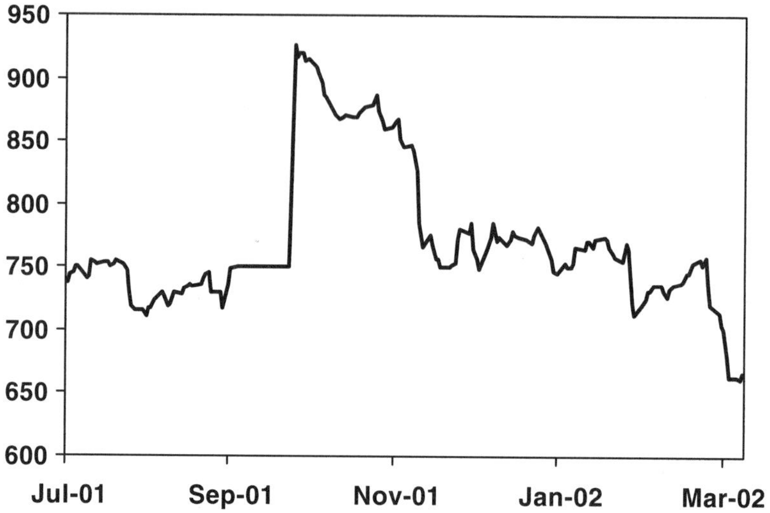

Figure 8-8. The September 11 Effect on High Yield Spreads over Treasuries, July 2001–March 2002. Spread of Merrill Lynch High Yield Master Index over Merrill Lynch Government Index. Sources: Merrill Lynch; Milken Institute.

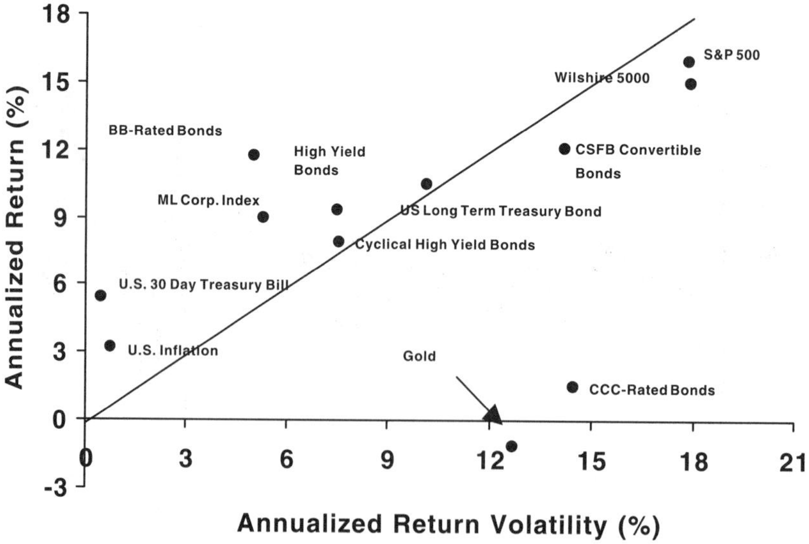

Figure 8-9. Risk and Return for Selected Assets, 1986–2000. Sources: Credit Suisse First Boston; Merrill Lynch; Milken Institute.

Table 8-3. Legislative and Regulatory Measures Inducing Rigidity in Capital Structures and Markets, 1985–1990

Date	Measure
1985	Congress makes a series of decisions on tender offers, lockups, contracts, and poison pills. Further, Congress takes action on such issues as taxes, "junk bonds," antitrust, tender offer rules, and disclosure requirements, all of which affect merger and acquisition (M&A) activity.
1986	Federal Reserve Board votes in January to apply the margin rules of Regulation G to high yield bond-financed takeovers by shell corporations. The Fed specifically exempts two types of situations: (1) when the shell and the target will merge, and (2) when an operating company issues or guarantees the bond.
	In the 100th Congress stricter regulations and new legislation are proposed (31 pieces of legislation) to check "excessive speculation" in securities markets, inasmuch as such speculation is damaging to corporations and converts too much equity into debt. Although the U.S. market system can tolerate many types of transactions, concern is expressed that economic and corporate behavior must be delineated from tolerating today's "runaway speculation."
	The Tax Reform Act of 1986 limits interest expense deductions. Tax treatment of interest deductions in leveraged redemptions involves (1) the so-called trade or business interest, (2) investment interest, (3) portfolio interest, (4) passive activity interest, and (5) personal interest. Initial public offerings and leveraged buyouts are affected by the tax changes. The tax changes increase overall corporate taxes by lowering tax rates while expanding the tax base. If inflation is ignored, the cost of debt is greater as the tax rate declines.
	The National Association of Insurance Commissioners (NAIC) approves an annual statement that requires all insurers to report the bonds they own, categorized by investment grade and quality as determined by the NAIC Securities Valuation Office.
1987	Congressional hearings detail the buildup of corporate debt and the impact of overnight restructuring, and result in a call for stricter federal controls in four areas: (1) "greenmail," (2) tender offers mechanics, (3) defense tactics, and (4) "junk bonds."
	The role of thrifts in the high yield bond market and the role of high yield bonds in corporate takeovers are addressed by the Senate Banking Committee. As legislation is developed, the focus is on the social and economic benefits of corporate takeovers as well as the role of savings and loans.
	Long-standing congressional prohibition against a binding vote that would modify any core term of a bond indenture—such as principal amount, interest rate, and maturity date—should be repealed and replaced with a simple and flexible standard, implemented by SEC rulemaking, that would prohibit fraud and distortion in bond recapitalizations.
	A proposal in the Revenue Act of 1987 curbs the use of pension funds as a source of financing for real estate.

(*continued*)

Table 8-3. (*continued*)

Date	Measure
1989	Federal legislation is proposed to curb the "excessive" use of debt in buyouts that could include partial deductibility of interest and dividends, increased disclosure requirements from managers seeking buyouts, and new limits on participation in buyouts by investment bankers.
	From a tax law perspective, concerns voiced about leveraged buyouts focus on the fact that there is a tax incentive for corporations to use debt rather than equity. To help rectify this situation, the joint Committee on Taxation considers the integration of corporate and individual tax systems. The problem with any form of integration, however, is that the federal government cannot afford it. Another option discussed by the joint committee is limiting the deductibility of corporate interest expenses.
	The Financial Institutions Reform, Recovery, and Enforcement Act (FIRREA) limits the percentage of assets that can be held by thrifts in high yield bonds, and also requires that high yield bonds be marked-to-market for regulatory accounting.
	In August, Congress gives thrifts five years to get rid of their high yield bonds; mark-to-market thrift accounting rules require immediate divestment.
	The Revenue Reconciliation Act of 1989 is a large piece of legislation containing a separate title of specifically targeted revisions to the Internal Revenue Code and lacks any coherent overall tax policy. Some of the provisions reflect an anti-takeover mood, whereas others attempt to close loopholes. The addition of special rules for original issue discount (OID) on certain high yield obligations results from congressional concern about "junk bonds," virtually removing the deduction for interest paid.
	Tax legislation is proposed that would remove the tax advantages of two categories of high yield debt: high yield zero-coupon bonds and payment-in-kind bonds. An amendment to the thrift recovery bill is also introduced to prohibit thrifts from purchasing or holding high yield bonds.
	Congress reduces the tax shields related to mergers as part of the latest tax revision legislation. Restraints are placed on the deduction of interest on the riskiest types of debt securities with deferred interest payments, and on tax refunds for portions of net operating losses caused by leveraged transactions, including recapitalizations and acquisitions. The new law does not affect the tax benefits for employee stock ownership programs as acquisition vehicles, but it could have significant effects on the establishment of defensive programs.
1990	An SEC decision in February forces additional disclosure rules for high yield bond issuers.
	In March, New York State limits insurance companies' holdings of high yield bonds to 20 percent of total assets as of 1987. Arizona limits high yield bonds to 20 percent of an insurer's assets or 200 percent of its net worth. New Jersey and Illinois are considering regulations similar to New York's.
	Although the "junk bond era" is over, politicians are still passing anti-takeover legislation. The states' latest anti-takeover laws typically prevent holders of more than 20 percent of an incorporated firm's shares from

Table 8-3. *(continued)*

Date	Measure
1990	voting on a merger or takeover. In effect, the laws deprive those with the largest ownership interest of a vote.
	NAIC moves to accelerate the rate of accumulation of reserves for insurers holding high yield securities. The NAIC sees the need to accelerate the rate of reserving because of concern that the accumulation periods were set 30 years ago, when there were no new high yield bonds.
	NAIC's loss reserve regulation requires most property-casualty insurers to have an actuary, or a loss reserve specialist, approved by an insurance commissioner certify the adequacy of loss reserves reported in annual statements. Insurers must begin complying with the regulation in their 1990 annual statements.
	NAIC examines proposals concerning whether or not to use reserve requirements to curb the amount of noninvestment-grade debt that an insurance company could carry in the future. Also, the reserve requirements would be cut in half, from 2 percent to 1 percent, on debt rated A or better. The NAIC also considers three industry proposals concerning the transition period and proposes a six-tier system that more closely parallels the brackets used by the rating agencies.
	Congress ends the tax break on lending to employee stock ownership plans, but allows them to issue debt in public markets.
	Congress, in an extreme departure from years of established judicial principles and administrative rulings, enacts legislation on October 27 that determines the cancellation of indebtedness income and original issue discount consequences in debt-for-debt exchanges by comparing the old debt to the current value of the new debt, without regard to the new debt's face amount.
	Tax liability is incurred on preferred stock issued in exchange for debt if the shares carry a redemption price that is greater than the issue price. The new tax legislation opts to treat such shares the way original issue discount bonds are treated, in that the difference will be amortized over the life of the issue and taxed annually as a dividend. A troubled company that exchanges old debt for new debt or stock now will have to pay tax on "discharge of indebtedness," computed as the difference between the face value of the old debt and the issue price of the new security. Another change outlaws the use of tax refunds for loss carrybacks as a source of equity in buyout using leverage.
	A proposed New York State amendment to high yield bond regulations reflects a rating system instituted by the NAIC in June, in which bond quality was divided into six categories. Category 1 represents the highest grade bonds and Category 6 the lowest grade, those in or near default. Category 3 bonds were assigned a description of medium quality. Repeatedly, speakers at the November hearing testify that Category 3 bonds should not be included with Category 4, 5, and 6 bonds (i.e., a small firm that has demonstrated reliability and that has a sound credit history may

(continued)

Table 8-3. (*continued*)

Date	Measure
1990	not be investment grade, but should not be considered "junk" from an investment standpoint).
	A Minnesota task force recommends that state regulators have more authority to scrutinize insurers' finances and to take quicker action against financing ailing insurers.
	Tax provisions of the new congressional budget package mandate that a debtor who exchanges new debt for existing debt generates cancellation-of-indebtedness income to the extent that the principal amount of the retired debt exceeds the issue price of the new.

rigidities in corporate capital structures made it difficult for some corporations to adapt to changing circumstances, particularly in the late 1980s. Defaults and distressed credits became an outcome of this process.

As the market recovered in the 1990s and the United States returned to growth, the high yield market—which many commentators had written off as dead—returned to health with rapidly falling yields and a sharp increase in issuance (figure 8-3). Additionally, the rise of structured finance (chapter 7) opened up opportunities for regulatory arbitrage.

The weakening U.S. economy of 2001 and the huge shock to Wall Street resulting from the terrorist attacks of September 11 saw an increase in the yield to maturity of high yield bonds as well as a sharp decrease in interest rates that resulted in the widening of high yield spread to over 900 basis points. The September 11 effect, seen in figure 8-8, was short-lived, however, and the spread fell from its postattack heights to below 700 basis points as investors were buoyed by improving economic news and the rapid defeat of the Taliban and their al Qaeda allies.

Despite the volatility in the flow of funds and the occasionally sharp increases in noninvestment grade debt yields, the asset class has been one of the best-performing fixed-income investments of the past few decades. The risk-return profile of a variety of securities is shown in figure 8-9. High yield bonds offer a risk-reward ratio not dissimilar to the U.S. long bond.

9

The 1980s Users' Performance in the 1990s

In assessing the impact of high yield financing on corporate performance, aggregate industry and economic data can help us identify general trends. But to learn how particular companies have benefited from the use of high yield financing, we need to look at the companies individually.

In this chapter, we describe actual cases of high yield companies and the strategies they have pursued to maximize the value of their assets, labor force, products, and markets. Our examples show how businesses have responded to the pressures of economic change by modifying their strategies, adopting new technologies, and changing their supply chains and distribution channels. The companies studied also show how high yield issuers have responded to increasing competition in both domestic and international markets.

A common story appears to repeat itself throughout the case studies. In utilizing the high yield market, firms not only went beyond traditional sources of capital, they also created functions that went beyond traditional industrial categories. We place these companies in the historical context of their foundations to give a sense of their place in their industries and in the economy as a whole. The histories show that innovation was not new to any of them. Stone Container opened the first plant devoted to cardboard boxes in 1936. McCaw purchased the cellular licenses in 1981 that AT&T didn't have any use for until 1993. Viacom revamped Nickelodeon to take it from the least popular channel on basic cable in 1985 to the one that was watched by more children than similar programming on all four major networks combined in 1993. From the mythical Lee Iacocca, who reduced his salary to $1 a year until he made Chrysler profitable to the visionary Martin Wygod, who established a company to contain the cost of prescriptions at a time when medical expenses were spiraling out of control—these are stories that exemplify the American dream.

STONE CONTAINER

The paper industry is characterized by very high utilization requirements for profitability (about 95 percent of capacity) and extreme price inelasticity. As a result, at times of decreased demand companies continue to manufacture products at almost full capacity and prices decrease significantly as they attempt to unload the produced goods. These factors make the industry highly cyclical, with years of high profitability followed by years of substantial losses.

Working in this environment, Stone Container, a Chicago-based pulp and paper company, nearly went bankrupt in 1993 under the weight of $4.6 billion in debt resulting from ambitious acquisitions. The company's strategy for growth had been to acquire distressed companies at discounted prices during cyclical downturns and then to reap the profits from their production as growth in manufacturing resumed.[1] Implementing this strategy had brought Stone extremely high returns on its investments in the 1980s, allowing the company to recover acquisition costs within one to two years. The very same strategy brought the company to near bankruptcy in the early 1990s due to a poorly timed acquisition. Stone managed to remain solvent with the help of creative financing methods, among which was the use of high yield securities, enabling the company to resume growth.

Company Growth

Stone Container originated in 1926 when Joseph Stone used $1,500 in savings to found J.H. Stone & Son's, a jobber of packing material and office supplies. The business proved to be an immediate success, generating sales of $68,000 and a profit of $13,500 for the first full year of operation. In 1933 the Great Depression pushed J.H. Stone & Sons into manufacturing. The National Recovery Act, signed into law by President Franklin Roosevelt, outlawed price-cutting and thus prevented jobbers from getting their merchandise at a discount. As a result, Stone's customers had to pay a premium for Stone's services. Needing a cheaper source of supplies, the company spent $7,200 on five machines that converted corrugated sheets into boxes.

In 1936, Joseph Stone died and complete control of the company passed to his three sons, Norman, Marvin, and Jerome. They then purchased a second-hand corrugator for $20,000. Two years later the Stones began to build their own plant. The 150,000-square-foot Chicago building was the first plant to be devoted exclusively to the manufacturing of corrugated boxes. Stone funded the $382,000 project by taking out a twenty-year loan at 6 percent. With sales continuing to increase (they reached the $1 million mark in 1939), Stone managed to pay off the entire loan in less than three years.

During World War II, Stone & Sons thrived. The government sent shipments of aid and arms overseas, almost all of which were packed in corrugated boxes. As a result, there was high demand for Stone & Sons products. The company's high war priority rating allowed it to receive a continuous supply of raw materials. In 1943 the company acquired Light Corrugated Box for $1.2 million. David Lipper, the first nonfamily member in upper management, became general manager at the newly purchased

1. Growth in sales of box products is very highly correlated with that of manufacturing.

facility. Two years later the business incorporated, changing its name to Stone Container Corporation.

Following the war, demand for Stone Container products skyrocketed and raw materials grew short. As a result, the company acquired two mills: a $1.2 million boxboard mill in Franklin, Ohio, and a $575,000 corrugating medium mill (the fluted material sandwiched between linerboard layers in corrugated containers) in Coshocton, Ohio. The purchase of these two mills was financed through a $2 million loan, which Stone Container paid off within one year. In 1947 Stone Container issued 250,000 shares of common stock and became a publicly owned company. Having relinquished complete family ownership, the brothers began searching for outsiders to fill management positions. Three years later the company built a new facility in the industrial area of Mansfield, Ohio. The plant was completed just prior to the Korean War, which brought another rise in demand. Within a year Stone bought another mill and converted it to a jute linerboard manufacturing facility.

Throughout the early 1950s supermarkets and self-service outlets enjoyed tremendous growth. At the same time, Stone pioneered the use of containers for advertising (by way of ads on box exteriors) in addition to carrying merchandise. Given that at the time it was not profitable to transport corrugated boxes more than about 125 miles, Stone focused on acquiring box companies near its main customers. Among the companies acquired at the time were W.C. Ritchie of Chicago and Western Paper Box of Detroit.

By 1960 Stone Container extended its product offerings to include folding cartons, fiber cans and tubs, tags, and special paper packages. This was made possible primarily by the acquisition of W.C. Ritchie. Around this time Stone's jute linerboard began losing market share to the lighter and stronger kraft linerboard. To stay competitive, Stone had to buy kraft linerboard from other paper companies. In order to reduce this cost, Stone took a 65 percent equity share in South Carolina Industries (SCI). Through SCI, Stone planned the construction of a new kraft linerboard mill at Florence, South Carolina, that would produce 400 tons of board a day.

In 1962 Stone was listed on the New York Stock Exchange. In the midst of an economic recession the company began construction on the SCI mill. The project, which would be completed in three years, was financed through Northwestern Mutual Life Insurance at a cost of $24 million, a sum greater than Stone Container's total net worth. Once this mill opened, Stone supplied virtually all of its own raw materials.

During the late 1960s and early 1970s Stone's expansion continued, and the company began to diversify toward a plastics packaging division. In 1974 the company purchased Lypho-Med, a dry-freeze pharmaceutical manufacturer. The following year Roger Stone, son of Marvin Stone, became president and chief operating officer (COO) of the firm. At the time Jerome Stone, the youngest of the three Stone brothers, served as company chairman and chief executive officer (CEO).

The company's extensive expansion took its toll on profitability. By 1978 Stone experienced a 50 percent decrease in earnings, compared to 1974 figures. The following year Roger Stone was named CEO. Boise Cascade proposed a merger, offering approximately $125 million in cash and stock—more than twice the company's market value—to buy Stone Container's outstanding shares. The Stone family, owning about 60 percent of the company's outstanding shares, chose to decline the offer and remain a public company. That same year the firm intensified its expansion campaign in a growth spurt that would eventually make it one of the world's largest paper manufacturers.

In 1981 Stone Container bought an equity position in Dean-Dempsy, a wood-chip fiber source, and the company grew to become the thirteenth largest producer of boxes in the United States. Two years later Stone paid $505 million for Continental Group's containerboard and brown-paper divisions, taking advantage of the latter's need for cash in a weak year for industry. This purchase, which was paid for with a $600 million loan (boosting the company's debt to 79 percent of capital) and an equity offering (cutting the family's share in the company from 57 to 49 percent), more than doubled the company's size and made Stone the nation's second largest producer of brown paper behind International Paper (table 9-1).

In October 1985 Stone paid $457 million to buy three containerboard mills and fifty-two box-and-bag plants from Champion International. The deal gave Champion the option to buy 12–14 percent of Stone's stock at a higher price within ten years. Two years later Stone purchased Southwest Forest Industries, a containerboard and newsprint company. In 1987 the company grew to be the nation's largest producer of brown paper, including corrugated boxes, paper bags, linerboard, and kraft paper, through the acquisition of Southwest's two large pulp and paper mills, nineteen corrugated container plants, and assorted plywood and veneer plants, lumber mills, and private fee timber. That year the family's share in the company fell to 30 percent.

Though the acquisitions to this point gradually increased its debt, the company was able to pay it down quickly. In all its acquisitions thus far, management purchased the target companies at low points in the economic cycle and then reaped the benefits of the increased capacity during the cyclical upturn that followed. However, the company's fortunes were about to change.

In March 1989 Stone borrowed $3.3. billion in floating-rate bank debt. The company used these funds to make its biggest acquisition yet, paying $2.7 billion in cash and securities for Consolidated-Bathurst (CB), Canada's fifth largest pulp and paper company.[2] This purchase, which increased Stone's production of pulp, paper, and newsprint, was most important strategically in that it gave Stone a foothold in the European market through CB's Europa Carton subsidiary and U.K. plants.[3]

2. The rest of the loan was used to consolidate and re-fund existing bank debt.

3. At the time management feared that increased U.S. market share would bring regulatory prohibitions. As a result, they sought to expand overseas.

Table 9-1. Stone Container Financials

Stone Container Corporation

Adjusted Debt/Cap Ratio	Market Cap (in Millions of US$)	Interest Coverage
93	4,212	-0.194

Business Description

Stone Container Corporation is a multinational unbleached paper and paper packaging producer. The company's products include containerboard, corrugated containers, kraft paper, and paper bags and sacks. Stone Container operates in North America, Europe, Central and South America, Australasia and Asia. On 11/18/98, Stone Container Corporation was acquired by Jefferson Smurfit.

Security Price History

Date	Stock High	Stock Low	Stock Close
1988	38.726	20.262	31.373
1989	35.662	21.691	23.407
1990	24.755	7.966	11.275
1991	25.490	8.824	25.368
1992	31.985	12.500	16.750
1993	19.500	6.375	9.625
1994	21.125	9.625	17.375
1995	24.625	12.500	14.375
1996	17.375	12.125	14.875
1997	17.812	9.500	10.875

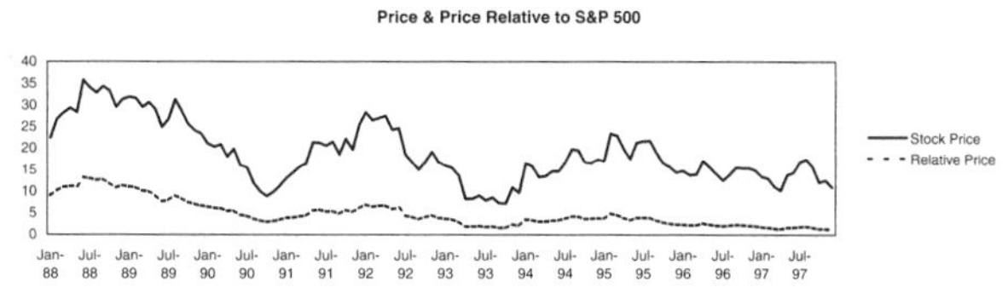

Market Ratios

	1997	1994	1991	1988
P/E Ratio	-2.719	-5.569	-646.874	
Earnings Yld	-0.383	-0.092	-0.031	0.178
MV/Sales	0.223	0.273	0.290	
MV/BV	6.925	2.947	1.026	
MV/EBITDA	5.082	2.549	2.883	
Cash Per Share	1.134	1.201	0.905	0.139
EPS	-4.160	-1.600	-0.775	5.578

Interest Coverage Model

Year	EBITDA / Interest	Return on Capital	Leverage
1988	6.855	18.690	0.719
1991	1.129	-0.874	2.580
1994	1.338	-2.658	6.838
1997	0.462	-9.793	14.213

Free Cash Flow

	1997	1994	1991	1988
EBITDA	213	616	541	762
Cash Interest	420	374	370	105
Taxes Paid	-34	-4	36	154
Capex	137	233	430	137
WC Change	-165	-24	331	56
Cash Dividends	2	8	45	21
Total	-148	30	-671	290

Financial History

	1997	1994	1991	1988
Income Statement				
Sales	4,849	5,749	5,384	3,742
COGS	4,070	4,564	4,320	2,627
SG&A	567	568	523	353
EBITDA	213	616	541	762
Interest Expense	460	461	479	111
Taxes	-201	-36	31	208
Net Income	-404	-129	-49	342
Balance Sheet				
Cash & Cash Equivaler	113	109	64	9
Acct. Receivable	653	825	642	441
Inventory	716	673	821	368
Intangible Assets	460	886	1,128	
Total Assets	5,824	7,005	6,903	2,395
Current Liabilities - To	1,089	1,032	915	426
Long Term Debt	3,936	4,432	4,046	765
Equity	277	648	1,569	1,064
Working Capital	507	785	771	440

Capitalization

	1997	1994	1991	1988
Cash & Equivalents	113	109	64	9
Subordinated Debt	594	818	846	447
Other Indebtedness	1,131	1,157	2,803	136
Total Debt	4,351	4,745	4,174	781
Preferred Stock	115	115	31	0
Total Debt + Preferred	4,466	4,860	4,205	781

Competitive Analysis

Inventory Turnover

Ticker Symbol	1997	1994	1991	1988
STO	5.584	6.556	5.459	7.687
BCC	7.560	7.938	6.937	7.696
CDP	7.332	7.954	7.082	9.349
GP	7.522	8.148	7.516	8.610
MEA	7.606	8.726	8.128	9.760

SGA/Sales

	1997	1994	1991	1988
STO	0.117	0.099	0.097	0.094
BCC	0.126	0.081	0.104	0.089
CDP	0.050	0.062	0.071	0.054
GP	0.088	0.090	0.094	0.066
MEA	0.116	0.119	0.139	0.126

Operating Income/Sales

	1997	1994	1991	1988
STO	0.044	0.107	0.100	0.204
BCC	0.066	0.084	0.049	0.185
CDP	0.201	0.209	0.232	0.295
GP	0.094	0.139	0.111	0.151
MEA	0.110	0.087	0.108	0.123

Gross Margin

	1997	1994	1991	1988
STO	16.075	20.603	19.759	29.809
BCC	19.243	16.584	15.321	27.359
CDP	25.123	27.119	30.245	34.898
GP	18.160	22.892	20.531	21.727
MEA	22.565	20.621	24.633	24.889

Operating Performance Ratios

	1997	1994	1991	1988
EBITDA/Sales	0.044	0.107	0.100	0.204
EBITDA/Assets	0.036	0.088	0.078	0.318
FCF/Sales	-0.030	0.005	-0.125	0.078
FCF/Assets	-0.025	0.004	-0.097	0.121
Gross Margin	0.161	0.206	0.198	0.298
SG&A/Sales	0.117	0.099	0.097	0.094
Net Profit Margin	-8.340	-2.241	-0.912	9.133
ROE	-254.787	-26.430	-3.193	32.136
ROA	-7.083	-2.011	-0.711	14.271
Inventory Turnove	5.584	6.556	5.459	7.687
Days Sales in Rec.	49.130	52.350	43.501	42.973
Sales/Assets	0.833	0.821	0.780	1.563

Capital Structure & Liquidity Ratios

	1997	1994	1991	1988
Assets/Equity	21.033	10.808	4.401	2.252
LT	7.767	5.643	5.252	1.740
LT Debt/Equity	14.213	6.838	2.580	0.719
LT Debt/EBITDA	18.520	7.192	7.478	1.004
(EBITDA-Capx)/I	0.165	0.833	0.232	5.627
EBITDA/Interest	0.462	1.338	1.129	6.855
Current Ratio	1.465	1.761	1.842	2.032
Acid Test Ratio	0.703	0.905	0.772	1.054
FCF/LT Debt	-0.038	0.007	-0.166	0.379
Funds Flow	-1.825	-0.024	0.508	3.191

Source: Compustat Research Insight, Milken Institute

The company disposed of some of its debt by selling $330.4 million in noncore assets, and management was confident that it would be able to pay off the rest of the debt after paper prices bounced back. Yet paper prices continued to drop dramatically (it would take them almost four years to recover), leading to the first ever successive years of reduced brown paper prices. Unexpectedly, newsprint prices declined as well. Unlike previous acquisitions, the CB purchase was at the midpoint of the paper price cycle. All the while, the U.S. economy was on the verge of a recession and the high yield bond market was collapsing.

In October 1990 the company's stock price fell to $8.50 from its 1988 high of $39.50. The company had sufficient cash flow to meet its obligations, yet deteriorating newsprint and brown paper prices caused investors to worry about Stone's $3.6 billion debt. The following year the company was forced to renegotiate with its financiers, issue new equity, and sell senior notes in order to decrease its acquisition debt. With sales of $5.38 billion, the firm lost $49.1 million.

By 1993, Stone was the world's largest manufacturer of containerboard for shipping boxes and was a major manufacturer of paper bags, newsprint, white papers, and wood products. Yet the company's debt was increasing and it was on the verge of bankruptcy. In that year alone Stone's cash flow fell short of annual interest costs by over $200 million, and $800 million in debt was coming due within a year. As a result, management did a $750 million refinancing that included the issuance of about $500 million in stock, cutting the Stone family's company ownership to 15 percent. To make matters worse, news of this dilutive offering sent the company's shares on a 67.3 percent decline to a low of $6.375 a share.

In 1994, the company's fortunes were changing. With the rising prices of linerboards, newsprint, and pulp, Stone was able to turn a profit. But if the company was to reverse its misfortune, it had to pay upcoming debt maturities. This was made possible by the resurgence of the high yield securities market.

Use of High Yield Bonds

In 1992, with the high yield market beginning to reemerge, Stone started to do small refinancings using convertible, exchangeable preferred stock and interest rate swaps. The deals were expensive, with coupons of 10.75 percent to 11 percent, yet they allowed the company to raise $475 million in much-needed cash. The following year, under extreme pressure from creditors, the company issued $150 million in convertible bonds, with coupons of 12.625 percent and a conversion rate of $11.55 per share.[4] In July of that year the company's bond rating was reduced from B to B– (table 9-2).

A mere two years later, during the company's transition year, Stone investors bought over $1.66 billion in newly issued Stone high yield bonds, and the company's stock price rose over 80 percent. This allowed it to refinance over $2 billion in debt, though it involved paying up to 11.5 percent in annual interest. The company still had over $4 billion in debt, yet it now had no major maturities due in the following three years. Finally, despite the company's aforementioned sizable new debt issuances, Stone's bond rating was upgraded to B+ in June 1995.

Growth after the Mid-1990s

The year 1995 was the best in Stone's history, with sales of $7.3 billion (up 27.8 percent from the previous year) and $444 million in net income (from a loss of $128 million the year before). That year Stone-Consolidated, a subsidiary of Stone, merged with Toronto-based Rainy River Forest Products. This provided Stone with three North American paper mills and access to the output of a fourth mill, which was also part of Stone-Consolidated's

4. During 1993, the company's stock price ranged from $7.125 to $16.00 (based on end of month prices).

Table 9-2. Stone Container Bonds

						Rating Changes					
Amount of Issue (MM)	Year of Issue	Description	Due Year	Company Issuing	Initial Rating	May-88 ↑	Aug-90 ↓	Dec-92 ↓	Jul-93 ↓	Jun-95 ↑	Apr-97 ↓
350	1985	SubNts 13 5/8	1995	Stone Container	B	BB–	B+	B	B–	Mat.	
230	1989	SrSubNts 11.5	1999	Stone Container	BB–		B+	B	B–	B	
240	1991	Sr Nts 11 7/8	1998	Stone Container	BB			BB–	B	B+	B
115	1992	6 3/4	2007	Stone Container	N/A						
200	1992	Sr Sub deb 10.75	2002	Stone Container	B+			B	B–	B	B–
150	1992	Sr Sub Nts 10.75	1997	Stone Container	B+			B	B–	B	Mat.
125	1992	Sr Sub Ns 11	1999	Stone Container	B+			B	B–	B	B–
150	1993	Sr Nts 12 5/8	1998	Stone Container	B+				B	B+	B
710	1994	Sr Nts 9 7/8	2001	Stone Container	B					B+	B
200	1994	Sr Nts 11 1/2	2004	Stone Container	B					B+	B
500	1994	1st Mtg Nts 10 3/4	2002	Stone Container	B+					BB–	B+
250	1994	8 7/8	2000	Stone Container	N/A						
125	1996	Sr Nts 11 7/8	2016	Stone Container	BB–						B
200	1996	11 1/2	2006	Stone Container	B						
275	1997	Sr Sub deb 10.75	2002	Stone Container	B–						
750	2001	9 3/4	2011	Stone Container	B						
300	2001	9 1/4	2008	Stone Container	B						
750	2001	9 3/4	2011	Stone Container	B						

Source: Moody's Investors Service, Bloomberg, Milken Institute

mill system, making Stone the world's largest marketer of newsprint and groundwood paper. In addition, Stone expanded its international exposure by purchasing voting control of Venepal, the largest producer of pulp, paper, and paper products in Venezuela.[5]

In 1996, Stone Container and Box USA purchased the assets of St. Joe Forest Products, which consisted of a 500,000 ton per year pulp and paper mill producing kraft and mottled linerboard, for $215 million. The joint venture company, based in Port St. Joe, Florida, was named Florida Coast Paper.

In 1997 Stone experienced a net loss of $404 million after a $122 million loss in 1996 due to industrywide overproduction, which led to continued paper price reductions. In November of the following year, Stone and Jefferson Smurfit merged to form Smurfit-Stone Container, the world's largest paper-packaging company. The combined Smurfit-Stone was 32 percent controlled by the Smurfit Group of Ireland, which merged its U.S. unit with Stone as a separate U.S.-based company.

Within a week of the deal acceptance, the merged company began capacity-cutting measures by closing four paper mills and making cuts in joint-venture mills. As a result, overall capacity was reduced by about 1.8 million tons annually (about 5 percent of total U.S. capacity). Smurfit-Stone also sold $2 billion of timberland and other assets to pay down its debt.

High Yield Bonds, Yet Again

Interestingly, high yield bonds played a crucial role in Stone's merger with Jefferson Smurfit. Initially, the two companies were reportedly planning to raise $4.8 billion of new bank debt and sell $750 million of high yield bonds. The proceeds would then allow them to pay down old debt and retire outstanding higher yielding bonds. Yet in September 1998 the high yield market was essentially closed and such a billion-dollar bank financing would have been extremely costly. Indeed, news of these circumstances led to a decline in Stone's bonds (for fear that the deal would fall apart), which in turn made the potential offering even more costly for Stone and thus further decreased the likelihood that the deal could be completed. The problem was solved through a restructuring of the deal between the companies, according to which Stone would become a sister organization to Jefferson Smurfit rather than a subsidiary of the company. As a result, both companies were able to maintain their debt. The new bank financing was then reduced to $550 million, about $300 million of which would be used as an equity infusion to Stone.

Conclusion

Stone Container's 1989 acquisition of Consolidated-Bathurst brought the company to near bankruptcy at a time of successive years of low paper prices and upcoming debt maturities. The extent of Stone's debt was not the main cause of the company's financial troubles. Instead, its difficulty

5. The purchase was made as a joint venture with Onofre Group.

in obtaining access to capital was. Previously, the company had been able to refinance its debts and thus maintain growth through cyclical industry downturns. Yet in the early 1990s, with the high yield securities market in shambles and the economy in recession, such funds were unavailable. As a result, Stone management had difficulty obtaining the funds necessary to refinance or pay off maturing debts. It is this problem—the lack of access to capital—that almost led to the company's demise. With this in mind, the recovery of the high yield securities market had a tremendous impact on the company's ability to remain solvent and to continue its growth.

MCCAW CELLULAR

Seattle-based McCaw Cellular experienced stellar growth as it built the nation's largest cellular telephone operation. The company's seamless network, providing cellular phone service primarily under the name Cellular One, reported $2.2 billion in sales during fiscal 1993, an increase of more than 25 percent over its previous fiscal year. The following year McCaw was acquired by AT&T for $12.6 billion. This acquisition made Craig McCaw, the company's visionary founder and CEO, a billionaire.

The story of McCaw Cellular is one of foresight and vision. Management's ability to understand the unmet needs of potential consumers helped McCaw grow to become a multibillion-dollar empire—the country's predominant cellular presence—in less than two decades. To understand this great success story, we must first understand the background and vision of its influential founder.

Forming the Company

The second of four brothers, Craig McCaw grew up in an entrepreneurial environment. His father, John Elroy McCaw, made his living buying and selling radio and TV stations, and cable systems. His mother was one of the first women to earn an accounting degree at the University of Washington.

In 1966, when Craig was sixteen, his father sold him and his brothers a small cable system in Centralia, Washington. Rather than receiving cash for the 2,000 subscriber system, John accepted preferred stock in the company from his sons. Three years later Craig McCaw, then a sophomore history student at Stanford, was running the cable company from his dorm room (along with operating a small aircraft leasing firm and attempting to take over the university's vending machine business). Craig McCaw acquired additional cable companies by using his father's strategy of securing loans against the company's existing business. He then increased the value of these companies by slashing costs, improving programming, and raising subscription fees.

Rapid Expansion

In 1981, McCaw received funding from Affiliated Publications (owner of the *Boston Globe*) to purchase cable systems in return for equity in McCaw.

Affiliated, which initially had a $12 million stake in the project, eventually raised its contribution to $85 million, resulting in Affiliated's owning 43 percent of McCaw.

Although at the time McCaw was undergoing rapid growth in its cable TV business, the company was about to undergo significant redirection in its expansion strategy as Craig McCaw began to realize the explosive growth potential of cellular technology. In 1981, with a mere $5 million in revenues, McCaw reassessed projections filed by AT&T with the Federal Communications Commission (FCC) that forecast only 900,000 cellular subscribers by the year 2000. These projections seemed ridiculously low to McCaw, so he began to turn his attention toward this market. In 1983, the company applied for and was granted licenses in six of the top thirty U.S. markets. In fact, by 1993 there were already 10 million cellular subscribers in the United States, and in 2000 the number of U.S. cellular phone users surpassed 100 million.

At that time AT&T could have been America's cellular service provider without paying a dime for franchises. During the Bell breakup, the FCC would have given the company these licenses for free. But AT&T did not care about the technology in its preoccupation with getting into the computer business, in which it would ultimately lose billions of dollars. Instead, the licenses went to the "Baby Bells" and independent companies such as McCaw. Thus AT&T's shortsightedness led to McCaw's fortune. Ironically, ten years later AT&T would pay a fortune to purchase McCaw and gain access to the cellular market that it passed up in 1983.

At the time of McCaw's license purchases the company was saddled with substantial debt from its cable companies and undeveloped demand for cellular phones, which at that time retailed for over $2,000 each. Yet management persisted in the belief that the low cost of licensing and the technology's extreme growth potential made for a tremendous business opportunity.

McCaw purchased the cellular licenses for about $4.50 per pop (per person in the market). Based on the numbers in the AT&T report, McCaw management calculated that the company could be profitable at $80 per pop, and thus the licenses were worth far more than their cost at the time. McCaw turned to bankers to request a loan, using the licenses as collateral. He explained the value of these licenses and the potential growth of the cellular market. The bankers agreed.

Use of High Yield Bonds

McCaw had succeeded in obtaining bank loans. Yet this money would not be sufficient to fuel the rapid expansion that was required if the company was to achieve its plan of creating several clusters of seamless cellular networks within the United States. This expansion would require purchasing additional licenses in areas adjacent to markets in which McCaw was already licensed. Such purchases required significant capital, which McCaw managed to raise primarily through selling company-owned licenses in markets that were remote from the clusters and through alternative sources of funding, chief of which was the high yield bond market.

McCaw raised $150 million in high yield securities in 1986, followed by a further $600 million in 1987 and $515 million in 1988. The coupon rates on all the securities the company issued were in the range of 12.95 percent to 14 percent.[6] The company's Moody's bond rating was CCC, suggesting that it was considered an extremely risky investment. However, the bonds were instrumental in the company's growth, and as a result of the purchases they funded, the company was able to access further capital and receive a slight rating upgrade in 1990 (changed to CCC+).

In total, the company raised $1.3 billion in high yield bonds between 1986 and 1988. It used the proceeds of these issues to fund internal growth and acquire additional companies.

Building the Nation's Largest Cellular Network

McCaw Cellular had its big break in 1986 when it succeeded in acquiring the cellular business of MCI for $120 million. A year later, McCaw bought the Washington Post Co.'s cellular business in Miami for $240 million and purchased a stake in Metro Mobile CTS. By 1988, McCaw would be the largest cellular telephone operator in the country, with 132,000 subscribers as a result of acquiring adjacent clusters of companies. However, the company's purchasing spree was taking a toll as its debt load increased to over $1.8 billion.

McCaw reduced the company's mounting debt in 1987 by selling its cable business, which by then had 434,000 subscribers, for $755 million. McCaw also offered 12 percent of McCaw Cellular (into which McCaw's cable-centered company merged) to the public. Around that time the Baby Bells began to realize the potential for cellular growth, and they started to buy independent cellular licenses. By then, however, McCaw had already secured licenses in many of the major cities. This allowed McCaw to use the Baby Bells as a source of financing, selling them cellular companies in areas that were not part of the firm's cluster plan and using the money to purchase companies whose licenses were in areas that fit McCaw's strategy.

In 1989, Affiliated distributed its stake in McCaw directly to its shareholders in a tax-free transaction. That year, as McCaw's debt approached 87 percent of its capital, the company sold a 22 percent stake to British Telecom, receiving $1.2 billion in fresh equity, and announced the sale of its southeastern cellular systems to Contel. That same year, McCaw outbid BellSouth for LIN Broadcasting, with licenses in New York, Los Angeles, Houston, and Dallas. McCaw paid $3.4 billion for the company, at the time an astonishing price of $350 per pop.

In 1991, McCaw reduced its debt by selling BellSouth cellular interests in eighteen midwestern markets in a deal valued at $410 million. The deal

6. One exception to this generalization was a 1988 issuance of $115 million in convertible senior debentures with a coupon rate of 8 percent.

also gave McCaw 100 percent of a Milwaukee mobile phone system. That same year McCaw sold to PacTel (a subsidiary of Pacific Telesis) its cellular properties in Wichita and Topeka for $100 million. As part of the deal the two companies agreed to combine their cellular systems in San Francisco, San Jose, Dallas, and Kansas City.

In November 1992, AT&T agreed to acquire 33 percent of McCaw Cellular for $3.73 billion. The deal involved AT&T paying $100 million for a seven-year option to buy out Craig McCaw's voting power, which would cost AT&T an additional $600 million. Moreover, McCaw agreed to convert his Class B supervoting stock shares to ordinary Class A shares if AT&T bought out the company. Negotiations stalled, however, over the issue of how to divide up strategic decisions and future profits. AT&T acquired all of McCaw Cellular's shares in 1993 for $12.6 billion in stock, an acquisition that provided AT&T with a 20 percent share in an industry that was growing at an annual rate of 35 percent. After the merger, McCaw became known as the AT&T Wireless Communications Services Division.

Financially, the purchase proved profitable even in the short term. Although McCaw Cellular's net income was negative, the company had solid profitability on an operating basis (table 9-3). The main cause for the company's loss was the interest payments on its $4.9 billion debt. With AT&T's ability to refinance McCaw's debt at investment grade interest rates, the new subsidiary would increase AT&T's earnings.

Conclusion

In today's information-intensive and extremely liquid market, the entrepreneur's ability to create value depends on his/her gaining some advantage over the competition in terms of proprietary information or a better understanding of consumer needs. McCaw's ability to become the largest cellular phone operator in the country was built on precisely this kind of advantage.

At a time when competitors viewed cellular technology as cumbersome and of limited usefulness, Craig McCaw had the vision to see that this technology would take off in the near future. His willingness to put his company on the line to ensure that it would have a dominant presence in the industry, and his ability to convince bankers of the technology's growth potential, led to McCaw Cellular having the resources to become a dominant force in the industry. With the initial infusion of capital, McCaw managed to secure licenses for the overlooked technology and use it, with the help of additional capital raised through the high yield market, to become the leader in cellular services (table 9-4). McCaw Cellular is a company that experienced tremendous growth and, as a result, had a tremendous need for access to capital markets. As with other rapidly growing companies in need of significant capital infusions, McCaw did not have the credit rating required for raising capital through "traditional" banking establishments. Consequently, it turned to the high yield securities market to secure the funds, then used them to create a phenomenal return for its stockholders.

Table 9-3. McCaw Cellular Financials

McCaw Cellular Communications

Adjusted Debt/Cap Ratio	Market Cap (in Millions of US$)	Interest Coverage
80	6,257	0.973

Business Description

McCaw Cellular Communications provides cellular mobile telephone service. The company also provides radio common services such as paging, conventional mobile phone and answering services. McCaw's services are provided throughout 12 states. On 9/20/94, McCaw Cellular was acquired by AT&T Corporation

Security Price History

Date	Stock High	Stock Low	Stock Close
1987	26.000	11.000	16.125
1988	28.125	16.250	27.000
1989	47.250	25.750	38.250
1990	38.500	11.000	17.250
1991	30.250	15.000	29.750
1992	36.000	20.250	33.500
1993	57.750	31.500	50.500

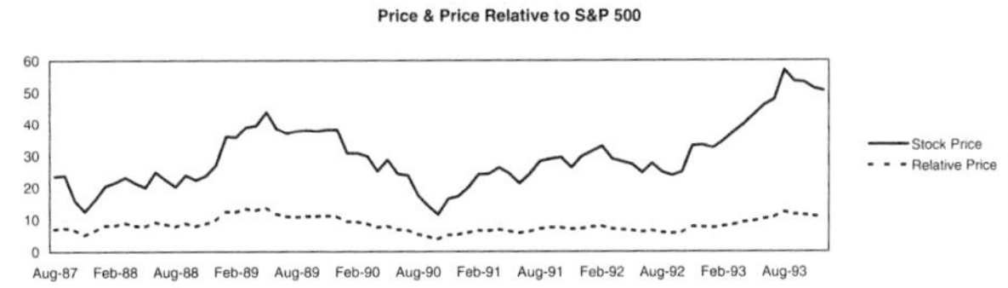

Market Ratios

	1993	1990	1987
P/E Ratio	-76.515	7.099	
Earnings Yld	-0.022	0.111	-0.081
MV/Sales	4.758	2.969	
MV/BV	-275.140	1.506	
MV/EBITDA	17.152	20.307	
Cash Per Share	0.943	2.294	3.764
EPS	-1.120	1.920	-1.310

Interest Coverage Model

Year	EBITDA / Interest	Return on Capital	Leverage
1987	-0.742	-11.400	8.634
1990	0.305	4.528	2.555
1993	1.545	-3.632	-131.642

Free Cash Flow

	1993	1990	1987
EBITDA	609	152	-77
Cash Interest	427	424	0
Taxes Paid	58	73	0
Capex	595	351	115
WC Change	-163	-484	399
Cash Dividends	0	0	0
Total	-309	-212	-592

Financial History

	1993	1990	1987
Income Statement			
Sales	2,195	1,037	150
COGS	1,586	886	111
SG&A			117
EBITDA	609	152	-77
Interest Expense	394	497	104
Taxes	98	315	0
Net Income	-227	562	-134
Balance Sheet			
Cash & Cash Equivaler	197	411	422
Acct. Receivable	363	203	78
Inventory	40	0	10
Intangible Assets			
Total Assets	9,065	8,714	1,333
Current Liabilities - Tot	721	362	132
Long Term Debt	4,990	5,225	1,006
Equity	-38	2,045	117
Working Capital	-91	289	382

Capitalization

	1993	1990	1987
Cash & Equivalents	197	411	422
Subordinated Debt	0	1,137	740
Other Indebtedness	4,990	3,644	280
Total Debt	5,149	5,262	1,020
Preferred Stock	0	0	0
Total Debt + Preferred	5,149	5,262	1,020

Competitive Analysis

Inventory Turnover

Ticker Symbol	1993	1990	1987
MCAWA	52.464		17.435
ROG	9.576	7.036	5.811
TCLB.CM			
MCIC			
USW3			10.518

SGA/Sales

	1993	1990	1987
MCAWA			0.778
ROG	0.207	0.184	0.207
TCLB.CM	0.274	0.196	0.203
MCIC			
USW3			0.330

Operating Income/Sales

	1993	1990	1987
MCAWA	0.277	0.146	-0.514
ROG	0.121	0.081	0.096
TCLB.CM	0.438	0.366	0.376
MCIC	0.199	0.249	0.179
USW3			0.464

Gross Margin

	1993	1990	1987
MCAWA	27.742	14.619	26.379
ROG	32.840	26.526	30.335
TCLB.CM	71.105	56.166	57.898
MCIC	19.881	24.909	17.923
USW3			79.399

Operating Performance Ratios

	1993	1990	1987
EBITDA/Sales	0.277	0.146	-0.514
EBITDA/Assets	0.067	0.017	-0.058
FCF/Sales	-0.141	-0.204	-3.941
FCF/Assets	-0.034	-0.024	-0.444
Gross Margin	0.277	0.146	0.264
SG&A/Sales			0.778
Net Profit Margin	-10.355	35.799	-89.257
ROE	599.625	18.164	-114.945
ROA	-2.507	4.262	-10.050
Inventory Turnov	52.464		17.435
Days Sales in Rec.	60.399	71.446	189.568
Sales/Assets	0.242	0.119	0.113

Capital Structure & Liquidity Ratios

	1993	1990	1987
Assets/Equity	-239.155	4.262	11.437
LT	-54.557	18.081	2.637
LT Debt/Equity	-131.642	2.555	8.634
LT Debt/EBITDA	8.195	34.449	-13.049
(EBITDA-Capx)/I	0.035	-0.402	-1.853
EBITDA/Interest	1.545	0.305	-0.742
Current Ratio	0.873	1.798	3.895
Acid Test Ratio	0.857	1.878	
FCF/LT Debt	-0.062	-0.041	-0.588
Funds Flow		-0.427	

Source: Compustat Research Insight, Milken Institute

VIACOM INCORPORATED

Multimedia giant Viacom is among the largest global entertainment and publishing companies in the world. The company operates numerous subsidiaries in four main areas: networks and broadcasting; entertainment; video, music and theme parks; and publishing. The subsidiaries include such household names as MTV, Nickelodeon, VH1, Showtime and The Movie Channel; the entertainment giant Paramount Pictures; the video and music retail chain Blockbuster; and Paramount Parks, which owns and operates five theme parks and a water park. The company's publishing group includes publishers such as Simon & Schuster, Macmillan, and Prentice-Hall. The story of Viacom's growth, from a medium-size cable operator to the second largest media company in the world, is inseparably tied to its senior management's growth strategy and its means of obtaining the funds required to remain in operation.

Table 9-4. McCaw Cellular Bonds

Amount of Issue (MM)	Year of Issue	Description	Year Due	Company Issuing	Initial Rating	Rating Change Apr-90 –	Notes
150	1986	Sr Sub Notes 13	1996	McCaw Cellular	B3/NR		Called in 7/1/89
600	1987	Sr Sub Deb 12.95s	1999	McCaw Cellular	CCC	CCC+	
400	1988	Sr Sub Deb 14s	1998	McCaw Cellular	CCC	CCC+	
115	1988	Conv Sr Debs 8	2008	McCaw Cellular	N/A		
285	1992	Conv Sr Sub discount debs 11.5	2008	McCaw Cellular	N/A		

Source: Moody's Investors Service, Bloomberg, Milken Institute

Company Growth

Viacom was formed in 1970 by CBS in an effort to comply with an FCC ruling that barred TV networks from owning cable stations and TV stations in the same market. The following year the company became a formally independent entity as CBS distributed Viacom stock to CBS shareholders at the rate of one Viacom share for every seven shares of CBS stock. At that time, Viacom had about 90,000 cable subscribers and annual revenues of $19.8 million, making it one of the largest cable operators in an extremely fragmented U.S. cable market. In 1973, there were about 2,800 cable systems in operation that served a total of about 7.5 million subscribers. Viacom also owned several syndicated CBS television series that were extremely popular, including *I Love Lucy*, which accounted for a sizable percentage of Viacom's income.

Viacom established the Showtime movie network in 1976 to broadcast feature films recently released in theaters, in order to compete with Home Box Office (HBO). Viacom and Warner Amex co-owned this venture, each having a 50 percent interest in the network. The following year, Showtime began transmitting its programming to local cable stations via satellite at a cost of $1.2 million a year. In its first year of operation the station lost $825,000 despite a federal ruling that removed many restrictions on the choice of movies and sports available on pay TV. Still, Viacom's other divisions made up for the loss, resulting in the company's earning $5.5 million on sales of $58.5 million. Most of these earnings represented sales of television shows, but they also reflected the growth of Viacom's cable systems, which by this time had about 350,000 subscribers.

In the early 1980s Viacom began to expand rapidly across a range of media categories. In pursuing this growth strategy, Viacom looked to different channels of communications and entertainment. In 1981 it bought Chicago radio station WLAK-FM for $8 million and took a minority stake in Cable Health Network, a new advertiser-supported cable service. It also bought Video Corp. for $16 million; the company's video production equipment could potentially save Viacom millions on production costs.

By 1982, Showtime had 3.4 million subscribers, earning about $10 million on sales of $140 million (table 9-5). At the same time Viacom had sales of about $210 million and syndication still accounted for 45 percent of the company's profits. However, the growth rate of the company's syndication was declining and that of cable was increasing. In 1982, Viacom was the ninth largest cable operator in the United States, with 540,000 subscribers.

In 1984, however, pay TV's popularity began to decline and growth in the industry was virtually halted. That year Showtime became a sister station to Warner Amex's The Movie Channel in a move to increase revenues for both channels. HBO and its sister channel, Cinemax, were being offered on 5,000 of the 5,800 cable systems in the United States, while Showtime and The Movie Channel were available on a mere 2,700. That year Viacom earned $30.9 million with sales of $320 million.

Table 9-5. Viacom Financials

Viacom Incorporated

Adjusted Debt/Cap Ratio	Market Cap (in Millions of US$)	Interest Coverage
18	67,481	2.456

Business Description

The Company (together with its subsidiaries and divisions) is a diversified entertainment and publishing company with operations in four segments: (i) Networks and Broadcasting, (ii) Entertainment, (iii) Video and Music/Theme Parks, and (iv) Publishing. Through the Networks and Broadcasting segment, Co. opertaes MTV: MUSIC TELEVISION, SHOWTIME, NICKELODEON / NICK AT NITE and VH1 MUSIC FIRST, among other program services, and 11 broadcast stations. Through the Entertainment segment, which includes PARAMOUNT PICTURES and the Co.'s approximately 75%-owned subsidiary SPELLING ENTERTAINMENT GROUP, INC> ("SPELLING"), Co. produces and distributes theatrical motion pictures and television programming. Through the Video and Music/Theme Parks segment, which includes the BLOCKBUSTER family of businesses and PARAMOUNT PARKS, Co. owns, operates and videocassette rantal and sales stores worldwide and owns and operates music stores in the U.S. In addition, PARAMOUNT PARKS owns and operates five theme parks and one water park in the U.S. and Canada. Through the publishing segment, which includes SIMON & SCHUSTER, MACMILLAN PUBLISHING USA and PRENTICE HALL, Co. publishes and distributes educational, consumer, business, technical and professional books, and audio-video software products.

Security Price History

Date	Stock High	Stock Low	Stock Close
1991	17.438	11.438	17.063
1992	20.938	13.500	20.938
1993	30.625	17.625	22.438
1994	22.500	10.875	20.375
1995	27.125	20.125	23.688
1996	23.813	14.875	17.438
1997	21.125	12.625	20.719
1998	37.125	20.250	37.000
1999	60.438	35.375	60.438
2000	75.875	44.312	46.750

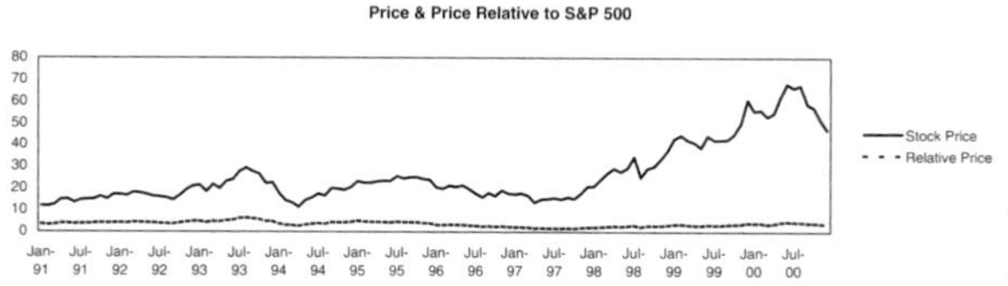

Market Ratios

	2000	1997	1994	1991
P/E Ratio	-292.188	-73.995	69.068	-34.821
Earnings Yld	-0.006	0.021	0.006	-0.012
MV/Sales	3.534	1.088	1.973	2.397
MV/BV	1.477	1.179	1.372	5.865
MV/EBITDA	16.696	9.462	17.626	10.731
Cash Per Share	0.625	0.420	0.833	0.119
EPS	-0.300	0.445	0.125	-0.205

Financial History

	2000	1997	1994	1991
Income Statement				
Sales	20,044	13,206	7,363	1,712
COGS	11,707	9,041	4,651	854
SG&A	4,094	2,647	1,888	476
EBITDA	4,243	1,518	824	382
Interest Expense	822	782	536	299
Taxes	730	690	280	42
Net Income	-364	375	131	-47
Balance Sheet				
Cash & Cash Equivaler	935	292	598	29
Acct. Receivable	3,964	2,398	1,639	323
Inventory	1,402	2,253	1,818	0
Intangible Assets	62,004	14,700	16,112	2,282
Total Assets	82,646	28,289	28,274	4,188
Current Liabilities - Tot	7,758	5,053	4,131	876
Long Term Debt	12,474	7,423	10,402	2,321
Equity	47,967	13,384	11,792	699
Working Capital	74	661	1,124	-158

Capitalization

	2000	1997	1994	1991
Cash & Equivalents	935	292	598	29
Subordinated Debt	704	646	633	1,047
Other Indebtedness	0	0	0	0
Total Debt	12,698	7,800	10,423	2,321
Preferred Stock	0	1,200	1,200	0
Total Debt + Preferred	12,698	9,000	11,623	2,321

Interest Coverage Model

Year	EBITDA / Interest	Return on Capital	Leverage
1991	1.280	-1.541	3.318
1994	1.537	0.250	0.882
1997	1.942	1.512	0.555
2000	5.160	-0.539	0.260

Competitive Analysis

Inventory Turnover

Ticker Symbol	2000	1997	1994	1991
VIA.B	6.965	3.935	5.117	
DIS	3.923		10.403	15.096
FOX	2.140			
SNE	7.511	4.177	3.879	3.426
3260B	6.331	5.163		

SGA/Sales

	2000	1997	1994	1991
VIA.B	0.204	0.200	0.256	0.278
DIS				
FOX	0.118	0.115		
SNE		0.200	0.235	0.241
3260B	0.183	0.218		

Operating Income/Sales

	2000	1997	1994	1991
VIA.B	0.212	0.115	0.112	0.223
DIS	0.292	0.396	0.339	0.291
FOX	0.128	0.086		
SNE	0.082	0.110	0.091	0.131
3260B	0.368	0.249		

Gross Margin

	2000	1997	1994	1991
VIA.B	41.592	31.538	36.837	50.129
DIS	29.159	39.616	33.931	29.092
FOX	24.531	20.181		
SNE	8.183	30.959	32.595	37.156
3260B	55.128	46.669		

Free Cash Flow

	2000	1997	1994	1991
EBITDA	4,243	1,518	824	382
Cash Interest	651	792	294	234
Taxes Paid	61	111	135	21
Capex	659	530	365	57
WC Change	-725	-788	-597	-13
Cash Dividends	0	60	73	0
Total	3,596	813	555	83

Operating Performance Ratios

	2000	1997	1994	1991
EBITDA/Sales	0.212	0.115	0.112	0.223
EBITDA/Assets	0.051	0.054	0.029	0.091
FCF/Sales	0.179	0.062	0.075	0.048
FCF/Assets	0.044	0.029	0.020	0.020
Gross Margin	0.416	0.315	0.368	0.501
SG&A/Sales	0.204	0.200	0.256	0.278
Net Profit Margin	-1.815	2.836	1.772	-2.720
ROE	-0.758	2.581	0.524	-6.656
ROA	-0.440	1.112	0.196	-1.112
Inventory Turnove	6.965	3.935	5.117	
Days Sales in Rec.	72.187	66.269	81.237	68.814
Sales/Assets	0.243	0.467	0.260	0.409

Capital Structure & Liquidity Ratios

	2000	1997	1994	1991
Assets/Equity	1.723	2.114	2.398	5.988
LT	168.111	11.230	9.255	-14.715
LT Debt/Equity	0.260	0.555	0.882	3.318
LT Debt/EBITDA	2.940	4.889	12.621	6.070
(EBITDA-Capx)/I	4.358	1.264	0.856	1.088
EBITDA/Interest	5.160	1.942	1.537	1.280
Current Ratio	1.010	1.131	1.272	0.820
Acid Test Ratio	0.631	0.532	0.541	0.401
FCF/LT Debt	0.288	0.110	0.053	0.036
Funds Flow				0.960

Source: Compustat Research Insight, Milken Institute

In September 1985, Viacom purchased MTV Networks and the remaining 50 percent interest in Showtime from Warner Communications. MTV Networks included MTV, a popular music and video channel; Nickelodeon, a channel geared toward children; and VH-1, a music video channel geared toward an older audience than that of MTV. As part of the deal, Viacom paid Warner $500 million in cash and $18 million in stock warrants. Viacom also offered $33.50 a share for the one-third of the publicly held MTV shares. Again, these purchases increased Viacom's debt load.

Viacom quickly revamped Nickelodeon, which had previously not achieved any notable success, giving it the slick and flashy look of MTV and unique programming that both appealed to children and distinguished the network from competitors. Viacom also introduced "Nick at Night," a block of classic sitcoms aired late in the evening, popular among an adult audience. These changes resulted in Nickelodeon's moving from being the least popular to the most popular channel on basic cable within a few years. Meanwhile, Showtime was deteriorating financially, losing an average of about 25,000 customers per month.

Weakened by the $2 billion debt load it incurred, Viacom lost $9.9 million on sales of $919.2 million in 1986, and the company became a takeover target. First Carl Icahn made an attempt to buy the company, and then a management buyout led by Terrence Elkes failed. Finally, in March 1986, after a six-month battle, Sumner M. Redstone, president of the National Amusements movie theater chain, bought Viacom for about $3.4 billion. Viacom was reincorporated in Delaware on November 10, 1986.

In an effort to return the company to profitability and turn Showtime around, Redstone brought in Frank Biondi, former chief executive of HBO, who began reorganizing the company's divisions. Biondi, in turn, brought in HBO executive Winston Cox to run the network, and Cox immediately doubled Showtime's marketing budget. Showtime also obtained exclusive contracts with Paramount Pictures and Walt Disney Films, which included the rights to air seven of the top ten films of 1986. By 1987, Redstone had purchased 83 percent of Viacom's stock for $3.4 billion.

At the time the company was in financial turmoil. Its Showtime continued to lose money, the company as a whole was in the red, and the company's high leverage created a need for cash, with $450 million in interest coming due within the next two years. In order to produce the cash required to service Viacom's debt load, and to resume company growth, Viacom management turned to the securities markets. In 1987 the company issued $399 million in bonds, followed by an additional $500 million the following year (table 9-6). In March 1989 the company's S&P debt rating was increased from B– to B, and that year the company issued a further $449 million in securities. These bond issuances allowed Redstone to pay off the $450 million in interest that was demanded by his banks in the two years following the takeover, to increase the company's marketing budget, and to fund its operations.

Recovery in the Late 1980s

In addition to the money raised by issuing debt, Viacom enjoyed unexpected revenue streams related to its operations. Shortly after the buyout, Viacom began to earn millions of dollars from television stations wanting to air reruns of *The Cosby Show*. Furthermore, when Congress deregulated cable in 1987, prices for cable franchises soared. Thus, Redstone could sell some of Viacom's assets for a sizable profit to help pay off its debt.

In February 1989, Viacom sold a couple of its cable systems to Cablevision Systems for $545 million. Cablevision also bought 5 percent of Showtime for $25 million, giving it a stake in the channel's success. Moreover, MTV experienced continued growth, fueled by Redstone's restructuring of the division and increasing its focus on sales and marketing. At the time, MTV was expanding throughout the world, broadcasting to Western Europe, Japan, Australia, and large portions of Latin America, with plans to con-

Table 9-6. Viacom Bonds

						Rating Changes			
Amount of Issue (MM)	Year of Issue	Description	Year Due	Company Issuing	Initial Rating	Jul-94 ↓	May-95 ↑	Jul-00 ↑	Apr-01 ↑
1,000	1995	Sr Nts 7.75	2005	Viacom	BBB–			BBB+	A–
350	1995	Sr Nts 6.75	2003	Viacom	BBB–			BBB+	A–
200	1995	Sr deb 7.625	2016	Viacom	BBB–			BBB+	A–
1,650	2000	Sr Nts 7.7	2010	Viacom	BBB+				A–
1,250	2000	Sr deb 7 7/8	2002	Viacom	BBB+				A–
1,000	2001	Sr Sub Nts 6 5/8	2011	Viacom	A–				
800	2001	Sr Sub Nts 6.4	2006	Viacom	A–				
700	2002	5 5/8	2007	Viacom	A–				

Source: Moody's Investors Service, Bloomberg, Milken Institute

tinue its expansion to Eastern Europe, Brazil, Israel, and New Zealand. These successes enabled Redstone and Biondi to significantly cut Viacom's debt by September 1989 and to negotiate more favorable terms on its loans. Even so, Viacom lost $154.4 million in 1987, with revenues of about $1 billion.

Viacom continued to expand its offerings. The company introduced Lifetime, a channel geared toward women, along with Hearst Corporation and Capital Cities/ABC. It also started its own production operations in 1989, Viacom Pictures, which produced about ten feature films that year at an average cost of about $4 million a film. These films initially appeared on Showtime. The company also spent heavily on new and acquired productions for Nickelodeon and MTV.

In October 1989, Viacom sold 50 percent of Showtime to TCI, a cable systems operator with six million subscribers, for $225 million. Viacom hoped the purchase would give TCI an increased incentive to market Showtime, thus giving the network a wider distribution. By the following year, Viacom owned five television stations, fourteen cable franchises, and nine radio stations. In November 1990, the company bought five more radio stations for $121 million. During that year, the company had $1.4 billion in revenues and a net income of $369 million.

In 1989 HBO introduced its Comedy Channel, which led to Viacom's beginning to transmit HA!, a channel similar in format, several months later. Both channels started with subscriber bases in the low millions, and most industry analysts believed that only one of them would survive. Viacom management expected to lose as much as $100 million over a three-year period before HA! broke even. The same year, Showtime filed a $2.4 billion antitrust lawsuit against HBO, alleging that HBO was trying to put Showtime out of business by intimidating cable systems that carried Showtime and by trying to corner the market on Hollywood films to prevent competitors from airing them.

In August 1992, after three years of legal battles costing both sides tens of millions of dollars, the lawsuit was settled out of court. Time Warner agreed to pay Viacom $75 million and buy a Viacom cable system in Milwaukee for $95 million, about $10 million more than its estimated worth at the time. Time Warner also agreed to distribute Showtime and The Movie Channel more widely on Time Warner's cable systems, the second largest in the United States. Furthermore, the two sides agreed to a joint marketing campaign to try to revive the image of cable, which had suffered since deregulation. Also during this time, HBO and Viacom agreed to merge their struggling comedy networks, HA! and the Comedy Channel, into one network called Comedy Central.

By 1993 Viacom was thriving, with revenues of $1.9 billion and net income of $66 million. Nickelodeon, meanwhile, was reaching 57.4 million homes and was watched by more children between ages two and 11 than the children's programming on all four major networks combined.

Redstone next began a company expansion into the motion picture and video rental markets. In July 1994, Viacom purchased Paramount Communications, one of the world's largest and oldest producers of motion pictures and television shows, for $10 billion, 25 percent more than originally planned. The deal, which made Paramount a wholly owned subsidiary of the company, made Viacom the fifth largest media company in the world and lowered its debt rating below investment grade. This acquisition vastly expanded the company's presence in the entertainment business, giving it a motion picture library that included movie classics such as *The Godfather*. This deal also gave Viacom ownership of the prominent book publisher Simon & Schuster. Later that year the company continued its expansion with the $8.4 billion acquisition of Blockbuster Entertainment. Viacom immediately wrote down about $318 million of tape inventory. In helping to finance the deal, the company issued $1.07 billion in bonds rated B by Standard & Poor's.

By February 1995 Viacom had grown to be the No. 2 entertainment company in the world. Yet the acquisition of Paramount and Blockbuster left it in significant debt. In order to relieve some debt and focus the company's energies, Viacom divested several of its businesses, including Madison Square Garden (sold to a partnership of ITT and Cablevision Systems for $1.07 billion). The same year, Viacom issued $1 billion in securities, rated BB+ by Standard & Poor's.

In January 1996, Redstone fired Viacom CEO Frank Biondi. The company also sold its cable systems, in a deal with TCI, to reduce Viacom's debt by $1.7 billion. The company issued $781.4 million in corporate bonds. The next year, Viacom divested its radio broadcasting business by selling ten radio stations to Evergreen Media. The deal, valued at approximately $1.1 billion, reduced Viacom's debt even further. Viacom also adopted a plan to dispose of its interactive game businesses, which included Viacom New Media and Virgin Interactive Entertainment. In October 1997, the company completed the sale of its interest in USA Networks, including the Sci-Fi Channel, to the Seagram Company for $1.7 billion in cash.

Although Viacom was no longer a cable service provider, and had expanded into the motion picture and video rental market, its cable networks remained a significant portion of its business. MTV Networks, which included MTV, Nickelodeon and VH1, accounted for almost $625 million in operating profits in 1997, approximately 32 percent of Viacom's estimated annual earnings.

On October 13, 1998, Viacom's long-term debt was upgraded to investment quality. For Viacom's studio, Paramount, this was a golden year. *Titanic* became the highest-grossing film in history and earned eleven Academy Awards. The company also produced the summer hits *Deep Impact* and *Saving Private Ryan* in a strategic risk-sharing partnership with DreamWorks SKG. The company sold its music retail stores to Wherehouse Entertainment for approximately $115 million in cash.

In November 1998 the company sold its nonconsumer publishing division to Pearson for $4.6 billion. Viacom kept its consumer publishing division, including Simon & Schuster. In June 1999, the company acquired

Spelling Entertainment Group for approximately $176 million. In December of that year the Justice Department announced that it was investigating MTV for alleged antitrust violations. The government was examining the company's business practices, including its requirement that music companies give MTV, MTV2, and VH1 exclusive rights to music videos.

In May 2000, Viacom acquired CBS Corporation in a merger that created the world's second largest media conglomerate behind Time Warner. The largest media merger to date, the $34.8 billion deal was announced about a month after the FCC loosened regulations concerning television station ownership. Two months later the company maintained an equity position of $30 million in World Wrestling Federation Entertainment.

Conclusion

Viacom's Redstone had succeeded, within a few years, in reviving a financially troubled, debt-ridden company and creating a profitable global media giant with programming that appeals to audiences in every demographic category across virtually all distribution of entertainment, news, sports, and music. In doing so, he benefited from the popularity of the company's syndicated programs and changes in governmental regulation. Yet in order to take advantage of these changes, he had to gain access to the cash required for the company's operations. In obtaining these funds the company turned several times to the high yield securities markets. Through the funds made available by these markets the company managed to maintain its media dominance and overcome extended periods of financial distress.

CHRYSLER CORPORATION

Walter Chrysler and His Company

Chrysler Motor Corp. was organized on the last day of 1923. A year and a half later it acquired the stock, assets, and properties of Maxwell Motors. This did not surprise anyone who knew the industry, since at the time Walter Chrysler was CEO of both companies.

By then Walter Chrysler was one of the industry's top executives. After a career as a railroad mechanic, he turned to automobiles in 1912, becoming plant manager for Buick. In two years he raised Buick's output from 40 cars a day to almost 600, and his personal salary grew from $6,000 to $500,000. In addition to heading Buick, he served as GM's executive vice president. Mr. Chrysler quit the company in 1920. After a brief retirement he took over an ailing Willys-Overland, which he nursed back to health, and in 1923 he became CEO at Maxwell, another troubled company.

In 1924 Walter Chrysler brought out the first Chrysler automobile, which borrowed from World War I aircraft in the design of its six-cylinder engine. The car was short, with a wheelbase of 112.75 inches, had a price tag of $1,565, and sold well. At the time, Chrysler was negotiating a $6 million bank loan. He received it with no trouble and set out to expand the company's offerings. The following year Walter Chrysler took over Maxwell and renamed it after himself.

By 1926 Chrysler had four models, the 50, the 60, the 70, and the Imperial 80, the model numbers indicating their top speeds. Chrysler had become the fourth largest automobile company by 1927, with 183,000 cars sold that year.

In 1928 Chrysler purchased Dodge Brothers for $176 million, all of which was in Chrysler common stock.[7] The company then introduced the Plymouth and the De Soto lines. Next came the announcement of the perfection of fluid drive, the first of the semiautomatic transmissions, and Chrysler's intention to construct the tallest building in the nation, the Chrysler Building, on 42nd Street in New York not far from the smaller GM building on Broadway. That year *Time* magazine named Chrysler "Man of the Year."

The Great Depression inflicted grievous harm on the automobile industry. Sales declined from 4.6 million cars in 1929 to 1.6 million cars in 1933. While the rest of the industry was prostrate, Chrysler actually sold more cars in 1933 than in 1929. In 1933 Chrysler's sales surpassed Ford's. At the time Chrysler had no long-term debt, relying solely upon bank loans, of which $19 million was outstanding. Two years later Walter Chrysler retired and was succeeded by his close associate, K. T. Keller. Walter Chrysler died in 1940.

During World War II, Chrysler produced no cars, but rather a wide variety of military products ranging from gyrocompasses to aircraft wings to Sherman tanks. By the end of the war Chrysler's annual sales rose to $994 million. Yet the company's operating profits had declined from $68 million to $55 million. The ratio of current assets to liabilities dropped to 2.4.

Decline

After the war, anticipating a return to the bleak depression, all the established auto companies were content to offer the same kinds of models that they made in the late 1930s, in some cases using the dies that had been stored. Once it became evident there would be no depression, the automakers rapidly redesigned their offerings.

Studebaker came first, in 1947, with its low-slung, "futuristic" Raymond Loewy-designed line. Hudson followed in 1948 with its longer, lower, sleeker cars. This was also the year that the Cadillac tail fins were introduced. In 1949, Ford offered radically redesigned cars and Nash came out with what appeared to be a garish bathtub. Chrysler held back.

The public had different aesthetic ideas, and as Chrysler's sales and market share declined, it became evident that Keller no longer fit in with the times. In 1953, Chrysler fell to third place behind Ford, and would never catch up again. Despite Keller's objections, Lester Colbert, who had become

7. Included was $5 million in Maxwell's 6 percent debentures, which were completely retired in 1935.

company president in 1950, hired the management consultant firm of McKinsey & Co. to make suggestions. The McKinsey report recommended that the authority of the engineering department be curbed and more power be given to the designers. The implementation of these recommendations showed in the 1953 models, which featured "the forward look" fashioned by chief stylist Virgil Exner. The new models were lower and longer than anything Chrysler had ever produced.

The changes were welcomed by the public. Company sales rose in all categories, with those for Plymouth hitting an all-time high. In 1954, Chrysler reported revenues of $2.1 billion and net profit of $20 million. The following year, revenues rose 62 percent, to $3.4 billion, and profits rose more than tenfold, to $224 million. Chrysler's market share expanded from less than 13 percent in 1954 to slightly below 17 percent in 1955.

Yet all of this came at a price. In 1954 Chrysler borrowed $62 million to help pay for the conversion and engineering. By 1957 the company's borrowings reached $250 million. Chrysler was using leverage in ways that Walter Chrysler had shunned. That year was later seen as a turning point for the company. In his attempt to outdo GM, Colbert had his team design models with more powerful engines and the longest, highest, and most bizarre tail fins ever seen. Once the most conservative of the Big Three, Chrysler was now the most flamboyant. Were Chrysler's cars reliable, this might have gone over well, but they were not. Rushed into production, the 1957 offerings had balky engines, leaky bodies, and erratic transmissions. As a result, Chrysler lost market share and money in the next two years.

In 1958 Chrysler took a major share in the French automobile manufacturer Simca, and purchased additional shares in 1963. By 1970, Chrysler would change the company's name to Chrysler France, which would form the foundation for Chrysler's European operations. The introduction of Simca cars was a failure in the American market, however, and in 1968 they were banned from the country for failing to comply with safety standards. Chrysler's buying a share in Britain's Rootes Group was also a failure. In 1960, in a move to meet the perceived interest in small cars, Chrysler introduced the Valiant, which was a success. This car, in addition to GM's Corvair and Ford's Falcon, enabled the Big Three to recapture more of the American market as imports' share of this market fell from 10.1 percent in 1959 to 4.9 percent in 1962. However, this did not suffice to bring Chrysler back to its formerly strong standing among U.S. automobile manufacturers.

Colbert was able to hang on until 1961, when he was replaced as CEO by George Love. But Love, unlike his predecessors, was unable to dominate the company. Rather, the key figure at Chrysler was now COO Lynn Townsend. At the time Chrysler had only 10 percent of the market and its share was slipping. Townsend devoted much of his time to reducing costs, while at the same time spending large amounts of money attempting to restore quality and to design cars that the public wanted. The strategy worked. Chrysler's market share, which had fallen to 8.3 percent in early 1962, rose to 12.4 percent by late 1964. Moreover, the company managed to do this without increasing its debt. By 1967, Chrysler's market share had reached 16 percent with an operating profit of $365 million on sales of $6.2 billion.

Townsend's major legacy at Chrysler had only an indirect relationship to the production of cars and was more associated with their marketing. Ever since 1919 customers had been able to purchase cars with payments over time. That year GM organized General Motors Acceptance Corporation, and several years later Ford reluctantly provided financing through Ford Motor Credit. Chrysler resisted; Walter Chrysler did not believe in consumer debt, but in 1928 he took an equity position in Universal Credit Company and in 1934 purchased a minority position in the Commercial Credit Corporation. This was where matters stood when Townsend arrived.

In 1964, with the creation of Chrysler Credit Corporation (later renamed Chrysler Financial), the company provided funding for dealers and customers. Chrysler Credit would essentially borrow money from banks at low rates, offer car loans to dealers and customers at higher rates, and profit from the difference. Both were important. Since the Chrysler dealer organization by then was not as strong as those of Ford and GM, it had to be assisted, and this was the task of Chrysler Credit. To do so, the company had to acquire the capabilities to provide credit to customers.

Under the leadership of Gordon Areen, Chrysler Credit Corporation purchased Redisco, the financing arm of ailing American Motors, in 1967. The following year it purchased Allied Concord Financial Corporation. The company grew rapidly. In 1965, it earned a mere $5,000 for Chrysler; by 1970 its earnings had expanded to $21.5 million.

When George Love retired in 1967, Townsend became Chrysler's CEO and Virgil Boyd was promoted to president. It was then that Townsend accelerated the company's manufacturing. Obsessed with the desire to increase Chrysler's market share, Townsend had the factories running full blast even though the cars could not be placed with the dealers. Instead, they were stored at various locations until they could be shipped. Meanwhile, there was a continual erosion of Chrysler dealerships. By the end of the decade Chrysler had 4,800 dealerships, compared to 6,700 and 11,500, respectively, for the much larger Ford and GM. Moreover, 600 of the Chrysler dealers handled half the company's sales.

In 1971, Townsend entered into a joint venture with Mitsubishi whereby Chrysler would import Mitsubishi's Colt compact and purchase 35 percent of Mitsubishi's stock. Embarrassingly, Chrysler was unable to come up with the needed cash, and wound up taking merely 15 percent of Mitsubishi's outstanding shares, leading both Japanese and Americans to conclude that Chrysler was on the ropes. By 1970, Chrysler's long-term debt was $791 million and the company's debt to equity ratio had risen from 14 percent in 1960 to 37 percent.

Feeling pressured to dress up the company's balance sheet, Townsend embarked on a cost-cutting program. He laid off 6,000 white collar workers, withdrew from the government's JOBS program (designed to provide work for the unemployed), and cut the company's dividend from $2.00 to

$0.60 per share. Despite these measures the company had to take on an additional $200 million in debt.

While all of this was happening at Chrysler, the entire industry was taking a beating. Environmentalists and their congressional supporters passed legislation to make safer and less polluting cars, which caused increases in manufacturing costs that were difficult to pass on to customers. Then, in 1973 OPEC increased the price of oil, making the large cars Chrysler and the others were producing less desirable. After earning $255 million in 1973, Chrysler lost $52 million in 1974 and $259 million in 1975. The following year, in an attempt to revive its reputation and increase sales, Chrysler offered an extended warranty for its new cars, causing one industry newsman to joke that the cars were to be guaranteed for 12,000 miles or until the company went out of business.

By then Townsend had stepped down as CEO and was succeeded by John Riccardo, while Eugene Cafiero became president. The company had profits of $473 million in 1976–1977, but this was due more to an industrywide bounce back from the horrors of 1974 than to anything Riccardo and Cafiero had done at the company. The following year the company had a loss of $205 million.

In its financial despair, Chrysler had to sell its European operations to Peugot-Citroen for $230 million in stock, abandoning its efforts to become a competitor of GM and Ford in Europe. The company also attempted to sell a majority interest in Chrysler Financial (CFC) for $320 million. It failed to find a buyer despite the fact that the company had a book value of $2.5 billion. In desperation, the board dismissed Cafiero in 1978 and replaced him with Lee Iacocca, who accepted on condition that Riccardo step down on November 1, 1979, and that he then became chairman and CEO.

In the late summer of 1979 it seemed as though Chrysler was headed for bankruptcy, and would be the largest industrial failure since the Penn Central collapse of 1970, due to violations of covenants in lending agreements by Chrysler and CFC. The company had reported a loss of $207 million in the second quarter and conceded that the losses might expand in the third quarter. Chrysler's lead banks were near their legal lending limits, and others were withdrawing from the corporation and its credit arm. Riccardo said that unless the government came up with assistance, in the form of either loans or loan guarantees, potential customers could be frightened and not purchase Chrysler cars, which on bankruptcy might become "orphans." He spoke of assistance at the level of $1 billion.

Lee Iacocca and the Myth of the Chrysler Bailout

No automobile industry figure had a better reputation than Lee Iacocca (except perhaps, Henry Ford II, who had fired him from Ford Motor Company in 1978). In particular, Iacocca was considered a marketing genius. On the day he was named to the Chrysler presidency, the company reported a $159 million loss for the third quarter, yet the company's stock rose 3/8 to close at $10.875.

There was little Iacocca could do with the product strategy that Chrysler had in place at the time. Riccardo and Cafiero had abandoned Townsend's hope to restore Chrysler as a full-line company. According to their plan, by 1982 more than half of Chrysler's output would be four-cylinder small cars with front-mounted transmissions. Iacocca kept the company's Omni / Horizon line—Chrysler's small cars based on the VW Rabbit design—and replaced the Volare / Aspen with the new Reliant / Aries models.

In January 1979, the shah of Iran was forced into exile and replaced by Ayatollah Ruhollah Khomeni. The new government, rabidly anti-American, led OPEC in another round of oil price increases that devastated the automobile industry in much the same way it had in 1973. As it happened, Chrysler's model line was better situated for such times than those of Ford and GM. The only trouble was that the company was unprepared to meet the heightened demand for Horizons and Omnis, with some dealers having to delay sales for as much as three months.

Chrysler's liquidity problem persisted, and by June 1979 it was in the process of firing more than 30 percent of its workforce. The trim plant in Lyons, Michigan, was closed down and the Dodge plant, which was acquired by the company during Walter Chrysler's Dodge takeover, was shuttered as well. By September, Iacocca had shaved $360 million in fixed costs, but, unlike Townsend, he did not cut back on research and development; the assembly line created for the K-cars was one of the most modern in the nation.

Meanwhile, Riccardo was attempting to win banker support for a financial infusion that was not forthcoming. Were Chrysler to go into bankruptcy, there seemed a possibility it would be purchased by Ford, given government approval. In the end, the Chrysler team approached Congress for financial assistance in the form of government loan guarantees. This was hardly a novel idea. Lockheed had received $250 million in government support in the early 1970s. Proponents of the plan highlighted estimates that a Chrysler failure would shave 0.5 percent from GNP, increase the unemployment rate by between 0.5 and 1.09 percent, and have a $1.5 billion negative impact on the balance of trade. Moreover, welfare payments would rise by $1.5 billion and tax receipts would fall by $500 million.

Faced with the potential loss of jobs by more than 100,000 of his union's members, United Auto Workers President Douglas Frazer agreed to concessions of $462.5 million, amounting to $5,000 per hourly worker, making Chrysler the lowest-cost American automobile producer. Further cuts plus a wage freeze followed, and in return Frazer was given a seat on the Chrysler board.

In late 1979 Congress agreed to grant the company $1.5 billion in federal loan guarantees, with the government receiving warrants to purchase 14.4 million shares of Chrysler common stock at $13 per share as a "sweetener." This agreement has been commonly referred to as the government's "bailout" of Chrysler. Yet what history has generally ignored is that the guarantee was contingent on Chrysler's raising *another* $2 billion in capital. Moreover, this capital would have to be subordinate to the government's loan. It is this capital, which Chrysler managed to raise through the issuance of high yield bonds, that in fact kept the company from bankruptcy. It was a more sizable sum than the government's loan and it was a substantially more risky source of finance (given that the government's component was senior to the private component).

In addition to the aforementioned forms of financing, the Canadian government added $100 million in loan guarantees in the hope of saving Chrysler jobs in Canada. French automaker Peugeot-Citroen, which in 1978 had exchanged company shares for Chrysler's France operations, provided an additional $100 million loan secured by that stock. Finally, suppliers granted close to $40 million in concessions.

The more than twenty banks that held over $4 billion in Chrysler's paper had to agree to a loan restructuring, which was part of the deal with the government. The company obtained $1.6 billion in bank credit at a rate that saved the company more than $655 million in interest payments. At the same time CFC, which had dealings with 282 banks that held $2.5 billion in its own paper, received $1.1 billion in receivable purchase agreements from its banks. While some banks had relations with both Chrysler and CFC, many had loaned funds to only one or the other. Under law, national banks were required to consider Chrysler and CFC as a single entity, but state-chartered banks could separate them when calculating legal lending limits. State banks that had loaned to CFC were eager to have it separated from Chrysler. While the car company might easily fall into bankruptcy, CFC was in better shape. Its loans were collateralized by cars on dealers' lots (some $700 million worth of cars and trucks in August 1979) and loans to purchasers.

CFC had just posted earnings of $48.5 million, its best year since 1964. Nonetheless, CFC's credit rating was lowered to below investment grade by Moody's and Standard & Poor's when Chrysler was downgraded due to a credit rating agency policy of not awarding credit arms higher ratings than their parent companies. The change meant that CFC was shut out of the market for prime commercial paper. With the lowered rating, CFC began to have trouble with its lending institutions. Unable to borrow to meet its needs, CFC was obliged to call upon its lines of credit rather than sell commercial paper, a more expensive way of raising money since at the time commercial paper rates were 10.75 percent and bank debt was at 13.5 percent.

As of August 13, 1979, the company's outstanding commercial paper totaled $481 million, down from $1.3 billion at midyear, while its bank loans increased from $420 million on June 30 to $1.16 billion. CFC also sold some $500 million in accounts receivable to Household Finance in exchange for $600 million in CFC's notes, an onerous deal, and another $230 million to GMAC. At that time Chrysler car sales began to pick up and the company's outlook improved. In late August, CFC was able to sell $100 million in two-year commercial paper at 9.625 percent, one of the few Baa offerings that found buyers. By November, CFC received a $1 billion line of credit for the next year.

Chrysler did poorly in 1980, losing $1.7 billion on revenues of $8.6 billion, but CFC did well, showing a small profit and ending the year with $5 billion in assets. Because of this, there was much talk of a possible deal with the banks whereby they would obtain a majority ownership position in this company in return for concessions. However, this plan was not put into operation due to an inability to come to terms. Instead, in 1981 CFC arranged to provide financing services to American Motors and Volkswagen of America, a further sign of revival. That year Chrysler reported another deficit, this time of $476 million. And while the following year was profitable, this was due to the sale of Chrysler's defense operations and a tax loss carryforward. Even so, an improving environment for sales enabled CFC to enter into arrangements with 349 financial institutions to renew $4.2 billion in credit facilities. "These new agreements are evidence of the strengthened confidence in Chrysler throughout the financial community," said Chrysler Vice Chairman Clement Greenwald. "They will provide Chrysler Financial with additional leverage, lower costs for our borrowings, and added operating flexibility."

Revival

Sales continued to boom in 1983, coming in at $13.2 billion with profits at $700 million, enabling the corporation to repay the government loan and making Iacocca a company hero. The signs were there even before the year's results were in. In April, Chrysler purchased an idle VW plant to meet the need for additional capacity, and in August, Iacocca offered to purchase the warrants that the government had received in the loan arrangement for $250 million, even though they were then worth only $187 million. The recovery continued into 1984, when earnings came to a record $2.4 billion, much of which was made possible by the introduction of a highly successful minivan. Iacocca celebrated by having Chrysler purchase a 5 percent stake in Maserati, which was increased to 15.5 percent in 1986. The following year Lamborghini came into the Chrysler fold.

This performance encouraged the parent company to seek additional outlets for CFC. This was a period when the financial arms of several major corporations, including Ford, GM, and General Electric, were entering a wide variety of fields, not only as lenders but also as equity holders. The vibrant area of currency dealings also beckoned, and after 1982 Chrysler executives hinted that they, too, might take the plunge. Robert Baker, who became vice chairman of CFC in 1985, told a reporter that while the automobile financing business was expanding rapidly, the company as exploring "opportunities to offer financing services that would diversify our portfolio." This would not be a new area of opportunity, he said. CFC had been in some of these areas before 1979, but was restricted to automobile financing by covenants in the loan arrangements. Now that the corporation was on a firm financial foundation, the covenants were removed, and CFC was preparing to reenter old areas and find new ones as well.

The move began on May 17, 1986, when CFC announced it was entering into a joint venture with GE Credit to finance real estate, equipment, and machinery purchases. Iacocca made the announcement at the firm's annual meeting, and in response to questions said CFC was considering diversification into financial services and even aerospace. In the past year, he said, CFC had financed 65 percent of dealer purchases and 20 percent of retail purchases. The following month the company reported that it had been granted investment grade ratings by Standard & Poor's and Moody's. Soon after, CFC purchased BankAmerica's consumer finance arm and E.F. Hutton Credit, which were united under the name of Chrysler Capital Corp. These new units, which financed a wide variety of enterprises and investments, taken together with CFC, contributed more than $200 million to Chrysler's earnings. Chrysler saw continued good sales and profits as the domestic automobile industry took larger market share and seemed to have significantly blunted the Japanese onslaught.

More purchases followed, including Gulfstream Aerospace and the Thrifty, Snappy, Dollar, and General car rental companies. Importantly, American Motors (AM) was acquired in 1987 in exchange for 14.9 million shares of common stock, 300,000 shares of a convertible preferred stock, and $200 million in cash. As part of the deal, Chrysler agreed to pay Renault, which had a 46 percent interest in AM, a contingency compensation of up to $350 million, depending upon profitability (table 9-7). That same year, Chrysler purchased Electrospace Systems for $372 million. Soon after, its Jeep Cherokee became the company's leading moneymaker.

Disaster Redux

While the company's outlook seemed quite rosy, underneath the veneer of good news were some major weaknesses. Sales of the company's minivan and Jeep were good, and profit margins were high, yet sales of passenger cars were slipping. The K-Car chassis, developed in the late 1970s, was still in use a decade later. While piling up a large cash position, Iacocca had cut back on product development, relying instead on a joint venture with Mitsubishi (Diamond-Star) according to which Chrysler would sell the Japanese company's automobiles in the United States. He deferred work on a new six-cylinder engine and ended up buying them from Mitsubishi. In 1985, he had restructured Chrysler as a holding company with Motors, CFC, Gulfstream Aerospace, and Technologies as operating subsidiaries. Iacocca placed his second in command, Clement Greenwald, in charge of Chrysler Motors. Later Iacocca admitted this was a mistake. Though a competent second in command, Greenwald lacked the marketing skills for which Iacocca was renowned. "If I made one mistake," he said in 1988, "it was delegating all the product development and not going to a single meeting."

Soon after, he undid the arrangement. Car sales fell in 1989 and 1990, and the Jeep Grand Wagoneer, once a hot seller, was discontinued. Ford rolled out its Explorer, a direct threat to the Jeep Cherokee. Several executives resigned, including Greenwald, Treasurer Frederick Zuckerman, and Michael Hammes, vice president in charge of international operations. This opened the way for the next generation at Chrysler, which included Robert

Table 9-7. Chrysler Financials

Chrysler Corporation	Adjusted Debt/Cap Ratio	Market Cap (in Millions of US$)	Interest Coverage
	44	20,368	2.916

Business Description

Chrysler Corporation and its consolidated subsidiaries ("Chrysler") operate in two principal industry segments: automotive operations and financial services. Automotive operations include the research, design, manufacture, assembly and sale of cars, trucks and related parts and accessories. Financial services include the operations of Chrysler Financial Corporation and its consolidated subsidiaries ("CFC"), which are engaged principally in providing consumer and dealer automotive financing for Chrysler's products. Chrysler also participates in short-term vehicle rental activities through certain of its subsidiaries (the "Car Rental Operations") and engages in aircraft modification and the manufacture of electronics products and systems through its Chrysler Technologies Corporation subsidiary.

Security Price History

Date	Stock High	Stock Low	Stock Close
1988	13.938	10.250	12.875
1989	14.813	9.063	9.500
1990	10.188	4.563	6.313
1991	7.938	4.875	5.875
1992	16.938	5.750	16.000
1993	29.188	15.875	26.625
1994	31.750	21.563	24.500
1995	29.063	19.125	27.563
1996	36.375	25.625	33.000
1997	38.562	28.125	35.187

Price & Price Relative to S&P 500

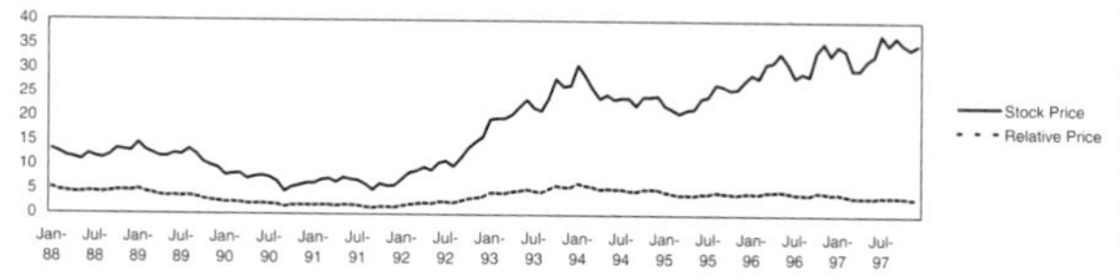

Market Ratios

	1997	1994	1991	1988
P/E Ratio	8.299	5.426	-4.401	
Earnings Yld	0.118	0.206	-0.189	0.181
MV/Sales	0.398	0.342	0.105	
MV/BV	2.053	1.767	0.485	
MV/EBITDA	3.763	2.405	4.113	
Cash Per Share	7.554	7.245	3.491	3.526
EPS	4.150	5.055	-1.110	2.330

Interest Coverage Model

Year	EBITDA/ Interest	Return on Capital	Leverage
1988	2.136	4.612	1.962
1991	0.355	-2.542	2.452
1994	6.484	19.805	0.715
1997	5.163	13.767	0.793

Free Cash Flow

	1997	1994	1991	1988
EBITDA	6,195	7,223	720	5,535
Cash Interest	955	928	1,943	2,314
Taxes Paid	1,230	910	49	260
Capex	7,150	3,843	2,348	2,016
WC Change	0	0	0	467
Cash Dividends	1,096	399	169	225
Total	-4,236	1,143	-3,789	254

Financial History

	1997	1994	1991	1988
Income Statement				
Sales	58,622	50,736	28,162	35,473
COGS	47,470	39,580	24,533	27,436
SG&A	4,957	3,933	2,909	2,501
EBITDA	6,195	7,223	720	5,535
Interest Expense	1,200	1,114	2,031	2,592
Taxes	1,752	2,117	-272	642
Net Income	2,805	3,713	-538	1,050
Balance Sheet				
Cash & Cash Equivaler	4,898	5,145	2,041	1,644
Acct. Receivable	15,164	14,258	14,239	27,689
Inventory	4,738	3,356	3,571	2,971
Intangible Assets	1,573	2,162	5,191	2,688
Total Assets	60,418	49,539	43,076	48,567
Current Liabilities - Tot	25,708	18,864	13,854	21,409
Long Term Debt	9,006	7,650	14,980	14,877
Equity	11,362	10,694	6,109	7,582
Working Capital	0	0	0	0

Capitalization

	1997	1994	1991	1988
Cash & Equivalents	4,898	5,145	2,041	1,644
Subordinated Debt	0	27	585	2,329
Other Indebtedness	702	1,801	8,742	1,898
Total Debt	15,485	13,106	19,438	27,147
Preferred Stock	0.0	2.0	0.0	0.3
Total Debt + Preferred	15,485	13,108	19,438	27,147

Competitive Analysis

Inventory Turnover

Ticker Symbol	1997	1994	1991	1988
C.1	9.558	11.333	7.300	9.934
4165A	4.523	4.442	3.494	3.321
F	19.734	17.136	11.481	11.606
GM	12.063	11.170	9.141	11.417
TM	15.842		22.110	23.104

SGA/Sales

	1997	1994	1991	1988
C.1	0.085	0.078	0.103	0.071
4165A	0.082	0.115	0.075	0.104
F				
GM				
TM	0.135 @NA		0.114	0.105

Operating Income/Sales

	1997	1994	1991	1988
C.1	0.106	0.142	0.026	0.156
4165A	0.351	0.360	0.571	0.483
F	0.221	0.198	0.133	0.186
GM	0.142	0.142	0.100	0.158
TM	0.104		0.090	0.101

Gross Margin

	1997	1994	1991	1988
C.1	19.024	21.988	12.886	22.656
4165A	43.355	47.516	64.638	58.725
F	22.130	19.782	13.323	18.649
GM	14.210	14.171	10.040	15.836
TM	23.909		20.411	20.578

Operating Performance Ratios

	1997	1994	1991	1988
EBITDA/Sales	0.106	0.142	0.026	0.156
EBITDA/Assets	0.103	0.146	0.017	0.114
FCF/Sales	-0.072	0.023	-0.135	0.007
FCF/Assets	-0.070	0.023	-0.088	0.005
Gross Margin	0.190	0.220	0.129	0.227
SG&A/Sales	0.085	0.078	0.103	0.071
Net Profit Margin	4.785	7.318	-1.910	2.961
ROE	24.679	33.979	-8.807	13.843
ROA	4.641	7.334	-1.249	2.161
Inventory Turnove	9.558	11.333	7.300	9.934
Days Sales in Rec.	94.416	102.574	184.548	284.909
Sales/Assets	0.970	1.024	0.654	0.730

Capital Structure & Liquidity Ratios

	1997	1994	1991	1988
Assets/Equity	5.318	4.632	7.051	6.405
LT				
LT Debt/Equity	0.793	0.715	2.452	1.962
LT Debt/EBITDA	1.454	1.059	20.806	2.688
(EBITDA-Capx)/I	-0.796	3.034	-0.802	1.358
EBITDA/Interest	5.163	6.484	0.355	2.136
Current Ratio	1.000	1.000	1.000	1.000
Acid Test Ratio				
FCF/LT Debt	-0.470	0.149	-0.253	0.017
Funds Flow	0.853	1.549	1.214	1.894

Source: Compustat Research Insight, Milken Institute

Lutz and Robert Miller, who shared Greenwald's former job. Everything seemed to hinge on the success of the LH models, which were due out in 1992. In automobile circles, it was suggested that LH stood for "last hope." In order to raise cash, Iacocca sold Gulf Aerospace for $825 million.

The Kerkorian Factor

The vultures were gathering. Several leveraged buyout firms seemed interested in Chrysler. Financier Kirk Kerkorian purchased slightly less than 10 percent of the company's common shares, indicating that unless something was done to resurrect the company, he might try to take it over.

In the midst of all of this, rumors spread that Chrysler was attempting to sell a minority share in CFC. The bank loans and lines of credit were renegotiated, with several banks dropping out. In January 1991, CFC's paper was downgraded to BB– by Fitch and Standard & Poor's (tables 9-8 and 9-9). The

Table 9-8. Chrysler Corporation Bonds

Amount of Issue (MM)	Year of Issue	Description	Year Due	Initial Rating	Rating Changes Aug-79 ↓	Jan-81 ↓	Jun-83 ↑	Jul-84 ↓	Nov-84 ↑	Jun-90 ↓	Feb-91 ↑	Jun-91 ↓	Jan-92 ↑	Jan-93 ↓	Feb-93 ↑
500	1980	Sec SF Nts 10.35s	1990	NR											
300	1980	Sec SF Nts 11.40s	1990	NR											
22	1970	SF Deb 8 7/8s	1995	BBB	B	CCC	B	BB–	BBB	BBB–	BB+	BB–	B+	BB	BB+
56	1973	SF Deb 8s	1998	BBB	B	CCC	B	BB–	BBB	BBB–	BB+	BB–	B+	BB	BB+
699	1985	SF Deb 12s	2015	BB–					BBB	BBB–	BB+	BB–	B+	BB	BB+
267	1987	SF Deb 10.95s	2017	BB–					BBB	BBB–	BB+	BB–	B+	BB	BB+
300	1985	Deb 13s	1997	BB–					BBB	BBB–	BB+	BB–	B+	BB	BB+
350	1987	Nts 9.6s	1994	BB–					BBB	BBB–	BB+	BB–	B+	BB	BB+
350	1985	Nts 12 3/4	1992	BB–					BBB	BBB–	BB+	BB–	B+		
245	1987	Nts 10.40s	1999	BB–					BBB	BBB–	BB+	BB–	B+	BB	BB+

Chrysler Corporation issued all bonds.
Source: Moody's Investors Service, Bloomberg, Milken Institute

Table 9-9. Chrysler Financial Bonds

Amount of Issue (MM)	Year of Issue	Description	Year Due	Initial Rating	Rating Changes Aug-79 ↓	Jan-81 ↓	Jun-83 ↑	Jul-84 ↓	Nov-84 ↑	Jun-90 ↓	Feb-91 ↑	Jun-91 ↓	Jan-92 ↑	Jan-93 ↓	Feb-93 ↓
27	1971	SFDeb 8.35s	1991	BBB	BB	CCC	B	BB–	BBB	BBB–	BB+				
18	1972	SF Deb 7.70s	1992	BBB	BB	CCC	B	BB–	BBB	BBB–	BB+	BB–	B+		
100	1972	Notes 7s	1979	BBB											
125	1976	Notes 10s	1981	BBB	BB	CCC									
125	1977	Notes 8 7/8s	1982	BBB–	BB	CCC									
100	1976	Notes 9 1/2s	1983	BBB	BB	CCC									
50	1977	Nts 8 7/8s	1984	BBB–	BB	CCC	B	BB–							
125	1976	Nts 9s	1986	BBB–	BB	CCC	B	BB–	BBB						
90	1971	xw Sub Deb 7 3/8s	1986	BB											
90	1971	Sub Deb 7 3/8s	1986	BB–	B	CCC		B							
51	1977	Sub SF Nts 9 3/8	1987	BB–	B	CCC		B							
100	1984	Nts 12.35s	1987	BBB											
400	1985	Nts 9.80s	1988	BBB											
300	1983	Nts 13 1/4s	1988	BBB											
250	1986	Nts 9 3/8s	1989	BBB											
200	1986	Nts 7 1/4s	1989	BBB											
200	1985	Nts 12s	1992	BBB						BBB–	BB+	BB–	B+		
250	1987	Nts 7 5/8s	1992	BBB						BBB–	BB+	BB–	B+		
300	1990	Nts 10.30s	1992	BBB						BBB–	BB+	BB–	B+		
225	1987	Nts 8 3/4s	1992	BBB						BBB–	BB+	BB–	B+		
250	1987	Nts 9 1/2s	1992	BBB						BBB–	BB+	BB–	B+		
200	1988	Put-Ext'd Nts 8.95s	1992	BBB						BBB–	BB+	BB–	B+		
300	1988	Remkt Res. Nts 9.30s	1992	BBB						BBB–	BB+	BB–	B+		
200	1984	Nts 13 1/4s	1999	BB–					BBB	BBB–	BB+	BB–	B+	BB	BB+
200	1985	Nts 11 3/4s	1990	BBB											
200	1985	Nts 9 3/4s	1990	BBB						BBB–					

200	1987	Nts 8 3/8s	1990	BBB						
250	1985	Nts 10.60s	1990	BBB						
200	1985	Nts 9 3/4s	1990	BBB						
200	1986	Nts 9 3/8	1991	BBB	BBB–					
200	1986	Nts 7 7/8	1991	BBB	BBB–					
200	1988	Nts 8 3/4s	1993	BBB	BBB–	BB+	BB–	B+	BB	BB
200	1989	Nts 9.65s	1993	BBB	BBB–	BB+	BB–	B+	BB	BB
200	1987	Nts 8 1/8s	1994	BBB	BBB–	BB+	BB–	B+	BB	BB
250	1989	Nts 9 1/2s	1994	BBB	BBB–	BB+	BB–	B+	BB	BB
250	1984	Nts 9s	1994	BBB	BBB–	BB+	BB–	B+	BB	BB
100	1989	F/R Nts (var. interest)	1991	BBB	BBB–	BB+	BB–			
80	1985	Nts Zero Cpn	1990	BBB	BBB–					
200	1985	Nts 12 3/4s	1999	BBB	BBB–	BB+	BB–	B+	BB	BB
300	1988	Ext's Nts 8.95s	1993	BBB	BBB–	BB+	BB–	B+	BB	BB
300	1988	Ext'd Nts 9 1/2s	1993	BBB	BBB–	BB+	BB–	B+	BB	BB
200	1985	F/R Ext'd Nts 9.312s	1989	BBB						
80	1985	Nts Zero Cpn s	1989	BBB						
300	1985	Ext's Nts 9.65	1993	BBB	BBB–	BB+	BB–	B+	BB	BB
200	1988	F/R Ext's Nts 4 3/4	1993	BBB	BBB–	BB+	BB–	B+	BB	BB
200	1988	Put-Ext'd Nts 8 1/2s	1996	BBB	BBB–	BB+	BB–	B+	BB	BB
300	1986	Nts 10.34s	1996	BBB	BBB–	BB+	BB–	B+	BB	BB
100	1985	SubNts 12 1/8s	1990	BBB–						
150	1986	SubNts 9 1/4s	1991	BBB–	BB+					
200	1987	Sub Nts. 9.3s	1994	BBB–	BB+	BB–	B	B–		
90	1985	Sub Nts 8 3/4	1997	BBB–	BB+	BB–	B	B–		
200	1984	Sub Ex V/R Nt 14s	1989	B						
60	1985	F/R Sub Nts 9.44s	1990	BBB–						
100	1985	F/R Jr Sub Nts 9.56s	1990	BBB–						
50	1985	V/R Jr Sub Nts 10.94s	1990	BBB–						
250	1990	F/R Jr Sub Nts 4 1/8	1995	BBB-	BB+	BB–	B	B–	B+	BB–

Chrysler Financial issued all bonds.
Source: Moody's Investors Service, Bloomberg, Milken Institute

company had $1.1 billion in commercial paper outstanding in March; a year earlier it had been $10.1 billion. VW Credit withdrew from its alliance with CFC. The company announced it would discontinue all nonautomotive operations.

In late 1991 the company's cash balances dipped below $1.3 billion. While this may sound like a plump cushion, Chrysler needed at least $800 million to handle day-to-day operations. Things were not improving. For that year, Chrysler would report a loss of $538 million. Iacocca sold stock to raise money and took on long-term debt. In late 1991, it seemed as though Chrysler would face a shortfall of $1.2 billion for the year, which would oblige it to sell assets, tap into its $1.75 billion credit line, or do both. Negotiations with Mitsubishi were initiated for an asset sale, and in 1993 Diamond-Star was sold for slightly more than $100 million. The stake in Mitsubishi itself was sold for $329 million. Once again, there were rumors of a marriage between Chrysler and a foreign company; this time the candidates were Fiat and Renault. Finally, Chrysler had to pledge the assets of CFC as collateral for its credit line. CFC spokesman Robert Heath was obliged to explain, "We're not an investment-grade company."

Iacocca announced his retirement in 1992 and was succeeded by Robert Eaton, just as a revamped Jeep Cherokee and the LH cars were prepared for their debut. Eaton, formerly in charge of GM's European operations, was a dark horse candidate at a time when the betting was that Greenwald would return as CEO or that Lutz would take over. Eaton had major successes in boosting quality while cutting costs, both of which were needed at Chrysler in 1992. The cost-cutting that would save Chrysler $4 billion in annual operating costs over a three-year period was already in its second year, however. Eaton was merely implementing Iacocca's program.

As it happened, Iacocca retired in glory. The new models were well received, and the entire industry's sales picked up. Chrysler earned $505 million in 1993 and went on to earn $2.4 billion the following year, as the LH cars won many awards. There were also waiting lists for the Cherokees. The company announced a new subcompact, to be called the Neon, which went on sale in late 1994 and enjoyed an excellent reception.

The situation at CFC remained a problem, however. Even with the resurgence, the company's paper remained high yield, and so CFC had difficulties matching the deals that the higher rated GM and Ford could provide. The company also had similar problems in financing purchases by the company's rental car businesses.

Chrysler experienced troubles in another area. Kerkorian told reporters he was displeased with the way Chrysler was being run. Eaton had amassed a war chest of more than $7 billion in preparation for the next downturn in sales. While saying he had "high regard for the company's management," and praising the company's "excellent operating performance in recent years," Kerkorian was disappointed with the stock's performance. He felt its price would rise if its dividends were boosted and a large-scale stock buyback program was initiated. "This program should deliver substantial value to all of the company's shareholders," he said.

Three years earlier Chrysler had placed a "poison pill" provision in its charter, preventing any shareholder from acquiring more than 10 percent of the company's common shares. Kerkorian demanded the poison pill be rescinded, indicating that unless he got his demands acted upon, he would make a hostile bid. How much would it take to buy Chrysler? The financial community guessed it would be between $17 billion and $23 billion.

Together with Gary Wilson, cochairman of Northwest Airlines, Kerkorian moved into action in early 1995. At the edge of the deal was Iacocca, who was bored with retirement and seemed eager to return to his old office. In April, Kerkorian announced he would pay $55 a share for a company whose stock then was in the mid-40s, and demanded that management permit shareholders to vote on the matter. In the end, Kerkorian and Wilson settled for a dividend hike and the share repurchase program that increased the value of their shares. In addition, a Kerkorian nominee went on the board.

Toward the end of the 1990s, Chrysler was in better financial shape than GM and close to Ford. Market share, which had been 12 percent in 1990, was 17 percent by 1998. The company was the leader in minivans, which together with light trucks accounted for 65 percent of sales. The company's Jeep brand was also the leader in the high-margin SUV market. At the same time, the company lacked branding for a family sedan (surveys indicated that except for the Neon and Intrepid, car buyers didn't know the names of the company's offerings) and a premium product, like Nissan's Infiniti and Toyota's Lexus.

Daimler-Chrysler

In May 1998, Chrysler's new CEO, Robert Lutz, and Daimler-Benz Chairman Juergan Schrempp announced the two companies would merge in a deal estimated at $55 billion. The new company, Daimler-Chrysler, was second only to Toyota in market capitalization. The new concern was 57 percent owned by Daimler's shareholders and 43 percent by Chrysler's. Thus, after close to three-quarters of a century, Chrysler ceased to exist as an independent entity.

Conclusion

The seventy-five years of Chrysler's existence were marked by extreme volatility in company profitability and access to capital. While management had used many means of securing funds for the company, the times in which it most needed an infusion of funds were those in which conventional sources of finance failed to secure sufficient funds to ensure the company's survival. It was in these times that the ability to access the high yield market proved crucial to Chrysler, allowing the company to access the capital that was necessary to avoid two major insolvency threats and remain a strong competitor among automobile manufacturers.

MEDCO CONTAINMENT SERVICES

In 1993, Merck agreed to pay $6 billion in stock and cash for a mail-order prescription drug company that was formed a mere ten years earlier with a $30 million purchase. The acquired company, New Jersey's Medco Containment Services, achieved stellar growth through a combination of management insight, fortunate timing, and capital raised by the issuance of high yield securities. These factors allowed the company to develop the infrastructure, brand recognition, and customer base required to establish Medco as the nation's largest marketer of mail-order medicine.

Understanding this great success story requires understanding both the history of its creator, Martin Wygod, and the prevailing industry trends. Wygod had entered the medical services industry sixteen years prior to the acquisition with a mere $2 million. He had the foresight to use his limited funds to position himself so that he could benefit from the changing drug industry. Wygod met the high capital demands for setting up a nationwide medical distribution system by focusing on key allegiances and issuing a total of $250 million in high yield securities. Through a combination of key acquisitions, allegiance formation, and innovative strategies for capturing value, Wygod created the company that became the dominant force in the mail-order prescription drug industry.

Company Growth

Born and educated in New York, Wygod began working on Wall Street with a $20,000 stake from his mother. He spent the following twenty years working in small-scale investment banking and acquisitions. In 1977 Wygod turned to medical services, gaining control of Glasrock, a producer of plastic products for the medical industry, for $2 million. Six years later Wygod sold Glasrock for a huge profit.

Wygod soon realized that the medical industry could provide profit-making opportunities. The population was aging and patients were spending less time in hospitals. As a result, there would be an increased need for written prescriptions, and the choice of provider for these prescriptions would be determined primarily by price.

In 1983, Wygod formed Porex Technologies, manufacturer of plastic medical devices, and through it he acquired National Pharmacies, a small mail-order drug company that supplied funded benefit health plans. At the time, National Pharmacies had revenues of about $25 million and was profitable (about $400,000 in net income). Wygod bought the company for $30 million in Porex stock, and cash and began to expand its client base.[8] In less than a year, Wygod succeeded in signing up Fortune 500 companies such as General Motors, Alcoa, and Georgia-Pacific for corporate-funded drug benefit plans provided by National.

8. Four years later, National (at the time under the name Medco) bought out Porex, after generating about 90 percent of Porex's sales.

Wygod's idea was simple: reduce the cost of delivering prescription drugs to workers whose drug expenses are picked up by their corporate health plans. With this in mind, the company developed a specialty in maintenance medication drugs (arthritis, diabetes, gastrointestinal problems, and other chronic ailments). By buying and selling in mass quantity, Wygod was able to negotiate heavily discounted prices from drug manufacturers. Increased automation allowed the company to keep its operating costs low. For example, pill-counting machines allowed pharmacists and technicians to fill as many as seventy prescriptions an hour, compared to less than thirteen an hour at standard pharmacies. The reduced cost structure was then passed on to the company's customers, resulting in drug prices that were significantly lower than those of the competition. At the time Medco claimed that it saved its customers 20 percent or more, relative to retail pharmacy prices. Not surprisingly, independent retail pharmacists and state pharmacy boards lobbied vigorously to restrict mail-order drug services.

In 1984, Wygod sold 1.4 million shares of National Pharmacies to the public, about 20 percent of the company, at $14 per share.[9] That year the company changed its name to Medco Containment Services. The following year Medco acquired Paid Prescriptions, a company that processed retail drug claims, gaining access to a national network of 40,000 drugstores that accepted Paid Prescriptions' health care card. This allowed Medco to provide its customers with a choice of filling acute illness prescriptions at a discount at participating drugstores, in addition to receiving chronic illness medication by mail. The acquisition also gave Medco access to medical histories and other proprietary information on millions of cardholders, allowing the company to inform plan sponsors of their employees' buying patterns.

Medco's tremendous growth was, in part, a result of the explosive growth in funded drug benefit plan coverage. In the first eight years of the company's operations, the percent of the population that was covered through such plans rose from under 5 percent to about 40 percent.

Use of High Yield Bonds

Maintaining Medco's tremendous growth required significant capital inflow. To meet these needs, the company issued $100 million in convertible high yield bonds on July 29, 1988, with regular scheduled call dates, for $20 per share. Thus, at any of the scheduled call dates, Medco was able to call its bond issuance in return for 5 million shares of common stock.

Medco called these bonds in December 1990, as part of a company refinancing, converting the entire issuance into the company's common stock. This conversion, which did not require any capital (e.g., through the buyback of company shares), was financed through the issuance of further

9. Adjusted for splits, the public offering was at $2.25 a share. These shares were worth $39 nine years later, when the company was bought out.

company stock. Between 1990 and 1991 Medco had increased the number of outstanding company shares by 19.7 million.[10] Thus the company's issuing and then calling of the bonds was essentially a way to raise money without having to pay it back from earnings.[11] Medco was also able to raise cash on demand through an agreement with Citibank that provided Medco with an unsecured line of credit in the aggregate amount of $20 million.

In September 1991 Medco offered a further $150 million in convertible bonds. At the time these bonds were not rated (and thus considered high yield) and were issued in the Rule 144A market.[12]

Medco's bond issues were used to fuel the company's rapid expansion and their impact is reflected in the company's financials (table 9-10). From June 1988 to June 1989 Medco's working capital had changed from $99.5 million to $200.3 million, increasing during the following two years by a further 100 percent (cumulatively). During these years, inventory levels rose from $71 million in mid-1988 to $247.5 million in mid-1991. The company's annual net income, which fell to negative $8 million in fiscal 1990 (primarily due to the liquidation at a loss of $43 million of a large portfolio of bonds that Porex had held), grew to $103 million by mid-1992.

Given that the company's main asset was goodwill (the extensive mailing lists, customer database, and brand name), the contribution of the bond issuance to Medco's growth can be ascertained more precisely by considering the company's market-to-book ratio. This ratio, which measures the value that the market places on each dollar of the company's book value, grew from 2.9 in mid-1989 to 4.9 the following year, and to 8.9 by mid-1991. In other words, within two years the market increased its valuation of Medco from roughly three times the company's book value to nine times its book value, a clear indication that investors were confident in the company's growth strategy and its implementation.

In 1990, Medco introduced a controversial program called Prescriber's Choice. Medco would promote a drug as the top choice in its category in exchange for a heavily discounted price from the manufacturer of that drug. When doctors prescribed a competing drug, Wygod's pharmacists would call the customer and make a cost-effectiveness pitch. This program proved extremely successful, much to the dislike of several major drug manufacturers (those which did not participate).

The following year Medco bought the institutional division of Rix Dunnington and Dunnington Super Drug, which provided pharmaceutical services to nursing homes and institutions in the Northeast. The com-

10. In December 1990 the company had 119.1 million shares outstanding, compared to 138.8 million the following year.

11. Of course the company's issuing further stock should have diluted the value of its outstanding shares, which then should have reduced the value of the equity owned by the company. However, the increase in demand for the company's stock was sufficient to offset the dilution's impact on total market value.

12. SEC Rule 144A allowed companies to issue debt with limited public disclosure, provided it is sold only to qualified institutional buyers: prequalified buyers with a portfolio of at least $1 million.

Table 9-10. Medco Financials

Medco Containment Services

Adjusted Debt/Cap Ratio	Market Cap (in Millions of US$)	Interest Coverage
22	1,303	11.541

Business Description

Medco Containment Services Inc. through its subsidiaries, provides drug benefit management behavioral healthcare services to medical benefit plans of employers and insurers. Medco's programs provide integrated delivery systems including retail pharmacy network management and mail service, comprehensive drug utilization review and drug formulary programs. On 11/19/93, Medco Containment Services was acquired by Merck & Co.

Security Price History

Date	Stock High	Stock Low	Stock Close
1987	7.520	3.040	4.600
1988	7.250	4.000	5.350
1989	7.550	4.650	7.300
1990	12.900	6.150	12.100
1991	31.900	11.400	31.600
1992	38.625	25.000	37.750
1993	40.375	24.500	40.000

Price & Price Relative to S&P 500

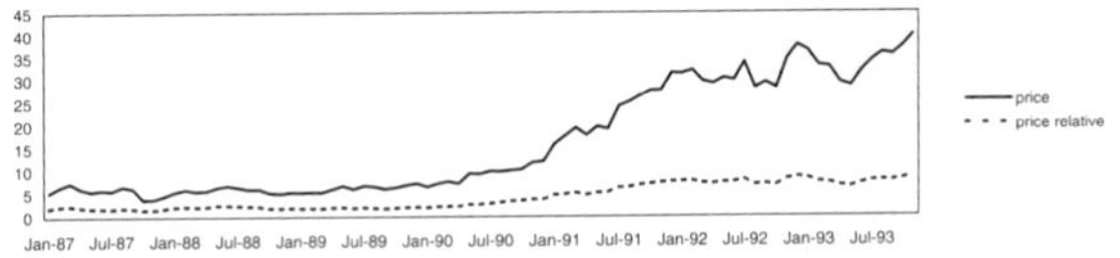

Market Ratios

	1993	1990	1987
P/E Ratio		159.211	
Earnings Yld	0.028	-0.007	0.018
MV/Sales		1.439	
MV/BV		4.922	
MV/EBITDA		21.869	
Cash Per Share	3.788	1.662	0.639
EPS	0.880	-0.064	0.107

Financial History

	1993	1990	1987
Income Statement			
Sales	2,624	1,004	283
COGS	2,198	871	245
SG&A	170	66	17
EBITDA	257	66	22
Interest Expense	19	8	0
Taxes	91	19	13
Net Income	141	-8	12
Balance Sheet			
Cash & Cash Equivaler	586	198	68
Acct. Receivable	205	94	66
Inventory	350	134	58
Intangible Assets	189	48	51
Total Assets	1,675	546	277
Current Liabilities - To	347	132	76
Long Term Debt	281	103	0
Equity	947	293	193
Working Capital	815	300	119

Capitalization

	1993	1990	1987
Cash & Equivalents	586	198	68
Subordinated Debt	0	0	0
Other Indebtedness	0	1	0
Total Debt	282	103	20
Preferred Stock	0	0	0
Total Debt + Preferred	282	103	20

Interest Coverage Model

Year	EBITDA/ Interest	Return on	Leverage
1987		6.026	0.000
1990	8.436	-1.959	0.349
1993	13.182	10.850	0.297

Competitive Analysis

Inventory Turnover

Ticker Symbol	1993	1990	1987
MCCS	6.479	6.950	6.202
9970B	9.194	6.974	8.518
MRK	1.522	1.850	2.026
PFE	1.417	1.853	1.810
AMS	64.941	53.314	18.725

SGA/Sales

	1993	1990	1987
MCCS	0.065	0.066	0.060
9970B	0.264	0.269	0.238
MRK	0.389	0.423	0.444
PFE	0.540	0.483	0.423
AMS	0.173	0.146	0.166

Operating Income/Sales

	1993	1990	1987
MCCS	0.098	0.066	0.077
9970B	0.215	0.243	0.155
MRK	0.406	0.376	0.308
PFE	0.255	0.196	0.224
AMS	0.111	0.230	0.256

Gross Margin

	1993	1990	1987
MCCS	16.243	13.201	13.664
9970B	47.978	51.119	39.299
MRK	79.528	79.838	75.188
PFE	79.527	67.850	64.736
AMS	28.373	37.578	42.167

Free Cash Flow

	1993	1990	1987
EBITDA	257	66	22
Cash Interest	19	8	0
Taxes Paid	32	17	0
Capex	69	16	12
WC Change	358	99	4
Cash Dividends	6	2	2
Total	-227	-76	4

Operating Performance Ratios

	1993	1990	1987
EBITDA/Sales	0.098	0.066	0.077
EBITDA/Assets	0.153	0.121	0.078
FCF/Sales	-0.086	-0.076	0.013
FCF/Assets	-0.135	-0.140	0.013
Gross Margin	0.162	0.132	0.137
SG&A/Sales	0.065	0.066	0.060
Net Profit Margin	5.390	-0.794	4.109
ROE	14.935	-2.716	6.026
ROA	8.442	-1.460	4.207
Inventory Turnov	6.479	6.950	6.202
Days Sales in Rec.	28.494	34.248	84.704
Sales/Assets	1.566	1.839	1.024

Capital Structure & Liquidity Ratios

	1993	1990	1987
Assets/Equity	1.769	1.860	1.433
LT Debt/Working	0.345	0.342	0.000
LT Debt/Equity	0.297	0.349	0.000
LT Debt/EBITDA	1.095	1.553	0.000
(EBITDA-Capx)/I	9.654	6.411	
EBITDA/Interest	13.182	8.436	
Current Ratio	3.347	3.266	2.565
Acid Test Ratio	3.414	2.378	2.581
FCF/LT Debt	-0.806	-0.744	
Funds Flow	4.319	48.020	

Source: Compustat Research Insight, Milken Institute

pany also bought American Biodyne, a managed mental health services provider. Also in 1991, Medco made an IPO of its Medical Marketing Group subsidiary, which was created to draw upon the company's extensive database in order to sell information and marketing programs based on doctors' prescribing patterns to drug companies. During this year Medco reported sales of $1.81 billion.

In 1992 Medco and United Healthcare agreed to market each other's products and services to their customers. At the time Medco offered medications for 25 percent less than retailers, which led Wygod to describe the company as "the Wal-Mart of pills" in the *Wall Street Journal*.

The following year the ex-head of Citibank, Richard Braddock, joined Medco as CEO. Later that year the company was acquired by pharmaceutical giant Merck for $6 billion in cash and stock, and became the subsidiary Merck-Medco Managed Care. At the time Medco made about $2.5

billion in revenues and $138 million in net income, owned relatively few physical facilities, and held no patents. The deal, which was the industry's first merger between a drug manufacturer and a distributor, united the world's largest pharmaceutical maker with the nation's leading mail-order pharmacy company.

By this time Medco's clients included more than one hundred Fortune 500 companies, federal and state benefit plans, 132 union groups, and 58 Blue Cross/Blue Shield groups and insurance companies, for a total of 33 million people.

Conclusion

Medco's story is one of tremendous growth resulting from the foresight of its management team and an understanding of the shifting needs of the company's customer base. Throughout its short existence as an independent company, Medco's main asset was essentially a mailing list with 33 million customer names and prescription histories.[13] Yet in an era in which drug prescribing was shifting away from doctors and to managed care outfits with emphasis on the reduction of medical costs, a ready-made mass distribution system was an extremely valuable asset.

In creating Medco's infrastructure, extensive capital was needed within a short period of time. Because the company was relatively new and thus could not show a substantial earnings history, it could not obtain these resources in the investment grade bond market. As a result Wygod turned to the high yield market and secured the funds that enabled Medco to increase its value 200-fold in just ten years (table 9-11).[14]

IMPROVING EFFICIENCY: MERGERS AND ACQUISITIONS

From 1980 to 1989, high yield bond financing was used in 8 percent of all mergers and acquisitions (M&A) in the United States. In the same period, high yield bonds accounted for 19 percent of the value of all M&A (Hogan and Huie 1992). The disparity in the two measures indicates that high yield bonds were instrumental in financing the merger of particularly large firms. The percent of cash payments financed with high yield bonds could be higher, because these statistics don't differentiate M&A by method of payment. Also, some firms issued high yield bonds for "possible future acquisitions" (Yago 1991a), making it difficult to precisely assign bond issuance to M&A.

Despite repeated efforts at regulation and increasingly robust defenses by targets, mergers in the United States can trace their origins to the mid-1800s (Pound 1992a). Among the 1980–1997 members of the Fortune 500, more than 30 percent were merged out by 1997. In addition, more than half

13. Interestingly, in 1993 (the acquisition year) changes in the tax code allowed companies to treat "customer lists" as goodwill for amortization.

14. The company was bought for $30 million in 1983 and sold for $6 billion in 1993.

Table 9-11. Medco Bonds

Amount of Issue (MM)	Year of Issue	Description	Year Due	Company Issuing	Initial Rating	Rating Change
100	1988	Convertible subordinated debentures 7 1/2s	2000	Medco Containment Services, Inc.	Ba3	–

Source: Moody's Investors Service, Bloomberg, Milken Institute
12/27/90: All convertible debenture 7 1/2, 2000 called at 105.357.

of them had purchased another firm. Such a prominent role for mergers in reallocating control over capital in the U.S. economy gave rise to a vigorous debate over whether mergers actually improve the allocation of resources. This debate focused on two issues: the relative premerger performance of targets and their postmerger changes in performance.

The debate about the postmerger performance of merged firms is fueled by conflicting empirical and anecdotal evidence. Mergers are both believed to create long-term value and improve the efficient use of assets, and to dramatically increase overhead and reduce corporate focus. While the earliest studies showed no consistent change in postmerger performance (Meeks 1977), later studies showed a significant deterioration in performance (Mueller 1980) or significant improvements in performance (Lichtenberg 1992). Analyses separating postmerger performance by the "mood" of the merger (hostile or friendly) produced similar contradictions (Fowler and Schmidt 1989; Healy, Palepu, and Ruback 1992; Powell 1997).

In this part, which draws heavily on material in Trimbath (2002), we need to focus our attention on the efficiency effects of mergers. If we consider the cost for each dollar of revenue generated, then we can directly measure the efficient use of resources in the production, distribution, and sale of goods and services. This "cost per unit of revenue" can be used to measure the economic efficiency of firm performance.[15]

Regulations Against Financing and Mergers

Trimbath (2002) shows that regulatory activity affecting the availability of financing for mergers had an effect on the relationship between mergers and the size of firms. Prior to the regulatory interference that took place in the mid-to-late-1980s, relatively larger firms were more likely to receive merger offers. Trimbath's results show that this gradually changed over time. The change was to make size a deterrent to takeover after restrictions were placed on the use of debt for financing.[16] Although relatively inefficient firms had a higher risk of takeover, a failure in efficiency performance eventually could be offset with size. This size-efficiency trade-off was created when regulations were enforced against the use of high-yield securities in mergers.

In 1983, HR 4170 was introduced in the U.S. House of Representatives for the express purpose of stopping all large mergers by eliminating the deduction for interest paid on debt used in acquisitions. With the introduction of this bill, Representative Byron L. Dorgan of South Dakota sought to "amend the Internal Revenue Code to deny any deduction for interest paid or incurred on loans in connection with corporate takeovers or attempted takeovers" (*Congressional Record*, May 25, 1983, page 14004). Although Representative Dorgan's bill was not approved, a similar bill was

15. This interpretation distinguishes efficiency from profitability and market valuation, which are indicative of the distribution of the firm's financial gains from production.

16. This result is not found in prior statistical studies of mergers because few have examined changes in merger determinants in a dynamic setting.

introduced virtually every year after that until it was passed. By 1987, support for the proposal had become strong enough that the Brady Commission listed consideration of the bill as a contributing factor to the stock market disturbance in October of that year (Lichtenberg 1992).

The version of the bill that finally passed was contained in the Revenue Reconciliation Act of 1989. The effect was to eliminate tax deductions for interest paid on high yield bonds, raising the cost of financing for mergers. Also in 1989, the New York State legislature eliminated the deduction for interest on debt used in takeovers (Yago 1991a). Similar tax bills were under consideration in other states at the same time. Meanwhile, in January 1986 the Board of Governors of the Federal Reserve System passed a rule to limit high yield bonds issued by shell corporations to 50 percent of the value in takeovers.

In addition to congressional action against merger financing, at least six separate bills were introduced into the House of Representatives and the U.S. Senate in 1985 and 1987 specifically designed to tax any profits realized in a merger. Figure 9-1 shows the number of bills mentioning "takeover" that were introduced in the House and Senate during the period. State legislatures were virtually barred from interfering with federal antitrust regulations covered by the Williams Act after the 1982 Supreme Court decision in *Edgar* v. *MITE Corp*. (457 U.S. 624 [1982]). An explosion of antitakeover laws were enacted in the states (Roe 1993) after the 1987 reversal of that decision. Table 9-12 presents a chronology of this activity.

The Federal Reserve rule and tax code changes were aimed at merger financing that was critical for approaching larger targets. Other congres-

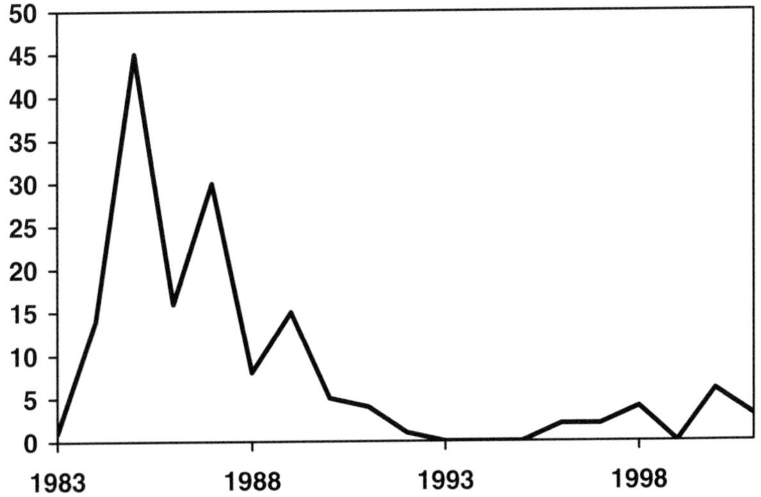

Figure 9-1. Congressional Actions Against Takeovers, 1983–2001. Sources: Compiled from data available in History of Bills, GPO Access Gateway, New York State Library; Trimbath 2000.

Table 9-12. Chronology of State Anti-takeover Statutes, 1982–1990

State	Type of Statute	Prompted by[a]	Introduced	Passed by Legislature	Signed by Governor
Ohio	1	Marathon Oil[b]	1/7/1982	11/17/1982	11/18/1982
Michigan	3	Supported by Chamber of Commerce	11/3/1981	5/9/1984	5/25/1984
Pennsylvania	2	Scott Paper Co. (drafted by PA Chamber of Commerce)	11/16/1983	12/13/1983	12/23/1983
Maryland	3	Martin Marietta[c], McCormick, PHH Group, Foremost-McKesson (vetoed 5/26/83)		4/3/1983	6/21/1983
Wisconsin	3		6/9/1983	3/22/1984	4/18/1984
Connecticut	3	Aetna Casualty & Life[c]	2/15/1984	5/7/1984	6/4/1984
Louisiana	3		4/30/1984	6/25/1984	7/13/1984
Minnesota	1		3/6/1984	4/18/1984	4/25/1984
Missouri	1	TWA[b]	5/28/1984	5/29/1984	5/30/1984
Georgia	3	(amended first-generation law)	1/22/1985	2/7/1985	3/27/1985
Mississippi	3	First MS Corporation	1/11/1985	2/13/1985	3/29/1985
Hawaii	1	International Holding Capital Corporation	2/11/1985	4/12/1985	4/23/1985
Illinois	3	Abbott Laboratories	2/28/1985	6/24/1985	8/24/1985
Utah	2	Northwest Pipeline	11/13/1985	2/26/1986	3/18/1986
Maine	2	Great Northern Nekoosa	3/8/1985	6/10/1985	6/21/1985
New York	4	CBS (drafted by Business Council of NY)	3/8/1985	6/27/1985	Vetoed 8/13/85
New York	4		10/30/1985	12/10/1985	12/16/1985
Indiana	1,4	Arvin Industries	1/8/1986	2/28/1986	3/5/1986
Kentucky	3,4	Ashland Oil[c]	3/27/1986	3/27/1986	3/28/1986
Missouri	4	TWA[d]	2/6/1986	4/22/1986	6/23/1986
New Jersey	4	Schering-Plough, Merck[c], Becton Dickinson, Johnson & Johnson	1/27/1986	6/26/1986	8/5/1986
Ohio	1	Marathon Oil[b], Goodyear[c]	11/19/1986	11/20/1986	11/22/1986

Virginia	3	Dan River Mills (drafted by Hutton & Williams Law firm)	1/15/1985	2/21/1985	3/24/1985
Washington	3	Weyerhaeuser[c]	2/5/1985	4/18/1985	5/13/1985
Wisconsin	1		2/11/1986	3/26/1986	4/10/1986
Missouri	1,4	[e]	1/14/1987	6/15/1987	8/11/1987
Florida	1,3	Harcourt-Brace	3/3/1987	7/2/1987	(no signature required)
Oregon	1		3/9/1987	6/27/1987	7/18/1987
North Carolina	1,3	Burlington Industries (revised 5/01, 5/13)	4/14/1987	4/23/1987	(no signature required)
Louisiana	1,3	[e]	5/4/1987	6/10/1987	6/11/1987
Nevada	1,3		5/6/1987	6/1/1987	6/6/1987
Utah	1	[e]	5/20/1987	5/20/1987	5/29/1987
Massachusetts	1	Gillette[c]	6/30/1987	7/16/1987	7/21/1987
Minnesota	1,4	Dayton-Hudson[c]	6/25/1987	6/25/1987	6/25/1987
Arizona	1,4	Greyhound[c]	7/20/1987	7/21/1987	7/22/1987
Washington	4	Boeing[c] (proposed by Boeing 8/4/87)	8/10/1987	8/10/1987	8/11/1987
Wisconsin	4	G. Heilman	9/15/1987	9/16/1987	9/17/1987
New York[f]			3/1989	4/1989	4/1989
Pennsylvania	1,2, 3,4	PA Chamber of Business & Industry and AFL-CIO	1989	4/5/1990	4/1990
Ohio	5		1990	1990	Never adopted
Delaware	5		1988		
California			1989		

Types of statutes are as follows: 1 = control share acquisition; 2 = control share cashout; 3 = fair price; 4 = five-year freeze-out fair price; 5 = business combination statute.

[a] Target of corporate control contest.

[b] indicates the target's BR membership was through USX at the time of the legislation

[c] indicates the target is a member of the Business Roundtable (BR).

[d] indicates the target's BR membership is active at the time of the legislation.

[e] Amendments to existing second-generation statutes.

[f] New York eliminated interest deductibility on acquisition-related debt; eliminated the use of net operating losses in acquisitions; eliminated debt equity exchanges and franchise tax credits.

sional and state actions had the effect of raising the transaction costs of mergers by erecting barriers to their timely execution. The combination undermined the effective workings of the market for corporate control.

Contrary to Popular Belief

Some definition of efficiency has been associated with U.S. government policy toward business combinations since the 1970s. Efficiency enhancement was added to the Federal Trade Commission Merger Guidelines in 1984 as a defense for mergers, regardless of size. This was in contrast to the "antitrust" period of regulation in which size was a primary consideration for opposing business combinations. We believe that putting aside size considerations in favor of efficiency was a natural step toward motivating the buyers in mergers. Enhancing the efficient allocation of resources in the economy would not motivate the rational management of any firm to be the buyer in a merger unless profits could be realized in the transaction. If a buyer could realize gains by taking over and reducing the costs of a small firm, then those gains should be even greater in a larger firm.

For nearly twenty years, however, economists had accepted as fact the idea that merger targets had to be small because of imperfections in capital markets. The failure to recognize changes in the structure of risk across time led to an overemphasis in the economics literature on the potential for large, inefficient firms to escape disciplinary mergers. Trimbath (2002) shows that there was no trade-off between size and efficiency in the early 1980s. Yet, as regulatory changes took effect in the mid-to-late-1980s, there was increasing opportunity for a firm to reduce the risk of takeover without improving efficiency simply by achieving a sufficiently large size.

Evidence about size and inefficiency shows differences in the effect of size on the probability of takeover for firms with relatively high costs during and after the introduction of regulations on mergers financed with "high yield bonds." When financing was available and the regulatory atmosphere was just beginning to change, only the top 1 percent of firms was large enough to have costs above the industry standard and not face an increased probability of takeover. After the regulations were fully enacted, this was true for the top 30 percent. What economists thought was true throughout the 1980s actually did not happen until nearly the end of the decade.

Despite the concerns of policy makers that mergers created too much debt, many of those financed with the high yield securities which were targeted for regulation were in a sector of the economy that could best afford to carry the debt.

Postmerger Changes in Efficiency

Trifts (1991) showed that method of payment and changes in the level of debt in mergers have independent effects in merger studies. An additional complication occurs when firms use equity issues to finance cash payments. In that case, the increase in debt will not directly correspond to cash financing for the merger. This is not to say that the two are not highly correlated.

When all cash is paid, the correlation coefficient with changes in debt is 0.32. When all stock is paid, the correlation coefficient with changes in debt is –0.29. Therefore, Trimbath (2002) uses both a method of payment indicator and a change in debt variable to check for separate effects.

In the study, debt is defined as [(long-term debt *plus* debt due in one year) *divided* by revenue]. Changes in debt are measured as the change from the year before to the year after the merger. As one would expect, cash payments were used statistically significantly more often in the years before 1989 (table 9-13).

Table 9-14 displays descriptive statistics for the efficiency measure used in the Trimbath study. The mean and median postmerger performance show improvement over the mean and median premerger performance of the pairs in the sample. The mean shows pairs achieved the same level of efficiency, though starting at different places. Firms combined in 1981–1989 made greater percentage improvements than those combined in later years. The median shows that firms start at about the same place, but the firms combined in 1990–1995 made greater absolute improvements, despite the fact that their percentage improvement was lower than those combined in earlier years.

Although method of payment and changes in debt are not perfectly synchronized, there are substantial differences in their impact on costs. We can see this more clearly by highlighting the impact of debt on the changes in efficiency attributed to mergers. Table 9-15 breaks out the means and medians by period and the level of the change in debt.

The overall gain in efficiency (from lower costs) for all observations is 2.1 percent. The gains in efficiency for firms with above median changes in debt are better at the mean than those with below median changes in debt. It is possible that firms with higher debt are forced to make greater improvements in cost efficiency in order to meet debt payments. This evidence is not conclusive, however, because it is not possible to definitely know if the financing was used for the merger event or to finance investment in the target's productive capacity after the merger (Trifts 1991).

The Impact of Regulations on Corporate Efficiency

Whereas firms combined in a merger before the regulatory restrictions enjoyed a 2.7 percent reduction in costs, the gain in the later years of the

Table 9-13. Frequency of Method of Payment by Period

	Any Cash	All Stock	All Cash	Total
All Years	115 (71%)	47 (29%)	94 (58%)	162
1981–1989	81 (76%)	26 (24%)	70 (65%)	107
1990–1995	34 (62%)	21 (38%)	24 (44%)	55

Note: "All cash" pairs are included in the "Any cash" column. "Any cash" and "All stock" are mutually exclusive designations for the method of payment.
Source: Trimbath 2000.

Table 9-14. Premerger and Postmerger Efficiency of Pairs

	All Years		1981–1989		1990–1995	
	Pre	Post	Pre	Post	Pre	Post
Mean	–0.031	–0.061	–0.024	–0.060	–0.040	–0.061
Median	–0.013	–0.042	–0.011	–0.044	–0.015	–0.028

Note: Premerger performance based on pro forma combined target and buyer before merger. Postmerger performance based on combined firm after merger. Efficiency measured as (cost of goods sold *plus* selling and administrative expenses) *divided by* revenue.
Source: Trimbath 2000

Trimbath study is only 1 percent. Considering the revenue of an average-sized target firm in that study, the U.S. economy benefited an average of $46 million just in cost reductions from each merger completed before the regulations and only $15 million on average after government interference in the market for corporate control. These are cost savings that may have been passed on to consumers in the form of lower product prices. The economic loss to the U.S. economy is even higher if we consider the large, inefficient firms that did not experience a change in ownership and control, and therefore continued to function in inefficient ways. Trimbath's analysis of Fortune 500 firms indicates that the elimination of "high yield bond"–financed mergers had a deleterious effect on the ability of the market for corporate control to discipline large, inefficient firms.

Table 9-15. Efficiency by Change in Debt and Period

	Premerger		Postmerger		Change	
	Below	Above	Below	Above	Below	Above
1981–1989						
Mean	–0.019	–0.020	–0.032	–0.051	–0.013	–0.031
Median	–0.010	–0.005	–0.033	–0.033		
N	169	184	140	200		
1990–1995						
Mean	–0.070	–0.015	–0.084	–0.032	–0.014	–0.017
Median	–0.047	–0.008	–0.055	–0.012		
N	156	91	110	59		
All Years						
Mean	–0.043	–0.019	–0.055	–0.046	–0.012	–0.027
Median	–0.020	–0.006	–0.040	–0.027		
N	325	275	250	259		

Note: "Below" refers to pairs with changes in the level of debt below the sample median. Similarly for "Above."
Source: Trimbath 2000.

The reduced gains in efficiency from mergers completed after 1989 could indicate two possible views. One possibility is that the regulations against mergers, both the financing regulations and the anti-takeover statutes passed at the state level, had the effect of limiting the opportunity for buyers to take over and improve inefficient firms. An alternative view is that even without the regulatory interference, opportunities for efficiency-enhancing mergers were virtually exhausted in the active corporate control market of the 1980s. There is no evidence that merger opportunities are cyclical in nature. However, this remains a popular belief.

Several other studies have looked for transfers of wealth from employees and bondholders in search of evidence that any merger gains are private in nature. None of these has produced significant evidence. Trimbath's approach reveals significant social gains in the form of reduced costs per unit of revenue in the postmerger firms. She identified the impact of regulations on the risk of takeover in size that are related to the availability of merger financing. Given that the cost efficiency gains are less robust in the postregulatory period, she suggests that an additional effect of antitakeover regulation was to reduce the social gains from mergers.

Support for Trimbath's findings are provided by examining the performance measures used in other studies that find postmerger improvements in merged firms. Total factor productivity, used in a study by Lichtenberg (1992), also is not affected (in an accounting sense) by changes in leverage, and thus avoids measurement problems. That study reported significant improvements in the long-run postmerger performance of merged firms.

Trimbath's work shows the impact of exogenous events on the market for corporate control. By accounting for temporal changes in the determinants, strategic value, and effects of mergers, more of the process can be understood. Conflicting evidence of the economic effect of mergers in previous studies has resulted from measuring performance only through accounting profits (which are sensitive to capital structure) across periods of significant changes in merger financing.

Evidence in Trimbath (2002) shows that all relatively inefficient firms had a higher risk of takeover in the early 1980s and that larger relatively inefficient firms had a reduced risk of takeover after anti-financing regulations. In addition, it shows that the postmerger gains from improved firm efficiency were significantly lower in the postregulatory period. In the postmerger analysis, there are significant merger gains in efficiency from lower costs per unit of revenue. This supports the hypothesis that buyers are motivated by the potential for unrealized gains evidenced by target inefficiencies. It also provides evidence of postmerger improvements in the use of resources. The postmerger efficiency gains are significantly lower after 1989. We can attribute this to the reduced risk of takeover due to size for relatively inefficient firms after 1989, as a result of restrictions on merger financing and of strengthened anti-takeover regulations in the states.

10

Industrial Restructuring

> **Manufacturers**
> When Anthony J. F. "Tony" O'Reilly, the chief executive of H.J. Heinz, called the company's 100 top managers to Pittsburgh in February for what was billed as the Low-Cost Operator Conference, most of them expected to hear some corporate cheerleading about turning off the lights. . . . O'Reilly's surprising message to his managers: it isn't enough. The food industry is in big trouble, the chief executive told them, and for Heinz, "the party is over." . . . The industry problems he recounted are nothing new: little or no growth in the number of units being sold, intense pressure on operating-profit margins, and low return on capital.
>
> *Fortune*, June 24, 1985, p. 44
>
> **Wholesalers**
> In an economy dominated by rising fuel prices and a business climate as competitive as ever, wholesale [food] distributors are cautious going into 1991 because, they say, the downward pressure on margins has never been greater.
>
> *U.S. Distribution Journal*, Dec. 15, 1990, p. 39
>
> **Retailers**
> Declining rates of population growth, higher labor costs . . . and stiffer competition are making life tough for the folks [in retail food]. . . . The 800-pound gorilla here is Wal-Mart, which now has supermarket sections at 432 of its 2,337 U.S. outlets, up from only a few ten years ago. How do you compete with that kind of expansion? You grow your own 800-pound gorilla.
>
> *Forbes*, Jan. 12, 1998, p. 160

Since 1980, the impact of low growth in both U.S. population and consumer real income has been felt at every level of the food industry. Starting with manufacturing, through wholesalers and on to retailers, firms in the food industry have had to become leaner and meaner to survive. This meant pushing efficiency to its limits and merging for growth. Intense price competition was met with the implementation of increasingly sophisticated technologies to enhance industry efficiency. That competition brought with it financial difficulties for many firms, sending them to the high yield market to finance both their growth through acquisitions and the purchase of the capital-intensive technology they required to remain competitive.

Industry growth, as measured by total expenditures on food, was below real GDP growth in all but three years of the period 1980–2000 (see figure 10-1). The basic determinant of growth in the food industry is the underlying annual U.S. population growth. As figure 10-1 shows, food expenditures have had an average annual real growth rate of about 1.99 percent, while the U.S. population has grown at about 1 percent per year since 1980. The additional growth has come through the introduction of new products, some of which were made possible by the application of newly developed technologies specialized for the food industry.

The share of food and beverages in personal consumption expenditures fell dramatically from 18.3 percent in 1980 to 16.1 percent in 1990 and 13.9 percent in 2000. The food industry's share of nondurable expenditures also fell sharply: from 54.9 percent to 52.7 percent and 46.9 percent in the same years. So how does an industry with an intrinsic growth factor of less than 1 percent flourish in a world in which firms strive for growth rates of 10 percent or more? The need for growth in a slow-growing industry was a driving force behind the corporate control activity in the food sector.

INDUSTRY COMPOSITION OF THE FORTUNE 500

Let's take a direct look at the industrial restructuring that occurred in the 1980s in the U.S. economy. Table 10-1 shows a breakout of consumer products into cyclical and noncyclical groups. The food industry is in the noncyclical group, which increased its share of revenues while decreasing its share of firms in the Fortune 500. Figure 10-2 displays the percent of Fortune 500 revenues (panel A) and firms (panel B) in 1980, 1989, and 1996.

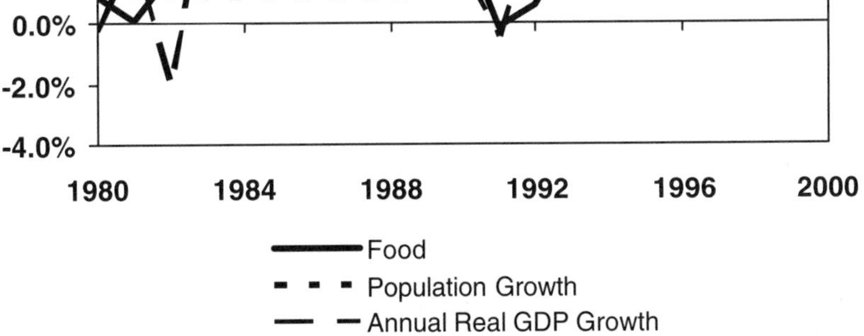

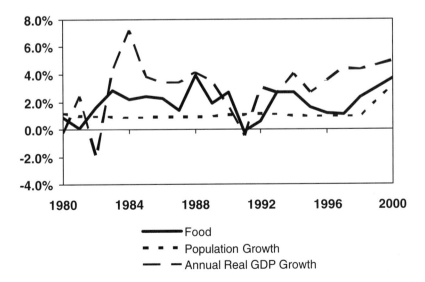

Figure 10-1. U.S. Real Growth in Food Expenditures, 1980–2000. Source: Department of Commerce, Bureau of Economic Analysis and Census Bureau.

Table 10-1. Sectoral Distribution of Revenue and Firms in Fortune 500, 1996

Sector	Basic Resources	Cyclical Consumer Products	Noncyclical Consumer Products	Energy	Industrial	Technology
Revenue						
1996 Share	10%	31%	19%	12%	12%	17%
% change from 1980	–15%	44%	18%	–58%	–7%	69%
Firms						
1996 share	20%	25%	17%	6%	19%	14%
% change from 1980	11%	8%	–17%	–12%	–13%	33%

% change is defined as (1996 share *minus* 1980 share) *divided by* 1980 share.
Source: Trimbath 2000.

The figures in the legend show the percentage change in the sectors' shares from 1980 to 1996. Not surprisingly, technology was the big winner, increasing its share of revenue by nearly 70 percent and its share of firms by about one-third. This is a reflection not only of growth in the technology sector itself but also of the increasing use of technology throughout the economy. Consumer products, on the other hand, increased their share of revenue while actually reducing their share of firms in the Fortune 500 between 1980 and 1996.

Put another way, in the consumer products sector *fewer firms* generated a *greater percentage of revenue* among U.S. corporations in 1996 than they did in 1980. During the period 1979–1994, fifteen well-known companies were dropped from Standard and Poor's listing of representative firms in the food industry (Weston and Chiu 1996). The names of the firms and the year in which they were removed are shown in table 10-2. Thus the M&A market has been important for the food industry.

In chapter 9 we presented the results of a merger study, the details of which are available in Trimbath (2000). The study examined mergers of Fortune 500 firms from 1980 to 1996. Twenty-eight percent of the mergers among food manufacturers studied by Trimbath were horizontal. In 1950, the Clayton Act was amended to close loopholes in preventing horizontal acquisitions. From 1950 to 1980, major horizontal acquisitions were prohibited by the antitrust authorities. Antitrust regulations were applied vigorously in the food industry, where by the mid-1950s companies like Beatrice and Borden were subject to Federal Trade Commission orders restricting further horizontal acquisitions and, in fact, requiring some food company divestitures. After 1980, the antitrust authorities changed their guidelines to include economic analysis of competitive processes, especially the impact of international competition (Weston and Chiu 1996).

a. % of Fortune 500 Revenues

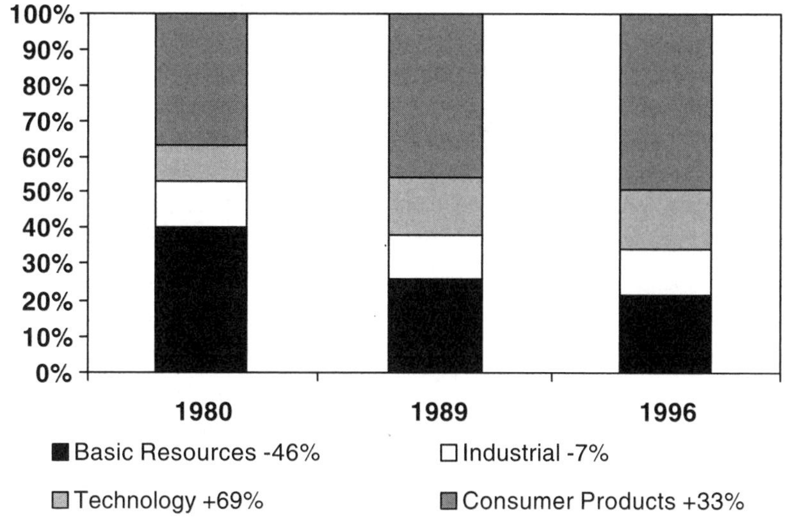

b. % of Fortune 500 Firms

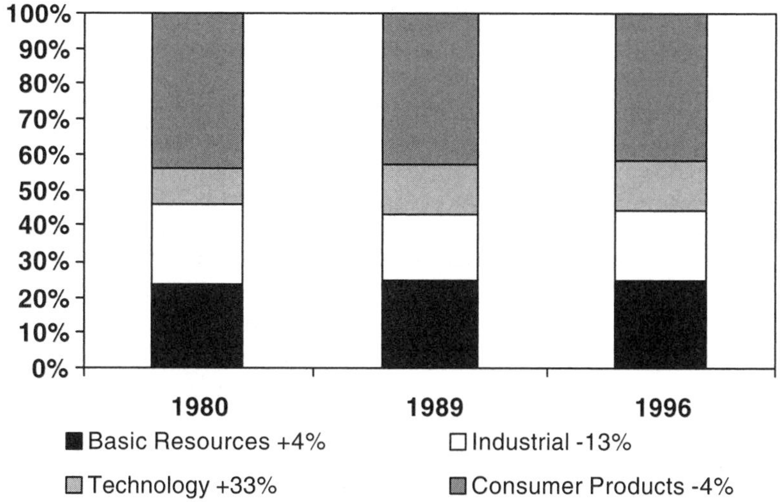

Figure 10-2. Sectoral Distribution of Fortune 500 Revenues and Firms, 1980–1996
Sectors are as defined elsewhere in the text, except that for purposes of this display Consumer Products includes both cyclical and noncyclical products, and Energy is included in Basic Resources. Source: Trimbath 2000.

Table 10-2. Food Firms Removed from S&P

Company	Year Removed	Buyer (if Merged)
Del Monte Corp.	1979	
Standard Brands	1981	Nabisco
Iowa Beef Processors	1981	Occidental Petroleum
Norton Simon	1983	Esmark
Stokely-Van Camp	1983	Quaker Oats
Oscar Mayer & Co.	1984	General Foods
Amstar	1984	KKR
Nabisco Brands	1985	RJ Reynolds
Pillsbury	1985	Grand Metropolitan PLC
Carnation	1985	Nestle
General Foods	1985	Philip Morris
Beatrice Foods	1986	KKR
Kraft Inc.	1988	Philip Morris
Whitman Corp.	1991	sold Pet Food group
Borden	1994	

Sources: Standard and Poor's; Milken Institute.

Figure 10-3 shows the trend in increasing size for firms in the food industry, using the "survivors" from the Trimbath study, that is, firms which remained active through 2000. Manufacturers saw their growth in the 1980s, and leveled off in the 1990s. The average size of retail firms declined slightly in the late 1980s and then increased steadily until the mid-1990s, so that they are now larger than wholesalers and are rivaling manufacturers.

Retail food was becoming the "800-pound gorilla" of the industry. Its size could also be seen in the number of products carried in the average store. The number of supermarkets in the United States declined slightly, from 26,815 stores in 1980 to 24,548 in 1993. The variety of unique brands, package sizes, and flavors carried was an estimated 14,000 products in 1985. By 1993, the figure had grown to about 25,000, and then doubled by 1997 to about 50,000 products. Retail food floor space grew to accommodate this increasing array of products and services. Supermarkets' average selling area rose from 23,000 square feet in 1980 to 35,000 square feet by 1996 (Kaufman 1996).

CONSOLIDATION THROUGH MERGERS AND ACQUISITIONS

In any given year more than 50 percent of corporate control activity is accounted for by five or six industries. However, the composition of the five or six industries changes from year to year, with different industries form-

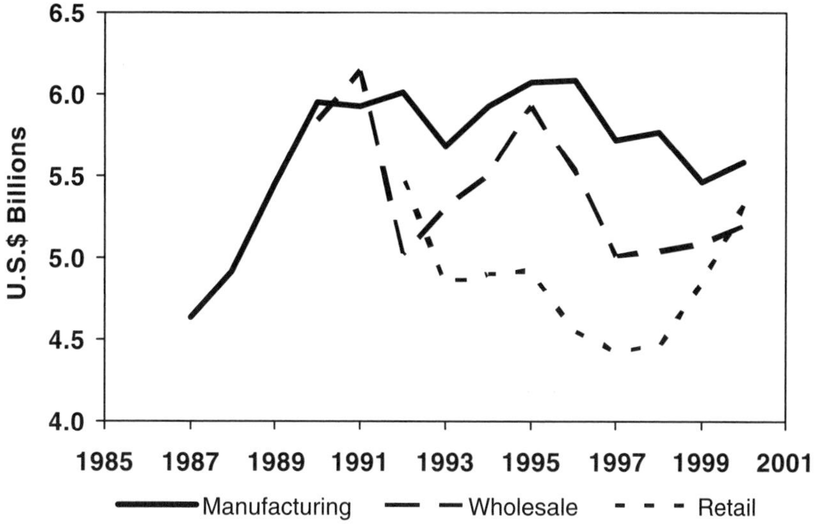

Figure 10-3. Average Food Industry Firm Size, 1987–2000. Sources: Compustat Research Insight; Milken Institute.

ing the top five in each year. Mitchell and Mulherin (1996) analyzed the patterns for the years 1982–1989. Among their fifty-one sample industries, they found significant differences in the rate of corporate control activity as well as in the timing of the activity. Most of the corporate control activity occurred in relatively few industries with clearly identifiable major shocks. One example was the oil price shocks occurring in 1973 and in 1979. These shocks affected not only the oil industry but also the structure of industries in which energy represented 10 percent or more of input costs. The industry patterns in takeovers and restructuring reflect the relative economic shocks to those sectors. A major influence on takeover activity has been broad underlying economic and financial forces.

Another example is the late 1990s effect of deregulation in financial services, utilities, and media. Those three areas accounted for 49 percent of the dollar value of corporate control activity in 1997. Food processing remained in the upper half of the fifty industry classifications ranked by Mergerstat throughout the 1990s. If you combine manufacturing, wholesale, and retail, the food industry ranked in the top ten until 1995. The rank of the food industry declined steadily in the 1990s, by about ten positions, as computers, financial services, and media firms became more active in the market for corporate control. Not that mergers and acquisitions in the food industry disappeared altogether. The purchase of RJR Nabisco in 1988 stood as the largest in history until 1997, seven years after KKR retired the high yield bonds it used to pay for the company. Food processing was the fourth most active sector ranked by value in the last quarter of 2000.

Food also was a leading industry in the manufacturing sector in terms of worldwide cross-border merger and acquisition activity in 1999 (UNCTAD 2000): "Most of these were horizontal, aiming at economies of scale, technological synergies, . . . consolidating and streamlining innovation strategies and R&D budgets" (Overview, p. 13). The second largest U.K. target in 2000 was Diageo's Pillsbury Company, which was purchased by General Mills for $5.12 billion. Just as the active sectors vary from time to time within a country, so there are also differences in cross-border activity among countries. Food and beverages were targeted industries across the European Union in 1999. Food (along with finance) was also the principal target industry in Central and Eastern Europe.

The Firm Efficiency Model (Revisited)

Slow growth in consumer real income served to increase price sensitivity in the food industry, forcing firms to become more efficient or lose sales to low cost competitors. Manufacturers, wholesalers, and retailers waged serious price competition. Recall the model of mergers discussed in chapter 9. Firms that were relatively inefficient in the use of resources were more likely to experience a change in ownership during the 1980s. And firms in the noncyclical consumer products sector were half again as likely to have a change in ownership if their costs were out of line for the industry (Trimbath 2002).

The food industry, which accounts for many of the firms in the consumer products sector studied by Trimbath, was a case of an industry with a high volume of corporate control activity. Table 10-3 shows how food's share of revenues held up despite the fact that the share of firms fell by one-quarter between 1980 and 1995.

Overall, no one sector in the Trimbath study had a significantly different risk of takeover than the full sample. Accounting for cost inefficiency in the model, however, firms in the noncyclical consumer products sector had a significantly higher probability of takeover. For firms with costs above industry in the noncyclical sector, the probability of takeover rose 350 percent above that in other sectors in 1981, then declined to the level of all other sectors by 1990. In addition to food, this sector includes cosmetics and personal care, other retailers and wholesalers, consumer and household products and services, medical supplies, tobacco, health care providers, and pharmaceuticals. Of the sixty targets in the noncyclical consumer prod-

Table 10-3. Cumulative Percentage Change From 1980 in Food Industry, 1985–1995

	1985	1990	1995
Revenues	1%	–3%	–7%
Firms	–19%	–22%	–25%

Percent of Fortune 500; Food Industry includes manufacturers, wholesalers, and retailers
Source: Trimbath 2000.

ucts sector among the Fortune 500 studied by Trimbath, however, two-thirds were in the food industry (thirty-two manufacturers and eight retailers). Twenty-four of the targets in the food industry (60 percent) were bought by other food industry firms, providing additional evidence of the horizontal mergers seen in cross-border activity. The next largest group (twelve) was taken private.

The significantly higher probability of takeover in this sector indicates an increased risk that is not explained by a model which does not account for cost inefficiency. To identify the source of the difference, separate measures were constructed for firms in the noncyclical sector and all other firms. There was no difference in the effect of size on takeover risk for firms in this sector. Only the noncyclical firms with costs above the industry median had a significantly higher risk of takeover. When costs rise above the industry median, the risk of takeover for a firm in the noncyclical consumer products sector is significantly higher than that of firms in other sectors. This strong positive effect of costs above industry decreases with time. By about 1990, the increased effect would be reduced to zero so that the risk is not different from firms in other sectors with costs above industry. This increased risk is associated with efficiency before the 1989 merger financing regulations, and the subsequent decrease appears in the postregulatory period. In the noncyclical sector, there were thirty-eight targets from 1981 through 1989; no targets from 1990 to 1993; and fourteen targets in 1994–1997 in the Trimbath study.

MONEY MATTERS

Financial innovations enabled these changes in the food industry. The ability to use public markets for leveraged financing increased both the rate of mergers and the size of merged firms. There is some evidence that firms in the noncyclical sector relied more heavily on high yield bond financing than other firms. Yago (1991a) found that the food industry accounted for 1.4 percent of corporate high yield bonds issued in 1983–1986 but only 0.5 percent of GNP, indicating that their participation in the high yield bond market was disproportional to their participation in the economy as a whole. This could account for the increased risk in that sector before merger financing regulations and the decrease in the significance of that risk through 1989 found in Trimbath (2002). In addition, while industries in the period used an average of 7 percent of high yield financing for mergers and acquisitions, the food industry used its high yield financing for mergers at more than double that rate (17 percent).

Figures 10-4 through 10-6 show the shift in the peak high yield bond usage by the three areas of the food industry. Figure 10-7 shows that manufacturers (food processing) dominated the industry's share of high yield bonds in the early years of the study. This is also reflected in figure 10-8, which shows a high rate of mergers and acquisitions in the food-processing industry during the same period. This also brings into focus the increas-

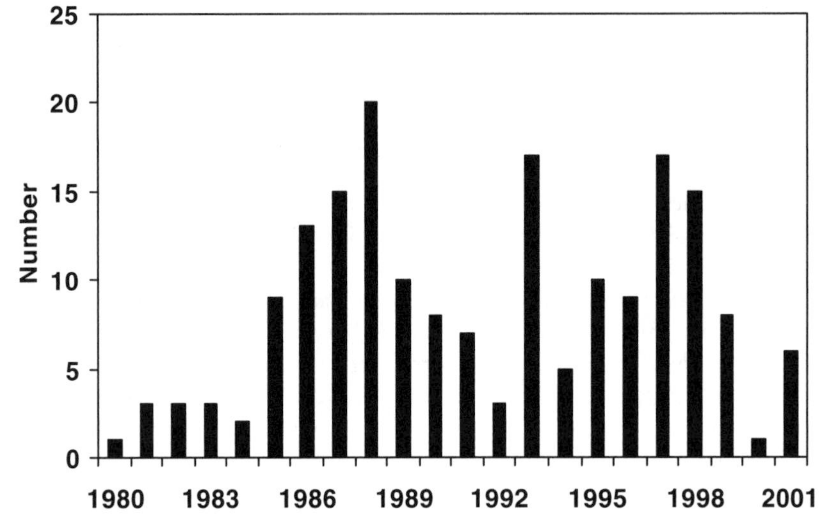

Figure 10-4. Number of High Yield Issues for Food Manufacturers, 1980–2001. Source: Securities Data Corporation.

ing use of high yield by food-processing companies during the 1980s. There was a noticeable shift to the use of high yield in the retail area in 1988 and 1992. Again, there was an accompanying increase in M&A activity. However, food retailers were a more modest number of firms, in absolute terms, so their activity does not show the dramatic percentage of all M&A activity that the food processors do.

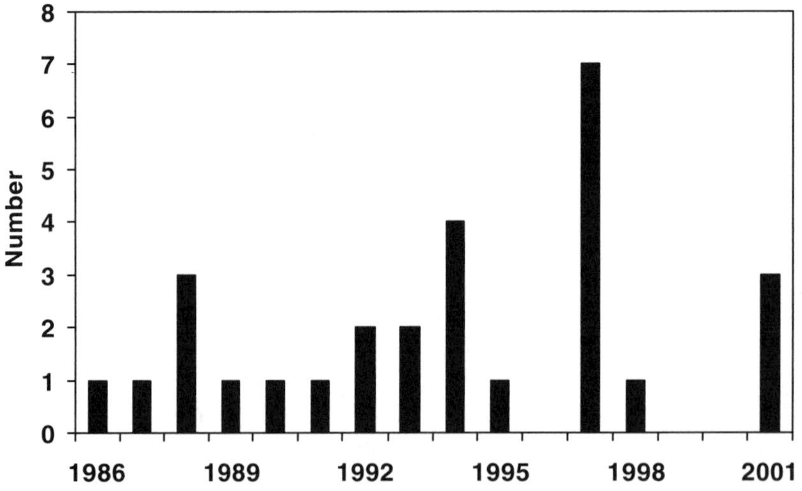

Figure 10-5. Number of High Yield Issues for Food Wholesalers, 1986–2001. Data not available before 1986. Years indicated as empty had no issues for that year. Source: Securities Data Corporation.

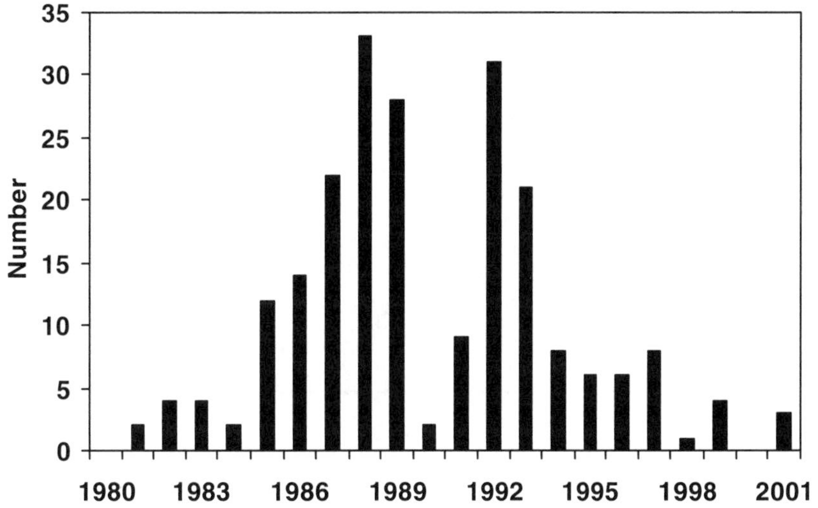

Figure 10-6. Number of High Yield Issues for Food Retailers, 1980–2001. Years indicated as empty had no issues for that year. Source: Securities Data Corporation.

This increasing reliance on high yield financing in the food industry, demonstrated in figure 10-9, is particularly interesting because it addresses an argument that the increase in debt from mergers had an adverse effect on U.S. corporations. Some economists believe that high yield bond debt could be used more heavily in the noncyclical sector with no adverse effect, because these firms were less vulnerable to economic fluctuations. A

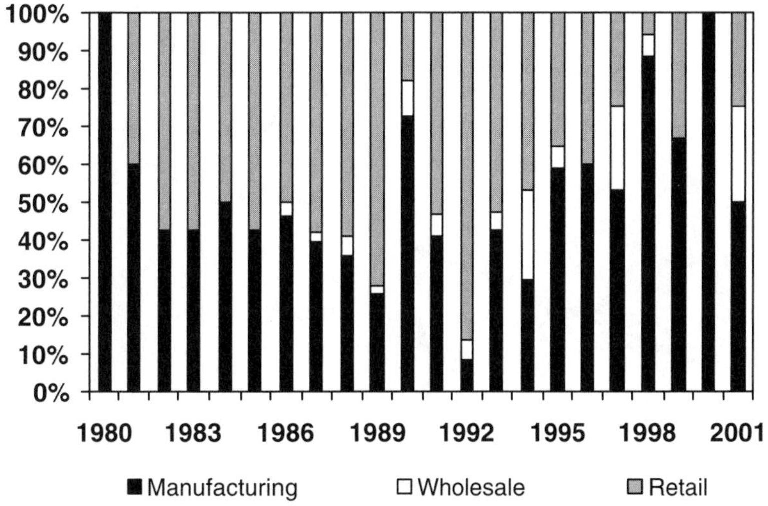

Figure 10-7. Percent of High Yield Issues in Food Sector by Producer Segment, 1980–2001. Source: Securities Data Corporation.

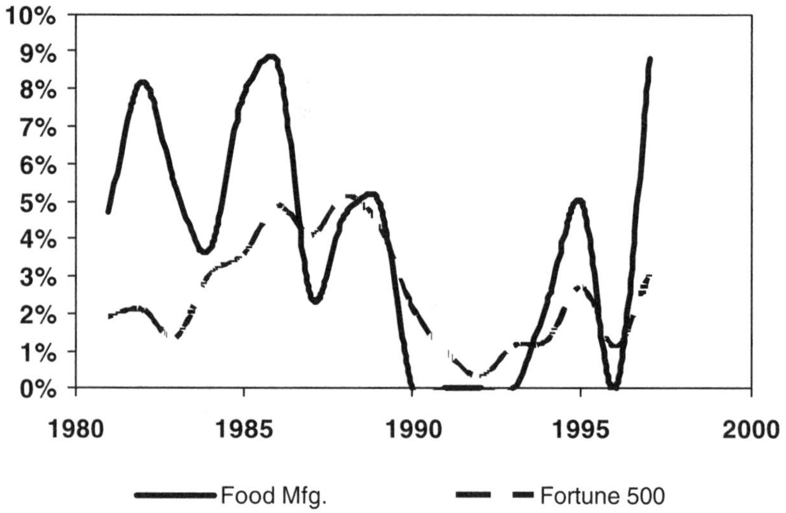

Figure 10-8. Takeover Rate, Food Manufacturing versus Fortune 500, 1981–1997. Source: Trimbath 2000.

1989 article in *U.S. News & World Report* (Feb. 13, 1989, p. 61), cited the work of Morgan Stanley economist Stephen Roach:

> most of the debt growth had occurred in businesses that historically suffer less than others during recessionary downdrafts. Sorting out LBO's [leveraged buyouts] by area, Roach found that food and tobacco firms, which boast steady incomes no matter what the economic climate, alone accounted for one fifth of

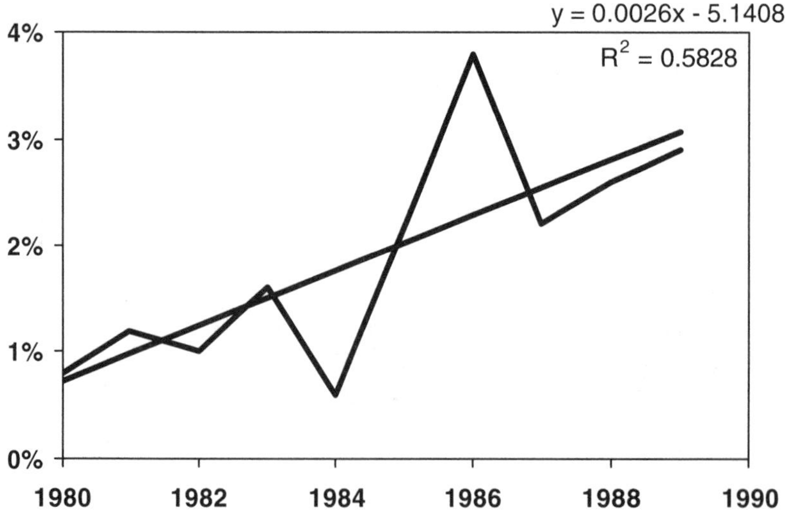

Figure 10-9. Focus on the 1980s: High Yield Issues by Food Companies as Percent of All Issues, 1980–1989. Source: Securities Data Corporation.

> the deals from 1982 to 1987. Over 95 percent of the rise in interest expense came in sectors comprising just one third of the nation's total output. "American industry is not running amok," says Roach. "The debt is being carried by those who can handle it best."

About 20 percent of the top fifty grocers issued debt in the high yield market in 1999. That percentage of the largest U.S. grocers accessing the high yield market hadn't changed since 1990, though the names of the issuers had.

TECHNOLOGY + CAPITAL = EFFICIENCY

Biotechnology was being applied to food production in the 1980s, but it was expensive to implement, with little if any innovation capital available from the government. R&D money was being spent to "invent" new products, like toaster pastries and microwavable meals. A *U.S. Distribution Journal* survey in 1990 painted a picture of an industry that was seemingly entering a "back-to-basics" period characterized by operational cost-cutting, an emphasis on buying more effectively, and a greater sense of strategic selling, all of which was made possible by the use of enhanced technologies at the retail level. By 1997 topics like shopping over the Internet and genetic engineering became commonly associated with the food industry, perhaps portents of further changes to come.

The consolidation in the number of firms was noticeable in the food industry. In addition, firms in the food industry became leaner, more efficient. The consolidation in the number of firms producing the nation's supply of ready-to-eat food was driven by the need for efficiency. Assisting that efficiency was the impact of the rapidly expanding use of technology.

We know from Trimbath (2002) that firms in the food industry paid a risk premium for having costs above the industry median. This is the initial evidence of corporate restructuring that took place through the joint effect of financing availability and an active corporate control market. Although the share of total revenue in the noncyclical sector increased across time, the number of firms represented in the sample decreased (see table 10-1). This is the only sector for which consolidation of this nature is evidenced.

Goodwin and Brester (1995) report that the food industry experienced crucial transitions in the structure of production, technological capabilities, and competitiveness. Their results confirm a significant gradual structural change in the U.S. food industry that was initiated in 1980:

> Between 1972 and 1990, labor's share of total variable production costs fell over 26 percent while capital's share rose almost 46 percent. Over the same period, raw food material's cost share fell 19 percent while energy's share rose 47 percent.

Goodwin and Brester specifically mention the "merger movement" of the 1980s as one of the significant changes in the business environment that "may have contributed to structural change in the food and kindred products sector." They emphasize the expanding use of new technologies for the processing, packaging, and marketing of food products. The efficiency enhancements in the food industry are largely attributable to the application of technology. In addition, Morrison and Siegel (1998) report finding evidence that the expansion of external technological capital in the food industry resulted in short- and long-run cost savings. Thus, unit cost changes or cost efficiency, motivated in the context of scale economies, were augmented by technological externalities in the food industry. Figure 10-10 shows that, again, food manufacturers dominated in the decline in cost per unit of revenue, with retailers showing only a slightly stronger decline. These figures are for the "survivors" only; the increase in efficiency would be even more dramatic if the targets and failed firms were included.

The science of preparing, preserving, and reshaping packaged food is a bigger business today than ever: food-related companies and the government allotted some $28 billion to research and development in 2000, up from about $1 billion in 1985.[1] The application of technology to the improvements in cost efficiency in the food industry was largely responsible for the consolidation described earlier. Much of the food industry's R&D money went to increase the efficiency of huge, sophisticated production lines. The second largest share of R&D was devoted to developing new products and adapting them to the appliances in the family kitchen—the toaster, the refrigerator, and especially the microwave oven. Processing

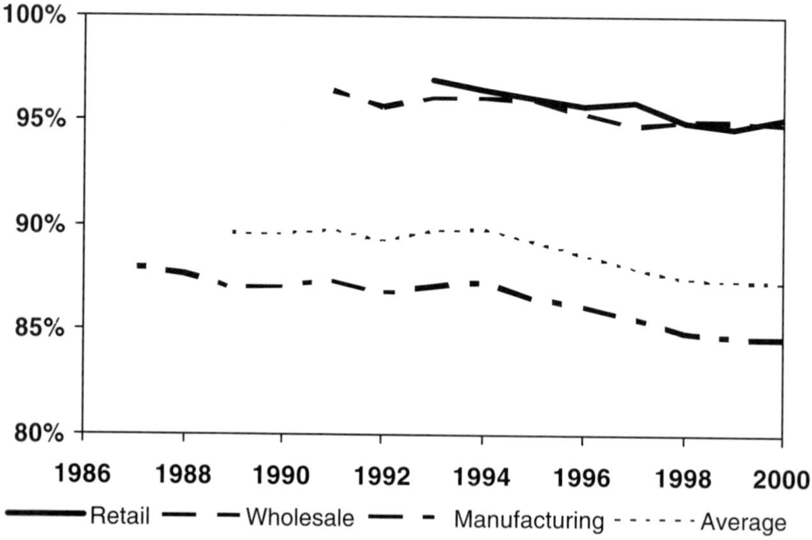

Figure 10-10. Total Cost per Unit of Revenue, 1987–2000. Source: Compustat Research Insight; Milken Institute.

1. General Foods, the biggest private spender in 1985, accounted for about 12 percent of total industry R&D (*Fortune*, Dec 23, 1985, p. 85).

techniques that consumers take for granted are often more complex than they seem. Keeping ingredients from separating in frozen foods, for example, requires a patented way of using emulsifiers to control ice crystal formation and maintain texture (*Fortune*, Dec. 23, 1985, p. 85[4]). Microwavable meals drove and were driven by the increased use of microwave ovens in consumer homes. About half of all U.S. households had a microwave oven in 1985 (*Financial World*, Dec. 25, 1985, p. 43). By 1999, the number had reached 90 percent (*Technology Review*, Jan. 1, 1999).

About 15,000 new food products were introduced on average each year during 1993–1995: quick snacks for busy people who want to buy time more than nourishment; ready-made meals for heating in the microwave; low-fat, low-calorie foods for dieters; special foods for babies and the elderly; health foods for the fitness oriented (Weston and Chiu 1996). By comparison, around 3,000 new products are launched each year in the United Kingdom. Today's new product rate is up astronomically from the rate of about 1,400 in 1982 (*Progressive Grocer*, Sept. 1983, p. 25). The number of new food products introduced fell 21 percent, from 16,863 in 1995 to 13,266 in 1996—the sharpest yearly decline since the early 1970s. This is in sharp contrast to an average 8 percent growth per year between 1992 and 1995. By 1997, there were over 320,000 packaged food products available in the United States (Gallo 1997). Manufacturers may have pulled back on the number of products offered in order to save costs, or they may have concentrated their marketing efforts on their core products. Fifty-two percent of respondents to the Food Processing Top 100 R&D survey indicated that they outsourced R&D to contractors. While 9 percent of respondents indicated that they had increased outsourcing of R&D projects, none of the respondents reported decreases. The business of R&D had become more efficient.

The U.S. retail market is now dominated by the major supermarkets. The top four retail supermarkets also dominate in the United Kingdom, where they account for about 50 percent of all sales, and the top ten have 80 percent of the food sales. The technology implemented at the retail level included scanners connected to computers that let store owners manage inventory and reduce waste. The use of this technology was particularly responsible for the shift in the balance of economic power away from the food manufacturers to the retailers. Hooked up to computers, the scanners gave retailers specific and highly detailed knowledge about sales and inventories.

The first operational scanning of the UPC (universal product code) was on June 26, 1974 at the Troy, Ohio, unit of Marsh Supermarkets, a Depression era success, one of the top fifty grocers in the United States, and a current participant in the high yield market. It used NCR registers and an NCR computer with the scanners.[2] The choice of city was no accident. Troy headquarters Hobart, the maker of UPC label printers and applicators for in-store marking, and is only half an hour from Dayton, NCR headquarters.[3] In 1975, only forty stores in the country were scanning (Walsh 1991).

2. NCR was purchased by AT&T in 1991.

3. Hobart was purchased by Dart & Kraft in 1981.

By 1985, the supermarket chains that accounted for 40 percent of retail food sales were using checkout scanners (*Forbes*, Aug 26, 1985, p. 76[1]). In 1989, 62 percent of all store sales were scanned. In 2001, you would have to look very far to find even one grocer that does not use a checkout scanner.

Many of the technology budget dollars in the food industry are going toward business reengineering efforts. Chief information officers (CIOs) in the InformationWeek 500 said that on average, slightly more than 17 percent of their information systems (IS) budgets in 2000 were dedicated to support for reengineering or business-process redesign projects. More than 46 percent of the CIOs said departments or business processes at their companies had undergone reengineering in the past five years. Two examples of high yield issuers using information technology are shown in the boxes: Chiquita Banana and Del Monte Foods.

Computers, in turn, were making possible comprehensive new product analysis programs and systems. The systems allow retailers to measure handling costs, warehousing expenses, the amount of space a product takes up on the shelf, how quickly an item sells, and so forth to calculate pre-

BOX 10-1. CHIQUITA BANANA

In 1999 Chiquita turned to the Internet to reduce communications costs with its associates around the world, including more than 30,000 who live and work in Latin America. "You can't run a leased line to all these places," Chiquita's Ledford says. With a mix of terrestrial, satellite, wireless, radio, and virtual private networking systems, the company can route payroll transactions, e-mail, and more to remote areas that four years ago didn't even have electricity. Chiquita's biggest project—which could net $1.2 million by reducing ongoing client PC support—is centralizing control of its PC operations. The company adheres to a standard desktop platform, which is a mixture of Microsoft NT and Novell print-and-file servers. Mandating standard desktops that employees can't change means updates will run more smoothly. "It prevents us from having to employ 30 people to do updates, and we can do application rollouts in minutes, as opposed to days and months," Ledford says.

Chiquita also implemented Citrix Systems Inc. application server software that lets client sessions run on a server. "People dialing in to the network where they don't have a dedicated line and only a 28.8 modem can now run full-blown applications," he says. Like most companies in the food and beverage industry, Chiquita—in spite of the enormous financial pressures—is preparing to participate in e-business. Key suppliers can directly access Chiquita's intranet systems to test product specifications; third-party brokers and customs offices can access Chiquita's internal tracking systems via the Web; and the company is exploring opportunities with online marketplaces.

Source: *InformationWeek*, Sept. 11, 2000, p. 237.

BOX 10-2. DEL MONTE FOODS

The nation's largest producer and distributor of branded processed fruit, vegetable and tomato products made a major move to improve its operating efficiencies and effect substantial cost savings through online procurement. Del Monte Foods Company, which markets products under the Del Monte, Contadina and Sunfresh brands, elected to use the iProcure network from Datastream Systems Inc. Del Monte identified an improved procurement strategy as critical to its effort to streamline its operations, eliminate unnecessary practices in its facilities and its supply chain, and improve asset management.

The Datastream's iProcure network automates electronic commerce for maintenance, repair and operations procurement. This purchasing is a key element in the asset management cycle. "Del Monte is dedicated to providing superior quality products while incorporating improved business processes," says Glen Lewis, western region procurement manager for Del Monte Foods, which had sales of $1.5 billion in 2000. The iProcure purchasing network provides simple and quick access to critical materials and supplies. Lewis also claims efficiency gains in both direct and indirect procurement.

"Leading companies such as Del Monte are reaping the benefits of streamlined procurement processes," says Greg Jackson, vice president of iProcure. "By automating their asset procurement process via the iProcure network, Del Monte can optimize its administrative processes, purchasing procedures and vendor management."

Source: FoodProcessing.com, June 2001.

cisely how much profit—per inch of space and per dollar invested—the item generates. The data allow retailers to choose from among various brands with unprecedented precision. This linking of suppliers and retailers with the use of computers helped to reduce the time it takes for a product to get from the manufacturer to the retail store from 104 days to 61 days (Weston and Chiu 1996).

A WORD ON THE TECHNOLOGY SECTOR

The combination of high yield with high tech is well documented. Every major brokerage firm and dealer in the high yield market has a weekly publication dedicated to the topic, with telecommunications being front and center. Here we choose to examine the use of high yield in the food industry to show the broader impact of that combination. Questions have been raised about the forces driving these changes and the implications of consolidation for both consumers and food market suppliers, such as grower-shippers, food processors, and wholesalers. The mergers and acquisitions effect on farmers from the consolidation in the food sector is being decried (and studied by the Small Business Administration and the U.S. Department of Agriculture). Yet those same groups applaud technology's growth and contribution to the economy. We've attempted to show how the two are related, using food as an example of an industry that is implementing the technology that is being funded by high yield, an industry that is financing its own growth and changes with high yield as well.

Firms in the technology sector were at a significantly greater risk for takeover, after controlling for size, inefficiency, and low market value, after 1989 than they were before. This result is also reflected in the significant risk premium put on low market value industries in the technology sector after the 1980s. The technology sector increased its share of both revenue and firms in the study, leading all sectors in growth in both categories (see table 10-1). Nearly 70 percent (seventeen out of twenty-five) of the technology firms among the Fortune 500 from 1980 through 1997 were taken over by other corporations in the technology sector. Those not taken by technology buyers were taken over by foreign corporations, financial firms, or management.

Most economic studies of the food industry tend to rely on the use of firms in the 2000 to 2099 range of standard industrial classification (SIC) codes, which includes only the food-processing industry (manufacturers). Here we include wholesalers and retailers to capture a broader flavor of the changes that are taking place. A more thorough examination could include even farming (agriculture) and restaurants (food service) (box 10-3). While many industry analysts make a separate study of food processing and restaurants, only a few break out retail food (primarily supermarkets), and virtually none make separate studies of the wholesale food segment.

The structure of the food wholesaling sector is changing dramatically. Consolidation, especially among food service distributors, continues to reshuffle the ranks of the leading distributors. For example, JP Foodservice was the fifth largest food service distributor in 1996. After a series of acquisitions, the company moved to become the second largest. Forward integration into retailing by leading wholesalers helps to blur the line between wholesalers and retailers. For example, Richfood Holdings, primarily a wholesaler, acquired the supermarket chain Farm Fresh, increasing the number of Richfood supermarkets sixfold. Richfood was subsequently purchased by Supervalu, the nation's largest wholesaler and twelfth largest food retailer.

The consolidation and structural change in U.S. food retailing in recent years through mergers, acquisitions, divestitures, internal growth, and new competitors has been unprecedented. Since 1996, almost 3,500 supermarkets have been purchased, representing annual grocery store sales of more than $67 billion. Two of the largest food retailing combinations in history were announced in 1998: the merger of Albertson's (the nation's fourth largest food retailer) with American Stores (the second largest) and the acquisition of sixth largest Fred Meyer by first-ranked Kroger Company.

BOX 10-3. DEFINITIONS OF INDUSTRIES IN THE FOOD SECTOR

Manufacturers

Food processing plants transform raw agricultural materials into intermediate foodstuffs or edible products through the application of labor, machinery, energy, and scientific knowledge. In 1998, food processing plants accounted for 12 percent of the value of shipments from all U.S. manufacturing plants. Because intermediate inputs (primarily agricultural materials) account for a relatively large share of food processors' costs, value-added in food processing represents a smaller share of all value-added in manufacturing at 8.5 percent.

There is a very large number of food processing establishments (plants)—over 26,000, according to the most recent comprehensive data in the Census of Manufactures. The plants employ 1.47 million workers, about 8 percent of all manufacturing employment and just over 1 percent of all U.S. employment. Most processing establishments are very small: only 4 percent have 100 or more employees. Those few large establishments, however, account for 80 percent of value-added in food processing. Moreover, the number of small establishments has fallen over time, along with their relative contribution to value-added in food processing.

Wholesalers

Food wholesaling in the U.S. is a $589 billion business. It is the part of the food system in which goods are assembled, stored, and transported to retailers, food service outlets, institutions (for example, schools and government), farmers, other wholesalers, and other types of businesses. There are three basic types of wholesalers: merchant wholesalers, manufacturers' sales branches and offices, and agents and brokers.

Merchant wholesalers are firms primarily engaged in buying groceries and grocery products from processors or manufacturers and reselling to retailers, institutions, and other businesses. Manufacturers' sales branches and offices are wholesale operations maintained by grocery manufacturers or processors to market their own products. Brokers and agents are wholesale operators who buy or sell as representatives of others for a commission and typically do not physically handle the products. They may serve as representatives of manufacturers or processors but do not take title to the goods. Merchant wholesalers' sales account for the largest percentage (56 percent) of food wholesale sales.

Wholesalers may be further classified as broad line, specialty, or limited line. Broad line distributors handle a wide variety of groceries, health and beauty items, and household products. They are also referred to as general line or full line distributors. Important broad line distributors include Supervalu, Fleming, and Nash Finch. In contrast, specialty merchants are primarily engaged in the wholesale distribution of such items as frozen foods, dairy

(*continued*)

Box 10-3. *continued*

products, poultry products, fish, meat and meat products, or fresh fruits and vegetables. Limited line merchants are primarily engaged in the wholesale distribution of a narrow range of dry groceries, such as canned foods, coffee, bread, or soft drinks. Specialty wholesalers account for 43 percent of food wholesale sales, the largest share among the three groups.

Retailers

The nation's retail food stores and food service outlets provide food products, prepared food, and meals to consumers. Food stores (supermarkets, superettes, small grocery stores, convenience stores, and specialized food stores) account for 82 percent of all food sold in retail stores. Food service outlets (including restaurants, fast food outlets, cafeterias, and institutions) account for 84 percent of prepared food and meals sold.

Food store sales, including food and nonfood products, amounted to $458.3 billion in 1999. Supermarkets accounted for 70 percent of the total, followed by superette and small grocery stores at 15 percent.

Source: USDA, Economic Research Service, Briefing Room.

Widespread consolidation in the grocery industry has significantly affected the share of total grocery store sales accounted for by the largest food retailers. In 1999, the twenty largest food retailers captured more than 52 percent of national grocery store sales, an increase from 38.6 percent in 1987.

Therefore, the analysis here should be considered only suggestive of technology induced changes in the food industry. Erickson (1994) reviews recent findings which provide compelling evidence that accurate analyses of technology-based industrial restructuring cannot be built on a foundation of aggregated (even four-digit SIC) classifications of output or employment associated with the technology categories traditionally used by economists, geographers, and other researchers. Technologically induced structural changes in industry composition and contributions to national output and its growth have been massive and subject to both short-term cyclical and long-term secular swings. According to Erickson, attention has shifted to the long (fifty-plus years) Kondratieff waves of economic growth and decline that subsume shorter business cycles, the theory of which is firmly anchored in the industrial restructuring inherent in the bunching of new inventions and their applications to products and processes, creating differential impacts in various industries.

Still, Morrison and Siegel (1998) attempt to overcome this difficulty in a food industry study that includes an examination of private sources of capital. They find both internal and external capital factors to be substitutable with the variable inputs and with each other. Increases in these factors generate strong cost savings overall in the food industry. This is consistent with tendencies toward increasing capital intensity and high-tech capital intensity in the industry. It also suggests that relationships among internal and external capital factors are a strong driving force for such changes. Finally, the observed patterns suggest a greater scope for scale economies to motivate productivity, and thus cost efficiency, in the food industry than that suggested in earlier studies.

FOREIGN AND INTERNATIONAL INFLUENCES

Figure 10-11 shows the value of U.S. food imports and exports from 1980 to 2000. During the mid-1980s, the United States came very close to being a net importer of food. However, rapid income growth, especially in China and other Asian nations, boosted world average caloric intake to record levels in many regions after 1990. Average daily food use, measured as the calories available for human consumption, climbed to nearly 2,700 calories worldwide in the early 1990s, from just under 2,400 calories in the 1970s. While U.S. exports surged ahead for several years, as the new millennium began, imports again approached exports.

Two of the displaced S&P firms mentioned earlier were taken over by foreign corporations. It has been argued that foreign firms have been favored in bidding for U.S. companies because of more liberal tax rules. Foreign firms may have an advantage over U.S. firms because of greater flexibility in handling goodwill (defined as the excess of purchase price over book value). Rules vary across countries, but broadly speaking, European

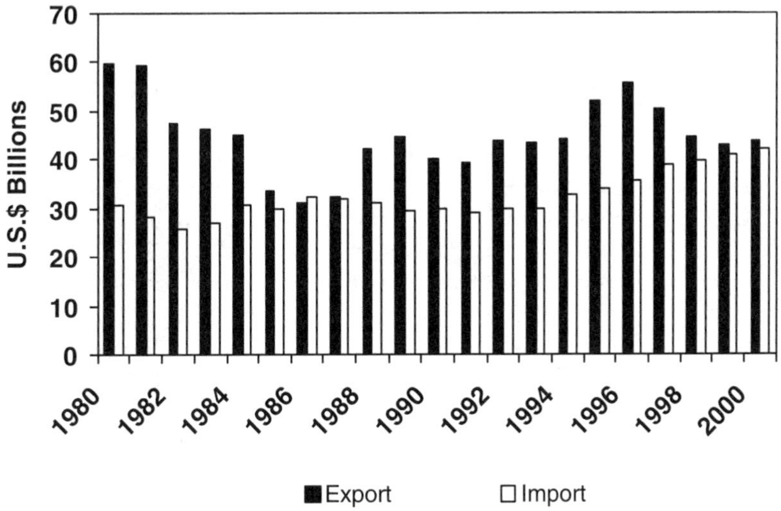

Figure 10-11. U.S. Food Exports and Imports, 1980–2000. In chained 1996 dollars. Source: Department of Commerce, Bureau of Economic Analysis.

countries allow goodwill to be charged off directly to shareholders' equity, and even this can be reversed later. Germany, Japan, and Canada go further. In these countries, a large portion of the charge-off is tax deductible; thus, the state subsidizes takeovers. Until 1993, U.S. accounting practices required that goodwill be amortized against earnings over a forty-year period, a charge to earnings that was not tax deductible. Thus U.S. firms have been required to decrease reported earnings without any tax benefit. But a tax law change helped to mitigate this tax disadvantage for U.S. companies. Under section 197 of the 1993 Clinton Budget Act (or the Investment Bankers Relief Act of 1993), a U.S. company can reduce taxable income by amortization of goodwill over a fifteen-year period, if the acquiring company purchases the assets (not the shares) of another company (Weston and Chiu 1996).

The food industry stood to benefit most from this change. Packaged food companies were already consolidating, and most of their stocks were trading at premiums averaging 4.3 times book value. The food companies with the ten largest market caps in 1991 were trading for $60 billion more than their combined book values. Indeed, acquisitions of food processing firms jumped 50 percent between 1993 and 1994 while overall activity rose only 12.5 percent (Mergerstat Review, 1996). Much of the value of a food company lies in its brand values, which are not captured on the balance sheet. For example, had goodwill been deductible when Philip Morris bought Kraft in 1989, the write-off would have come to nearly 95 percent of the $12.9 billion price tag (Taub 1991).

The U.S. food retailing firms are attractive to foreign investors for a variety of strategic reasons. The U.S. market is much larger than many foreign markets, with favorable overall growth prospects. The United States has a highly developed food distribution infrastructure, imposes fewer restrictions on overseas investors, and has less stringent regulations related to the building of new stores and support facilities than do many other countries. The United States also offers a stable political and business environment with lower investment risk (Kaufman 1996).

Food retailing sales by U.S. affiliates of foreign firms reached $48.2 billion in 1992, an increase of 2.3 percent over 1991. Affiliates were responsible for 12.8 percent of total U.S. grocery store sales in 1992. U.S. affiliates are companies having at least 10 percent of voting stock or equivalent equity owned by a foreign investor. The five largest U.S. affiliates of foreign food retailers were among the top thirty food retailers nationwide, generating sales of $39.5 billion in 1994. Albertson's, headquartered in Boise, Idaho, was the largest U.S. affiliate and the fourth largest food retailer in the United States, with sales of $11.9 billion in 1994 (table 10-4). U.S. affiliates have grown by building new stores and by acquiring other food retailers. Both Albertson's and Food Lion have relied almost exclusively on internal growth strategies, while Ahold USA, and the Atlantic and Pacific Tea Company (A&P) have grown through acquisition strategies.

Table 10-4. International Sales and Earnings of Food Companies, 1994

Companies	International Sources as a Percent of	
	Sales	Operating Earnings
CPC International	64	58
Ralston Purina	44	n.a.
Borden	n.a.	57
H.J. Heinz	42	37
Kellogg	40	34
Sara Lee	35	29

n.a.: not available.
Source: Weston and Chiu 1996.

The United States dominates the rest of the world with seven of the top twenty-five transnational corporations (TNCs). Four of the top twenty-five TNCs are in the food industry, but none of those are U.S. firms. In fact, only two U.S. food firms make the top 100: Coca-Cola (forty-seventh) and RJR Nabisco (sixty-first).[4] The largest transnational food firm in the world is Nestle (Switzerland), which ranks tenth, followed by Unilever (Netherlands/U.K.), which ranks twelfth (UNCTAD 2000).

4. Wal-Mart, which is adding grocery sections to its stores, is ranked fourteenth.

11

Financing the Future

It is clear that firms offering new technologies, old industries seeking new life, and countries emerging from the developing world or transitioning from socialism all require access to capital markets. With insufficient internal savings that can be transformed into investment, carving channels from global capital markets to economic development needs is central to keeping economic growth alive. The world remains largely below investment grade, and any strategy that can increase the quality of the future and its markets by enhancing capital access today is far from "junk." Moreover, the high yield market has developed and evolved. The financial technology innovations of this asset class have moved far beyond the borders of what was once considered to be the high yield market. Innovations in private equity deal structures, asset-backed securitizations, and other derivative markets all evolved within and extended beyond the junk bond market. Junk no more, these financial innovations are now mainstreamed into the diversified investment portfolios of institutions, mutual funds, and individuals.

As this book is being written, the U.S. economy hovers between recession and recovery; the longest bull market in history has ended and a significant stock market slide is spooking investors in virtually every asset class. The global economy remains increasingly polarized and endangered by economic stagnation, instability, and inadequate job and capital formation. Extending the logic of financial innovation to new markets and assets is a significant challenge. In applying the logic and practice of high yield financial innovations to the future, it is worth recounting what we have learned and how the means and methods of high yield finance might be applied to future challenges.

The visionary work accomplished by Michael Milken and his pioneering colleagues and competitors in the new issue high yield market evolved from the lessons of bond markets in the 1930s and before. As financial professionals steeped in the corporate finance revolution spread to other sectors of financial services, and the fundamentals of the financial breakthroughs of scholarly work by Merton Miller, Harry Markowitz, William Sharpe, Michael Jensen, and many others (see appendix D) became respected and replicated in multiple markets, financial innovation became a core competence of business and public policy practice. How can we apply these important lessons?

WHAT HAVE WE LEARNED?

The emergence of high yield markets and the explosion of financial innovations to support them were important flash points in the corporate finance revolution that heralded the longest period of continuous economic growth in the twentieth century. Challenges for the twenty-first century high yield market continue unabated in the face of structural changes in markets, global financial instability, and issues of corporate governance. Unshackling capital and allowing it to flow to those who have the best business ideas and the best chance to create jobs must be the mission of entrepreneurs, financial innovators, and government regulators.

During the last quarter of the twentieth century, control of capital in America shifted away from private, concentrated financial institutions and toward decentralized, more competitive public capital markets, making the process of financing growth more forward looking and democratic. This democratization of capital meant that entrepreneurs were no longer limited to those few institutions which controlled capital access.[1]

The broadening and deepening of the high yield market in the 1990s was extraordinary, as we've documented, and not without continued growing pains of defaults, flawed capital structures, and external shocks. The dependency of entrepreneurs upon individual banks and insurance companies has been replaced. Companies can now turn to a market-based system with thousands of institutional buyers, including mutual funds, which have eclipsed banks in the financial services industry.

The difference between bank-based and market-based financing systems has proved to be profound for economic growth (Barth, Brumbaugh, and Yago 2001). Not only has the move toward open capital markets and financial innovations democratized the process of finance, it has also raised standards of disclosure and safeguards. Transparency and accountability are fundamental to market performance, as controversies and market disruptions caused by flawed governance and accounting scandals proved once again in 2002.

Transportation and communication have been transformed by the spread of digital technology. Global economies and markets must be transformed by continuous and permanent innovation in financial technology (Trimbath, forthcoming). More countries and regions must embrace these technologies in order to escape their dependence on foreign aid, government debt, and remittances by expatriate workers, and to create growth economies.

YIELD GAPS AND THE ROLE OF THE HIGH YIELD MARKET

After nearly two decades of high domestic equity market returns, we may now be entering a low yield environment. A gap between the expected

1. This discussion is largely based on Milken 1999a, 1999b, and 2000. See also *Democratizing Capital in the United States Conference Proceedings, Co-Sponsored by the Milken Institute, the Franklin D. Roosevelt Presidential Library, and the Ronald Reagan Presidential Library, June 1–2, 1998,* for a section of historical papers placing the phenomenon of the democratization of capital in a broader context.

return on equities and the return needed to meet long-term liabilities in pension funds is emerging (table 11-1). Endowments and foundations must earn an average annual return of 8.8 percent to pay retirement benefits in their defined benefit plans. Lower current returns and anticipated returns are creating a pension funding gap that will be important to bridge. While a combination of domestic equity and fixed income easily provided this return in the past, with neither asset class projected to provide such returns before 2005, asset managers must look to other investments. It is in this context that high yield securities and product extensions play an important role. Indeed, as Mark Yusko, chief investment officer at the University of North Carolina wrote in *Alternative Investment Research*, June 1999: "Institutions sometimes accept serious risk in more widely held asset classes, such as small cap equities or emerging markets, while overlooking strategies that exhibit sound returns and lower risk."

In order to bridge these yield gaps, future investment emerging from high yield markets and beyond will need to focus on new sources of economic growth and potential returns. Looking forward, we will review areas of potential market growth in the following:

- Emerging overseas markets
- Emerging domestic markets
- Environmental finance
- Intellectual capital securitization.

TOWARD GLOBAL MARKET DEVELOPMENT

Several macroeconomic problems have surfaced that are undermining future economic growth: (1) the concentration of financial control in many countries; (2) the absence of property rights and related incentive structures (de Soto 2000; North 1990); and (3) the lack of market transparency and corporate governance. These obstacles make tools of financial technology inaccessible in most of the world and have aborted market changes in many countries.[2] The intersection between financial technology and information technology is important here. Without a free flow of accurate operating and financial information and the oversight of investors, owners,

Table 11-1. The Emerging Yield Gap

	Domestic Equity	Fixed Income
Past five-year return	10.1%	7.4%
Expected five-year return	8.7%	6.4%

Source: Greenwich Associates, U.S. Aggregate Fixed Income.

2. The Milken Institute Global Capital Access Index (CAI) summarizes statistical measures for much of these. Each annual release of the CAI includes a companion essay on a topical issue. The CAI (current and historical) is available at www.milkeninstitute.org.

and regulators, economic and regulatory distortions occur that are difficult to remedy.

Without financial technology, the means to stimulate growth and create jobs do not exist. The sources of growth depend upon the inclusion of broader populations, geographies, and markets into the capital markets that can finance the future. Changes in ownership and control, technology innovations, restructured industries, and the mobilization of assets—intellectual and natural—not yet monetized all represent sources of growth for high yield financial innovations in the future.

Looking forward, further deployment of high yield financial innovations needs to address issues of global economic development and bridge the capital, job, and income gap between the developed and the developing worlds. Financial technology can enliven economies that are absorbing domestic demographic shifts through new waves of business formation, monetizing and developing environmental goods and services, and addressing the emerging knowledge-capital gap.

MISSING MARKETS

Several key issues are identified as emerging global risks to sustainable growth and the capacity of the global economy to finance its future. These are the issues that financial innovations and high yield markets, and capital markets in general, must address:

- Negative capital flows to developing and transition economies
- Inadequate demand growth and the absence of middle-class development in the developing world due to increasing income and wealth polarization
- Lack of markets to adequately and efficiently allocate capital for entrepreneurial finance and economic growth.

At present, capital flows into emerging markets remain volatile and relatively short term. In some countries, flows have turned negative. In most emerging markets, capital flows have yet to be restored to pre–Asian-crisis levels. Small and medium-size businesses, moreover, are denied access to the vast pool of capital that the savings of developed countries represent. This situation persists because the much-needed changes in economic policy and in the governance of firms in emerging economies still lack sufficient popular support. For market-oriented reforms to succeed and produce lasting stability, they must hold out the prospect that all citizens will directly benefit from them.

Financial technology has its enemies. Entrenched managers and elites in developing countries have yet to see their way clear to support reforms that might decentralize political and economic power to transform from statist financial institutions and economies into entrepreneurial ones. Reforms, for example, must be designed to allow ordinary people access to home ownership through the availability of affordable long-term financing and for private entrepreneurs to enter long-protected, government-directed business markets.

Expanding economic participation in home and business ownership is key to the expansion of consumption and production in developing economies. Not only will a program of middle-class-oriented development financed through the democratization of capital create a constituency that will support reform, but it will be the best guarantor of global stability. Fortunately, much of the world—indeed, most emerging market economies—is ready for middle-class-oriented policies. Despite the difficulties of 2001 and the overall decline in capital access, there is a favorable climate for launching policies and programs for broader global participation. Fifty-two countries with a combined population of some 1.5 billion have already achieved levels of GDP comparable to those at which the United States and other countries first enacted middle-class-oriented policies (Mead and Schwenninger, 2003). The key to the development of a large middle class is the access of ordinary people to affordable, long-term credit and equity investments enabling them to realize the hopes and dreams in their business, professional, and personal lives. This, in turn, requires well-functioning and adequately capitalized regional and international financial institutions.

CAPITAL FLOWS

The Asian crisis of 1997, the Russian default and subsequent near financial meltdown of 1998, the resulting problems in Brazil and Ecuador, and, most recently, the collapse of the Argentine economy have dramatically curtailed investors' appetite for investments in emerging market countries (EMCs), despite a recent upturn in such investments driven by excess liquidity and portfolio reallocation by some large funds. Counter to this, and perhaps most meaningful, was the recent decision by the largest U.S. pension fund, CALPERS, to withdraw from Thailand, Indonesia, Malaysia, and the Philippines (Wilshire Associates 2002). This fueled a disinvestment backlash that should be a focus of grave concern for the prospects of sustainable global growth. Each of the three large regions of EMCs—Eastern Europe, East Asia, and Latin America—has seen a collapse in capital flows since 1997. Both East Asia and Eastern Europe have seen net capital outflows (figure 11-1). As capital flight has drained the poorer regions of the global economy, money has flowed into the developed countries, particularly the United States where it funds investment not only but also a widening trade deficit (figure 11-2).

Capital formation and its impact upon job creation are critical issues in fostering sustainable development strategies. The negative flow of capital to developing nations and transition economies deserves significant attention. During the third quarter of 2001, the gross volume of capital raised by emerging markets in the international capital markets fell sharply, with quarterly issuance falling more than 50 percent over the previous quarter to levels last

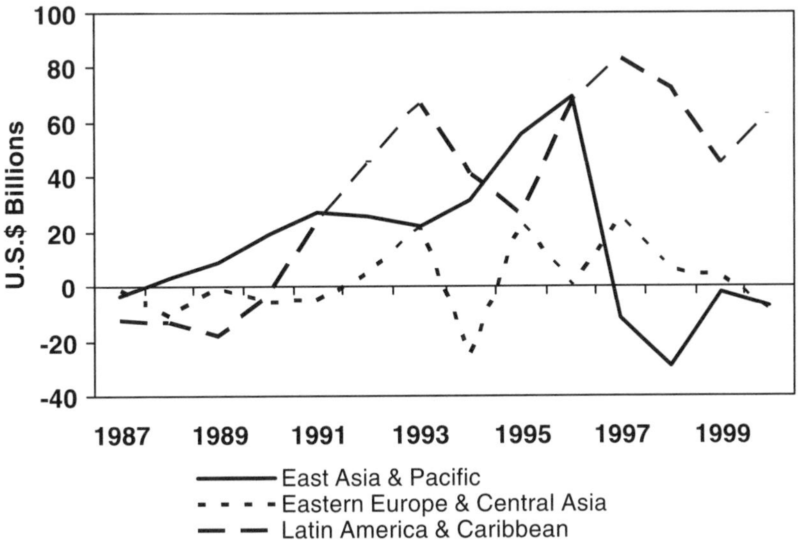

Figure 11-1. Total Net Capital Flows to EMCs, 1987–2000. Source: International Financial Statistics.

seen in the 1998 Russian Long Term Capital Management crisis. It is currently estimated that net private flows to emerging markets will continue to be slightly negative. Should this trend of weak capital flows continue through 2002, many emerging economies will have difficulty refinancing an estimated $160 billion due in private emerging market debt. These problems will resonate and amplify systemic risk for global financial markets.

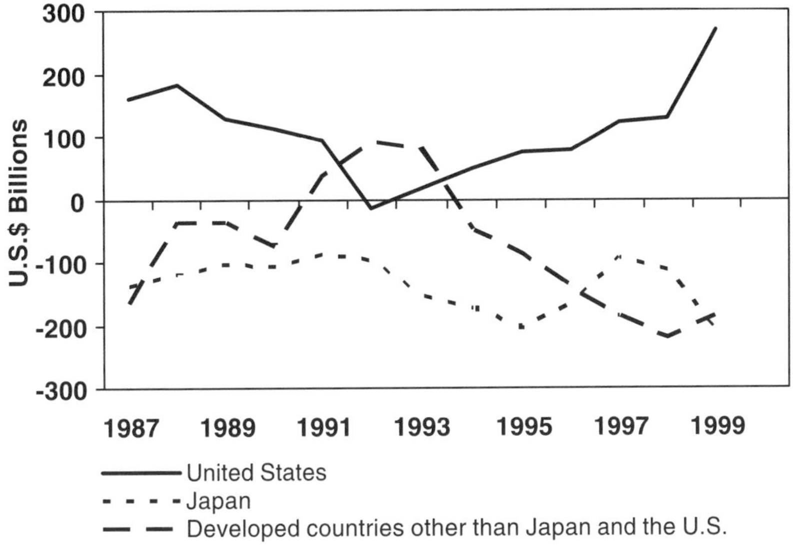

Figure 11-2. Net Capital Flight from Developed Countries to the United States, 1987–1999. Source: World Development Indicators, World Bank.

The shortage of capital is refracted most dramatically in the Asian countries by a collapse in per capita GDP (figure 11-3). In the four "tiger economies" of South Korea, Indonesia, Malaysia, and Thailand, per capita GDP remains lower than pre-crisis levels as a failure of reforms has left those nations unable to recover.

THE IMPORTANCE OF FINANCIAL INFRASTRUCTURE

Growth in jobs, income, and wealth is closely tied to the development of both financial institutions and markets (Levine 1997; Rajan and Zingales 1998; Beck, Loayza, and Levine 2000). Having a well developed financial system, as measured by the share of credit to GDP, has also been found to be negatively related to economic volatility (Easterly, Islam, and Stiglitz 2001).[3] Capital markets and access to them are key for mobilizing savings, facilitating investment risk reduction both over time and across industries, monitoring managerial behavior, and processing information for efficient asset pricing (Levine 1997; Beck and Levine 2002). A deep and liquid financial system that offers broader economic participation through equal access to capital would tend to favor the development of a middle class, bridging the yawning gaps of income polarization currently observed. Access to commodity futures markets allows farmers to hedge against price fluctuations, and the development of such markets would allow producers

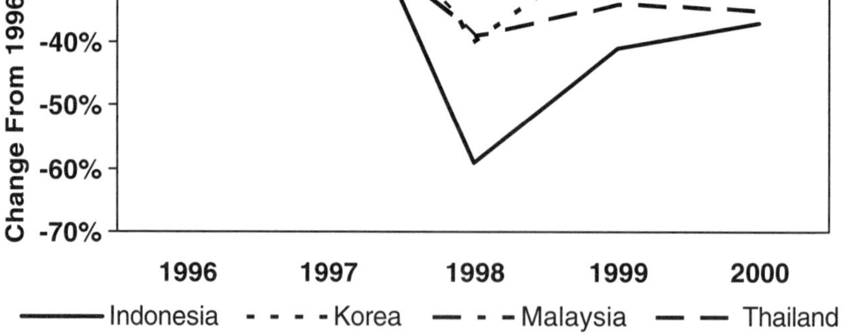

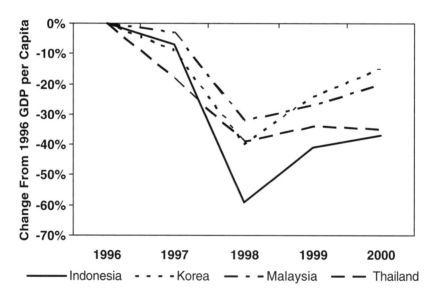

Figure 11-3. Post-Crisis per Capita GDP Change for Asian "Tigers," 1996–2000. Source: International Financial Statistics.

3. Except where the share of credit to GDP is excessively high.

in emerging markets to protect themselves against the idiosyncratic risks of farming just as their American and European peers are able to do.

There is increasing evidence from the financial research literature that an entrenched corporate elite exercises rent-seeking powers to limit property rights broadly, and outsiders' access to capital in general. Their presence serves to undermine the transparency and functionality of the domestic securities markets and financial institutions (Durnev, Morck, and Yeung 2001). Capital markets require transparency and information to operate effectively in order to restrain inept managerial behavior and self-dealing.

Asia is one example that illustrates the costs of a missing bond market. What is true of Asia is true of most developing countries where a major problem with financial systems development is inactive, and thus illiquid, financial markets. An examination of the role of financial markets in economic growth and development is an ongoing project at Milken Institute. (See, e.g., Barth, Trimbath, and Yago 2002.) Domestic financial intermediaries and markets in developing countries are often small and weak. Of EMCs, only China and Brazil have financial assets that amount to more than 1 percent of the world total. A market without activity is equivalent to the absence of a market. Small markets not only have higher per unit operating costs but also are more risky. Less liquidity leads to excessive volatility as prices fluctuate in the absence of market makers. Without liquidity, countries cannot reap the benefits of efficient markets that drive down the cost of capital. Inefficient markets combined with insufficient and poor quality regulation, ineffective supervision, and weak enforcement provides a perfect formula for inviting fraudulent opportunists, and subsequent bank and market runs.

Most of the world is below investment grade. The emerging and transition markets of the global economy began their entry into capital markets, but have been stymied by the lack of market participation. Building local and regional markets requires widespread participation by issuers, investors, and intermediaries. It requires building the necessary market infrastructure of reporting, information flows, and corporate governance as well. The extension of the logic of the high yield marketplace is critical in the next phase of economic growth. These emerging and transition markets are important not only because their downfalls shatter economic and political stability in an increasingly interdependent world, but also because they have most of the world's population and should account for most of the world's growth over the next few decades. Capital flows within and between those markets and the developed world become increasingly important—to fund not only projects and firms in the developing world, but also the pensions and well-being of the developed world.

The emergence of primary and secondary high yield securities markets in the developing and transition economies is key to sustainable growth in the twenty-first century. These markets would help provide a benchmark for pricing credit risk, bank loans, and public securities for domestic and foreign investors alike. The development of these markets would allow the transfer of risks through securitization. Repackaging loans and selling them as bonds would reduce developing and emerging market banks' exposure to liquidity risk and mitigate maturity mismatches for financing institutions in these countries as well. Funding costs for entrepreneurs and consumers would fall.

EMERGING DOMESTIC MARKETS

As we enter the twenty-first century, the United States faces the challenge of sustaining and expanding economic prosperity at home. It does so amid a rapidly changing marketplace, including several economic shifts that highlight the significance of emerging domestic markets (EDM) in terms of businesses and population trends.

Given the increasingly rapid rate of minority population growth, minority business ownership will continue to rise at an even sharper rate in the coming years. The size distribution of minority-owned businesses is quite similar to the distribution of all U.S. firms. Hence, the regenerative dynamics of the U.S. business system remain dependent upon the dynamic rates of small firm formation, and innovation associated with this process. Business firm formation and growth dynamics remain consistent, in this regard, across ethnic groups. This reinforces the frequently overlooked fact that the vast majority of U.S. firms are small: 99 percent have fewer than 500 employees, 98 percent have fewer than 100, and 78 percent have fewer than 20 (U.S. Census Bureau 1997).

Growing U.S. ethnic populations represent several important investment factors beyond supplying the pool of new entrepreneurs:

- As record numbers of business owners retire in the coming years, few with family succession in place, numerous companies will be available for sale (figure 11-4). The new management and ownership will increasingly draw from ethnic populations—in just the years between 1996 and 1998, the percent of minorities receiving business degrees grew over three times faster than the percent of whites.
- These ethnic owners, managers, and workers are critical to replenishing pension funds, which will be depleted by large numbers of retiring, largely white, baby boomers. Small and medium-sized businesses are already creating more than 75 percent of new jobs.
- Of the foregoing trends, perhaps as important as the growth in number and sales of EDM firms is their change in distribution across industries. At one time, minority firms were largely concentrated in personal services. Today, however, the distribution of minority-owned businesses generally reflects that of all U.S. businesses. Significant concentrations exist in construction, wholesale trade, transportation, communications, and utilities, with an increasing focus on export opportunities. Within the service sector,

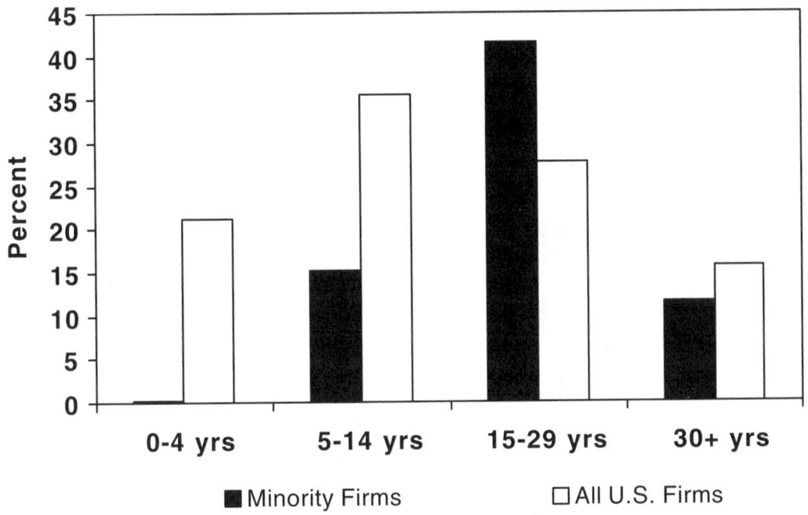

Figure 11-4. Age Distribution of Firms in the United States. Source: U.S. Census Bureau.

minorities show particular strength in the high-growth/high-skill health and business services, and engineering and management categories. In finance, insurance, and real estate, we find increasing numbers of securities and commodities brokers, and both depository and nondepository institutions.

Despite the tremendous advances, the vast majority of smaller EDM firms do not have access to the financing technologies that have fueled mainstream growth. In 1999, firms focusing on traditionally undercapitalized entrepreneurs managed only 2 percent of private equity funds. Given the rapid growth in the numbers of EDM businesses, the disparity between capital demand and capital availability is great, and a serious constraint on expansion: venture-backed companies experienced at least 40 percent average annual job growth in the 1990s, compared to a 2.5 percent decline among Fortune 500 companies. Annual sales per employee increased 16.5 percent on average, more than twice the rate of the Fortune 500 (PricewaterhouseCoopers 1998).

A critical factor in entrepreneurial business growth is the level and type of capital inputs. Small business finance relies heavily on both equity capital and bank loans. Figure 11-5 illustrates the fact that ethnic business owners generally use higher cost sources of capital than do nonethnic owners. Research has also determined that use of debt and equity are positively correlated: debt and equity are complements, not substitutes, in the context of small firm creation, where possessing equity increases one's access to institutional credit sources (Bates 1997).

In recent years, institutional investors have been increasingly attentive to emerging domestic markets. Institutional investors have taken a num-

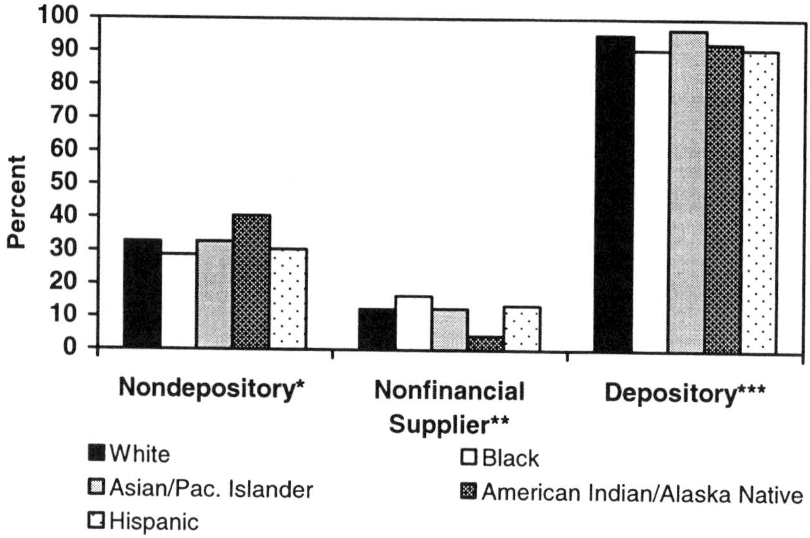

Figure 11-5. Small Businesses' Sources of Financial Services by Ethnic Group.
*Finance company, brokerage, leasing company, other,
**Family and individuals, other businesses, government,
***Commercial bank and thrift institution.
Source: "Survey of Small Business Finance," Federal Reserve 2001.

ber of paths to exploring the market, largely depending on how they define EDM: some use traditional fund managers, particularly those which have developed emerging manager programs; some use traditional institutions, particularly those which have alliances with fund managers (e.g., Hicks, Muse, Tate & Furst/21st Century); some work through banks that effectively screen the managers (e.g., Citicorp, Bank of America); some invest directly with minority-focused funds. As in emerging markets overseas, the importance of general investment expertise, training, and experience must be coupled with local market partners and knowledge for effective investing.

The continuing increase in the number and size of funds seeking women- and ethnic-owned businesses provides an indication of the increased interest in EDM among pension funds. Between 1990 and 2000, the capital invested in such funds rose from $550 million to $3.4 billion. More significantly, the variety of investors rose—from five sources of capital in 1990 (with the federal government providing 70 percent of invested funds) to nine in 2000 (of which only 19 percent came from the government).

STRUCTURED FINANCE FOR EDM

One example of the type of risk management structure that would apply the logic of structured finance vehicles to the emerging domestic marketplace would be the expansion of state capital access programs (CAP), small business-lending programs available in twenty-two states and two cities in the United States. They offer a mechanism to provide loans to small businesses that may not otherwise be able to get them. CAPs hold particular appeal to borrowers in EDM markets. Any federal or state-chartered bank, savings association, or credit union is eligible to participate in a CAP.

In order to create a private capital markets link to the CAP program, the state of California passed legislation in 1999 permitting the securitization and sale of CAP loans as asset-backed bonds. The U.S. Congress passed legislation in 2001 authorizing $200 million to be appropriated for a national CAP reserve.

The EDM market is a research-intensive asset class requiring detailed capacity building within the institutional investment community. Significant commitments have been made recently because this market represents a growing focus of interest. High yield issuance by EDM firms has already occurred in the entertainment (particularly radio), communications, and retail sectors. Using innovative structured finance technologies would allow for portfolio diversification and mitigate incumbent new market risk while capturing potential market returns. Indeed, there has already been some progress in the securitization of Small Business Administration loans (figure 11-6).

ENVIRONMENTAL FINANCE

In order to finance the future of a dynamically sustainable environment, the application of financial technologies that allow for the valuation and

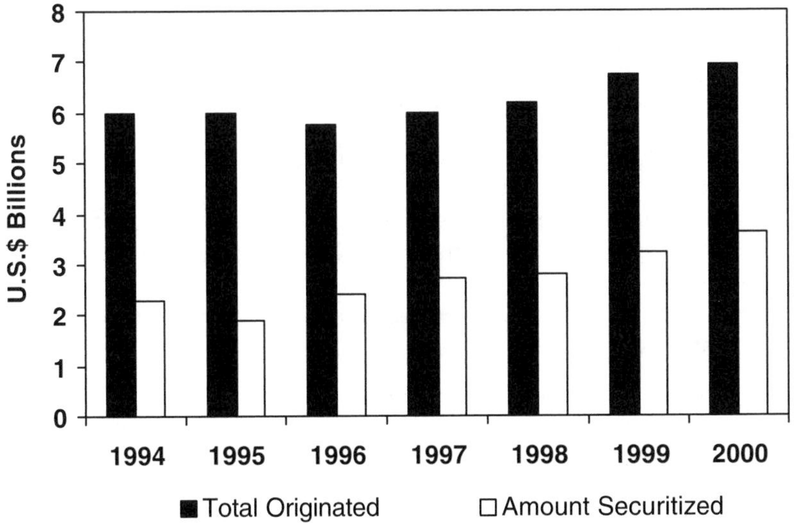

Figure 11-6. Securitization of Guaranteed Portion of SBA Loans, 1994–2000. Source: World Development Indicators, World Bank.

pricing of anticipated returns and expected growth from environmental "externalities" (as a means of pricing and mitigating them) needs to occur. Options, futures, hedging strategies, and a variety of hybrid financial instruments evolved in other areas of innovative capital markets are readily applied in what can become an environmental goods and services industry (Yago 2001). Creating optimal capital structures of instruments that will finance environmental growth and maximize the shareholder value of environmentally based enterprises is long overdue. Building the bridge to an adequate pricing mechanism for the environment requires mobilizing proven financial innovations for creating and developing environmental markets. The evolution of these markets promises great hope for emerging countries whose natural resource base continues to provide them, under adequate stewardship, with a comparative advantage in attracting capital flows to support environmental and economic sustainability. Job and capital formation through monetizing environmental assets could substantially increase income and wealth generation in poorer countries.

Since 1990, progress has been made in extending the benefits of new financial technologies to the solution of large-scale, persistent environmental problems. Applying the principles of corporate finance and economics to environmental issues demonstrates how aligning the interests of consumers, producers, and the general public can result in improved environmental outcomes. Active trading, public prices, and clear incentives have contributed to efficiency and innovation in reducing pollution at far lower cost than predicted. Market mechanisms allow emission sources to meet their emission reduction commitments either in-house or, if less costly, to pay others to reduce or sequester emissions elsewhere.

The application of market-based solutions for environmental policy covers several objectives and is quite interconnected. In this context, risk management and hybrid financial instruments integrate capital, commodity, and environmental markets by doing the following:

- Expanding markets in tradable emissions permits (SO_2, greenhouse gases, and other pollutants)
- Developing an ecosystem services market (market-based incentives to monetize biodiversity and its prospecting, ecotourism, water quality, etc.)
- Providing the monitoring, information, and innovation necessary to enhance market development.

The conditions necessary for financing the future are the same both for removing barriers to job and capital formation globally and specifically for sustaining the global environment. Environmental finance represents a special, but not unusual, case of the need to align interests of investors, entrepreneurs, and consumers tied to various layers of capital structure for specific projects, markets, and commodities. Indeed, the same conditions that promote environmental sustainability affect the sustainability of corporations as well. Environmental and corporate performances are increasingly found to be empirically related (Ameer, Feldman, and Soyka 1996).

INTELLECTUAL CAPITAL SECURITIZATION

Old models of capitalism were built around concentrated capital and control. A handful of capitalists marshaled a society's assets and mass labor to make things. The homogenization of labor and capital inputs made that possible through large-scale, high volume, standardized production which was organized hierarchically. Today, the expansion of economies runs largely on ideas and the ability to finance them. Scale economies have given way to scope economies in the technological evolution of processes and products. Organizational pyramids, as Alvin and Heidi Toffler have written, are transformed into pancakes.

Capital spending that used to be concentrated in basic industries now drives accelerating product and production process cycles in knowledge-based industries. Meanwhile, research and development budgets and basic science research have not been maintained at historic levels to generate future growth. Government spending for such efforts has declined, and consolidation in some industries (e.g., pharmaceuticals) has compromised research and development budgets.

In the late 1990s, businesses began to appreciate that their intellectual property and other forms of early stage technologies represent important assets.[4] Early stage corporate, small business, and university technologies have attracted unprecedented attention, valuations, and investments. While the potential inventory of intellectual property and knowledge capital has continued to grow, supplies of capital through both government and corporate budgets and from the public and private capital marketplaces have diminished after the technology market collapse of recent months.

An emerging knowledge capital gap exists for discovery and technologies to be spun out of large corporations, university or private laboratories, and the government. This financing gap adversely affects science and technology development, owners of intellectual property, financial services firms, and investors, and impairs the promise of technology development and its implications for macroeconomic markets. Financial innovations that could structure technology pools and diversify risk to advance commercialization are a key challenge to new markets. Securitizing intellectual property assets into liquid, secondary markets will be key for the future. Accelerating medical solutions to global health problems, resolving environmental and energy problems, and advancing material sciences can be funded by the application of financial innovations to resolving the issue of knowledge capital formation in the future.

4. This discussion is based on some pathbreaking work in Kossovsky 2002.

Inspired by the insight that "the best investor is a good social scientist," we've attempted to describe how the financial markets and the technologies that sustain them might move forward through understanding how they have survived, stumbled, and thrived in the recent past. As we measure and monitor the financial future, we can embrace it with greater certainty.

Appendix A

The Many Definitions of "Junk Bond"

REFERENCE BOOKS AND PUBLICATIONS

Business Encyclopedia (Knowledge Exchange)

Junk bond: A bond with a rating lower than investment grade.

The high-yield debt market dates back to the beginning of the securities market. Many of our nation's best known corporations were initially financed with junk bonds. Prior to 1920, U.S. Steel, General Motors, and Computing-Tabulating-Recording (which would later be known as IBM) all used high-yield debt to finance the expansion of their operations.

Until World War II, junk bonds accounted for 17 percent of all publicly issued straight corporate debt. The greatest increase occurred during the Depression due to the large number of companies that were downgraded from their original investment-grade ratings.

Spiraling inflation and increasing interest rates in the 1970s created a need for new financial products, which would provide investors with higher yields and companies with affordable, fixed-rate funding. The result was the birth of the new-issue junk bond market, which experienced its most explosive growth during the 1980s and continued to grow into the 1990s. According to the Securities Data Corporation, the high-yield market raised more than $50 billion in new underwritings for companies in its peak year 1993, up from about $1 billion in 1980.

Encyclopedia of Business, Second Edition (Crown Books)

Junk bonds are corporate debt securities of comparatively high credit risk, as indicated by ratings lower than Baa3 by Moody's Investor Service or lower than BBB– by Standard & Poor's. This usually excludes obligations that are convertible to equity securities, although the bonds may have other equity-related options (such as warrants) attached to them. Junk bonds are also known as high-yield, noninvestment-grade, below-investment-grade, less than investment-grade, or speculative-grade bonds.

The term "junk bonds" dates to the 1920s, apparently originating as traders' jargon. Financial publisher John Moody applied the less pejorative label, "high-yield bonds," as early as 1919, but non-investment-grade debt received little attention outside a small circle of professional specialists prior to the mid-1980s.

Financial Literacy for a Changing Market **(Houghton Mifflin)**

Junk Bond: A high-risk, high-yield debt security that, if rated at all, is graded less than BBB. These securities are most appropriate for risk-oriented investors. When LTV Corporation filed for bankruptcy in the summer of 1986, it listed liabilities of nearly $4.25 billion of debentures qualifying as junk bonds. LTV had been a major issuer of debentures qualifying as junk bonds. These high-yielding debentures suffered very large price declines immediately before and after the firm's bankruptcy filing. For example, its 5% subordinated debentures due in 1988 declined from a price near $700 on July 16 to $350 two days later. By October, the debenture sold for only $200. Other LTV debentures suffered similar large losses. In addition to sustaining the loss in market value, the owners of the securities received no interest income during the reorganization. The LTV junk bonds offered investors a high yield only for as long as the firm remained able to pay interest on the securities.

The Handbook of International Financial Terms **(Oxford University Press)**

Junk bond (USA). A high-yield bond with a credit rating below investment grade at issue which has become popular as means of financing corporate takeovers and management buyouts. In theory, it differs from the fallen angel bond in that the issuer was below investment grade at the time of issue (hence the idea of a junk bond credit). The term has come to mean all speculative grade bonds whether they were speculative or not at issue. The junk bond market was popularized by Drexel Burnham Lambert and Michael Milken in the USA in the 1970s, although many other securities firms have become active in the market. Milken found when looking at the experience of the fallen angel bond market that the risk (and liquidity) spread such issues commanded over investment grade bonds of a similar class were higher than the historical default record. Building on this finding, Drexel was able to build up large-scale distribution in such securities to yield-hungry investors. Many innovations have been tried out in an attempt to increase marketability, including pay-in-kind bonds and deep discount issues as well as step-up and convertibles. Also sometimes called speculative grade securities or non-investment grade securities.

Webster's Ninth New Collegiate Dictionary **(Merriam-Webster)**

The first time the term "junk bond" appeared in *Webster's Ninth New Collegiate Dictionary* was in the 1990 edition, page 655.

junk bond n (1976): a high-risk bond that offers a high yield and is often issued to finance a takeover of a company.

INTERNET SOURCES

Cornerstone Investment Consultants **(http://www.stonecorner.com)**

Junk bonds, also known as high-yield bonds, are bonds rated noninvestment grade by a major bond rating agency, such as Moody's or Standard & Poor's. The ratings . . . reflect an opinion of the bond issuer's ability to meet the required interest and principal payments.

Junk bonds became popular during the 1980s, when firms such as Drexel Burnham Lambert utilized them to finance large leveraged buyouts. Before Michael Milken became the poster boy for junk bonds, they were known by only the most sophisticated investors.

Investors purchase junk bonds because their yields are higher than investment grade bonds. The reason for this is simple: companies that issue them are generally perceived to have a greater risk of default.

Dow Publishing Company **(http://www.dows.com)**

Bonds are generally classified into two groups—"investment grade" bonds and "junk" bonds. Investment grade bonds include those assigned to the top four quality categories by either Standard & Poor's (AAA, AA, A, BBB) or Moody's (Aaa, Aa, A, Baa).

The term "junk" is reserved for all bonds with Standard & Poor's ratings below BBB and / or Moody's rating below Baa. Investment grade bonds are generally legal for purchase by banks; junk bonds are not.

Encyclopedia.com **(http://www.encyclopedia.com)**

Junk bond: A bond that involves greater than usual risk as an investment and pays a relatively high rate of interest, typically issued by a company lacking an established earning history or having a questionable credit history. Junk bonds became a common means for raising business capital in the 1980s, when they were used to help finance the purchase of companies, especially by leveraged buyouts; the sales of junk bonds continued to be used in the 1990s to generate capital.

Financial Pipeline **(http://www.finpipe.com)**

A high yield or "junk" bond is a bond issued by a company that is considered to be a higher credit risk. The credit rating of a high yield bond is considered "speculative" grade or below "investment" grade. This means that that chance of default with high yield bonds is higher than for other bonds. Their higher credit risk means that "junk" bond yields are higher than bonds of better credit quality. Studies have demonstrated that portfolios of high yield bonds have higher returns than other bond portfolios, suggesting that the higher yields more than compensate for their additional default risk.

High yield or "junk" bonds get their name from their characteristics. As credit ratings were developed for bonds, the credit rating agencies created a grading system to reflect the relative credit quality of bond issuers. The highest quality bonds are "AAA" and the credit scale descends to "C," and finally to the "D" or default category. Bonds considered to have an acceptable risk of default are "investment grade" and encompass "BBB" bonds and higher. Bonds "BB" and lower are called "speculative grade" and have a higher risk of default. . . .

Underwriters, being creative and profit-oriented, soon began to issue new bonds for issuers that were less than investment grade. This led to the Drexel-Burnham saga, where Michael Milken led a major investment charge into junk bonds in the late 1980s, which ended with a scandal and the collapse of many lower rated issuers. Despite this, the variety and number of high yield issues recovered in the 1990s and is currently thriving. Many mutual funds have been established that invest exclusively in high yield bonds, which have continued to have high risk-adjusted returns.

The Investing Guys **(http://www.investopedia.com)**

Junk bonds: These are bonds that pay high yields to bondholders because the borrowers don't have any other option. Their credit ratings are less than pristine, making it difficult for them to acquire capital at an inexpensive cost. The measuring stick for junk bonds is typically a bond rating of BB/Ba or less.

Although junk bonds pay high yields, they also carry higher than average risk that the company will default on the bond. Historically, average yields on junk bonds have been between 4 and 6 percentage points above those on comparable U.S. Treasuries.

Junk bonds can be further broken down into two or more categories:

- Fallen Angels—This is a bond that was once investment grade but has since been reduced to junk bond status as a result of poor credit quality of the issuing company.
- Rising Stars—The opposite of a fallen angel, this is a bond whose credit rating has been increased by a rating agency because of an improving credit quality of the issuing company. A rising star may still be a junk bond but on its way to being investment quality.

Investment.com **(http://investment.com)**

Junk bond: Bond with a credit rating of BB or lower by rating agencies. Although commonly used, the term has a pejorative connotation, and issuers and holders prefer the securities to be called high-yield bonds. Junk bonds are issued by companies without long track records of sales and earnings, or by those with questionable credit strength. They are a popular means of financing takeovers. Since they are more volatile and pay higher yields than investment grade bonds, many risk-oriented investors specialize in trading them.

Microsoft Network Money Central Glossary **(http://www.moneycentral.msn.com)**

A debt security that pays investors a high interest rate because of its high risk of default. Junk bonds aren't for everybody or even most people, but they aren't all bad. They provide less than rock-solid firms with access to credit, and a broadly diversified portfolio can reduce the risk of any one bond's default while providing high portfolio interest. But beware: junk bonds really are risky. In addition to the unusually high credit risk (and the usual interest-rate risk associated with all bonds), junk bonds are susceptible to the winds of economic fortune. When a downturn is anticipated, many investors shun the bonds of companies that might not be able to pay interest or principal if business should turn sour. Thus, the price of your junk holdings would fall under such circumstances. Given the uncertainties, some junk-bond investors prefer a good mutual fund, which will do the work of credit analysis and diversification for you.

Oxford English Dictionary (http://www.oed.com)

Junk bond (orig. U.S.), a stock with a high rate of interest and substantial risk, issued esp. to finance a corporate take-over or buy-out.

Power Investor Primer (Investors Alliance, http://www.powerinvestor.com)

High yield "junk" bonds were invented to enable smaller companies or big investors to use bonds and bond markets to finance takeovers. The original concept was good and legal; but unbelievably greedy brokers and arbitrageurs, aided by big investment firms, exploited and corrupted it. They used illegal inside information, deliberately planted misinformation, and market rigging to make millions and millions of dollars while, in some instances, destroying profitable old companies. Some of these multimillionaires are now in the penitentiary. Unfortunately, greed is still rampant.

The junk bond market grew exponentially. During the 1990–91 recession many of these bonds defaulted, helping bankrupt the S&Ls throughout the U.S. and helping to saddle U.S. taxpayers with a trillion dollar national deficit.

When the bonds defaulted, many investors complained that their brokers said they would get a 16 percent yield. They chose to ignore the axiom that high risks inevitably accompany high rewards. There are no free lunches, no guarantees.

We recommend avoiding junk bonds. However, if you must buy them, at least buy a junk bond fund; with a fund you have more diversification. In the junk bond fund you may lose only 25 percent of your principal versus 100 percent in an individual bond. We feel that investors have superior and safer opportunities in undervalued common stocks or stock mutual funds.

A research study completed in mid-1989 by Harvard professor Dr. Paul Asquith found that an incredible 34 percent of all high yield bonds defaulted. He started with bonds issued in 1977 and assumed that if a hypothetical investor bought every high yield bond issue between 1978 and 1986, 34 percent of the bonds would have defaulted by November 1988. Professor Asquith also found that the quality of bond issues has decreased over time, with higher quality issues in the early 1980s versus the late 1980s.

Stock Quest Glossary **(http://www.stocksquest.thinkquest.org)**

Junk bond: A weak bond, rated BB or lower, that has a high default risk, and thus carries a high interest rate.

OTHER SOURCES

Professor David Zalewski, Department of Finance, Providence College

Junk Bonds: Although high-yield bonds existed for years, the term "junk bonds" appeared during the rapid expansion of the market for these securities during the latter half of the 1980s. I am not sure who first coined the term "junk," although I heard somewhere that the columnist Art Buchwald may have been responsible. The term is most closely associated with Michael Milken and Drexel Burnham Lambert, who exploited the decline of the private placement market, the increase in corporate leverage, and the need to finance acquisitions by providing liquidity for junk bonds and aid to high-risk borrowers experiencing financial distress.

Appendix B

Technical Material From Chapter 4

ECONOMETRIC MODELS OF THE HIGH YIELD MARKET

This appendix presents the technical material used to generate the results reported in chapter 4. For ease of presentation, some of the explanatory material from chapter 4 is repeated here to provide the full context of the econometric material. Much of this material was published in another form in Yago and Siegel (1994).

We construct a model to test the hypothesis that the rate of return or month-to-month change in the rate of return on high yield issues is a function of the default rate on these bonds, the high yield spread over Treasury securities, credit availability, fluctuations in stock market indices, and general economic performance. We then test whether that model is structurally stable across time.

Under our main hypothesis:

$$HYR \text{ or } DHYR = f\,(DEF, SPREAD, CREDIT, WIL, ECONPER) \qquad (1)$$

or, as a linear regression equation:

$$HYR \text{ or } DHRY = \beta_1 + \beta_2 DEF + \beta_3 SPREAD + \beta_4 CREDIT + \beta_5 WIL + \beta_6 ECONPER + \mu \qquad (2)$$

where

HYR = the rate of return on high yield securities
$DHYR$ = the month-to-month change in the rate of return on high yield securities
DEF = the high yield default rate
$SPREAD$ = the high yield spread over Treasury securities
$CREDIT$ = credit availability
WIL = the Wilshire 5000 Index
$ECONPER$ = % change in GNP
μ = a classical disturbance term.

We conjecture that an increase in the default rate on high yield debt will reduce the attractiveness of these securities to potential investors. Thus, it is expected that $\beta_1 < 0$. Higher spreads should increase the relative attractiveness of, and thus the demand for, high yield debt such that we expect $\beta_2 > 0$. We also hypothesize that the demand for high yield securities is lower during periods of relatively tight credit conditions, so that $\beta_3 > 0$. An increase in stock prices is expected to increase prices of high yield issues because the market value of firms with outstanding debt will be higher and investors will have greater perceived or actual wealth. Both of these factors should increase the demand for high yield debt such that we expect $\beta_4 > 0$. A recession or a downturn in the economy is supposed to reduce the supply of and demand for these securities because investors and firms offering this debt may be concerned about the probability of repayment. Therefore, we expect that $\beta_5 > 0$.

We can also analyze the determinants of the number of high yield issues and capital flows into funds that specialize in investing in these securities. For that purpose we propose the following specifications:

$$HYR \text{ or } DHYR = f(DEF, SPREAD, CREDIT, WIL, ECONPER, LBONO, LHYR) \quad (3)$$

or, as a linear regression equation:

$$HYR \text{ or } DHYR = \beta_1 + \beta_2 DEF + \beta_3 SPREAD + \beta_4 CREDIT + \beta_5 WIL + \beta_6 LBONO + \beta_7 LHYR \quad (4)$$

where

$LBONO$ = the number of LBO transactions
$LHYR$ = the average value of the rate of return on high yield securities for the previous two months.

The expected signs of the coefficients β_1–β_5 are the same as in the previous model. An expansion in LBO activity is assumed to increase the number and value of high yield issues because, in part, these securities have been used to finance corporate control changes. Hence, the expected sign of β_6 is positive. Since higher returns in more recent months should induce additional investment in high yield securities, we expect β_7 also to be positive.

DATA

This section provides information on our data sources and details on the construction of variables.

1. High yield returns: Two monthly high yield indices of returns were provided to us. The first, constructed by Merrill Lynch (HYRM), is the High Yield 175 Index; the second (HYRS) is an index from Salomon Brothers. The Merrill Lynch index was normalized to a base of 100 in 1985.
2. Default rates: Default rates (DEF), which are available on an annual basis before 1989, and on a quarterly basis after 1989, were calculated by Edward Altman of New York University.
3. Spreads: Monthly data on high yield spread (SPREAD) were provided to us by Merrill Lynch. The spread is calculated as the difference between high yield bonds and ten-year Treasury bonds.

4. Credit and economic conditions: Our quarterly measure of credit availability (CREDIT) is defined as total credit market funds raised in the private sector, excluding corporate and foreign bonds. The data source is the Federal Reserve Board's flow of funds data. Quarterly data on the percentage change in GNP are used as our proxy for changes in economic conditions (ECONPER).
5. Stock market performance: Monthly data on the Wilshire 5000 Index from Dow Jones is chosen as the indicator of stock market performance. We chose this series because it provides the broadest measure of equity market performance.
6. Number and value of LBOs and high yield issues (LBONO, LBOVAL, and HYNO): Monthly data on the value and number of high yield issues and LBOs are taken from the Securities Data Corporation (SDC) database.
7. High yield investment capital: Monthly data on capital flows in high yield bond funds (NETFLOW) were provided to us by the Investment Company Institute.

EMPIRICAL RESULTS

In this section, we present estimates of equations (2) and (4) using monthly data on NETFLOW, HYR, HYNO, SPREAD, WIL, and LBONO, and quarterly data for DEF, CREDIT, and ECONPER.

Descriptive statistics and a matrix of correlation coefficients for variables included in the regression equations are presented in table A-1. As expected, there is a positive, statistically significant correlation between the spread and both indices of high yield returns. There is also a positive, statistically significant correlation between increases in stock market prices and these indices. A negative correlation between the default rate and the high yield indices is also observed, although this correlation is not statistically significant. The strong, positive association between the number of LBOs and the value and number of high yield bonds is also consistent with our expectations. The measure of credit availability and changes in economic conditions are both negatively correlated with returns, though neither coefficient is statistically significantly different from zero.

Table A-2 contains parameter estimates for equations (2) and (4). We have estimated equation (2) using two alternative series on monthly returns: a series constructed by Merrill Lynch and another provided by Salomon Brothers. Levels and month-to-month changes in returns were alternately included as dependent variables. The use of monthly observations raises concerns about autocorrelation, or the instance where the error terms are serially correlated. In this regard, we report Durbin-Watson statistics. The fact that our Durbin-Watson values are quite close to 2 indicates that the presence of autocorrelation is not a problem. Note that our use of month-to-month changes in variables as dependent and independent variables, and other transformation of the data (such as the calculation of averages),

Table A-1. Summary Statistics and Matrix of Correlation Coefficients for Variables Included in the Regression Analysis

Summary Statistics

Variable	Mean	Median	Std. Dev.	Minimum	Maximum
NETFLOW	259.540	240.470	481.210	–1064.920	1336.060
HYRM	1.030	0.980	3.060	–9.500	13.300
HYRS	1.060	0.960	3.300	–6.690	14.940
HYNO	6.450	4.000	6.280	0.000	27.000
DEF	2.340	1.480	2.420	0.160	11.400
SPREAD	5.050	4.650	1.510	2.700	9.700
CREDIT	0.088	0.035	0.632	–5.610	3.700
WIL	0.009	0.011	0.047	–0.230	0.127
ECONPER	0.010	0.009	0.014	–0.040	0.070
LBOVAL	2079.290	855.250	3951.420	0.000	37934.500

Matrix of Correlation Coefficients

	NETFLOW	HYRM	HYRS	HYNO	DEF	SPREAD	DCREDIT	DWIL	ECONPER	LBOVAL
NETFLOW	1.00									
HYRM	.56*	1.00								
HYRS	.53*	.93*	1.00							
HYNO	.27*	–.10	–.15	1.00						
DEF	–.05	–.08	–.09	–.09	1.00					
SPREAD	.15	.26*	.30*	–.19**	.02	1.00				
DCREDIT	.26*	–.19**	–.17**	–.03	–.00	.07	1.00			
DWIL	.36*	.41*	.45*	–.08	–.05	.14	–.06	1.00		
ECONPER	.08	–.14	–.10	.10	–.13	–.13	.13	–.06	1.00	
LBOVAL	.16	–.02	–.05	.68*	.09	–.08	–.06	.03	.09	1.00

*Significant at .01 level
**Significant at .05 level

reduces the likelihood of autocorrelation. For example, because the previous month's spread, as well as the contemporaneous value, may influence returns, we have calculated the average value of these terms and included it as a regressor.

Table A-2 reveals that the most powerful determinant of returns within this model is the average value of the spread. These coefficients are all positive and highly statistically significant. The point estimates on the stock market variable are also positive and statistically significant. The coefficient on the month-to-month change in the default rate is negative, as expected, although far from statistically significant. We also note that the variables

Table A-2. Determinants of Rates of Return on High Yield Securities, Net Capital Flows in High Yield Bond Funds, and the Number of High Yield Issues

	Equation 2				Equation 4	
Coefficient on Variable	HYRM	HYRS	DHYRM	DHYRS	NETFLOW	HYNO
DEF	–0.065	–0.177	0.116	–0.087	–26	–0.024
	–0.157	–0.18	–0.195	–0.224	–32.95	–0.05
SPREAD	1.556	1.851	2.007	2.69	325.19	1.133
	(.694)**	(.828)**	(.857)**	(1.020)*	(141.71)**	(0.387)*
CREDIT	0.621	0.421	0.147	–0.314	199.55	0.185
	–0.435	–0.52	–0.544	–0.629	–91.87	–0.142
WILSHIRE	0.007	0.009	0.006	0.008	1.12	0.0002
	(.001)*	(.002)*	(.002)*	(.002)*	(0.28)*	–0.0004
ECONPER	–0.003	0.003	–0.005	0.006	1.73	–0.014
	–0.011	–0.013	–0.015	–0.017	–2.46	–0.0039
LBOVAL					–97.41	–0.0143
					–117.34	–0.203
LHYRM					34.67	0.127
					–24.65	(0.034)*
INTERCEPT	0.547	0.509	–0.085	–0.204	274.97	0.135
	(.225)*	(.255)**	–0.267	–0.308	–322.36	–0.52
df	77	77	77	77	77	72
R_2	0.4538	0.4748	0.2893	0.2775	0.6201	0.8123
DW	1.78	1.57			1.71	1.64

Note: Standard errors in parentheses (each equation includes lagged values of the dependent variable).
* Denotes that the point estimate is statistically significant at the .01 level.
** Denotes that the point estimate is statistically significant at the .05 level.
df = degress of freedom.
R_2 = coefficient of determination.
DW = Durbin-Watson statistic.

measuring changes in credit conditions and economic performance do not explain variation in returns. Finally, given the marked difference in values of the coefficients of determination (R^2), the regression equation based on levels rather than growth rates has significantly more explanatory power.

Point estimates of the determinants of net flow of capital into high yield bond funds and the number of high yield securities (equation [4]) are also presented in table A-2. The significant increases in R^2 indicate that the fit of the models improves when we use these measures as dependent variables. The parameter estimate results are broadly consistent with the findings on returns. That is, we find that spreads are the most important determinant of high yield investment capital. Also, when NETFLOW is selected as the dependent variable, the coefficient of credit availability is positive and significant, which is also consistent with our expectations.

EVIDENCE OF REGULATORY DESTABILIZATION

We wish to test whether the regression model of high yield supply and returns is stable over time, and, if it has changed, to identify the point in time at which these changes occurred. One of the implicit assumptions in a standard regression equation is that the coefficients are stable over time. That is, estimation of equations (2) and (4) is contingent on the assumption that the coefficients are time-invariant. In this section, we analyze the structural stability of our econometric estimates.

The usual practice in assessing the constancy of regression coefficients (with respect to time) is to use prior information concerning the true point of structural change in the nature of the regression relationship. The researcher identifies an event or set of events that is hypothesized to cause structural change, estimates separate regressions, and examines whether the multiple sets of estimated coefficients are significantly different from each other using the Chow (1960) test.

A test for the structural stability of regression parameters has been developed by Brown, Durbin, and Evans (1975) that does *not* require prior information concerning the true point of structural change. An analysis of the cumulative sum of squared residuals from the regression determines where, if at all, a structural "break" or shift occurs. An attractive property of the Brown-Durbin-Evans "cusum" test is that it allows the data to identify when the true point(s) of structural change occur. In our context, the null hypothesis of this test is that the regression coefficients are constant over time.

The basic intuition behind the Brown-Durbin-Evans test is as follows: If the structure of equations (2) and (4) varies according to an index of time, a shift in the residuals will result, as compared to the constant coefficients model. The Brown-Durbin-Evans test uses the test statistic S_r, which is derived from the normalized cumulative sum of squared residuals from a recursive estimation model:

$$S_r = \frac{\sum_{k+1}^{r} W_i^2}{\sum_{k+1}^{N} W_i^2} \qquad r = k+1, \ldots, N,$$

where w_i are the orthogonalized recursive residuals, k is the number of regressors, and N is the number of observations. S_r has a beta distribution with expected value $\mu = \frac{(r-k)}{(N-k)}$. With constant coefficients, a graph of S_r will coincide with its mean-value line, within a confidence interval $\pm C_0 + \frac{(r-k)}{(N-k)}$, where C_0 is Pyke's modified Kolmogorov-Smirnov statistic (C_0).[1] We have calculated, for each observation, the actual and expected values of the test sta-

1. A precise definition of C_0 is presented in Durbin (1969) and values of C_0 for our sample were calculated from distributions of this statistic contained in Ben-Horim and Levy (1981).

tistic, S_r and $E(S_r)$. We have also computed the absolute value of the difference between S_r and $E(S_r)$. If the regression coefficients do not vary over time, then this difference will fall within the specified confidence region. When the value of $S_r - E(S_r)$ exceeds C_0, we have identified a point where structural change has occurred.

For each regression presented in table A-2, we have calculated values of S_r for each observation based on residuals from these regressions. We have also computed the values of $S_r - E(S_r)$ and plotted these differences against time, as measured in monthly intervals. Graphs of the test statistics for three dependent variables—the level and month-to-month change in monthly returns and the number of high yield issues—are presented in figures 4-4 through 4-6 in chapter 4. In addition to the plot of the difference between S_r and $E(S_r)$, each chart includes two horizontal lines representing the 95 percent and 99 percent confidence regions, respectively. If the test statistic exceeds the confidence bound, we can reject structural stability at the respective level of significance. Analysis of these figures reveals that structural stability can be decisively rejected in all instances.

Appendix C

Tools of the Trade Glossary

Like the paver's jackhammer or the miner's pick, a tool is an instrument for effecting changes on other objects. The corporate financial officer and the federal Secretary of the Treasury also have tools for making changes. Their process channels savings from investors to productive purposes that make possible the use of all the other tools. Below is a glossary of terms describing the tools of the trade used in finance.

EQUITY SECURITIES

An equity security represents a share of ownership in the issuing corporation.

Common Stock

Common Stock Class of ownership, or equity, security with residual claims on assets of a corporation after claims of bondholders and other creditors have been paid. Common stock is a form of permanent capitalization because a corporation has no obligation to redeem it at any time in the future. Generally, common stockholders elect the board of directors, who oversee company management, and from time to time stockholders make major policy decisions through the exercise of their voting rights.

Common Stock/Warrant unit A packaged security that combines a common stock and a warrant (see definition of warrant below).

Master Limited Partnership (MLP) Unit A limited partnership that provides an investor with a direct interest in a group of assets (generally, oil and gas properties). Master limited partnership units trade publicly like stock, and thus provide the investor significantly more liquidity than ordinary limited partnerships do. They also retain many advantages of the corporate form while eliminating double taxation of corporate earnings.

Option A right that enables the holder to buy a fixed quantity of a security, at a fixed price, within a specified time. Calls (right to buy) and puts (right to sell) are the most common types of options. Corporations also grant options to buy stock to selected corporate executives. Technically, rights, warrants, and convertibles also are options to buy but have time periods to exercise that are longer than options.

Preferred Stock

Preferred Stock A form of equity security that denotes some residual ownership after creditors. It rarely has a maturity date, so it is a permanent loan of capital. Preferred stock, however, has two very important differences from common stock. Normally common stock has voting rights, so that shareholders are really participating owners of a company; preferred stock usually has no voting rights. Also, preferred stock normally has a stated rate of return. This rate will be a percentage of par value or it will be stated in dollars per share per year. (Common stock has no stated rate of return.) In addition, preferred stock is usually considered senior to common. In the event that a company is liquidated, the preferred shareholders are paid before common shareholders. Certain issues of preferred stock have a predetermined time at which they must he repaid—redemption rights.

Preferred Stock/Warrant Unit A packaged security that combines a preferred stock and a warrant (see definition of warrant below).

Convertible Preferred Stock A form of preferred stock with a convertible feature that permits the stockholder, at his or her option, to exchange the convertible preferred stock into another form of security, usually a fixed number of common shares of the same issue. This feature gives the convertible shareholder the income protection afforded by a fixed-income security, plus the possibility of substantial capital gains if the underlying common stock increases in market value.

Convertible Exchangeable Preferred Stock A preferred stock that may be converted at the option of the stockholder into another predetermined security (usually stock) at a predetermined price and fixed amount within a specified time frame. Also may be exchanged in whole or in part at the option of the company into another predetermined security (usually debentures) with set amounts, terms, and rates, usually on an interest payment date.

Cumulative Preferred Stock On cumulative preferred stock, if for any reason the company is unable to pay the stated dividend, the unpaid dividend accumulates to the next payment date. In turn, all the accumulated dividends on the preferred must be paid before the common stockholders receive anything.

Depository Preferred Stock These are evidenced by depository receipts that are issuable pursuant to a deposit agreement among the issuing company, acting depository, and the holders from time to time of the depository receipts. They usually represent a percentage of a share (e.g., 10 percent of a share of preferred stock) and are held on deposit per the depository agreement. They also have a fixed annual dividend.

Exchangeable Preferred Stock A preferred stock that may be exchanged in whole or in part at the option of the company into another predetermined security (usually debentures) with set amounts, terms, and rates. The exchange usually occurs on an interest payment date.

Increasing Rate Preferred Stock A form of preferred stock on which, after a brief initial fixed interest period, the dividend increases at a predetermined rate at predetermined periods (usually quarterly).

Payment-in-Kind (PIK) Preferred Stock A preferred stock that gives the issuer the choice to pay the dividend in more shares of preferred stock or in cash. This gives the issuer flexibility, if it is in need of cash.

Variable Rate Preferred Stock A preferred stock that, after a brief initial fixed interest period, increases or decreases (floats) based upon predetermined interest rates or credit conditions, at predetermined periods (usually quarterly).

Rights (Offering) A privilege granted by some corporations to current common shareholders whereby they can purchase a proportionate number of new shares of common stock before the public is allowed to purchase the shares. A right normally has a subscription price lower than the current market value of the common stock and a life of thirty to sixty days.

Warrant

Warrant A security that permits the holder to purchase a specific number of shares of stock at a predetermined price for a stated period of time. For example, a warrant may give an investor the right to purchase five shares of XYZ common stock at a price of $25 per share until October 1, 1997. Warrants can originate as part of a new bond issue (a "unit"), but they trade separately after issuance. Their values are considerably more volatile than the values of the underlying stock. Thus, purchases of warrants, also called subscription warrants, can be risky investments.

Warrant–Into Public Stock A warrant that permits the holder to purchase a specific number of shares of common stock of a public company.

Warrant–Into Private Stock A warrant that permits the holder to purchase a specific number of shares of common stock of a private issuer at a predetermined price.

DEBT SECURITIES

General term for any security representing money borrowed that must be repaid and having a fixed amount, a specific maturity or maturities, and usually a specific rate of interest or an original purchase price discount. Examples include bills, notes, bonds, debentures, commercial paper, certificates of deposit, and banker's acceptances.

Bond

Bond Any interest-bearing or discounted government or corporate security that obligates the issuer to pay the holder a specified sum of money, usually at specific intervals, and to repay the principal amount of the loan at maturity. Bondholders have an IOU from the issuer, but no corporate ownership privileges (as stockholders do). A secured bond is backed by collateral that may be sold by the bondholder to satisfy a claim if the bond's issuer fails to pay interest and principal when they are due. An unsecured bond or debenture is backed by the full faith and credit of the issuer but not by any specific collateral.

Bond/Warrant Unit A securities package consisting of a long-term bond and a warrant (see definition above). Having a unit form allows the securities to be traded together or separately, with each trading on its own merit and value. When trading as a unit, it acts like a convertible security. The bond is "usable" with the warrants, which means the bond would be used in lieu of cash in order to purchase the shares of stock through the exercise of the warrant.

Bond/Warrant/Stock Unit An investment unit comprising three securities—a bond, a warrant (see definition above), and a common stock (see definition above).

Eurobond Convertible Security A bond of a domestic corporation sold overseas that may be converted into some other asset of the issuer (usually stock). These securities typically have a "put" feature that allows the holder to return them to the issuer for repayment within a certain period of time (e.g., three to seven years). Since the security is sold overseas, it is exempt from U.S. securities laws and cannot be sold within the United States.

Industrial Revenue Bond A special type of municipal bond (see "municipal debenture" below for definition) in which interest and principal payments are secured by the credit of a private firm rather than by the municipality or a public works project. Also called industrial development bond.

Commercial Paper Unsecured promissory notes with maturities usually ranging from 2 to 270 days issued by banks, corporations, and other borrowers. Commercial paper is issued to provide short-term financing, is sold at a discounted price, and is redeemed at face value. It is highly competitive with other money market instruments.

Commodity-Index Certificate A corporate bond whose payments are linked to the price of underlying assets, usually a commodity, or that may be convertible into that commodity. The value of the security itself is tied directly to the current market price of the underlying commodity.

Debenture

Debenture A longer-term bond issued by a corporation that is unsecured by other collateral and is documented by an agreement called an indenture, usually having a maturity of ten years or more.

Convertible Debenture A debt security that is convertible or exchangeable into another form of security, usually a fixed number of shares of common stock of the same company.

Convertible Puttable Debenture A convertible debenture with a put feature, which requires that the issuer repurchase the security on specified dates before maturity. The repurchase price, usually at par value, is set at the time of issuance. The put feature allows the investor to redeem a long-term bond before maturity.

Convertible Resettable Debenture A convertible debenture with terms that can also be changed (i.e., reset) at various times while the security is outstanding.

Convertible Subordinated Debenture A convertible debenture that is subordinate or junior to all existing debt in the case of liquidation. All other claims must be satisfied before subordinated holders can receive debt payment.

Discounted Debenture A security sold at a discounted price from face value that accrues, but does not pay, current interest payments until a predetermined date. After that date, the debenture will pay at a current rate of interest.

Discounted Convertible Debenture A convertible debenture that is sold at a discounted price from the face value. The issuer pays no cash interest for a specified period; interest is imputed (i.e., internally calculated, based upon the time to maturity or the time to which the security begins to pay cash interest).

Exchangeable Debenture A debt security that allows the holder to trade the bond for a predetermined number of shares of common stock of a company affiliated with the issuer. An exchangeable bond differs from an ordinary convertible bond in that a convertible permits the holder to convert into shares of the issuer only, not of an affiliate.

Municipal Debenture A debt security that is issued by a state, city, or other political subdivision chartered by the state. Funds raised may support a government's general financial needs or may be spent on a special public works project (e.g., a housing development or a sewage treatment plant). All municipal bonds have the following in common: (1) there is enabling legislation to permit their issuance and (2) interest payments are exempt from federal income taxes.

Participating Subordinated Debenture A debenture that is generally an unsecured obligation of the company and that is subordinate or junior in right to payment to senior debt in the event of liquidation. The lenders receive an added interest that is a percentage (calculated by a predetermined formula) of the increase of cash flow of the company.

Resettable Debenture A debt security with terms (including interest rate, maturity, call price, sinking fund, etc.) that can be changed (reset) on one or more dates during the life of the security.

Senior Subordinated Debenture A subordinated debenture that is senior to subordinated debt but junior to all other existing debt.

Subordinated Debenture An unsecured bond with a claim to assets that is junior to all existing debt. In the case of liquidation, all other debt claims must be satisfied before subordinated holders can receive debt payment.

Zero Coupon Convertible Debenture A convertible debenture offered at a substantially discounted price from its stated principal amount. The interest rate is calculated based upon accretion of principal (face value) over the outstanding period of time. It is usually subordinated or junior to all liabilities, including lease obligations, and has features similar to a typical convertible debenture, that is, it is exchangeable into a fixed number of shares at all times.

Leveraged Lease Obligation A lease that involves a third party (i.e., lender) in addition to the lessor and lessee. The lender, usually a bank or insurance company, puts up a percentage of the cash required to purchase the assets, usually more than half. The balance is put up by the lessor, who is both the equity participant and the borrower. With the cash, the lessor acquires the asset, giving the lender (1) a mortgage on the asset and (2) an assignment of the lease and lease payments. The lessee then makes periodic payments to the lessor, who in turn pays the lender. As owner of the asset, the lessor is entitled to all tax deductions for depreciation on the asset, interest on the loan, and investment tax credit.

Note

Note A corporate or government bond with a relatively limited maturity, as opposed to a long-term bond.

Adjustable Rate Note An intermediate-term, quarterly interest-paying note (usually subordinated) that, after a brief initial fixed interest period, become a note with an interest rate that adjusts quarterly (also known as a variable rate note). Following the initial interest rate period, the formula for determining the interest rate takes effect and the coupon changes: the notes become adjustable rate notes. They typically range in maturity from five to ten years. The coupon is redetermined each quarter based on a prespecified spread above commonly quoted base interest rates (usually one or more of the following benchmarks: the bond equivalent on three-month Treasury bills, three-month LIBOR, the prime rate, or ten-year Treasury notes).

Credit Sensitive Note A debt security whose interest rate will be adjusted if necessary in response to changes in the credit ratings by agreed upon services (Standard & Poor's or Moody's rating agencies). Therefore, the holder will receive a lesser rate of return if the bonds have a higher rating and will receive a higher rate of return if the bonds fall in their rating. This security provides the holder with some protection that the return will always match the credit of the issuer. For the issuer, it provides an incentive to improve and strengthen operations to receive a higher credit rating and thus benefit from the lower interest rates.

Employee Stock Ownership Plan (ESOP) Note An ESOP is a retirement plan in which employees receive shares of the common stock of the company for which they work, and the company receives an investment tax credit for providing the opportunity for employees to own common stock. The purpose of the ESOP is to give employees a future interest in the company, thereby providing them with an additional incentive toward greater productivity.

Eurocurrency Note Notes issued by a domestic corporation in a foreign currency. By their nature such securities are not registered with the Securities and Exchange Commission (SEC) and cannot immediately be sold in the United States. Eurocurrency is funds deposited in a bank that are denominated in a currency differing from that bank's domestic currency. Eurocurrency applies to any currency and to banks in any country. Thus, if a Japanese company deposits yen in a Canadian bank, the yen will be considered Eurocurrency.

First Mortgage Note A debt security secured by a first lien on real estate. This security has priority with respect to the payment of interest and repayment of principal in the event of liquidation.

Floating Rate Note (FRN) A note, usually with a five-to-seven year maturity, whose stated rate of interest is indexed to some preestablished money market rate. The money market rate may be an average of Treasury bill rates or some other sensitive market rate. Because the rate is variable, the holders of FRNs have substantially reduced interest rate risk.

Floating Rate Exchangeable Note A floating rate note that may be exchanged in whole or in part at the option of the issuer into a fixed rate (nonfloating rate) note with set amounts, terms, and rates. The exchange usually occurs on an interest payment date.

Guaranteed Subordinated Note A debt security whose principal and interest are guaranteed by a third party (another entity in addition to the issuer). Since there is another party who promises to pay principal and interest in the event that the borrower does not pay, this security has greater value than a similar security with no guarantee.

Increasing Rate Note Debt securities that have an incentive to be repaid as fast as possible by the issuer because their interest rate increases (usually every quarter) at specific intervals (basis points). The initial rate (base rate) is determined by the credit quality of the issuer and can be paid in cash or in kind (additional securities).

Mortgage Note A debt security that promises to pay interest and to repay principal, and that pledges real property, either land or plant or both, as collateral for the loan. Mortgage securities are always designated as such, and the indenture (agreement) will specify whether the mortgage is first or second (priority on claiming the underlying property) and will state the restrictions on the further issuance of bonds.

Participating Mortgage Note A mortgage security in which the holder of the security owns a claim to a portion of the equity appreciation of the underlying property. The percentage of participation is set when the security is issued and is a factor in determining the price of the security.

Payment-in-Kind (PIK) Note Debt securities that give the issuer the option to pay interest payments in additional securities or in cash. This option gives the issuer flexibility to regulate cash needs.

Promissory Note A long-term debt security secured by a lien on assets of the company (usually real estate). The note can be sold with various rankings based upon its priority of asset claims (first right to claim assets, second right, etc.).

Senior Note A note that has claim to the assets of the issuer prior to subordinated notes and equity securities in the event of liquidation. Unsecured senior note claims are subordinated to claims of any secured lien holder (i.e., mortgage, equipment trust certificate, secured bank debt, etc.). An equipment trust certificate is one form of secured senior note that is a secured debt obligation which has claim to specific assets of the issuer and which is issued in serial maturity (i.e., series 1 due 1991, series 2 due 1992, etc.), usually based upon the acquisition of the underlying assets. This security has been traditionally used to finance transportation assets (railroad cars, airplanes, trailer containers, etc.).

Senior Secured Note A debt security that has claim to the issuer's assets prior to the claims of the holders of an issuer's junior debt and equity securities. Senior secured notes are backed by the pledge of collateral, a mortgage, or other lien. The exact nature of the security is defined in the indenture.

Senior Subordinated Note/Convertible Exchangeable Preferred Stock Unit A securities package consisting of a senior subordinated note and convertible exchangeable preferred stock (see definition above). Having a unit form allows the securities to be traded together or separately, with each trading on their own merit and value.

Subordinated Note A debt security with a claim to assets that is junior to all existing debt. In the case of liquidation, all other debt claims must be satisfied before subordinated holders can receive debt payment.

Split Coupon Note A debt security that is sold at a discounted price from its face value. This security pays both part cash interest and part noncash interest (accreting interest) until a specific date. At that date, the security will pay the interest rate in cash only until maturity.

Zero Coupon Note A debt security that is sold at a reduced price from its face value (e.g., deep discount) because it makes no periodic cash interest payments. The interest instead is internally calculated (imputed), based upon time to maturity and credit quality. The buyer of such a bond receives the rate of return by the gradual appreciation of the security, which is redeemed at face value on a specified maturity date.

OTHER

Revolving Credit Facility

A contractual agreement between a bank and a company whereby the bank agrees to loan the company funds up to a specific maximum limit over a specific period of time (usually a year or more). As the borrower repays a portion of the loan, an amount equal to the repayment can be borrowed again under the terms of the agreement. Also called open-end credit or revolving line of credit.

Unit

A term used to describe securities sold as a "package." For example, a company offers two common shares and one convertible preferred share as a unit. Bonds and warrants are frequent unit offerings.

Appendix D

Literature Review

This literature review is organized by topic because the subject of an entire market is so broad. We begin with a brief summary of seven topics:

- Bond ratings
- Macroeconomic relationship
- Regulation
- Use of proceeds
- Drexel Burnham Lambert
- Default rates
- Risk.

Even the casual reader should take in this summary, although the more detailed coverage can be skipped without loss of continuity. We cover each topic in more detail in the sections that follow the summary. To help with topic-specific research, we've elected to repeat the most important references here from the main listing. Finally, we present a matrix that summarizes the important empirical work in the subject.

OVERVIEW

The market for high yield bonds has gone through cycles reflecting fundamental changes in composition. Prior to the 1980s the market, such as it was, was composed mostly of fallen angels—firms whose debt had been downgraded from investment to speculative grade. The 1980s saw rapid growth in the floating of bonds rated high yield at time of issuance, as well as the LBO boom that facilitated corporate restructuring. By 1990, regulators stepped in with restrictions that precipitated the collapse of the market. Resurgence of the high yield market in the 1990s can be attributed largely to the growth of emerging market issuance as well as to an SEC regulation—Rule 144A—which was intended for foreign rather than domestic issuance, but nevertheless provided a channel of easy access to credit for domestic high yield issuers as well.

The high yield market experienced a remarkable growth spurt between 1994 and the first half of 1998. This growth was interrupted by the Asian financial crisis in August, when spreads widened so much that the market for new issues virtually dried up. A modest recovery ensued following interest rate cuts by the Federal Reserve. An article by Henk Bouhuys and

Stephan Yeager of Bank of America Securities (1999) outlines these developments. One significant trend has been the division of the market into two distinct categories—while larger issues and issuers had easy access to capital, smaller issues and issuers (with revenue less than $250 million and EBITDA (earnings before interest, taxes, depreciation, and amortization) under $40 million) were subject to a much more restrictive environment. Proposals for regulatory changes to Rule 144A further threatened access to capital for the smaller high yield issuers by shutting off the market for private placements and forcing them to go through an elaborate process of registering their securities (Yago and Ramesh 1999).

The literature on bond ratings is diverse, and results can vary depending on the time period covered, the methodology employed, and the ratings systems followed. Two papers in particular are detailed below. The first (Helwege and Kleiman 1997) uses ratings to explain fluctuation in default rates, while the second (Blume, Lim, and MacKinlay 1998) suggests an explanation for why ratings downgrades exceed upgrades during some periods of time.

The premium on high yield bonds (over prime lending, for example) provides a measure of the financial accelerator (a theoretical construct that characterizes how financial factors may amplify and propagate business cycles). In the section on macroeconomic relationships between high yield bonds and other measures of economic activity, we examine studies such as that of Gertler and Lown (2000), which shows that the high yield spread has significant explanatory power for the business cycle. Other sources find significant relationships between various measures of the high yield market and the output gap, movements in output, and the net interest burden.

Studies on the impact of regulations on the high yield market were discussed at length in chapters 3 and 4. For completeness, we make a brief summary below and include the references on the topic. The next body of work pertains to the use of proceeds from high yield bond issuance. Kaplan and Stein (1993) compare buyouts in the late 1980s with the early 1990s and conclude that they were more risky in the earlier period. Simonson (1997) shows that small firms did not use proceeds from high yield bonds to finance growth, although Gilson and Warner (1998) look at approximately the same period and arrive at the opposite conclusion. According to their study, firms grew rapidly after they used bond issues to pay down bank debt. This was followed by Andrade and Kaplan (1998), who studied firms engaging in highly leveraged transactions that become financially distressed and estimated the cost of distress. This important article distinguishes between economic and financial distress.

To make our survey complete, we include literature that specifically studied the lead underwriter of high yield securities in the 1980s—Drexel Burnham Lambert (DBL). For high yield bond issues floated between 1977 and 1988, Harlan Platt (1993) finds that high yield bonds underwritten by DBL had a lower default rate than bonds issued by other underwriters. Livingstone, Pratt, and Mann (1995) show that while DBL's fees were about

26 basis points higher than those charged by other underwriters, interest rates on DBL issues were 22 basis points lower.

The literature on defaults covers issues pertaining to the duration of default and to recovery. Helwege (1999) concludes that banks do not facilitate the process of negotiation and may even slow it down. In contrast, a large fraction of the liability structure of the firm in the form of high yield bonds appears to speed up the process considerably. In explaining recovery, Altman and Kishore (1997) argue that the seniority factor dominates, and neither the size of the issue nor the time to default from its original date of issuance has any association with the recovery rate. They conclude that since 1991 almost 70 percent of all new issuance in the high yield market was senior in priority, so that average recovery rates can be expected to continue to be above the historical average.

Finally, the survey addresses the question of risk. Fridson and Jónsson (1994) identify variables that might affect credit risk and the risk arising from illiquidity. A later study by Garman and Fridson (1996) expands on the earlier analysis to include monetary indicators. They conclude that this modification enhances the explanatory power of the model. Lea Carty (1996) aims to characterize and measure credit risk while emphasizing the information structure of the debt market. Using nonparametric estimation techniques, Carty concludes that default risk first rises, then falls as investors and managers learn more about the quality of the enterprise. Moreover, for each rating category, the growth rate of the S&P 500 Stock Index and the change in nominal rates are positively correlated with the risk of exiting the public bond market without defaulting, while the growth rate of real GDP is negatively correlated with risk.

The following sections cover these and other research results on the seven topics from the literature in the high yield market and securities.

BOND RATINGS

Helwege and Kleiman (1996) look at the distribution of ratings (using data from S&P and Moody's) at the beginning of each year. They seek to explain fluctuations in default rates over time. They hypothesize that ratings are a proxy for underlying indicators of financial strength and, therefore, the distribution of ratings should provide information about the aggregate default rate. Helwege and Kleiman (1997) calculate the expected default rate for three categories: BB, B, and CCC.

An indicator variable is included for weak economies that takes into account the influence of initial conditions on default rates, using actual GDP growth instead of forecasted growth. When the economy dips below a critical level of GDP growth, the aggregate default rate would be expected to rise. Since one would expect more defaults in a downturn if a greater percentage of companies had low ratings, a recession indicator dummy (1 if slow / negative growth, 0 otherwise) is multiplied by the expected default rate to produce an interaction variable that helps explain the difference in the aggregate default rates of 1981–1982 and 1990–1991. In 1986, however, speculative defaults increased sharply even though the economy was not in recession, the credit quality of the market was not tilted toward the lower end, and lagged new issuance had not peaked. This is explained by the authors as arising from industry specific factors such as the decline in oil and gas prices. According to Salomon Brothers, half of the defaults on original issue high yield bonds were in the energy industry in 1986.

In recent years, downgrades in corporate bond ratings have exceeded upgrades. A study by Blume, Lim, and MacKinlay (1998) investigates whether this is due to a decline in credit quality or to an increase in the stringency of ratings standards. They study bond ratings from 1978 to 1995 and assess the impact of various measures of firm performance and credit quality on the probability that a bond migrates into a particular rating category. The data on bond ratings come from files of individual bonds that make up the Lehman Brothers Bond Index assembled by Arthur Warga. The Warga file also contains S&P corporate bond ratings for all the bonds in the Lehman Brothers Bond Corporate Index. Virtually all of these bonds represent senior investment grade debt.

To measure credit quality, the study takes into consideration financial ratios measuring interest coverage, profitability, and leverage, following practices used by Standard and Poor's. It also looks at accounting ratios such as pretax interest coverage, operating income to sales, long-term debt to assets and total debt to assets. Since larger firms tend to be older, with more established product lines and more varied sources of revenue, they consequently have higher ratings. Therefore, firm size is also taken into consideration and measured as the natural log of the market value of equity (in real dollars). Beta coefficients and standard errors (obtained from CRSP daily stock files) are significant for the study, too, since firms are less able to service debt as equity risk increases.

An ordered probit analysis reveals that more stringent ratings standards have resulted in downgrades exceeding upgrades. The evidence also suggests that accounting ratios and market-based risk measures are more informative for larger companies than for smaller ones.

Bibliography

Blume, M. E., Lim, F., and MacKinlay, A. C. (1998). "The Declining Credit Quality of U.S. Corporate Debt: Myth or Reality?" *The Journal of Finance* 53, no. 4: 1389–1413.

Fons, J. S., Carty, L., and Kaufman, J. (1994). *Corporate Bond Defaults and Default Rates, 1970–1993*. Moody's Special Report.

Hawley, D. D., and Walker, M. M. (1993). "Speculative Grade Ratings and the Investment Decision Process: A Survey of Institutional Money Managers." *Financial Practice and Education*, Fall, pp. 39–46.

Helwege, J., and Kleiman, K. (1997)."Understanding Aggregate Default Rates of High Yield Bonds." *The Journal of Fixed Income*, June, pp. 55–61.

Hickman, W. B. (1958). *Corporate Bond Quality and Investor Experience*. Princeton, NJ: Princeton University Press.

Wigmore, B. A. (1990). "The Decline in Credit Quality of New-Issue Junk Bonds." *Financial Analysts Journal*, September/October, pp. 53–62.

MACROECONOMIC RELATIONSHIPS

Until the early 1980s, only the highest quality borrowers were able to issue market debt; most firms relied heavily on external finance through bank debt, secured at the prime lending rate. With the development of a market for below investment grade debt, the rate on high yield bonds came to be market determined, providing a more accurate measure of the premium on external funds. This premium provides a better measure of the financial accelerator (a theoretical construct that characterizes how financial factors may amplify and propagate business cycles) than various other monetary indicators that reflect policy decisions.

Gertler and Lown (2000) show that the high yield spread (between high yield bonds and the highest quality AAA bonds) has significant explanatory power for the business cycle, outperforming other leading financial indicators, such as the term spread (between ten-year and one-year government bonds), the paper-bill spread (between commercial paper and Treasury bills), and the Federal Funds rate. This is because the high yield spread is extremely sensitive to default risk and may detect a greater variety of factors that influence the macroeconomy than do the other indicators. This proposition is tested in various regressions and vector autoregressions (VARs).

Results of a regression of the high yield spread on the output gap (measured as the log difference of real GDP and potential output by the Congressional Budget Office) indicate that there has been a strong inverse relation between the two variables since 1985. Moreover, the high yield spread leads movements in output by one or two years. Movements in the spread on high yield bonds are also closely related to the net interest burden, indicating an inverse relation between firms' balance sheet strength and the premium for external funds. Similarly, the weakness in bank balance sheets constrains the availability of credit to firms and raises the premium on external funds. Thus, periods where the terms of credit tightened were also associated with an increase in the spread on high yield, supporting evidence of the financial accelerator effect. Consequently, the study shows that the high yield spread has significant explanatory power for the business cycle, with the caveat that the short sample period of 1985–1999 included only one major recession.

Bibliography

Altman, E. I. (1990a). "How 1989 Changed the Hierachy of Fixed Income Security Performance." *Financial Analysts Journal*, May/June, pp. 9–12, 20.

Altman, E. I. (ed.) (1990c). *The High Yield Debt Market: Investment Performance and Economic Impact*. Homewood, IL: Dow Jones-Irwin.

Altman, E. I., and Nammacher, S. A. (1987). *Investing in Junk Bonds: Inside the High Yield Debt Market*. New York: John Wiley & Sons.

Barclay, M. J., and Smith, C. W., Jr. (1999). "The Capital Structure Puzzle: Another Look at the Evidence." *Journal of Applied Corporate Finance* 12, no. 1: 8–20.

Becketti, S. (1990). "The Truth About Junk Bonds." *Economic Review, Federal Reserve Bank of Kansas City*, July / August, pp. 45–54.
Bouhuys, H., and Yeager, S. (1999). "Recent Developments in the High Yield Market." *Journal of Applied Corporate Finance* 12, No. 1:70–77.
Corcoran, P. J. (1994). "The Double-B Private Placement Market." *The Journal of Fixed Income*, June, pp. 42–51.
Fabozzi, F. J. (ed.). (1990). *The New High-Yield Debt Market: A Handbook for Portfolio Managers and Analysts*. New York: HarperCollins.
Fitzpatrick, J. D., and Severiens, J. T. (1978)."Hickman Revisited: The Case for Junk Bonds." *The Journal of Portfolio Management*, Summer, pp. 53–57.
Fridson, M. S. (1992a). "High Yield Indexes and Benchmark Portfolios." *The Journal of Portfolio Management*, Winter, pp. 77–83.
Fridson, M. S. (1993). "High Yield Bonds: Markets Work." In G. Kaufman (ed.), *Research in Financial Services: Private and Public Policy*, vol. 5. Greenwich, CT: JAI Press.
Fridson, M. S. (1994b). "The State of the High Yield Bond Market: Overshooting or Return to Normalcy?" *Journal of Applied Corporate Finance*, Spring, pp. 85–97.
Fridson, M. S. (1994c)"Fraine's Neglected Findings: Was Hickman Wrong?" *Financial Analysts Journal*, September / October, pp. 43–53.
Fridson, M. S., and Bersh, J. A. (1994). "Spread Versus Treasuries as a Market-Timing Tool for High-Yield Investors." *Journal of Fixed Income*, June, pp. 63–69.
Fridson, M. S., Cherry, M. A., Kim, J. A., and Weiss, S. W. (1992). "What Drives the Flows of High Yield Mutual Funds?" *The Journal of Fixed Income*, December, pp. 47–59.
Fridson, M. S., and De Candia, A. (1991). "Trends: Follow, Buck or Ignore?" *The Journal of Portfolio Management*, Winter, pp. 50–55.
Garman, M. C., and Fridson, M. S. (1996). *Monetary Influences on the High-Yield Spread Versus Treasuries*. New York: Merrill Lynch.
Garvey, G. T., and Hanka, G. (1999)."Capital Structure and Corporate Control: The Effect of Antitakeover Statutes on Firm Leverage." *The Journal of Finance* 54, no. 2: 519–546.
Gertler, M., and Lown, C. S. (2000). "The Information in the High Yield Bond Spread for the Business Cycle: Evidence and Some Implications." Prepared for the Conference on Financial Instability, Oxford University, July 1999.
Gilson, S. C., and Warner, J. B. (1998). "Private Versus Public Debt: Evidence from Firms That Replace Bank Loans with Junk Bonds." Harvard Business School Working paper.
Jefferis, R. H., Jr. (1990). "The High-Yield Debt Market: 1980–1990." *Economic Commentary, Federal Reserve Bank of Cleveland*. April.
Klein, W. A. (1997). "High Yield ('Junk') Bonds as Investments and as Financial Tools." *Cardozo Law Review* 19, 22: 505–510.
Knowledge Exchange. (1991). *High Yield 500*. Beverly Hills, CA: The Knowledge Exchange.
Lederman, J., and Sullivan, M. P. (eds.) (1993). *The New High Yield Bond Market: Investment Opportunities, Strategies and Analysis*. Chicago: Probus.
Lindo, D. J. (1989). "High Yield Bonds: Junking the Myths." *Best's Review*, February, pp. 22–24.
Ma, C. K., Rao, R., and Peterson, R. L. (1989). "The Resiliency of the High Yield Bond Market: The LTV Default." *The Journal of Finance* 44, no. 4: 1085–1097.

Platt, H. D. (1994). *The First Junk Bond: A Story of Corporate Boom and Bust*. Armonk, NY: M. E. Sharpe.

Pound, J. (1992a). "Raiders, Targets, and Politics: The History and Future of American Corporate Control." *Journal of Applied Corporate Finance* 5: 6–18.

Regan, P. J. (1990). "Junk Bonds—Opportunity Knocks?" *Financial Analysts Journal*, May/June, pp. 13–16.

Reilly, F. K., and Wright, D. J. (1994). "An Analysis of High-Yield Bond Benchmarks." *The Journal of Fixed Income*, March, pp. 6–25.

Shane, H. (1994). "Comovements of Low-Grade Debt and Equity Returns of Highly Leveraged Firms." *The Journal of Fixed Income*, March, pp. 79–89.

Simonson, M. (1997)."Junk Bond Financing and the Value of the Firm: The performance of Junk Bond Issuers." Ph.D. dissertation, University of Oregon.

Winch, K. F. (1990). *High Yield Bond Market*. Washington, D.C.: Congressional Research Service.

Yago, G. (1991a). *Junk Bonds: How High Yield Securities Restructured Corporate America*. New York: Oxford University Press.

REGULATION

In the late 1980s, the high yield market experienced regulatory intervention with drastic consequences for the market. Yago and Siegel (1994) provide evidence to suggest that specific regulatory events led to a temporary contraction in liquidity and trading in the high yield bond market that resulted in a price collapse. Descriptive data plotting capital flows in high yield bond funds indicates a substantial unexpected withdrawal of funds before the steep reductions in returns.

The Brown-Durbin-Evans test statistic indicates that functional economic relationships between cyclical factors, credit quality, defaults, and market yields—factors that drove the high yield market—changed dramatically during the 1980s. Larger high yield spreads over Treasury securities should increase the demand for high yield debt. This, too, is empirically validated, and there is a positive, statistically significant correlation between the spread and both indices of high yield returns. An increase in the default rate will reduce the attractiveness of securities to potential investors. This result is validated empirically in the study. Higher stock prices should stimulate increases in the price of high yield issues because the market value of firms will be bid up as a result of higher perceived wealth. In the study, stock prices are indeed strongly, positively correlated with returns. A structural break is identified at 1989–1990 for three dependent variables over time—the level and monthly change in the rate of return on high yield securities, and the number of high yield issues. This period was one of dramatic increases in government regulatory intervention in the high yield market.

Bibliography

Hawley, D. D., and Walker, M. M. (1992). "An Empirical Test of Investment Restrictions of Efficiency in the High Yield Debt Market." *Financial Review*, May, pp. 273–287.

Smythe, W. (1989). "Insurer Investigations in Junk or Below—Investment Grade Bonds: Some Questions and Answers for Regulators." *Journal of Insurance Regulation*, September, pp. 4–15.

Yago, G., and Ramesh, L. (1999). *Raising Regulatory Costs of Growth Capital: Implications of the Proposal to Amend Rule 144A*. Santa Monica, CA: Milken Institute.

Yago, G., and Siegel, D. (1994). "Triggering High Yield Market Decline: Regulatory Barriers in Financial Markets." *Extra Credit: The Journal of High Yield Bond Research* 21 March/April, pp. 11–24.

USE OF PROCEEDS

The leveraged buyout boom of the late 1980s gave way to bust in the early 1990s. Due to too much financing chasing too few good deals, by the end of the 1980s many transactions were overpriced, recklessly structured, or both. The aim of Kaplan and Stein (1993) is to determine whether there were important differences ex ante between management buyouts done in the latter part of the decade and those done earlier. The study looks at a sample of 124 large management buyouts between 1980 and 1989. Of the forty-one deals in the period between 1980 and 1984, only one defaulted. In contrast, twenty-two of eighty-three deals completed between 1985 and 1989 had defaulted by August 1991.

The authors examine the hypothesis that the market had overheated, using three broad measures: overall prices paid to take companies private, buyout capital structure, and the incentives of buyout investors. Prices paid increase relative to the fundamental value of a company's assets in an overheated market, and investors earn lower returns regardless of capital structure. A poorly designed capital structure (the study looked at debt and coverage ratios in relation to risk) may also reflect overheating and raise the probability and costs of financial distress. The incentives of buyout investors refer to the equity stake of management. If managers "cash out" their pre-buyout equity holdings, this might indicate their intention to take part in an overpriced transaction.

The study found that buyout prices rose relative to fundamentals in the 1980s, but were largely in line with the stock market. Moreover, the premiums paid showed no significant trend, providing mixed support for the overheating hypothesis. However, measures of total risk indicated that buyout companies in the late 1980s were riskier than those in earlier years, and that prices were particularly high in deals financed with high yield bonds. The use of these bonds was associated with statistically and economically significant increases in the probability of distress, default, and Chapter 11 filings.

Interestingly, banks took smaller positions in later deals, at the same time accelerating required principal repayments, which led to sharply lower ratios of cash flow to total debt obligations. Management and other interested parties, such as investment bankers and deal promoters, on the other hand, were able to take more money up front out of later deals.

Andrade and Kaplan (1998) studied firms engaging in highly leveraged transactions that became financially distressed in the latter half of the 1980s, and the cost of this distress. Isolating firms whose leverage is the primary source of capital, they find that distressed highly leveraged transactions increased in value ex post. Financial distress has net costs on average of 10 percent and with a maximum of 23 percent. Firm leverage (and not any of the other explanatory variables) is the primary cause of financial distress when operating income falls below interest expense. Their analysis reveals that poor industry performance has a positive rather than a negative effect. They find that some of the quantitative costs of distress include an increase in operating and net cash flow margins. The three most common qualitative costs include curtailing capital spending, selling assets at depressed prices, and postponing a restructuring or Chapter 11 filing. The cost of financial distress declines with capital structure complexity, and the use of high yield bonds is specifically associated with a lower cost of financial distress.

According to Jensen (1989, 1993), high yield bonds eliminated size as a deterrent to takeover and strengthened the credibility of takeover threats. (We present empirical evidence on the first point in chapter 3.) Pound (1992a) argued that these bonds were used to finance valuable large-scale projects, such as mergers and acquisitions. To address these issues, Simonson (1997) investigates two hypotheses. The first is that high yield bond issuers undertake capital investment projects that the market believes have positive net present values, but they usually have lower than expected realized values. The second is that high yield bond issuers undertake acquisitions that the market believes to have positive net present values but that usually have lower than expected realized values.

Using a listing of all firms issuing public, nonconvertible, below investment grade bonds at least once between January 1, 1977, and December 31, 1989, Simonson's analysis suggests that stock performance is negatively related to the level of capital expenditures for high yield bond issuers. Simonson also studies time series of valuation multiples and accounting performance measures in the years surrounding issuance. The data indicate that both the market to book and price to earnings ratios fell significantly below comparison firms in the five years post issuance. While this supports the idea that many firms are funding value-decreasing projects in the postissue period, the evidence is also consistent with the idea that the market tends to overvalue many firms before they issue high yield bonds. While the largest firms have positive adjusted returns, smaller firms have negative ones. According to Simonson, the finding that these firms perform poorly is not consistent with the idea that they utilized the new ability to issue publicly traded bonds to finance valuable growth. Together with the earlier conclusion that high capital-spending firms have worse postissue stock returns, this finding implies that high spending firms invest in value-decreasing projects.

Gilson and Warner (1998), however, study firms over an approximately overlapping period to arrive at the opposite conclusion. They consider firms that reduced private debt by repaying bank loans with proceeds from high yield bonds. These firms were profitable but experienced declining operating earnings just prior to high yield bond issues. Since a decline in earnings tightens restrictions on bank debt, this study demonstrated that high yield bond issuance enabled firms to maintain their ability to grow rapidly. High yield bonds have a number of advantages over bank debt. Not only do they carry fewer restrictive covenants, but high yield bonds also have longer maturities than bank loans (a median of 10 years versus 4.7 years). They also have no sinking fund provisions, so that principal payments are not due until maturity, considerably easing cash flow for companies issuing debt.

The study selected a sample of 164 non-acquisition related high yield issues for the period January 1, 1980–December 31, 1992. The sample was truncated at 1992 so that firms could be tracked for several years after the issue. Background information (on bank loan interest rates, maturity, etc.) and ratings information were obtained from sources such as 10-K reports, shareholder proxy statements, and bond issue propectuses, in addition to automated sources such as Compustat. From the sample, it was observed that firms experienced declines in their stock price at the announcement of bank debt paydowns. This was because of a decline in operating performance rather than manager-shareholder conflicts arising from bank debt reduction. Stock price declines were smallest for firms that were closest to violating their bank debt covenants, and these firms grew most rapidly after the issues. The study also breaks out the primary use of high yield proceeds. It is interesting that most of it was used to repay debt of some kind. Of the proceeds, 29.7 percent was used to repay bank debt and 26.2 percent was used to repay other debt.

Bibliography

Andrade, G., and Kaplan, S. (1997). "How Costly Is Financial (Not Economic) Distress? Evidence from Highly Leveraged Transactions That Became Distressed" *Journal of Finance*, 53, 5: 1443–1493.

Fridson, M. S. (1991c). "What Went Wrong with the Highly Leveraged Deals? (Or, All Variety of Agency Costs)." *Journal of Applied Corporate Finance*, Fall, pp. 57–67.

Gilson, S. C., and Warner, J. B. (1998). "Private Versus Public Debt: Evidence from Firms That Replace Bank Loans with Junk Bonds." Harvard Business School Working paper.

Jensen, M. (1989). "Active Investors, LBOs, and the Privatization of Bankruptcy." *Journal of Applied Corporate Finance* 2: 35–44.

Jensen, M. (1993). "Presidential Address: The Modern Industrial Revolution, Exit, and the Failure of Internal Control Systems." *The Journal of Finance* 48: 831–880.

Kaplan, S., and Stein, J. (1993). "The Evolution of Buyout Pricing and Financial Structure." Working Paper 3695, National Bureau of Economic Research.

Loeys, J. (1986). "Low-Grade Bonds: A Growing Source of Corporate Funding." *Business Review, Federal Reserve Bank of Philadelphia*, November/December, pp. 3–12.

Pound, J. (1992a). "Raiders, Targets, and Politics: The History and Future of American Corporate Control." *Journal of Applied Corporate Finance* 5: 6–18.
Simonson, M. (1997)."Junk Bond Financing and the Value of the Firm: The Performance of Junk Bond Issuers." Ph.D. dissertation, University of Oregon.
Sobel, R. (1989). "The Use of High Yield Securities in Corporate Creation: A Hundred Years of Financing and Reshaping America's Industries." Presented at Drexel Burnham Lambert's Eleventh Annual Institutional Research Conference, Beverly Hills, CA, April 6.

DREXEL BURNHAM LAMBERT

We found several studies that specifically examined high yield securities underwritten by Drexel Burnham Lambert (DBL). Platt (1993) finds that high yield bonds underwritten by DBL had a lower default rate than bonds issued by other underwriters. The study included 557 high yield bonds issued between 1977 and 1988, of which 263 (46.8 percent) were underwritten at DBL. A model of default risk at time of issuance investigates the impact on the probability of future default of variables such as cash flow to sales, net fixed assets to total assets, total debt to total assets, short-term debt to total debt, and one-year revenue growth. The data indicate that the probability of default increased dramatically after 1986. Until then, high yield bonds were a relatively safe investment. The increase in defaults is attributed to increased merger and acquisition activity and fierce competition among underwriters as DBL's role in the market waned through 1989.

In another study, Livingston, Pratt, and Mann (1995) investigated the impact of DBL on underwriter fees. Underwriter spreads were regressed against a number of risk and cost factors. The three measures used to study performance were underwriter fees, yield to the bondholder, and the sum of the two, which encapsulates the cost to the issuer. The study uses data on all nonconvertible industrial and utility bond issues (2,700) from Moody's bond survey between 1980 and 1993 for which complete data is available. Data on underwriter spreads are obtained from the Directory of Corporate Financing. The study found that underwriter fees were substantially higher for high yield bonds compared to their investment grade counterparts. In particular, DBL's fees exceeded those charged by other underwriters by 26 basis points. On the other hand, interest rates were 22 basis points lower on DBL issues. Therefore, on balance, the total cost to the issuer was the same.

Bibliography

Alcaly, R. E. (1994). "The Golden Age of Junk." *The New York Review of Books* 26: 28–34.
Livingston, M., Pratt, H., and Mann, C. (1995). "Drexel Burnham Lambert's Debt Issues." *The Journal of Fixed Income*, March, pp. 58–75.
Platt, H. D. (1993). "Underwriter Effects and the Riskiness of Original-Issue High-Yield Bonds." *Journal of Applied Corporate Finance* 6, no. 1: 89–94.

DEFAULT RATES

Helwege (1999) analyzes high yield bond defaults from 1980 to 1991 to determine factors that affect the length of time spent in default. The study uses the list of defaults compiled by the Salomon Brothers High Yield Research Group, which includes bonds that were rated speculative grade or unrated at issuance. This sample includes only bonds originally offered in the public high yield market and private placements with registrations that entered the public market prior to default. A bond is considered in default for the purposes of the study not only if an interest payment is missed, but also if a troubled exchange or tender offer is announced. The sample includes 127 firms and 129 defaults (two firms defaulted twice). Default experience is investigated through the financial press and financial databases (from Securities Data Corporation and Moody's Investors Service), operating performance, and firm value variables (from Compustat, Compact Disclosure, analyst reports, etc.). The dependent variable studied is the time to default, which includes only the period from default to acceptance of new securities or emergence from bankruptcy, and disregards subsequent financial distress or subsequent efforts to restructure the firm.

The study looks at the impact of various factors on the time to default. The first of these is bargaining opportunities, which is influenced by the complexity of capital structure, contingent claims, and lawsuits. The latter presents opportunities to debate the rankings of creditors claims. Such bargaining opportunities are expected to slow the restructuring process as the number and types of claimants increases. This is possible when the firm has bank debt or more than one class of public bonds in addition to other sources of credit. Opportunities for negotiating a favorable outcome for a particular creditor at the expense of another are greater when there is uncertainty about the value of creditors' claims because restructuring cannot proceed until a compromise is reached.

The second factor influencing the time to default is the holdout problem, which has to do with incentives to restructure debt. Bondholders have an incentive not to participate in out-of-court restructuring because the untendered bonds of the holdouts will be paid in full at maturity on original terms. One proxy for holdouts is the public debt the company has in its liability structure. This indicates a greater potential for a holdout problem than bank loans or private placements.

Information problems are identified as another factor that might extend the time to default. Differential information between managers and creditors (or different creditor classes) may lead to bargaining problems. An indicator variable for highly leveraged transactions is also used to assess its impact on the time to default. Firms engaging in these activities are likely to be fundamentally profitable companies at the time of distress (because less equity has been eroded). These firms are less likely to have entrenched managers because of their highly concentrated equity ownership. These managers may cause a delay in restructuring, whereas creditors are more likely to preserve firms with a high value of assets in place or growth opportunities.

Finally, the institutional environment has an important influence on the time to default. This encapsulates developments such as revisions in tax codes, rulings against exchange offers, and increases in the number of distressed firms whose restructurings involve outside support. In order to examine Milken's role in debt restructuring, an indicator variable is used as a proxy. It is set to 1 for firms whose bonds were underwritten by DBL and defaulted before DBL's troubles in 1989. In many cases, firms that renegotiated their debt with the help of Milken appear to have ended their default spells earlier.

The conclusion of this study is that size, lawsuits, and contingent claims lengthen the default spell. However, the number of bond classes and whether the debt is publicly held do not appear to present severe bargaining hurdles. Bondholders apparently are not a particularly difficult group to negotiate with, compared to banks and private debtholders. Counter to Gilson, Kose, and Lang (1990), but consistent with Asquith, Gertner, and Scharfstein (1994), banks in this sample do not facilitate the process of renegotiation and may even slow it down. In contrast, a large fraction of the liability structure in the form of high yield bonds appears to speed up the process considerably, consistent with Jensen's (1989) assumptions.

A study by Altman and Kishore (1996) examines the recovery experience at default and provides important information on pricing of debt securities. A measure of the severity of default is based on recoveries because they influence the expected loss from defaults. They calculate the recovery rate by industry from 1971 to 1995. SIC codes are assigned corresponding to the product group that accounts for the firm's greatest value of sales. Since some sectors had too few data points to be meaningful, several SIC codes were combined into logical groups to arrive at reasonable aggregations.

Industry affiliation is important because it dictates the type of assets and the competitive conditions of firms within different industries. For example, the more tangible and liquid the assets, the higher their liquidation value. If firms in certain industry classifications have a higher proportion of higher rated, senior secured and senior unsecured original debt, then one might expect higher recovery rates. The study documents the severity of bond defaults stratified by industry and by debt seniority. The highest average recoveries came from public utilities (70 percent) and firms in the chemical and petroleum-related products industry (63 percent). The differences between sectors are statistically significant even when adjusted for seniority.

A subsequent study by the same authors (Altman and Kishore, 1997) documents the high yield debt market's risk and return performance by presenting default and mortality statistics and providing a matrix of average returns and performance statistics. They investigate the period from 1971 to 1996 for defaults and 1978 to 1995 for returns. They also take into account historical average recovery rates by seniority (from 1977 to 1996) and by original bond rating (from 1971 to 1996). Carty (1996) utilizes a hazard model to improve on default description and prediction.

The study found that all the seniority levels recovered higher amounts in 1996 than the historical nineteen-year average. The original rating had virtually no effect on recoveries after controlling for seniority. For example, senior secured investment grade defaults had an average weighted price recovery of $48.58, compared to $48.13 for senior secured non-investment grade original issues. Therefore the original rating was probably not the relevant factor in expected recovery—the seniority factor dominated. Altman and Kishore argue that since almost 70 percent of all new issuance in the high yield market since 1991 had been senior in priority, recovery rates would continue to be above the historical average. In addition, neither the size of the issue nor the time to default from its original date of issuance had any association with the recovery rate.

Bibliography

Altman, E. I. (1990b). "Setting the Record Straight on Junk Bonds: A Review of Research on Default Rates and Returns." *Journal of Applied Corporate Finance 3*, no. 2: 82–95.

Altman, E. I., and Kishore, V. M. (1996). "Almost Everything You Wanted to Know About Recoveries on Defaulted Bonds." *Financial Analysts Journal*, November/December, pp. 57–64.

Altman, E. I., and Kishore, V. M, (1997). *Defaults and Returns on High-Yield Bonds*. New York: Salomon Center.

Andrade, G., and Kaplan, S. (1998). "How Costly Is Financial (Not Economic) Distress? Evidence from Highly Leveraged Transactions That Became Distressed." *Journal of Finance* 53(5), pp. 1443–1493.

Asquith, P., Gertner, R., and Scharfstein, D. (1994). "Anatomy of Financial Distress: An Examination of Junk Bond Issuers." *Quarterly Journal of Economics* 109: 625–634.

Asquith, P., Mullins, D., Jr., and Wolff, E. (1989). "Original Issue High Yield Bonds: Aging Analysis of Defaults, Exchanges and Calls." *The Journal of Finance*, September, pp. 923–952.

Bencivenga, J., Cheung, R., and Fabozzi, F. J. (1992). "Original Issue High-Yield Bonds: Historical Return and Default Experience, 1977–1989." *The Journal of Fixed Income*, September, pp. 58–75.

Blume, M. E., and Keim, D. B. (1991a). "Realized Returns and Defaults on Low-Grade Bonds: The Cohort of 1977 and 1978." *Financial Analysts Journal*, March/April, pp. 63–72.

Carty, Lea V. (1996). "An Empirical Investigation of Default Risk Dynamics." Ph.D Dissertation, Columbia University.

DeRosa-Farag, S., Blau, J., Matousek, P., and Chandra, I. (1999). "Default Rates in the High Yield Market." *Journal of Fixed Income*, June, pp. 7–31.

Fons, J. S. (1987). "The Default Premium and Corporate Bond Experience." *The Journal of Finance*, March, pp. 81–97.

Fons, J. S. (1991). *An Approach to Forecasting Default Rates*. Moody's Special Report.

Fons, J. S. (1994). "Using Default Rates to Model the Term Structure of Credit Risk." *Financial Analysts Journal*, September / October, pp. 25–32.
Fons, J. S., Carty, L., and Kaufman, J. (1994). *Corporate Bond Defaults and Default Rates, 1970–1993*. Moody's Special Report.
Fons, J. S., and Kimball, A. E. (1991)."Corporate Bond Defaults and Default Rates 1970–1990." *The Journal of Fixed Income*, June, pp. 36–47.
Fraine, H. G., and Mills, R. H. (1961). "Effects of Defaults and Credit Deterioration on Yields of Corporate Bonds." *The Journal of Finance*, September, pp. 423–434.
Fridson, M. S. (1991b). "Everything You Ever Wanted to Know About Default Rates." *Extra Credit: The Journal of High Yield Bond Research*, July / August, pp. 4–14.
Fridson, M. S., Garman, M. C., and Wu, S. (1997). "Real Interest Rates and the Default Rate on High-Yield Bonds." *The Journal of Fixed Income*, September, pp. 29–34.
Gilson, S. C., Kose, J., and Lang, L. H. P. (1990). "Troubled Debt Restructurings: An Empirical Study of Private Reorganization of Firms in Default." *Journal of Financial Economics* 27: 315–353.
Goodman, L. S. (1990). "High-Yield Default Rates: Is There Cause for Concern?" *The Journal of Portfolio Management*, Winter, pp. 54–59.
Helwege, J. (1999). "How Long Do Junk Bonds Spend in Default?" *The Journal of Finance* 54, no. 1: 341–357.
Helwege, J., and Kleiman, K. (1997). "Understanding Aggregate Default Rates of High Yield Bonds." *The Journal of Fixed Income*, June, pp. 55–61.
Jónsson, J. G., and Fridson, M. S. (1996). "Forecasting Default Rates on High Yield Bonds." *The Journal of Fixed Income*, June, pp. 69–77.
Keegan, S. C., Sobehart, J., and Hamilton, D. T. (1999). *Predicting Default Rates: A Forecasting Model for Moody's Issuer-Based Default Rates*. Moody's Special Comment.
Vanderhoof, I. T., Albert, F. S., Tenenbein, A., and Verni, R. F. (1990). "The Risk of Asset Default: Report of the Society of Actuaries C-1 Risk Task Force of the Committee on Valuation and Related Areas." *Transactions* 41: 547–582.

RISK

The most widely used technique for valuing the high yield market is to compare the prevailing spread over Treasuries against its historical average. An underlying presumption of this technique of mean reversion is that the "correct" spread is the historical average spread. If the spread is truly a risk premium, then it must vary with risk. Therefore, a high yield bond is "cheap" only if its yield premium is larger than warranted by prevailing risk. As is borne out by Altman and Bencivenga (1995), the spread is not a useful market timing tool in the short run. Fridson and Jónsson (1994) investigate alternative measures of risk by studying their impact on spread (operationalized as changes in the Merrill Lynch High Yield Master Index's yield versus ten-year Treasuries).

One measure of credit risk is captured in Moody's Trailing-Twelve-Months Default Rate (since investors demand increased compensation when credit failures rise) and in the Index of Lagging Economic Indicators published by the Bureau of Economic Analysis. The latter is considered significant on the assumption that high yield spreads anticipate changes in default rates but change only after the fact. Lagging indicators may read favorably even though the economy is already in decline (Carty 1996).

Risk can also arise from illiquidity, measured by high yield mutual fund flows as a percentage of fund assets, which serves as a proxy for high yield investment. A negative correlation coefficient indicates that net inflows tend to improve liquidity and reduce the risk premium. Illiquidity risk is also measured by cash as a percent of high yield mutual fund assets, since fund managers may temporarily increase cash positions when they expect large outflows. Therefore, large liquidity premiums tend to coincide with large cash positions of high yield mutual funds. Another measure is the three-month Moving Average Price of the Merrill Lynch High Yield Master Index. A negative price trend may encourage investors to sell and reduce liquidity. In this way, it affects the willingness of dealers to take risk positions.

The Fridson-Jónsson model generated a fairly high R^2 of 0.72, and all variables were statistically significant at the 95 percent confidence level. Of the plausible variables that lacked explanatory power, one was the term structure. Between the end of 1987 and the end of 1992, the index's average maturity declined steadily from 10.9 to 8.8 years. Over the same period, end-of-year basis point spreads versus Treasuries tightened from 454 to 405, widened to 933, then narrowed to 457, indicating that variability in term risk had little to do with changes in spread.

Similarly, a study by Fridson and Kenney (1994) indicated that the level of Treasury rates had no statistical correlation with the spread. Likewise with the Merrill Lynch High Yield Master Index, whether expressed in terms of yield-to-maturity or in terms of price. Other factors that lacked explanatory power were the Index of Leading Economic Indicators, the broker loan rate, the monthly count of news articles on high yield bonds from the Business Periodicals Index, and new issuance.

Garman and Fridson (1996) subsequently refined the model of Fridson and Jónsson to include indicators of monetary conditions. One such indicator is the change in the consumer price index. One effect of inflation is that it benefits debtors by reducing the real cost of liabilities. However, the predicted response of the Federal Reserve to higher inflation is to tighten monetary policy, resulting in a higher risk premium. Regression results indicate that the net effect is positive.

Other variables included are the treasury yield curve (ten year minus three month bond yields), money supply (which had the greatest explanatory power), and a proxy for the ratings mix of the Merrill Lynch High Yield Master Index. The last variable yielded unsatisfactory results in that a higher quality mix was associated with a larger risk premium, and was therefore rejected as an explanatory variable. Another variable included in this model was capacity utilization. The risk premium decreases when capacity utilization rises or when the yield curve steepens, indicating a strengthening economy and less risk of business failure.

Fridson, Garman, and Wu (1997) look at the impact of real interest rates on the default rate over the period 1971–1995. They take into consideration the twelve-month default rate on high yield bonds from Moody's Investors Service and compute the real interest rate from the yield on ten-year Treasuries and the change in the consumer price index from the Bureau of Labor Statistics. They also test for lags because an increase in the cost of capital will not immediately render companies insolvent if they have substantial liquidity on their balance sheets. Moreover, a contraction in economic activity resulting from a rise in real interest rates may occur only gradually.

The study, along with earlier ones (Helwege and Kleiman 1997; Jónsson and Fridson 1996), indicates that, on average, three-quarters of the current year's default rate is "locked in" by the economic and financial forces of two to three years ago. They find that the correlation of default rates and the real interest rate is high (nominal rates show a low correlation). A two-year lag produces the maximum correlation between real interest rates and default rates.

Carty (1996) aims to characterize and measure credit risk. An important determinant of risk is the information structure of the debt market. Two contrasting models of default behavior are empirically examined. The Diamond model of moral hazard implies that default risk declines over time as the firm develops a reputation. In the Jovanovic matching model with incomplete information, default risk first rises and then falls as investors and managers learn more about the quality of the enterprise.

This study uses a time-varying hazard model to estimate the timing of defaults. The random variable of fundamental interest is the period from when a firm enters the public debt market until it defaults or exits without defaulting. The hypothesis tests the polynomial equation $a + bt_1 + ct_2$, to see whether the parameters are such that $b>0$ and $c<0$ (implying a default pattern similar to the Jovanovic model) or $b<0$ and $c<0$ (as implied by the Diamond model). The study concludes in favor of the Jovanovic-type model, which indicates that very few firms default initially. Subsequently, the number of defaults increases and then falls back to a zero hazard rate.

The study also takes into consideration other explanatory variables, such as the growth rate of the S&P 500 stock price index. The relationship is negative, as would be expected, since high expectations of future earnings would lower the risk of default. Also considered is the growth rate of GDP, which is significant, indicating that it is easier to sell debt during an expansion. In addition, the study also includes a proxy for real interest rates, and the interaction between the change in nominal interest rates and the duration of the firm's spell in the public bond market. Increases in nominal interest rates reduce the value of fixed debt obligations, resulting in capital gains. This variable is highly significantly related to the risk of a firm exiting the debt market without defaulting at each credit rating. The number of issuers entering the bond market (a proxy for capturing economic cycles) does not appear to be an economically significant determinant of default risk—evidence against the hypothesis that the duration dependence of default can be attributed to the cyclical nature of bond issuance.

Bibliography

Altman, E. I. (1989). "Measuring Corporate Bond Mortality and Performance." *The Journal of Finance*, September, pp. 909–922.

Altman, E. I., and Bencivenga, J. C. (1995). "A Yield Premium Model for the High Yield Market." *Financial Analysts Journal*, September/October, pp. 49–56.

Atkinson, T. R. (1967). *Trends in Corporate Bond Quality*. New York: Columbia University Press.

Barnhill, T. M., Jr., Maxwell, W. F., and Shenkman, M. R. (eds.). (1999). *High Yield Bonds: Market Structure, Portfolio Management, and Credit Risk Modeling*. New York: McGraw-Hill.

Blume, M. E., and Keim, D. B. (1991b). "The Risk and Return of Low-Grade Bonds: An Update." *Financial Analysts Journal*, September/October, pp. 85–89.

Blume, M. E., Lim, F., and MacKinlay, A. C. (1998). "The Declining Credit Quality of U.S. Corporate Debt: Myth or Reality?" *The Journal of Finance* 53, no. 4: 1389–1413.

Bookstaber, R., and Jacob, D. P. (1986). "The Composite Hedge: Controlling the Credit Risk of High-Yield Bonds." *Financial Analysts Journal*, March/April, pp. 25–36.

Buell, S. G. (1992). "The Accuracy of the Initial Pricing of Junk Bonds." *The Journal of Fixed Income*, September, pp. 77–83.

Carty, L. V. (1996). "An Empirical Investigation of Default Risk Dynamics." Ph.D. dissertation, Columbia University.

Christensen, D. G., and Faria, H. J. (1994). "A Note on the Shareholder Wealth Effects of High-Yield Bonds." *Financial Management*, Spring, p. 10.

Cooper, R. A., and Shulman, J. M. (1994). "The Year-End Effect in Junk Bond Prices." *Financial Analysts Journal*, September/October, pp. 61–65.

Cornell, B. (1992). "Liquidity and the Pricing of Low-Grade Bonds." *Financial Analysts Journal*, January/February, pp. 63–67.

Cornell, B., and Green, K. (1991). "The Investment Performance of Low-Grade Bond Funds." *The Journal of Finance*, March, pp. 29–48.

Datta, S., Iskandar-Datta, M., and Patel, A. (1997). "The Pricing of Initial Public Offers of Corporate Straight Debt." *The Journal of Finance*, March, pp. 379–396.

Fraine, H. G. (1937). "Superiority of High-Yield Bonds Not Substantiated by 1927–1936 Performance." *Annalist*, October, pp. 533–547.

Fridson, M. S. (1989). *High Yield Bonds: Identifying Value and Assessing Risk of Speculative Grade Securities*. Chicago: Probus.

Fridson, M. S. (1992b). "Modeling the Credit Risk of Nonrated High Yield Bonds." *Risks and Rewards: The Newsletter of the Investment Sector of the Society of Actuaries*, March, pp. 6–11.

Fridson, M. S. (1994a) "Do High-Yield Bonds Have an Equity Component?" *Financial Management*, Summer, pp. 76–78.

Fridson, M. S. (1995). "Loads, Flows, and Performance in High-Yield Bond Mutual Funds." *Journal of Fixed Income*, December, pp. 70–78.

Fridson, M. S., and Cherry, M. A. (1990). "Initial Pricing as a Predictor of Subsequent Performance of High Yield Bonds." *Financial Analysts Journal*, July/August, pp. 61–67.

Fridson, M. S., and Cherry, M. A. (1991b). "Explaining the Variance in High Yield Managers' Returns." *Financial Analysts Journal*, May/June, pp. 64–72.
Fridson, M. S., and Gao, Y. (1996). "Primary Versus Secondary Pricing of High Yield Bonds." *Financial Analysts Journal*, May/June, pp. 20–27.
Fridson, M. S., and Garman, M. C. (1997). "Valuing Like-Rated Senior and Subordinated Debt." *The Journal of Fixed Income*, December, pp. 83–93.
Fridson, M. S., and Garman, M. C. (1998a). "Determinants of Spreads on New High-Yield Bonds." *Financial Analysts Journal*, March/April, pp. 28–39.
Fridson, M. S., and Garman, M. C. (1998b). "Erosion of Principal and the Rebasing Illusion." *The Journal of Fixed Income*, December, pp. 85–98.
Fridson, M. S., Garman, M. C., and Wu, S. (1997). "Real Interest Rates and the Default Rate on High-Yield Bonds." *The Journal of Fixed Income*, September, pp. 29–34.
Fridson, M. S., and Jónsson, J. G. (1994). *Spread Versus Treasuries and the Riskiness of High-Yield Bonds*. New York: Merrill Lynch.
Fridson, M. S., and Jónsson, J. G. (1995). "Spread Versus Treasuries and the Riskiness of High-Yield Bonds." *Journal of Fixed Income*, December, pp. 79–88.
Garman, M. C., and Fridson, M. S. (1996). *Monetary Influences on the High-Yield Spread Versus Treasuries*. New York: Merrill Lynch.
General Accounting Office. (1988). *High Yield Bonds: Nature of the Market and Effect on Federally Insured Institutions*. Washington DC: U.S. General Accounting Office.
Gudikunst, A., and McCarthy, J. (1997). "High-Yield Bond Mutual Funds: Performance, January Effects, and Other Surprises." *The Journal of Fixed Income*, September, pp. 35–46.
Helwege, J., and Kleiman, K. (1998)."The Pricing of High-Yield Debt IPOs." *Journal of Fixed Income*, September, pp. 61–68.
Howe, J. (1988). *Junk Bonds: Analysis and Portfolio Strategies*. Chicago: Probus.
Hradsky, G. T., and Long, R. (1989). "High Yield Losses and the Return Performance of Bankrupt Debt." *Financial Analysts Journal*, July/August, pp. 38–49.
Jensen, M. (1993). "Presidential Address: The Modern Industrial Revolution, Exit, and the Failure of Internal Control Systems." *The Journal of Finance* 48: 838–880.
Jónsson, J. G., and Fridson, M. S. (1996). "Forecasting Default Rates on High Yield Bonds." *The Journal of Fixed Income*, June, pp. 69–77.
Kahan, M., and Tuckman, B. (1993). "Do Bondholders Lose from Junk Bond Covenant Changes?" *The Journal of Business*, October, pp. 499–516.
Kao, D. (1993). "Illiquid Securities: Issues of Pricing and Performance Measurement." *Financial Analysts Journal* 77: 28–35.
Kaplan, S., and Stein, J. (1990). "How Risky Is the Debt in Highly Leveraged Transactions?" *Journal of Financial Economics* 27: 215–246.
Kihn, J. (1994). "Unraveling the Low-Grade Bond Risk/Reward Puzzle." *Financial Analysts Journal*, July/August, pp. 32–42.
Kwan, S. H. (1996). "Firm-Specific Information and the Correlation Between Individual Stocks and Bonds." *Journal of Financial Economics* 40: 63–80.
Maxwell, W. F. (1998). "The January Effect in the Corporate Bond Market." *Financial Management*, Summer, pp. 18–30.
Platt, H. D. (1993). "Underwriter Effects and the Riskiness of Original-Issue High-Yield Bonds." *Journal of Applied Corporate Finance* 6, no. 1: 89–94.
Platt, H. D., and Platt, M. (1991). "A Linear Programming Approach to Bond Portfolio Selection." *Economic and Financial Computing*, Spring, pp. 71–84.

Ramaswami, M. (1991). "Hedging the Equity Risk of High Yield Bonds." *Financial Analysts Journal*, September / October, pp. 41–50.

Reilly, F. K. (ed.). (1990). *High Yield Bonds: Analysis and Risk Assessment*. Charlottesville, VA: The Institute of Chartered Financial Analysts.

Rogalski, R. J., and Sunder, L. (1990). "An Analysis of the Equity Component of Low-Grade Bonds." Presented to the Eastern Finance Association in Charleston, WV, April 7.

Shulman, J., Bayless, V., and Price, K. (1993). "The Influence of Marketability on the Yield Premium of Speculative Grade Debt." *Financial Management*, Autumn, pp. 132–141.

Waite, S. R., and Fridson, M. S. (1989). "Do Leveraged Buyouts Pose Major Credit Risks?" *Mergers and Acquisitions*, July / August, pp. 43–47.

Weinstein, M. I. (1987). "A Curmudgeon's View of Junk Bonds." *The Journal of Portfolio Management*, Spring, pp. 76–80.

Willis, M. (1995). "High Yield Corporates Defy Conventional Wisdom." *Bondweek*, December 4, p. 9.

Table D-1. Annotated Table of Literature

Issues Addressed	Methods and Measures	Results
Ratings 1. Helwege and Kleiman (1997) The aggregate default rate includes a fraction of all high yield issuers that default in a given year. What explains the wide fluctuations in default rates over time?		Finds that during 1981–1994, expected default rate had significant explanatory power.
Refines variables used in Fons (1991) and Fridson and Jónsson (1995) (see below) to determine relative importance of these factors from 1981 to 1994.	Looks at distribution of ratings (S&P and Moody's) at the beginning of the year since ratings are a proxy for underlying indicators of financial strength. Expects distribution to provide information about aggregate default rate. Fons, Carty, and Kaufman (1994) indicate that B3 bonds are three times more likely to default than B1 bonds.) Calculates expected default rate for categories BB, B, and CCC.	All three factors—the riskiness of bonds outstanding, the length of time they have been outstanding in the market, the state of the economy—play an important role in determining aggregate defaults, but credit quality appears to be the most influential factor.
	Includes indicator variable for weak economy (dummy variable for slow or negative real GDP growth), accounts for influence of initial conditions on default rate. Aggregate default rate would be expected to rise during recessions. Interacting recession indicator with expected default rate helps explain difference in aggregate default rates of 1981–1982 and 1990–1991.	Downturn in the economy leads to many more defaults when the composition of the high yield market is skewed toward riskier bonds. Early high yield market consisted of mostly fallen angels and had few risky bonds vulnerable to recessionary pressures. Since 1991, many high yield firms have raised ratings by issuing equity and lowering debt burdens. Lower leverage reduces the riskiness of the market.

(continued)

Table D-1. (*continued*)

Issues Addressed	Methods and Measures	Results
	1986 puzzle: Speculative defaults increased sharply even though the economy was not in recession, the credit quality of the market was not tilted toward the lower end, and lagged new issuance had not peaked.	Can be explained by industry specific factors such as decline in oil and gas prices. Half of defaults on original-issue high yield bonds were in energy industry in 1986 (Salomon Brothers).
Fons (1991)	Independent variables include change in credit quality of speculative-grade bonds, state of economy (blue chip GDP forecast).	
Fridson and Jónsson (1996)	Independent variables include aging effect (fraction of high yield bond issuance rated B3 or lower by Moody's, lagged 3 years).	Companies that recently raised money in bond markets are likely to have cash to pay creditors. Bond markets do not lend to companies in immediate danger of default.
	Macro variables closely tied to financial health of company.	Corporate profits are significant only when liabilities of failed firms are included.
2. Blume, Lim, and MacKinlay (1998) Downgrades in corporate bond ratings exceeded upgrades in late 1990s. Authors investigate whether due to decline in credit quality or because ratings standards have become more stringent. Larger firms tend to be older, with more established product lines, varied sources of revenue, and hence higher ratings. Dependent variable: probability that a bond falls into a particular rating category.		On the basis of an ordered probit anlaysis on firms from 1978 through 1995, concludes that more stringent ratings standards have resulted in downgrades exceeding upgrades. Also finds evidence that accounting ratios and market-based risk measures are more informative for larger companies than for smaller ones.

Macro		
1. Gertler and Lown (June 1999) Shows that the high yield spread has significant explanatory power for the business cycle, outperforming other leading financial indicators such as the term spread, the paper-bill spread and the federal funds rate. Dependent variable: output gap (log difference of real GDP and the CBO measure of potential output).	1985:1–1999:1 quarterly data on spread between high yield bonds and AAA (highest quality firms) bonds. Regressions and VARs included commercial paper/T-bill spread and term spread between ten-year government bond and one-year bond. Since the HY spread is extremely sensitive to default risk, it may detect a greater variety of factors that influence the macroeconomy than do other indicators. Caveat: Sample period short and includes only one major recession.	(1) Since 1985 there has been a strong inverse relation between the HY spread and the output gap. (2) HY spread leads movements in output by one or two years. (3) Movements in the HY spread are closely related to the net interest burden, indicating inverse relation between firms' balance sheet strength and premium for external funds. (4) Weakness in bank balance sheets constrains availability of credit to firms and raises premium on external funds. (5) Periods where terms of credit tightened were associated with increases in HY spread.
Regulation		
1. Yago and Siegel (1994) Provides evidence to suggest that specific regulatory events led to a temporary contraction in liquidity and trading in the high yield bond market, and resulted in a price collapse and possibly induced an economic downturn.	Descriptive data plotting capital flows in high yield bond funds indicate substantial withdrawal of funds "before" the steep reductions in returns. Test for structural stability using Brown-Durbin-Evans statistic. Identified 1989–1990 structural break for three dependent variables over time—the level (returns) and month-to-month changes (mutual fund capital flows) in monthly returns and the number of high yield issues.	Test statistic indicates that functional economic relationships between cyclical factors, credit quality, defaults, market yields changed dramatically during the 1980s.

(continued)

Table D-1. *(continued)*

Issues Addressed	Methods and Measures	Results
Dependent variable: Rate of return on high yield securities/month-to-month changes (Merrill/Salomon).	Independent variables include default rate.	Statistically significant negative coefficient. Increase in default rate will reduce attractiveness of securities to potential investors.
	High yield spread over Treasury securities	Positive, statistically significant correlation between spread and both indices of high yield returns. Higher spreads should increase demand for high yield debt.
	Credit availability	Coefficient statistically, significantly different from zero. Results differ if capital flows are dependent variable. Demand for high yield securities lower during tight credit conditions.
	Fluctuations in stock market indices	Stock prices strongly, positively correlated with returns. Higher stock prices expected to stimulate increases in price of high yield issues because market value of firms will be higher, given higher perceived wealth.
	General economic performance	Coefficient not statistically, significantly different from zero. Recession does not appear to reduce demand for high yield bonds.
Leveraged buyout activity could increase number and value of high yield bonds, which were popularly used for financing. Dependent variables: Number of high yield issues or capital flows in high yield bond funds.		Strong, positive association between number of LBOs and value and number of high yield bonds consistent with model.

	Average rate of return on high yield securities for previous two months	Higher returns in recent months should induce additional investment in high yield securities.
Use of Proceeds		
1. Kaplan and Stein (1993) How did buyout prices vary over time relative to fundamentals? Aim of study to determine whether important differences exist ex ante between deals done in the latter part of 1980s and those done earlier. Overheating hypothesis studied using three broad categories: (1) Overall prices paid to take companies private. As prices paid increase relative to fundamental value of a company's assets, investors earn lower returns regardless of capital structure. (2) Buyout capital structure. Poorly designed capital structure raises probability and costs of financial distress. (3) Incentives of buyout investors. If managers cash out pre-buyout equity holdings, might indicate incentive to take part in overpriced transaction.	Data used 124 large management buyouts executed between 1980 and 1989. Of 41 deals in sample between 1980 and 1984, only one defaulted. In contrast, 22 of 83 deals completed between 1985 and 1989 defaulted as of August 1991. Independent variables: EBITDA and EBITDA less capital expenditures to measure cash flow. Debt and coverage ratios in relation to risk (defined as standard deviation of growth rate of operating margin – EBITDA/sales).	Buyout prices rose relative to fundamentals in the 1980s, but largely in line with stock market. Premiums showed no significant trend. Mixed support for overheating hypothesis. Measures of total risk indicate buyout companies in late 1980s were riskier than in earlier years. Prices particularly high in deals financed with high yield bonds. Banks took smaller positions in later deals, accelerating required principal repayments, leading to sharply lower ratios of cash flow to total debt obligations. Public high yield bond financing replaced private subordinated debt beginning in 1985, more likely to include deferred interest securities and less likely to involve equity strips. Management and other interested parties able to take more money upfront out of later deals. Use of high yield bonds associated with statistically and economically significant increases in probability of distress, default, and Chapter 11 filings.

(continued)

Table D-1. *(continued)*

Issues Addressed	Methods and Measures	Results
2. Andrade and Kaplan (1998)		
Study of highly leveraged transactions that became financially distressed—firms whose operating margins are positive and generally greater than industry median. Addresses two questions: (1) performance of firms engaging in highly leveraged transactions (HLTs) in latter half of the 1980s; (2) cost of financial distress. Dependent variable: Cost of financial distress.	Qualitative measures include firms forced to curtail capital expenditures, firms that appear to sell assets at depressed prices, firms that delay restructuring, market value of equity, book value of long-term and short-term debt, book value of capitalized leases, dummy variable for high yield bond presence, fraction of debt that is bank debt in year before HLT becomes distressed, dummy variable for presence of buyout sponsor.	Isolating firms whose leverage is primary source of capital, finds that distressed HLTs increase in value. Moreover, HLTs during 1980s were successful in creating value. Financial distress has net costs on average of 10% and maximum of 23%. Only firm leverage found to cause financial distress, when EBITDA falls below interest expense. Analysis reveals poor industry performance has positive effect. Finds that some quantitative costs of distress include increase in operating and net cash flow margins. Three most common qualitative costs are: (1) curtailing capital spending, (2) selling assets at depressed prices, (3) postponing restructuring or Chapter 11 filing. Cost of financial distress declines with capital structure complexity, use of high yield bonds specifically associated with lower cost of financial distress.
3. Simonson (1997)		
Hypothesis 1: High yield bond issuers undertake capital investment projects that market believes have positive net present values, but that usually have lower than expected realized values. Hypothesis 2: High yield bond issuers undertake acquisitions that market believes	Uses a listing of all firms issuing public, nonconvertible, below investment-grade bonds at least once between January 1, 1977, and December 31, 1989. Issues rated BB+ or below from Calender on New Security Offerings in S&P's Bond Guide. Firms unrated by S&P	Regression (1) shows a negative association between the level of capital spending and a firm's average annual adjusted stock return, and a positive association between spending on acquisitions and the dependent variable. Regression (2) displays similar relations

have positive net present values, but usually have lower than expected realized values. Shows stock returns of firms issuing below investment-grade bonds between 1977 and 1989 were significantly lower than those of size-matched comparison firms in the five years following the issuance. Evaluates hypothesis that firms time their high yield bond issues after a stock price run-up, which leads to an over-valuation that is corrected by negative stock returns following issuance. Dependent variable: average annual adjusted stock return	were identified in Moody's Bond Survey, and those rated Ba1 or below were retained. Also retained were firms issuing bonds unrated by both rating agencies. Firms not listed with CRSP Daily Returns File at the date of issuance and firms undergoing a leverage buyout and no longer having any publicly traded stock were dropped. Also dropped were firms for which Compustat data was not available. Final sample 262 firms. Cross-sectional regression on independent variables controlled for size (measured as the natural log of the market value of equity in the year before initial issuance, in 1983 dollars).	between the rates of growth of the explanatory variables and the dependent variable. Regressions (3), (4), and (5) permit a comparison between preissue and postissue stock performance. None are statistically different from zero. Underperformance concentrated in the smallest firms and the firms with the lowest ratings. Firms issuing high yield bonds and simultaneously undertaking large capital spending projects experience a significant decline in the level of cash flow per dollar of assets relative to the year before they issue, and have particularly poor postissue stock performance. Larger firms, firms with higher bond ratings, firms that have a low rate of capital spending, and firms making acquisitions show no underperformance.
Dependent variable: Adjusted operating cash flow to assets		Regression (1) shows that the level of capital spending and the change in operating performance are negatively correlated. Regression (2) shows an insignificant association between acquisition spending and changes in operating performance. Regression (3) combines both variables, and the results are unchanged. Concludes that firms with the highest levels of capital spending have the worst change in postissue operating performance and the worst postissue stock returns, implying that they are investing in value-decreasing projects.

(continued)

Table D-1. (*continued*)

Issues Addressed	Methods and Measures	Results
Investigates possibility that firms spending large amounts on capital investment projects are generally overvalued by the market, regardless of whether they issue high yield bonds or not. Includes both the high yield bond issuers and the size-matched firms in the analysis.	Independent variables include level of capital spending in the year of issuance, three-year preissue stock return, and an interaction term between the high yield bond issuer dummy and each of the independent variables. Interaction terms test if there is a difference in the performance of issuers and nonissuers.	Regression (2) shows the interaction between the high yield bond issuer dummy and the level of capital spending is negative and significant at 5%. Regression (4) shows that there is no significant relation between preissue stock performance and postissue returns for either issuers and nonissuers.
Dependent variable: annual geometric average adjusted stock return.		Analysis suggests that stock performance is negatively related to level of capital spending for high yield bond issuers but not for firms in general.
4. Gilson and Warner (1998)		
Study firms that reduced private debt by repaying bank loans with proceeds from high yield bonds. Sample firms are profitable but experience operating earnings declines just prior to high yield issuance. Earning declines tighten restrictions on bank debt. Dependent variable: Two-day cumulative abnormal return (measuring stock market response).	Sample of 164 nonacquisition-related high yield bond issues drawn from SDC for the period January 1, 1980, to December 31, 1992. Sample truncated at 1992 so that firms can be tracked for several years after the issue. Background information (on bank loan interest rates, maturity, etc.) and ratings info provided by 10-K reports, shareholder proxy statements, bond issue prospectuses, Compustat, Moody's manuals, and S&P's Creditweek. High yield bonds mature later than bank loans (median of 10 vs. 4.7 years). High yield bonds have no sinking fund provisions, so no principal payments are due until maturity, freeing up	This study indicates that high yield bond issuance enabled firms to maintain their ability to grow rapidly. Firms also experienced declines in stock price at the announcement of bank debt paydowns, resulting from decline in operating performance rather than manager–shareholder conflicts due to bank debt reduction. Stock price declines were smallest for firms closest to violating bank debt covenants and those that grew most rapidly after the issues. Primary use (largest dollar use) of HY proceeds: repay bank debt (29.7%), repay other debt (26.2%), general purposes (20.3%), finance acquisitions (19.1%).

	cash flows. Explanatory Variables: (1) Dummy for pre-issue interest coverage ratio compared to the sample median (differentiates firms that want value-enhancing flexibility since they face the tightest debt constraints); (2) postissue sales growth (measure of investment activities); (3) Value Line earnings forecast errors; (4) dummy variables for insider ownership and use of proceeds (other than paying down bank debt) on real estate and working capital used as proxies for reduced bank monitoring.	
Literature on Drexel Burnham Lambert (DBL)		
1. Platt (1993) Studies 557 high yield bond issues floated between 1977 and 1988. Of these, DBL underwrote 263 (46.8%). Model of default risk at time of issuance. Dependent variable: Probability of future default.	Independent variables: Cash flow to sales, Net fixed assets to total assets, Total debt to total assets, Short-term debt to total debt, One-year revenue growth. Also looks at underwriters' share of total defaults relative to market share.	DBL's cumulative default rate was fourth highest of the group. Probability of default increased dramatically after 1986. Finds that DBL underwritten high yield bonds had a lower default rate than bonds issued by other underwriters.
2. Benveniste, Singh, and Wilhelm (1993) Argues that bank loans and publicly traded sub-investment-grade debt are close substitutes for one another and that the failure of DBL created a competitive opportunity for commercial banks.		Observes within the commercial banking industry a positive wealth effect associated with DBL's failure. Distribution of wealth effect across commercial banks and DBL's investment banking rivals is consistent with wealth effect being primarily a reflection of market expectation of return to traditional intermediated funding for sub-investment-grade issuers.

(*continued*)

Table D-1. (*continued*)

Issues Addressed	Methods and Measures	Results
3. Livingston, Pratt, and Mann (1995)		
Historical study of DBL impact on underwriter fees. Dependent variables: underwriter spreads from Directory of Corporate Financing (US = (PB - Pc)/ PB), yield to the bondholder and sum of the two (cost to the company).	Independent variables: ratings, issue size, maturity, shelf registration, industrial vs. utility issue, competitive bids, option features, Treasury yield spread, time period, and a DBL dummy. Data set includes all nonconvertible industrial and utility bond issues (2,700) for which complete data are available from Moody's bond survey from mid-1980 to 1993.	Substantially higher underwriter fees for high yield bonds compared to investment grade. DBL's fees higher than other underwriters by 26 points. Interest rates 22 basis points lower on DBL issues. Therefore, on balance, total cost to the issuer was the same.
Default		
1. Helwege (1999)		
Analyzes high yield bond defaults. Hypotheses include: Bargaining opportunities expected to slow restructuring process as number and types of claimants increases. Opportunities for negotiating favorable outcome for particular creditor at expense of another are greater when uncertainty exists about value of claims. Lawsuits present opportunities to debate rankings of creditors' claims. Bondholders have incentive not to participate in out-of-court restructuring (holdouts) because untendered bonds will be paid in full at maturity. Asymmetric information between managers and creditors (or different creditor classes) may lead to bargaining problems, incentives to hasten/	Data from list of defaults compiled by Salomon Brothers High Yield Research Group (1992) include bonds rated speculative grade or unrated at issuance. Includes only bonds originally offered in public high yield market and private placements with registrations that entered public market prior to default. Bond is considered in default if an interest payment is missed, but also if a troubled exchange or tender offer is announced. Final sample includes 127 firms and 129 defaults (2 firms defaulted twice) from 1980 to 1991. Default experience investigated through financial press and financial databases (SDC, Moody's Investors Service), operating performance,	Size, lawsuits, and contingent claims lengthen default spell. However, the number of bond classes and whether the debt is publicly held do not appear to present severe bargaining hurdles. Counter to Gilson et. al. (1990), but consistent with Asquith et al. (1994), banks in this sample do not facilitate the process, and even slow down renegotiation. In contrast, a large fraction of the liability structure, in the form of high yield bonds, appears to speed up the process considerably. Finally, firms that renegotiated their debt with the help of DBL (Milken) may have ended default spells earlier.

delay restructuring process. HLT firms likely to be fundamentally profitable at time of distress because less equity has been eroded. Creditors try to preserve firms with high value of assets in place or growth opportunities. Entrenched managers may cause delay in restructuring. HLT firms less likely to have entrenched managers because of highly concentrated equity ownership. Institutional factors include revisions in tax codes, rulings against exchange offers, and increase in number of distressed firms. Dependent variable: Time to default (period from default to acceptance of new securities or emergence from bankruptcy.)	firm value variables (Compustat, Compact Disclosure, analyst reports, etc.), indicator variable for presence of lawsuits. One proxy for holdouts is public debt company has in its liability structure. Indicator variable for HLTs indicates time to default. Indicator variable for firms whose bonds were underwritten by DBL that defaulted before 1989.	
2. Altman and Kishore (1996) This study examines the recovery experience at default and provides important information on pricing debt securities. Severity of default based on recoveries because they influence expected loss from defaults. Industry affiliation likely to be important because it dictates the type of assets and the competitive conditions of firms within different sectors. If firms in certain industries have a higher proportion of higher-rated, senior secured and senior unsecured original debt, one might expect higher recovery rates.	Calculates recovery rate by industry (1971–1995). SIC codes assigned corresponding to product group that accounts for firm's greatest value of sales. Since some sectors had too few data points to be meaningful, several SIC codes were combined into logical groups.	Original rating of bond issue as investment grade or below investment grade has virtually no effect on recovery once seniority is accounted for. Study documents severity of bond defaults stratified by SIC sector and by debt seniority. Highest average recoveries came from public utilities (70%), chemical and petroleum related products (63%). Differences between sectors are statistically significant even when adjusted for seniority.

(continued)

Table D-1. *(continued)*

Issues Addressed	Methods and Measures	Results
3. Altman and Kishore (1997)		
Documents high yield market's risk and return performance by presenting default and mortality statistics. Provides matrix of average returns and performance statistics. Since almost 70% of all new issuance in high yield market since 1991 has been senior in priority, average recovery rates should continue to be above historical average.	Data use annual default rates 1971–1996, historical average recovery rates by seniority (1977–1996) and by original bond rating (1971–1996). Also looks at yield spreads (Merrill Lynch HYMI vs. 10-yr. Treasuries).	Neither size of issue nor time to default from original date of issuance has association with recovery rate. All seniority levels recovered higher amounts in 1996 than historical 19-year average. Original rating has virtually no effect on recoveries once seniority is accounted for. Senior secured investment grade defaults had average weighted price recovery of $48.58 compared to $48.13 for senior secured non-investment grade original issues.
Risk		
1. Fridson and Jónsson (1994)		
How is risk measured? High yield market valuation widely used is comparing spreads over Treasuries to historical average (with underlying assumption of mean reversion). If spread is a risk premium, it must vary with risk. Therefore, a high yield bond is cheap only if its yield premium is larger than warranted by prevailing risk. Investors demand increased compensation when credit failures rise. Dependent variable: Changes in Merrill Lynch High Yield Master Index's spread versus ten-year Treasuries.	Credit risk measured by Moody's Trailing-Twelve-Month Default Rate (percentage of issuers basis), Index of Lagging Economic Indicators (BEA).	Fridson-Jónsson model generates R^2 of 0.72. All variables statistically significant at 95% confidence level. Spread not a useful market timing tool in the short run. (Also borne out by Altman and Bencivenga 1995). Evidently, high yield spreads anticipate changes in default rates but change only after the fact. Lagging indicators read favorably even though economy is already declining.

	Illiquidity risk measured by mutual fund flows as percentage of fund assets (ICI); cash as % of high yield mutual fund assets (ICI/AMG Data Services); three-month moving average price of Merrill Lynch High Yield Master Index (Bloomberg daily data).	–0.47 correlation coefficient. Negative sign indicates net inflows tend to improve liquidity and reduce risk premium. When fund managers expect large outflows, they may temporarily increase cash positions. Therefore, large liquidity premiums tend to coincide with large cash positions. Positive sign and 0.56 correlation with spread.
	Additional variables include term structure, level of Treasury rates, High Yield Master Index (expressed in terms of yield-to-maturity or in terms of price), Index of Leading Economic Indicators, broker loan rate, monthly count of news articles on high yield bonds (Business Periodicals Index), new issuance	–0.46 correlation coefficient. Negative sign indicates that price decline makes investors wary, leading to contraction in liquidity. Disparity between actual and estimated values very pronounced during first half of 1996. Estimated > actual indicates inadequate risk premium and overvalued market. Additional variables lacked explanatory power. Fridson and Kenney (1994) also found no statistical correlation with spread. A negative price trend may encourage investors to sell, less liquidity.
Other Studies		
1. Ma, Rao, and Peterson (1989) Analyzed new issue spreads on high yield bonds.	Data used 506 high yield bonds issued from January 1980 to May 1987. Independent variables include use of proceeds for specific M&A, use of proceeds for unspecified M&A, Moody's Rating, duration to first call, issue size, convertibility, yield spread between Moody's 30-year Aaa bonds and 30-year Treasury bonds	Explained 79% of variance in spreads.

(continued)

Table D-1. (*continued*)

Issues Addressed	Methods and Measures	Results
Shulman, Bayless, and Price (1993) Analyzed bonds to develop a default risk model. Tested default probability and yield spreads jointly.	Data used 107 bonds of 78 issuers. Independent variables include cash from operations/total sources, net liquid balance/total assets, amount of debt outstanding, market value of stock/liabilities, standard deviation of stock returns, frequency of bond trades, volatility of bond prices.	Explained 77% of variance in default risk and spreads.
2. Garman and Fridson (1996) January 1985–May 1996 Refinements on Fridson-Jónsson model to include indicators of monetary conditions, instability of high yield index's composition (ratings mix), general level of interest rates. Risk premium decreases when capacity utilization rises or yield curve steepens, implying strengthening economy and less risk of business failure. Spread narrows when money supply expands, indicating easier credit conditions. Cash flows into high yield mutual funds should enhance market liquidity. Inflation benefits debtors by reducing real cost of liabilities. Dependent variable: Changes in Merrill Lynch High Yield Master Index's spread over 10 year-Treasuries.	Independent variables include default risk measured by Moody's trailing-twelve-months default rate (percentage of issuers basis) and capacity utilization. Illiquidity risk measured by mutual fund flows as percent of fund assets (ICI) and cash as percent of high yield mutual fund assets (ICI). Monetary conditions measured as year-over-year change in CPI (Federal Reserve Board), Treasury yield curve (10-year minus 3-month), money supply (M2 minus M1, year-over-year change), ratings mix of Merrill Lynch High Yield Master Index.	$R^2 = 0.89$. Positive correlation between spread and CPI. Useful when viewed in conjunction with other variables. Greatest explanatory power from monetary aggregates. Between January 1995 and May 1996, two out of three key monetary indicators suggested narrower-than-average spreads. Once these are considered, high yield market ceases to appear overvalued. Rejected as explanatory variable. Regression indicates positive net effect. Introducing ratings mix proxy (par weighted quality, Bloomberg) into multivariate model yields unsatisfactory results—higher-quality mix associated with larger risk premium.

3. Fridson, Garman, and Wu (1997) Looks at impact of real interest rates on default. Increase in cost of capital will not immediately render companies insolvent if they have substantial liquidity on balance sheets. Contraction in economic activity resulting from rise in real interest rates may occur only gradually. Dependent variable: default rate.	Data for 1971–1995. Default rate: twelve months' default rate from Moody's Investors Service; nominal interest rates: yield on 10-year Treasuries from FRB; inflation: change in CPI from Bureau of Labor Statistics. Test for lags.	High correlation of default rates and real interest (low correlation with nominal rates). Two-year lag produces maximum correlation between real interest rates and default rates. Study, along with Helwege and Kleiman (1997), Jónsson and Fridson (1996), indicates that, on average, three-quarters of current year's default rate is locked in by economic and financial forces of two to three years ago. Despite close fit, model characterizes 1996 trailing twelve-month rate as surprisingly low.
4. Carty (1996) Aims to characterize and measure credit risk. Important determinant is information structure of debt market. Empirically examines two contrasting models of default behavior. Diamond model of moral hazard implies default risk declines over time as firm develops reputation. In Jovanovic matching model with incomplete information, default risk first rises and then falls as investors and managers learn more about quality of enterprise.	Time-varying hazard model estimated with additional conditioning variables. Fundamental interest in length of time from firm entering public debt market to default or exit. Competing risks could terminate firm's spell in market, captured in polynomial $a + bt + ct^2$. Jovanovic's Hypothesis: $b>0$, $c<0$. Diamond's hypothesis: $b<0$, $c<0$. Specifies hazard function of duration random variable that gives instantaneous risk of exit, conditional on no prior exit. Nonparametric estimates of probability of default for firms by rating category, based on standard life table methods (Kalbfleisch & Prentice 1980). Other explanatory variables: Growth rate of S&P 500 stock price index, growth rate of GDP, proxy for	For each rating category, growth rate of S&P 500 stock index and change in nominal rates positively correlated with risk of exiting public bond market without defaulting, while growth rate of real GDP negatively correlated with risk. Weakly significant determinant of risk of default for riskier companies. Variable is highly significantly related to risk of firm exiting debt market without defaulting at each credit rating. Results favor Jovanovic-type model. Growth rate of S&P 500 stock prices index negative coefficient. High expectations of future earnings lowers risk of default (except for Baa-rated firms). Increases in nominal interest rates reduce value of fixed debt obligations, resulting in capital gains.

(continued)

Table D-1. (*continued*)

Issues Addressed	Methods and Measures	Results
	real interest rate (ex post rate = average yearly yield on long-term government bonds and yearly growth in CPI), interaction between change in nominal interest rates and duration of firm's spell in public bond market.	
	Number of issuers entering bond market (proxy for capturing booms and busts). Dummy to capture regime shifts (bankruptcy code changes coincide with development of modern high yield bond market). Industry dummy (some change in riskiness, depending on rating of firm in industry).	Does not appear to be economically significant determinant of default risk. Evidence against hypothesis that duration dependence of default attributable to cyclical nature of bond issuance.

References

Alcaly, R. E. (1994). "The Golden Age of Junk." *The New York Review of Books*, May 26, pp. 28–34.

Altman, E. I. (1989). "Measuring Corporate Bond Mortality and Performance." *The Journal of Finance*, September, pp. 909–922.

Altman, E. I. (1990a). "How 1989 Changed the Hierarchy of Fixed Income Security Performance." *Financial Analysts Journal*, May/June, pp. 9–12, 20.

Altman, E. I. (1990b). "Setting the Record Straight on Junk Bonds: A Review of Research on Default Rates and Returns." *Journal of Applied Corporate Finance* 3, no. 2: 82–95.

Altman, E. I. (ed.) (1990c). *The High Yield Debt Market: Investment Performance and Economic Impact*. Homewood, IL: Dow Jones-Irwin.

Altman, E. I. (1991). *Distressed Securities: Analyzing and Evaluating Market Potential and Investment Risk*. Chicago: Probus.

Altman, E. I., and Bencivenga, J. C. (1995). "A Yield Premium Model for the High Yield Market." *Financial Analysts Journal*, September/October, pp. 49–56.

Altman, E. I., Hukkawala, N., and Kishore, V. (2000). "Defaults and Returns on High-Yield Bonds: Lessons from 1999 and Outlook for 2000–2002." *Business Economics* 35, no. 2: 27–38.

Altman, E. I., and Kishore, V. M. (1996). "Almost Everything You Wanted to Know About Recoveries on Defaulted Bonds." *Financial Analysts Journal*, November/December, pp. 57–64.

Altman, E. I., and Kishore, V. M, (1997). *Defaults and Returns on High-Yield Bonds*. New York: Salomon Center.

Altman, E. I., and Nammacher, S. A. (1987). *Investing in Junk Bonds: Inside the High Yield Debt Market*. New York: John Wiley & Sons.

Altman, E. I., Resti, A. and Sironi, A. (2001). "Analyzing and Explaining Default Recovery Rates." Submitted to the International Swaps and Derivatives Association.

Ameer, P., Feldman, S. J., and Soyka, P. A. (1996). "Does Improving a Firm's Environmental Management System and Environmental Performance Result in Higher Stock Price?" Mimeograph.

Amihud, Y., and Mendleson, H. (1988). "Liquidity and Asset Prices: Financial Management Implications." *Financial Management* 17: 5–15.

Amihud, Y., and Mendleson, H. (2000). "The Liquidity Route to a Lower Cost of Capital." *Journal of Applied Corporate Finance* 12, no. 4: 8–25.

Andrade, G., and Kaplan, S. (1998). "How Costly Is Financial (Not Economic) Distress? Evidence from Highly Leveraged Transactions That Became Distressed." *Journal of Finance* 53, 5: 1443–1493.

Arthur, B. (1990). "Positive Feedbacks in the Economy." *Scientific American*, February, 262: 92–97.

Arthur, B. (1994). *Increasing Returns and Path Dependence in the Economy*. Ann Arbor: University of Michigan Press.

Arthur, B. (1995). "Complexity in Economic and Financial Markets." *Complexity* 1: 20–25.

Asquith, P., Gertner, R., and Scharfstein, D. (1994). "Anatomy of Financial Distress: An Examination of Junk Bond Issuers." *Quarterly Journal of Economics* 109: 625–634.

Asquith, P., Mullins, D., Jr., and Wolff E. (1989). "Original Issue High Yield Bonds: Aging Analysis of Defaults, Exchanges and Calls." *The Journal of Finance*, September, pp. 923–952.

Atkinson, T. R. (1967). *Trends in Corporate Bond Quality*. New York: Columbia University Press.

Auerbach, A. J. (ed.) (1988). *Corporate Takeovers: Causes and Consequences*. Chicago: University of Chicago Press.

Barclay, M. J., Marx, L. M., and Smith, C. W., Jr. (forthcoming). "The Joint Determination of Leverage and Maturity." *Journal of Corporate Finance*.

Barclay, M. J., and Smith, C. W., Jr. (1996). "On Financial Architecture: Leverage, Maturity, and Priority." *Journal of Applied Corporate Finance* 8, no. 4: 4–29.

Barclay, M. J., and Smith, C. W., Jr. (1999). "The Capital Structure Puzzle: Another Look at the Evidence." *Journal of Applied Corporate Finance* 12, no. 1: 8–20.

Barnhill, T. M., Jr., Maxwell, W. F., and Shenkman, M. R. (eds.). (1999). *High Yield Bonds: Market Structure, Portfolio Management, and Credit Risk Modeling*. New York: McGraw-Hill.

Barth, J., Brumbaugh, D., and Yago, G. (eds.) (2001). *Restructuring Regulation and Financial Institutions*. Boston: Kluwer Academic Press.

Barth, J., Trimbath, S., and Yago, G. (2002). "Institute View." *Milken Institute Review*, Second Quarter: 86–95.

Barth, J., Trimbath, S., and Yago, G. (eds.) (2003). *What Can be Learned from an Examination of S&Ls?* Boston: Kluwer Academic Press.

Bates, T. (1997). "Unequal Access to Financial Institution Lending to Black- and White-owned Small Business Startups." *Journal of Urban Affairs* 19, no. 4: 487–489.

Beck, T., and Levine, R. (2002). "Industry Growth and Capital Allocation: Does Having a Market- or Bank-Based System Matter?" *Journal of Financial Economics* 64: 147–180.

Beck, T., Loayza, N., and Levine, R. (2000). "Finance and the Sources of Growth." *Journal of Financial Economics*, 58, no. 1–2: 261–300.

Becketti, S. (1990). "The Truth About Junk Bonds." *Economic Review, Federal Reserve Bank of Kansas City*, July / August, pp. 45–54.

Ben-Horim, M., and Levy, H. (1981). *Statistics: Decisions and Applications in Business and Economics*. New York: Random House.

Bencivenga, J., Cheung, R., and Fabozzi, F. J. (1992). "Original Issue High-Yield Bonds: Historical Return and Default Experience, 1977–1989." *The Journal of Fixed Income*, September, pp. 58–75.

Bennett, P., and Kelleher, J. (1988). "The International Transmission of Stock Price Disruption in October 1987." *Federal Reserve Bank of New York Quarterly Review* 13: 17–33.

Benveniste, L. M., Singh, M., and Wilhelm, W. J., Jr. (1993). "The Failure of Drexel

Burnham Lambert: Evidence on the Implications for Commercial Banks." *Journal of Financial Intermediation* 3: 104–137.

Bernanke, B. (1983). "Nonmonetary Effects of the Financial Crisis in Propagation of the Great Depression." *American Economic Review* 73, no. 3: 257–276.

Bernanke, B., Gertler, M., and Gilchrist, S. (1996). "The Financial Accelerator and the Flight to Quality." *Review of Economics and Statistics* 78: 1–15.

Bernanke, B., and Lown, C. S. (1991). "The Credit Crunch." *Brookings Papers on Economic Activity* no. 2: 205–247.

Bhagat, S., Shliefer, A., and Vishny, R. (1990). "Hostile Takeovers in the 1980s: The Return to Corporate Specialization." *Brookings Papers on Economic Activity: Microeconomics*, Special Issue: 1–84.

Birch, D., Haggerty, A., and Parsons, W. (1993). *Corporate Almanac*. Cambridge, MA: Cognetics, Inc.

Bizer, D. S. (1993). "Regulatory Discretion and the Credit Crunch." Working paper, U.S. Securities and Exchange Commission.

Blackwell, D., Marr, W., and Spivey, M. (1990). "Plant-Closing Decisions and the Market Value of the Firm." *Journal of Financial Economics* 26: 277–288.

Blume, M. E., and Keim, D. B. (1991a). "Realized Returns and Defaults on Low-Grade Bonds: The Cohort of 1977 and 1978." *Financial Analysts Journal*, March/April, pp. 63–72.

Blume, M. E., and Keim, D. B. (1991b). "The Risk and Return of Low-Grade Bonds: An Update." *Financial Analysts Journal*, September/October, pp. 85–89.

Blume, M. E., Keim, D. B., and Patel, S. A. (1991). "Return and Volatility of Low-Grade Bonds 1977–1989." *Journal of Finance* 46, no. 1: 49–74.

Blume, M. E., Lim, F., and MacKinlay, A. C. (1998). "The Declining Credit Quality of U.S. Corporate Debt: Myth or Reality?" *The Journal of Finance* 53, no. 4: 1389–1413.

Bookstaber, R., and Jacob, D. P. (1986). "The Composite Hedge: Controlling the Credit Risk of High-Yield Bonds." *Financial Analysts Journal*, March/April, pp. 25–36.

Bouhuys, H., and Yeager, S. (1999). "Recent Developments in the High Yield Market." *Journal of Applied Corporate Finance* 12, no. 1, pp. 70–77.

Brealey, R., and Myers, S. (2000). *Principles of Corporate Finance*. New York: Irwin McGraw-Hill.

Breeden, R. C. (1990). Letters to Chairman of Senate Committee on Banking Housing, and Urban Affairs dated March 15 and August 14.

Brown, C., and Medoff, J. (1988). "The Impact of Firm Acquisitions on Labor." In A. Auerback (ed.), *Corporate Takeovers: Causes and Consequences*. Chicago: University of Chicago Press.

Brown, R. L., Durbin, J., and Evans, J. M. (1975). "Techniques for Testing the Constancy of Regression Relationships over Time." *Journal of the Royal Statistical Society*, December, pp. 149–163.

Buell, S. G. (1992). "The Accuracy of the Initial Pricing of Junk Bonds." *The Journal of Fixed Income*, September, pp. 77–83.

Bygrave, W., and Timmons, J. (1991). *Venture Capital at the Crossroads*. Cambridge, MA: Harvard University Press.

Carey, M., Prowse, S., Rea, J., and Udell, G. (1993). *The Economics of the Private Placement Market*. Federal Reserve Board of Governors Staff Study 166. Washington, DC: Federal Reserve.

Carpenter, R. E., Fazzari, S. M., and Petersen, B. C. (1994). "Inventory (Dis)Investment, Internal Finance Fluctuations and the Business Cycle." *Brookings Papers on Economic Activity* no. 2, pp. 75–138.

Carty, L. V. (1996). "An Empirical Investigation of Default Risk Dynamics." Ph.D. diss., Columbia University.

Chen, G. (1993). "Minority Business Development: Where Do We Go from Here?" *Journal of Black Political Economy*, 22, 2: 5–16.

Chew, D. (1998). *The New Corporate Finance: Where Theory Meets Practice*. New York: McGraw-Hill.

Chou, Y. K., and Chin, M. S. (2001). "Financial Innovations and Endogenous Growth." Working paper, University of Melbourne.

Chow, G. C. (1960). "Tests of Equality Between Sets of Coefficients in Two Linear Regressions." *Econometrica*, June, pp. 591–605.

Christensen, D. G., and Faria, H. J. (1994). "A Note on the Shareholder Wealth Effects of High-Yield Bonds." *Financial Management*, Spring, p. 10.

Cooper, R. A., and Shulman, J. M. (1994). "The Year-End Effect in Junk Bond Prices." *Financial Analysts Journal*, September / October, pp. 61–65.

Corcoran, P. J. (1994). "The Double-B Private Placement Market." *The Journal of Fixed Income*, June, pp. 42–51.

Cornell, B. (1992). "Liquidity and the Pricing of Low-Grade Bonds." *Financial Analysts Journal*, January / February, pp. 63–67.

Cornell, B., and Green, K. (1991). "The Investment Performance of Low-Grade Bond Funds." *The Journal of Finance*, March, pp. 29–48.

Datta, S., Iskandar-Datta, M., and Patel, A. (1997). "The Pricing of Initial Public Offers of Corporate Straight Debt." *The Journal of Finance*, March, pp. 379–396.

Datta, S., Iskandar-Datta, M., and Patel, A. (1999). "The Market's Pricing of Debt IPOs." *Journal of Applied Corporate Finance* 12, no.1: 86–91.

Davenport, K. A. (1999). *Public vs. Private Markets: A Review of High Yield Financing Techniques*. Los Angeles: Latham and Watkins.

DeAngelo, H., DeAngelo, L., and Gilson, S. C. (1993). "The Collapse of First Executive Corporation: Junk Bonds, Adverse Publicity, and the 'Run on the Bank' Phenomenon." Working paper, University of Southern California.

Denis, D., and Kruse, T. (2000). "Managerial Discipline and Corporate Restructuring Following Performance Declines." *Journal of Financial Economics* 55: 391–424.

DeRosa-Farag, S., Blau, J., Matousek, P., and Chandra, I. (1999). "Default Rates in the High Yield Market." *Journal of Fixed Income*, June, pp. 7–31.

De Soto, H. (2000). *The Mystery of Capital: Why Capitalism Succeeds in the West and Fails Everywhere Else*. New York: Basic Books.

Duffie, D., and Gârleanu, N. (2001). "Risk and Valuation of Collateralized Debt Obligations." Working paper, Stanford University Graduate School of Business.

Durbin, J. (1969). "Tests for Serial Correlation in Regression Based on the Periodogram of the Least Squares Residuals." *Biometrika*, March, pp. 1–15.

Durnev, A. A., Morck, A. R., and Yeung, B. (2001). "Capital Markets and Capital Allocation: Implications for Economies in Transition." Working paper, University of Michigan Business School, November 27.

Easterly, W., Islam, R., and Stiglitz, J. (2001). "Shaken and Stirred: Explaining Growth Volatility." Presented at the Annual Bank Conference on Development Economics, April.

Easterwood, J., and Seth, A. (1993). "Strategic Restructuring in Large Management Buyouts." *Strategic Management Journal* 13, no. 2: 25–37.

Erickson, R. A. (1994). "Technology, Industrial Restructuring, and Regional Development." *Growth & Change* 25, no. 3: 353–379.

Fabozzi, F. J. (ed.). (1989). *Advances and Innovations in the Bond and Mortgage Markets*. Chicago: Probus.

Fabozzi, F. J. (ed.). (1990). *The New High-Yield Debt Market: A Handbook for Portfolio Managers and Analysts*. New York: HarperCollins.

Fazzari, S. R., Hubbard, R. G., and Petersen, B. C. (1988). "Finance Constraints and Corporate Investment." *Brookings Papers on Economic Activity* 1: 141–195.

Fenn, G. W. (2000). "Speed of Issuance and the Adequacy of Disclosure in the 144A High-Yield Debt Market." *Journal of Financial Economics* 56, no. 3: 383–406.

Finnerty, J. D. (1992). "An Overview of Corporate Securities Innovation." *Journal of Applied Corporate Finance* 4, no. 4: 23–39.

First Boston. (1991). *High Yield Handbook*. New York: First Boston.

Fitzpatrick, J. D., and Severiens, J. T. (1978). "Hickman Revisited: The Case for Junk Bonds." *The Journal of Portfolio Management*, Summer, pp. 53–57.

Fons, J. S. (1987). "The Default Premium and Corporate Bond Experience." *The Journal of Finance*, March, pp. 81–97.

Fons, J. S. (1991). *An Approach to Forecasting Default Rates*. Moody's Special Report. New York: Moody's Inc.

Fons, J. S. (1994). "Using Default Rates to Model the Term Structure of Credit Risk." *Financial Analysts Journal*, September / October, pp. 25–32.

Fons, J. S., Carty, L., and Kaufman, J. (1994). *Corporate Bond Defaults and Default Rates, 1970–1993*. Moody's Special Report. New York: Moody's Inc.

Fons, J. S., and Kimball, A. E. (1991). "Corporate Bond Defaults and Default Rates 1970–1990." *The Journal of Fixed Income*, June, pp. 36–47.

Fowler, K. L., and Schmidt, D. R. (1989). "Determinants of Tender Offer Post Acquisition Financial Performance." *Strategic Management Journal* 10: 339–350.

Fraine, H. G. (1937). "Superiority of High-Yield Bonds Not Substantiated by 1927–1936 Performance." *Analyst*, October, pp. 533–547.

Fraine, H. G., and Mills, R. H. (1961)."Effects of Defaults and Credit Deterioration on Yields of Corporate Bonds." *The Journal of Finance*, September, pp. 423–434.

Fridson, M. S. (1989). *High Yield Bonds: Identifying Value and Assessing Risk of Speculative Grade Securities*. Chicago: Probus.

Fridson, M. S. (1991a)."This Year in High Yield." *Extra Credit: The Journal of High Yield Bond Research*, February, pp. 4–15.

Fridson, M. S. (1991b). "Everything You Ever Wanted to Know About Default Rates." *Extra Credit: The Journal of High Yield Bond Research*, July / August, pp. 4–14.

Fridson, M. S. (1991c). "What Went Wrong with the Highly Leveraged Deals? (Or, All Variety of Agency Costs)." *Journal of Applied Corporate Finance*, Fall, pp. 57–67.

Fridson, M. S. (1992a). "High Yield Indexes and Benchmark Portfolios." *The Journal of Portfolio Management*, Winter, pp. 77–83.

Fridson, M. S. (1992b). "Modeling the Credit Risk of Nonrated High Yield Bonds." *Risks and Rewards: The Newsletter of the Investment Sector of the Society of Actuaries*, March, pp. 6–11.

Fridson, M. S. (1993). "High Yield Bonds: Markets Work." In G. Kaufman (ed.), *Research in Financial Services: Private and Public Policy*, vol. 5. Greenwich, CT: JAI Press.

Fridson, M. S. (1994a). "Do High-Yield Bonds Have an Equity Component?" *Financial Management*, Summer, pp. 76–78.

Fridson, M. S. (1994b). "The State of the High Yield Bond Market: Overshooting or Return to Normalcy?" *Journal of Applied Corporate Finance*, Spring, pp. 85–97.

Fridson, M. S. (1994c). "Fraine's Neglected Findings: Was Hickman Wrong?" *Financial Analysts Journal*, September / October, pp. 43–53.

Fridson, M. S. (1995). "Loads, Flows, and Performance in High-Yield Bond Mutual Funds." *Journal of Fixed Income*, December, pp. 70–78.

Fridson, M. S., and Bersh, J. A. (1994). "Spread Versus Treasuries as a Market-Timing Tool for High-Yield Investors." *Journal of Fixed Income*, June, pp. 63–69.

Fridson, M. S., and Cherry, M. A. (1990). "Initial Pricing as a Predictor of Subsequent Performance of High Yield Bonds." *Financial Analysts Journal*, July / August, pp. 61–67.

Fridson, M. S., and Cherry, M. A. (1991a). "A Critique of the Spread-Versus-Treasuries Concept." *Extra Credit: The Journal of High Yield Bond Research*. July / August, pp. 41–45.

Fridson, M. S., and Cherry, M. A. (1991b). "Explaining the Variance in High Yield Managers' Returns." *Financial Analysts Journal*, May / June, pp. 64–72.

Fridson, M. S., Cherry, M. A., Kim, J. A., and Weiss, S. W. (1992). "What Drives the Flows of High Yield Mutual Funds?" *The Journal of Fixed Income*, December, pp. 47–59.

Fridson, M. S., and De Candia, A. (1991). "Trends: Follow, Buck or Ignore?" *The Journal of Portfolio Management*, Winter, pp. 50–55.

Fridson, M. S., and Gao, Y. (1996). "Primary Versus Secondary Pricing of High Yield Bonds." *Financial Analysts Journal*, May / June, pp. 20–27.

Fridson, M. S., and Garman, M. C. (1997). "Valuing Like-Rated Senior and Subordinated Debt." *The Journal of Fixed Income*, December, pp. 83–93.

Fridson, M. S., and Garman, M. C. (1998a). "Determinants of Spreads on New High-Yield Bonds." *Financial Analysts Journal*, March / April, pp. 28–39.

Fridson, M. S., and Garman, M. C. (1998b). "Erosion of Principal and the Rebasing Illusion." *The Journal of Fixed Income*, December, pp. 85–98.

Fridson, M. S., Garman, M. C., and Wu, S. (1997). "Real Interest Rates and the Default Rate on High-Yield Bonds." *The Journal of Fixed Income*, September, pp. 29–34.

Fridson, M. S., and Jónsson, J. G. (1994). *Spread Versus Treasuries and the Riskiness of High-yield Bonds*. New York: Merrill Lynch.

Fridson, M. S., and Jónsson, J. G. (1995). "Spread Versus Treasuries and the Riskiness of High-Yield Bonds." *Journal of Fixed Income*, December, pp. 79–88.

Gale Group. (2001). *History of Viacom* and *History of Fort James Corp*. Farmington Hills, MI: Gale Group.

Gallo, A. E. (1997). "First Major Drop in Food Product Introduction in over 20 Years." *Food Review* 20, no. 3: 33.

Garman, M. C., and Fridson, M. S. (1996). *Monetary Influences on the High-Yield Spread Versus Treasuries*. New York: Merrill Lynch.

Garvey, G. T., and Hanka, G. (1999). "Capital Structure and Corporate Control: The Effect of Antitakeover Statutes on Firm Leverage." *The Journal of Finance* 54, no. 2: 519–546.

General Accounting Office. (1988). *High Yield Bonds: Nature of the Market and Effect on Federally Insured Institutions*. Washington, DC: U.S. General Accounting Office.

Gertler, M., and Lown, C. S. (1999). "The Information in the High Yield Bond Spread for the Business Cycle: Evidence and Some Implications." Prepared for the Conference on Financial Instability, Oxford University, July 1999.

Gilson, S. C., Kose, J., and Lang, L. H. P. (1990). "Troubled Debt Restructurings: An Empirical Study of Private Reorganization of Firms in Default." *Journal of Financial Economics* 27: 315–353.

Gilson, S. C., and Warner, J. B. (1998). "Private Versus Public Debt: Evidence from Firms That Replace Bank Loans with Junk Bonds." Working paper, Harvard Business School.

Goodman, L. S. (1990). "High-Yield Default Rates: Is There Cause for Concern?" *The Journal of Portfolio Management*, Winter, pp. 54–59.

Goodwin, B. K., and Brester, G. W. (1995). "Structural Change in Factor Demand Relationships in the U.S. Food and Kindred Products Industry." *American Journal of Agricultural Economics* 77: 69–79.

Grossman, S. J., and Hart, O. D. (1982). "Corporate Financial Structure and Managerial Incentives." In J. McCall (ed.), *The Economics of Information and Uncertainty*. Chicago: University of Chicago Press.

Gudikunst, A., and McCarthy, J. (1997). "High-Yield Bond Mutual Funds: Performance, January Effects, and Other Surprises." *The Journal of Fixed Income*, September, pp. 35–46.

Hall, R. (1993). "Macrotheory and the Recession of 1990–91." Working Paper, National Bureau of Economic Research and Stanford University.

Hancock, D., and Wilcox, J. (1993). "The Credit Crunch and the Availability of Credit to Small Businesses." Presented at Conference on Economics of Small Business Finance, New York University.

Hartzheim, P. (2000). *Canada's Nascent High Yield Market*. Calgary: University of Calgary Press.

Hawley, D. D., and Walker, M. M. (1992). "An Empirical Test of Investment Restrictions of Efficiency in the High Yield Debt Market." *Financial Review*, May, pp. 273–287.

Hawley, D. D., and Walker, M. M. (1993). "Speculative Grade Ratings and the Investment Decision Process: A Survey of Institutional Money Managers." *Financial Practice and Education*, Fall, pp. 39–46.

Healy, P., Palepu, K., and Ruback, R. (1992). "Does Corporate Performance Improve After Mergers?" *Journal of Financial Economics* 31: 135–175.

Heller, R. H., and Khan, M. S. (1979). "The Demand for Money and the Term Structure of Interest Rates." *Journal of Political Economy* 87: 109–129.

Helwege, J. (1999). "How Long Do Junk Bonds Spend in Default?" *The Journal of Finance* 54, no. 1: 341–357.

Helwege, J., and Kleiman, K. (1997). "Understanding Aggregate Default Rates of High Yield Bonds." *The Journal of Fixed Income*, June, pp. 55–61.

Helwege, J., and Kleiman, K. (1998). "The Pricing of High-Yield Debt IPOs." *The Journal of Fixed Income*, September, pp. 61–68.

Hickman, W. B. (1958). *Corporate Bond Quality and Investor Experience*. Princeton, NJ: Princeton University Press.

Hogan, S. D., and Huie, M. C. (1992). "Bigness, Junk, and Bust-ups: End of the Fourth Merger Wave?" *Antitrust Bulletin* 37, no. 4: 881–956.

Howe, J. (1988). *Junk Bonds: Analysis and Portfolio Strategies*. Chicago: Probus.

Hradsky, G. T., and Long, R. (1989). "High Yield Losses and the Return Performance of Bankrupt Debt." *Financial Analysts Journal*, July / August, pp. 38–49.

Hubbard, R. G., Kashyap, A. K., and Whited, T. M. (1995). "Internal Finance and Firm Investment." NBER Working Paper no. 4392.

Iannoconi, T. (1993). "The SEC's Expanded Role in Small Business Capital Formation." *Journal of Accountancy*, August, pp. 47–48.

Jefferis, R. H., Jr. (1990). "The High-Yield Debt Market: 1980–1990." *Economic Commentary, Federal Reserve Bank of Cleveland*, April.

Jensen, M. (1986). "Agency Costs of Free Cash Flow, Corporate Finance and Takeovers." *American Economic Review* 76: 323–329.

Jensen, M. (1989)."Active Investors, LBOs, and the Privatization of Bankruptcy." *Journal of Applied Corporate Finance* 2: 35–44.

Jensen, M. (1991). "Corporate Control and the Politics of Finance." *Journal of Applied Corporate Finance*, 4, no. 2: 13–33.

Jensen, M. (1993). "Presidential Address: The Modern Industrial Revolution, Exit, and the Failure of Internal Control Systems." *The Journal of Finance* 48: 831–880.

Jensen, M., Kaplan, S., and Stiglin, L. (1989). "The Effects of LBOs on the Tax Revenues of the U.S. Treasury. *Tax Notes*, 42, 6: 727–733.

Jensen, M., and Meckling, W. (1976). "Theory of the Firm: Managerial Behavior, Agency Costs, and Capital Structure." *Journal of Financial Economics* 3: 305–360.

Jónsson, J. G., and Fridson, M. S. (1996). "Forecasting Default Rates on High Yield Bonds." *The Journal of Fixed Income*, June, pp. 69–77.

JPMorgan Securities (2001). *CDO Handbook*. New York: JPMorgan Securities.

Kahan, M., and Tuckman, B. (1993). "Do Bondholders Lose from Junk Bond Covenant Changes?" *The Journal of Business*, October, pp. 499–516.

Kalbfleisch, J., and Prentice, R. (1980). *The Statistical Analysis of Failure Time Data*. New York: Wiley.

Kao, D. (1993). "Illiquid Securities: Issues of Pricing and Performance Measurement." *Financial Analysts Journal* 77: 28–35.

Kaplan, S. (1989). "The Effects of Management Buyouts on Operations and Value." *Journal of Financial Economics* 24: 217–254.

Kaplan, S. (1991). "The Staying Power of Leveraged Buyouts." *Journal of Financial Economics* 29: 287–314.

Kaplan, S. (1997). "The Evolution of U.S. Corporate Governance: We Are All Henry Kravis Now." *Journal of Private Equity*, Fall, pp. 7–14.

Kaplan, S., and Stein, J. (1990). "How Risky Is the Debt in Highly Leveraged Transactions?" *Journal of Financial Economics* 27: 215–246.

Kaplan, S., and Stein, J. (1993). "The Evolution of Buyout Pricing and Financial Structure." Working Paper 3695, National Bureau of Economic Research.

Karpoff, J., and Malatesta, P. (1989). "The Wealth Effects of Second Generation Takeover Legislation." *Journal of Financial Economics* 25: 291–322.

Kaufman, P. (1996). "Fewer but Larger Supermarkets." *Food Review* 18, no. 2: 26.

Keegan, S. C., Sobehart, J., and Hamilton, D. T. (1999). "Predicting Default Rates: A Forecasting Model for Moody's Issuer-Based Default Rates." *Moody's Special Comment*. New York: Moody's Inc.

Kihn, J. (1994). "Unraveling the Low-Grade Bond Risk/Reward Puzzle." *Financial Analysts Journal*, July/August, pp. 32–42.

Klein, W. A. (1997). "High Yield ('Junk') Bonds as Investments and as Financial Tools." *Cardozo Law Review*, 19, 2: 505–510.

Knowledge Exchange. (1991). *High Yield 500*. Beverly Hills, CA: The Knowledge Exchange.

Kossovsky, N. (2002). *Intellectual Property/Technology Securitization*. Pasadena, CA: Heisenberg Principals.
Krol, R., and Svorny, S. (1993). "The Effect of the Bank Regulatory Environment on State Economic Activity." Working Paper 93-8, Milken Institute.
Kwan, S. H. (1996). "Firm-Specific Information and the Correlation Between Individual Stocks and Bonds." *Journal of Financial Economics* 40: 63–80.
La Porta, R., Lopez-de-Silanese, F., Shleifer, A., and Vishny, R. W. (1998). "Law and Finance," *Journal of Political Economy*, 106: 1113–1155.
Lederman, J., and Sullivan, M. P. (eds.). (1993). *The New High Yield Bond Market: Investment Opportunities, Strategies and Analysis*. Chicago: Probus.
Lerner, J. (1999). "The Government as Venture Capitalist: The Long-Run Effects of the SBIR Program." *Journal of Business* 72, no. 3: 285–318.
Lerner, J., and Gompers, P. (1998). "Venture Capital Distributions: Short-Run and Long-Run Reactions." *Journal of Finance* 53: 2161–2183.
Lerner, J., and Gompers, P. (1999). *The Venture Capital Cycle*. Cambridge, MA: MIT Press.
Levine, R. (1997). "Financial Development and Economic Growth: Views and Agenda." *Journal of Economic Literature* 35: 688–726.
Lichtenberg, F. R. (1992). *Corporate Takeovers and Productivity*. Cambridge, MA: MIT Press.
Lichtenberg, F. R., and Siegel, D. (1987). "Productivity and Changes in Ownership of Manufacturing Plants." *Brookings Papers on Economic Activity* 3: 643–673.
Lichtenberg, F. R., and Siegel, D. (1991). "The Impact of R&D Investment on Productivity—New Evidence Using Linked R&D-LRD Data." *Economic Inquiry* 29: 203–229.
Lindo, D. J. (1989). "High Yield Bonds: Junking the Myths." *Best's Review*, February, pp. 22–24.
Link, A. N. (1981a). *Research and Development Activity in U.S. Manufacturing*. New York: Praeger.
Link, A. N. (1981b). "Basic Research and Productivity Increase in Manufacturing: Additional Evidence." *American Economic Review* 71: 1111–1112.
Livingston, M., Pratt, H., and Mann, C. (1995). "Drexel Burnham Lambert's Debt Issues." *The Journal of Fixed Income*, March, pp. 58–75.
Loeys, J. (1986). "Low-Grade Bonds: A Growing Source of Corporate Funding." *Business Review, Federal Reserve Bank of Philadelphia*, November / December, pp. 3–12.
Lown, C. S., Morgan, D. P., and Rohatgi, S. (2000). "Listening to Loan Officers: The Impact of Commercial Credit Standards on Lending and Output." *Economic Policy Review* 6, no. 2: 1–16.
Lown, P., Persitiani, S., and Robinson, K. (2001). "Capital Regulation and Depository Institutions." In J. S. Barth, D. Brumbaugh, and G. Yago (eds.), *Restructuring Regulation and Financial Institutions*. Boston: Kluwer Academic Press.
Ma, C. K., Rao, R., and Peterson, R. L. (1989). "The Resiliency of the High Yield Bond Market: The LTV Default." *The Journal of Finance* 44, no. 4: 1085–1097.
Mason, S., Merton, R. C., Perold, A., and Tufano, P. (1995). *Cases in Financial Engineering: Applied Studies of Financial Innovation*. New York: Prentice-Hall.
Maxwell, W. F. (1998). "The January Effect in the Corporate Bond Market." *Financial Management*, Summer, pp. 18–30.
Mead, W. R., and S. Schwenninger. (2003). *The Bridge to a Global Middle Class: Development, Trade and International Finance in the 21st Century*. The Milken In-

stitute Series on Financial Innovation and Economic Growth. Boston: Kluwer Academic Publishers.

Meakin, T. K. (1990). "Junk Bond Hysteria Hits Insurer Stocks." *National Underwriter* no. 7: 61–66.

Meeks, G. (1977). *Disappointing Marriage: A Study of the Gains from Merger*. Cambridge: Cambridge University Press.

Merton, R. C. (1990). "The Financial System and Economic Performance." *Journal of Financial Services Research* 4: 263–300.

Merton, R. C. (1992a). "Financial Innovation and Economic Performance." *Journal of Applied Corporate Finance* 4, no. 4: 12–22.

Merton, R. C. (1992b). *Continuous Time Finance*. Malden, MA: Blackwell.

Milken, M. R. (1992). "My Story." *Forbes*, March 16, p. 78.

Milken, M. R. (1999a). "Prosperity and Social Capital." *Wall St. Journal*, June 23, p. 26.

Milken, M. R. (1999b). "The Helical Ride to Global Prosperity." *Forbes ASAP*, October 4, p. 122.

Milken, M. R. (2000). "The Democratization of Capital." *California Lawyer*, July, pp. 57–60.

Milken, M. R. (2003). "The Corporate Financing Cube: Matching Capital Structure to Business Risk." In Joel Kurtzman (ed.), *Business Encyclopedia*. New York: Crown Books.

Milken Institute, The Franklin D. Roosevelt Library, and the Ronald Reagan Presidential Library. (1998). Democratizing Capital in the United States. Conference Proceedings Available at www.milkeninstitute.org

Miller, M. H. (1988). "Financial Innovation: The Last Twenty Years and the Next." *Journal of Financial and Quantitative Analysis*, 21, 4: 459–471.

Miller, M. H. (1996). "Financial Innovation: Achievements and Prospects." *Journal of Applied Corporate Finance*, 4: 4–11.

Miller, M. H. (1992). "Financial Markets and Economic Growth." *Journal of Applied Corporate Finance* 11, No. 3: 8–14.

Miller, M. H., and Modigliani, F. (1958). "The Cost of Capital, Corporation Finance and the Theory of Investment." *American Economic Review* 48: 261–297.

Miller, M. H., and Modigliani, F. (1961). "Dividend Policy, Growth and the Valuation of Shares." *Journal of Business* 34: 411–433.

Miller, M. H., and Modigliani, F. (1963). "Corporate Income Taxes and the Cost of Capital: A Correction." *American Economic Review* 53: 433–443.

Minority Business Development Agency (2000). *Minority Purchasing Power: 2000 to 2045*. Washington, DC: Minority Business Development Agency.

Mishkin, F. (1991). "Asymmetric Information and Financial Crises: A Historical Perspective." In R. G. Hubbard (ed.), *Financial Markets and Financial Crises*. Chicago: University of Chicago Press.

Mitchell, M. L., and Mulherin, J. H. (1996). "The Impact of Industry Shocks on Takeover and Restructuring Activity." *Journal of Financial Economics* 41: 193–229.

Mitchell, M. L., and Netter, J. M. (1989). *Triggering the 1987 Stock-Market Crash: Antitakeover Provisions in the Proposed House Ways and Means Tax Bill*. Washington, DC: Office of Economic Analysis, U.S. Securities and Exchange Commission.

Morck, R., Acs, Z., and Yeung, B. (1997). "Productivity Growth and Firm Size Distribution." In Acs, Z., Carlsson, B., and Carlsson, C. (eds.), *Entrepreneurship, Small and Medium-Sized Enterprises and the Macroeconomy*. Cambridge: Cambridge University Press.

Morck, R., Shleifer, A., and Vishny, R. (1990). "Do Managerial Objectives Drive Bad Aquisitions?" *Journal of Finance* 45, no. 1: 31–48.

Morrison, C. J., and Siegel, D. (1998). "Knowledge Capital and Cost Structure in the U.S. Food and Fiber Industries." *American Journal of Agricultural Economics* 80, no.1: 30–45.

Mueller, D. C. (1980). "The United States, 1962–1972." In D. C. Mueller, (ed.), *The Determinants and Effects of Mergers: An International Comparison*. Cambridge, MA: Königstein/TS, Oelgeschlager, Gunn & Hain, Verlag A. Hain.

North, D. C. (1990). *Institutions, Institutional Change, and Economic Performance*. Cambridge: Cambridge University Press.

Opler, T. C., Saron, M., and Titman, S. (1997). "Designing Capital Structure to Create Shareholder Value." *Journal of Applied Corporate Finance* 10, no. 1: 21–32.

Paulus, J. D., and Waite, S. R. (1990). "High-Yield Bonds, Corporate Control, and Innovation." In F. J. Fabozzi (ed.), *The New High-Yield Debt Market: A Handbook for Portfolio Managers and Analysts*. New York: HarperCollins.

Peek, J., and Rosengren, E. S. (1993). "Bank Regulation and the Credit Crunch." Working paper no. 93-2, Federal Reserve Bank of Boston.

Phillips, B. (1995). "Small Business in the Year 2005." Washington, DC: Office of Economic Research, U.S. Small Business Administration.

Platt, H. D. (1993). "Underwriter Effects and the Riskiness of Original-Issue High-Yield Bonds." *Journal of Applied Corporate Finance* 6, no. 1: 89–94.

Platt, H. D. (1994). *The First Junk Bond: A Story of Corporate Boom and Bust*. Armonk, NY: M.E. Sharpe.

Platt, H. D., and Platt, M. (1991). "A Linear Programming Approach to Bond Portfolio Selection." *Economic and Financial Computing*, Spring, pp. 71–84.

Pound, J. (1992a). "Raiders, Targets, and Politics: The History and Future of American Corporate Control." *Journal of Applied Corporate Finance* 5: 6–18.

Pound, J. (1992b). "Beyond Takeovers: Politics Comes to Corporate Control." *Harvard Business Review* 70, no. 2: 83–94.

Powell, R. G. (1997). "Modeling Takeover Likelihood." *Journal of Business Finance and Accounting* 24, no. 7/8: 1009–1030.

PricewaterhouseCoopers (1998). *Eighth Annual Economic Impact of Venture Capital*. New York: PricewaterhouseCoopers.

Rajan, R., and Zingales, L. (1995). "Is There an Optimal Capital Structure? Some Evidence from International Data." *Journal of Finance* 50: 1421–1460.

Rajan, R., and Zingales, L. (1998). "Financial Dependence and Growth." *American Economic Review* 88, no. 3: 559–586.

Ramaswami, M. (1991). "Hedging the Equity Risk of High Yield Bonds." *Financial Analysts Journal*, September/October, pp. 41–50.

Ravenscraft, D. J., and Scherer, F. M. (1987). *Mergers, Sell-Offs, and Economic Efficiency*. Washington, DC: Brookings Institution.

Regan, P. J. (1990). "Junk Bonds—Opportunity Knocks?" *Financial Analysts Journal*, May/June, pp. 13–16.

Reilly, F. K. (ed.). (1990). *High Yield Bonds: Analysis and Risk Assessment*. Charlottesville, VA: Institute of Chartered Financial Analysts.

Reilly, F. K., and Wright, D. J. (1992). "Analysis of High Yield Bonds: Evidence of Segmentation in the Bond Market." Working paper, University of Notre Dame.

Reilly, F. K., and Wright, D. J. (1994). "An Analysis of High-Yield Bond Benchmarks." *The Journal of Fixed Income*, March, pp. 6–25.

Roe, M. J. (1993). "Takeover Politics." In M. M. Blair (ed.), *The Deal Decade: What Takeovers and Leveraged Buyouts Mean for Corporate Buyouts*. Washington, DC: The Brookings Institution.

Rogalski, R. J., and Sunder, L. (1990). "An Analysis of the Equity Component of Low-Grade Bonds." Presented to the Eastern Finance Association in Charleston, WV, April 7.

Romer, P. (1986). "Increasing Returns and Long Run Growth." *Journal of Political Economy* 94: 1002–1037.

Romer, P. (1996a). "Science, Economic Growth and Public Policy." In Bruce Smith and Claude Barfield (eds.), *Technology, R&D, and the Economy*. Washington, DC: Brookings Institution and American Enterprise Institute.

Romer, P. (1996b). "Why, Indeed, in America? Theory, History, and the Origins of Modern Economic Growth." *AEA Papers and Proceedings* 86, no. 2: 202–206.

Ross, S. (1989). "Institutional Markets, Financial Marketing, and Financial Innovation." *Journal of Finance* 44: 541–556.

Securities and Exchange Commission. (1990). *Recent Developments in the High Yield Market*. Washington, DC: Securities and Exchange Commission.

Securities and Exchange Commission. (1991). *A Report by the Division of Market Regulation on Transparency in the Market for High Yield Debt Securities*. Washington, DC: Securities and Exchange Commission.

Securities and Exchange Commission. (1996). *Report of the Advisory Committee on the Capital Formation and Regulatory Processes*. Washington, DC: Securities and Exchange Commission.

Securities and Exchange Commission, Division of Market Regulation. (1988). *The October 1987 Market Break*. Washington, DC: U.S. Government Printing Office.

Shane, H. (1994). "Comovements of Low-Grade Debt and Equity Returns of Highly Leveraged Firms." *The Journal of Fixed Income*, March, pp. 79–89.

Sharpe, S. (1994). "Financial Market Imperfections, Firm Leverage, and the Cyclicality of Employment." *American Economic Review* 84: 1060–1074.

Shulman, J., Bayless, V., and Price, K. (1993). "The Influence of Marketability on the Yield Premium of Speculative Grade Debt." *Financial Management*, Autumn, pp. 132–141.

Simonson, M. (1997). "Junk Bond Financing and the Value of the Firm: The Performance of Junk Bond Issuers." Ph.D. diss., University of Oregon.

Smith, C. W., Jr. (2001). "Organizational Architecture and Corporate Finance." *Journal of Financial Research* 24, no. 1: 1–13.

Smith, C. W., Jr., and Watts, R. (1992). "The Investment Opportunity Set and Corporate Financing, Dividend, and Compensation Policies." *Journal of Financial Economics* 32, no. 3: 263–292.

Smythe, W. (1989). "Insurer Investigations in Junk or Below-Investment Grade Bonds: Some Questions and Answers for Regulators." *Journal of Insurance Regulation*, September, pp. 4–15.

Sobel, R. (1989). "The Use of High Yield Securities in Corporate Creation: A Hundred Years of Financing and Reshaping America's Industries." Presented at Drexel Burnham Lambert's 11th Annual Institutional Research Conference, Beverly Hills, CA, April 6.

Stulz, R. M. (1990). "Managerial Discretion and Optimal Financial Policies." *Journal of Financial Economics* 26: 3–26.

Stulz, R. M. (1999). "Globalization, Corporate Finance and the Cost of Capital." *Journal of Applied Corporate Finance* 12, no. 3: 8–25.

Taggart, R. A., Jr. (1990). "Corporate Leverage and the Restructuring Movement of the 1980s." *Business Economics* 25, no. 2: 12–18.
Taub, S. (1991). "Rostenkowski's Food for Takeover Thought." *Financial World* 160, no. 25: 12–13.
Trifts, J. W. (1991). "Corporate Takeover Bids, Methods of Payment and the Effects of Leverage." *Quarterly Journal of Business & Economics* 30, no. 3: 33–47.
Trimbath, S. (2000). *The Determinants and Effects of Takeovers in the US, 1981–1997.* UMI Microform 9970939. New York: New York University, Department of Economics.
Trimbath, S. (2002). *Mergers and Efficiency: Changes Across Time.* Boston: Kluwer Academic Press.
Trimbath, S. (forthcoming). "Progress Report on Promoting Global Financial Development: Vive la Différence!" *Progress in Development Studies.*
Trimbath, S., Frydman, R., and Frydman, M. (2001). "Cost Inefficiency, Size of Firms and Takeovers." *Review of Quantitative Finance and Accounting* 17, no. 4: 397–420.
Tufano, P. (1989). "Financial Innovation and First-Mover Advantages" *Journal of Economics* 25: 213–240.
U.S. Census Bureau. (1997). *Survey of Minority Owned Business Enterprises.* Washington, DC: U.S. Census Bureau.
U.S. Distribution Journal. (1990). "Going Back to Basics." *Journal Annual Report* 217, no. 12: 39.
UNCTAD (2000). *World Investment Report, Cross-border Mergers and Acquisitions and Development, United Nations Conference on Trade and Development.* New York and Geneva: United Nations.
Vanderhoof, I. T., Albert, F. S., Tenenbein, A., and Verni, R. F. (1990). "The Risk of Asset Default: Report of the Society of Actuaries' C-1 Risk Task Force of the Committee on Valuation and Related Areas." *Transactions* 41: 547–582.
Waite, S. R. (1991). "The Eclipse of Growth Capital." *Journal of Applied Corporate Finance* 4, no. 1: 77–85.
Walsh, J. P. (1991). "The Social Context of Technological Change: The Case of the Retail Food Industry." *Sociological Quarterly* 32, no. 3: 447–468.
Walter, J. E., and Milken, M. R. (1973). "Managing the Corporate Financial Structure." Working Paper no. 26-73, Rodney L. White Center for Financial Research, Wharton School, University of Pennsylvania.
Weinstein, M. I. (1987). "A Curmudgeon's View of Junk Bonds." *The Journal of Portfolio Management*, Spring, pp. 76–80.
Weston, J. F., and Chiu, S. (1996). "Growth Strategies in the Food Industry." *Business Economics* 31, no. 1: 21–27.
Wigmore, B. A. (1990). "The Decline in Credit Quality of New-Issue Junk Bonds." *Financial Analysts Journal*, September/October, pp. 53–62.
Willis, M. (1995)."High Yield Corporates Defy Conventional Wisdom." *Bondweek*, December 4, p. 9.
Wilshire Associates. (2002). "Permissible Equity Markets Investment Analysis and Recommendations." Prepared for the California Public Employees Retirement System, January.
Winch, K. F. (1990). *High Yield Bond Market.* Washington, DC: Congressional Research Service.
Wright, M., Wilson, N., and Robbie, K. (1997). "The Longer Term Performance of Management Buy-outs." *Frontiers of Entrepreneurship Research*, Spring, pp. 555–569.

Wright, M., Wilson, N., and Robbie, K. (1998)."The Longer Term Effects of Management-led Buy-outs." *Journal of Entrepreneurial and Small Business Finance* 5, no. 3: 213–234.

Yago, G. (1990). "Corporate Restructuring in the United States." In M. Smith (ed.), *Corporate Restructuring*. London: Euromoney Publications.

Yago, G. (1991a). *Junk Bonds: How High Yield Securities Restructured Corporate America*. New York: Oxford University Press.

Yago, G. (1991b). "The Credit Crunch: A Regulatory Squeeze on Growth Capital." *Journal of Applied Corporate Finance* 4, no. 1: 96–100.

Yago, G. (1993). "Financial Repression and the Capital Crunch Recession." In B. Zycher and L. Solmon (eds.), *Economic Policy, Financial Markets and Economic Growth*. Boulder, CO: Westview Press.

Yago, G. (1999). *The Jobs/Capital Mismatch: Financial Regulatory Chokeholds on Economic Growth*. Santa Monica, CA: Milken Institute.

Yago, G. (2001). "Financing Global Environmental Futures: Using Financial Market and Instruments to Advance Environmental Goals." *Milken Institute Policy Brief*, March 20.

Yago, G., Lichtenberg, F., and Siegel, D. (1989). "Leveraged Buyouts and Industrial Competitiveness: The Effects of LBOs on Productivity, Employment, and Research and Development." Working Paper, W. Averell Harriman School of Management and Policy, no. HAR90-003. State University of New York at Stony Brook.

Yago, G., and Ramesh, L. (1999). *Raising Regulatory Costs of Growth Capital: Implications of the Proposal to Amend Rule 144A*. Santa Monica, CA: Milken Institute.

Yago, G., and Siegel, D. (1994). "Triggering High Yield Market Decline: Regulatory Barriers in Financial Markets." *Extra Credit: The Journal of High Yield Bond Research* 21, pp. 11–24.

Young, H. (1993). *The Banks of the Future*. Washington, DC: Federal Deposit Insurance Corporation, Division of Resolutions.

Zycher, B. (1993). "Bank Capitalization Standards, the Credit Crunch, and Resource Allocation Under Regulation." In B. Zycher and L. Solmon (eds.), *Economic Policy, Financial Markets and Economic Growth*. Boulder, CO: Westview Press.

Index